Gaze-Following: Its Development and Significance

Gaze-Following: Its Development and Significance

Edited by

Ross Flom
Brigham Young University

Kang Lee
University of Toronto

and

Darwin Muir
Queens University

LEA LAWRENCE ERLBAUM ASSOCIATES, PUBLISHERS
2007 Mahwah, New Jersey   London

Senior Acquisitions Editor: Lori Stone Handelman
Editorial Assistant: Anthony Messina
Cover Design: Tomai Maridou
Cover image: "Como sube todo" by Sebastián Picker. Oil on canvas, 40″ × 32″, 2004
Full-Service Compositor: MidAtlantic Books & Journals, Inc.

This book was typeset in 10.5/12 pt. Goudy Old Style, Italic, Bold, and Bold Italic
with Americana.

Lawrence Erlbaum Associates, Inc., Publishers
10 Industrial Avenue
Mahwah, New Jersey 07430
www.erlbaum.com

**CIP information for this volume can be obtained by contacting the
Library of Congress**

ISBN 0-8058-4750-2 (casebound)

Books published by Lawrence Erlbaum Associates are printed on
acid-free paper, and their bindings are chosen for strength and durability.

Printed in the United States of America

10 9 8 7 6 5 4 3 2 1

Contents

      in early word learning   193
      Susan A. Graham, Elizabeth S. Nilsen, and Samantha L. Nayer

10   Eyes Wide Shut: The importance of eyes in infant gaze-
      following and understanding other minds   217
      Andrew M. Meltzoff and Rechele Brooks

11   Preschoolers' use of eye-gaze for "mind reading"   243
      Michelle Eskritt and Kang Lee

12   The inquisitive eye: Infants' implicit understanding
      that looking leads to knowing   263
      Diane Poulin-Dubois, Tamara L. Demke, and Kara M. Olineck

13   Look into my eyes: The effect of direct gaze on face
      processing in children and adults   283
      Bruce M. Hood and C. Neil Macrae

14   Gaze processing in nonhuman primates   297
      Shoji Itakura, Lopamudra Das, and Arash Farshid

      Author Index   313
      Subject Index   325

Foreword

John H. Flavell
Stanford University

Since Robert Fantz's pioneering work a half a century ago, developmental psychologists have been making important discoveries about infants' minds by observing where they look and for how long. For us, their eyes have been something akin to windows to their souls. As this book on the development and significance of gaze-following abundantly documents, infants are doing much the same thing with us. They gradually learn to look where we look and to predict our mental states and behaviors from what they see; our eyes are their windows, as well.

I was left with several impressions about infant and child gaze-following after reading this fine book.

First, it became very clear—clearer than it had been to me previously—just how developmentally significant this familiar and modest-seeming behavior is. It is a very powerful tool for learning all sorts of things about people. In Meltzoff and Brooks' words, it "entails the ascription of a mental life to a viewer. We follow where another person looks because we want to see what they are seeing. When we see people direct their gaze somewhere, we wonder what object is catching their attention . . ." (Chapter 5, p. 232). Other chapters offer similar, convincing testimonials to the importance of gaze-following as an engine of development.

Second, the development of gaze-following and attendant skills is surprisingly lengthy and complex. Rudiments or precursors of gaze-following are evident even in newborns. Visual perspective-taking skills, and some understanding that seeing is a visual experience that leads to knowing, develop later in infancy or early childhood. There may be still other, later-developing insights that could be added to those detailed in this book. One has to look to see but still may not see, when one looks (the object is camouflaged or too far away, the light is too dim, one's eyesight is too poor). The position and movements of a person's eyes may give clues that the person is reflecting, remembering, distracted, interested, uninterested, distracted, untrustworthy, or sleepy.

The effects of a visual input on a person depend complexly on both the nature of the input and the nature of the person. On the input side, visual information may be obscure, ambiguous, or deceptive; eyewitness error is always a possibility, even when eyewitness confidence is high. On the person side, individual differences of all sorts may lead to differences regarding what in the visual input is attended to and how what is attended to is interpreted (Flom and Pick, Chapter 5, pp. 102–106).

Third, I was also surprised to learn how much has already been discovered about the development of gaze-following, much of it by the authors of these chapters. Although as a retired but still interested, theory-of-minder I was already aware of some of these findings, many others were totally new to me. I also discovered some novel ways of thinking about the phenomena. For example, the distinction between endogenous and exogenous gaze-following (MacPherson and Moore, Chapter 3, pp. 54–57), the idea that gaze-following can be construed as a form of imitation (Van Hecke and Mundy, Chapter 2, pp. 38–39), and the notion that transitional periods of development in this area are akin to "tadpoles with legs" (Meltzoff and Brooks, Chapter 10, p. 218).

Finally, the chapters are also full of interesting suggestions for future research. They make it clear that this is an area with a rich past, as well as a rich future. As the authors of these chapters are well aware, perhaps the most important question in this general area is what infants and children know about people's mental experiences as the people perceive and act upon the world. If the study of gaze-following could answer that question, the eyes would truly be windows to the soul.

Preface

Gaze-following:
Its development and significance

Since Scaife and Bruner's (1975) seminal report that many 8- to 10-month-olds will follow an experimenter's change in eye-gaze, the field of developmental psychology has come a long way in understanding the development and significance of this behavior. From my perspective, it was the publication of Moore and Dunham's (1995) edited volume twenty-years later that placed the topic of following another's direction of gaze into the forefront of our field. Prior to Moore and Dunham's volume research in this area was rather sparse and was being conducted in a handful of labs. It was in this volume that many of us, including myself as a then first-year graduate student, came to recognize and understand something of the interconnected nature of joint visual attention and the rest of development. We learned of the association between autism and infants' inability to follow another's line of visual regard, we began to see the relation of joint attention and early word learning and theory of mind, and we saw this behavior as another way to examine the nature of early social communication and interaction.

In the nearly 12-years since the publication of Moore and Dunham we have continued to make substantial gains in understanding the development of joint attention. We have examined the relation of initiating joint attention and responding to joint attention and autism, the role of the superior temporal sulcus and other interconnected areas of the brain associated with face processing, the following of another's eye-gaze as it informs of us of attention and the flexibility of attention. We have begun to examine the connection between gaze-following and children's susceptibility to deception, non-human primates' proclivity for following another's direction of gaze, and recently the significance of gaze in face recognition and social exchanges between adults. Along with these more recent areas of inquiry we have continued to examine the links of joint visual attention and early language, theory of mind, and perceptual development. The current volume represents all of these areas, both the "old" and the "new". In preparing this volume it became clear that with each new and exciting result there came new and unexplored questions—thus we still have a long way to go!

Taken together, all of the chapters in this volume highlight what I believe to be two important points. First, if we are to draw nearer to understanding human development then we must study it *in situ*. Certainly we need to study the "individual" but we must also study what occurs *between* and even *among* people. I believe it is what occurs within the context of these social exchanges and relationships that so frequently involve looking where another is looking that holds many keys to our understanding of social, cognitive, perceptual and neurological development. Second joint visual attention/gaze-following is not merely a developmental precursor; rather these behaviors, their relations to other developmental achievements, are all part of the dynamic system that is Development.

My appreciation goes to each author for their contribution and patience with this volume. I express my gratitude to Lori Handelman at Lawrence Erlbaum Associates for her sense of humor and assistance with the editorial process, Steve Chisholm at MidAtlantic books in preparing the book for production, Sebastián Picker for the cover art, and to Kang Lee and Darwin Muir who provided assistance when needed. Enjoy!

Ross Flom

Gaze-Following: Its Development and Significance

1

The Neurodevelopmental Origins of Eye Gaze Perception

Mark H. Johnson
Birkbeck College

Teresa Farroni
Birkbeck College and University of Padua, Italy

Over the past decade many researchers have tried to understand the perceptual, cognitive, and neurological processes involved in extracting meaning from the human face. The perception of faces elicits activity in distributed regions of the brain involving several cortical and sub-cortical structures. Different parts of this distributed neural system for face perception seem to mediate different aspects of face perception (see Haxby, Hoffman, & Gobbini, 2002 for a review). The perception of faces and the understanding that faces can reflect internal states of social partners are vital skills for the typical development of humans. Of particular importance is processing information about eyes, and eye gaze direction. Perception of averted gaze can elicit an automatic shift of attention in the same direction (Driver et al., 1999), allowing the establishment of "joint attention" (Butterworth & Jarrett, 1991). Direction of gaze is a very good guide to the focus of another's attention. Further, mutual gaze (eye contact) provides the main mode of establishing a communicative context between humans (Kleinke, 1986; Symons, Hains, & Muir, 1998).

We begin this chapter by addressing three issues concerning the brain basis of eye gaze processing in adults. First, which regions of the brain are activated

1

by viewing the eyes of a person? Second, are these activated regions related to those involved in the perception of movement in general? Third, which of these regions are also activated during general face processing? In the next section of the chapter, we will turn to development and focus on behavioral and neural evidence pertaining to two different aspects of eye gaze processing: perceiving the direction of another's eye gaze and acting on another's eye gaze. Finally, we will attempt to synthesize data on the development of eye gaze perception and speculate on their relation to the available neuroscience data.

THE NEURAL BASIS OF EYE GAZE PERCEPTION

The first investigations of the brain basis of eye gaze processing involved electrophysiological recording in monkeys. In these species, eye gaze has an important regulatory influence on social interaction and can be used to assert dominance or submission. Perrett and colleagues (Perrett, Rolls, & Caan, 1982; Perrett et al., 1985; Perrett, Hietanen, Oram, & Benson, 1992) studied the responses of the macaque monkey's Superior Temporal Sulcus (STS) cells to the perception of gaze direction. They observed that neurons that were most responsive to viewing a full face preferred eye contact (direct gaze), while cells that were tuned to the profile view of a face preferred averted gaze. These results indicated that the brain has evolved mechanisms for interpreting the direction of eye gaze and that these mechanisms involve the activation of specific brain regions.

The advent of functional imaging has allowed the study of the neural basis of eye gaze processing in adults. Using these methods, several authors have established that the STS is also important for eye gaze perception in humans (see Allison, Puce, & McCarthy, 2000 for review). The STS region is defined as being the regions of adjacent cortex on the surface of the superior and middle temporal gyri and adjacent cortex on the surface of the angular gyrus (see Figure 1–1). Figure 1–1 also shows the distribution of areas of the Superior Temporal Sulcus that are related to eye gaze processing, body, and actions (i.e., regions related to biological movements).

Functional imaging studies have also revealed that a network of other cortical areas is activated during the processing of eye gaze. Since the perception of eye gaze involves the detection of movement, one issue is the extent of overlap between structures involved in motion perception and those engaged by eye gaze processing. For example, the "eye regions" of STS are very close to the MT/V5 area, a structure known to be important for the perception of motion in general. To examine the responses of this latter region, Puce, Allison, Bentin, Gore, and McCarthy (1998) run a functional magnetic resonance imaging (fMRI) experiment in which participants viewed moving eyes, moving

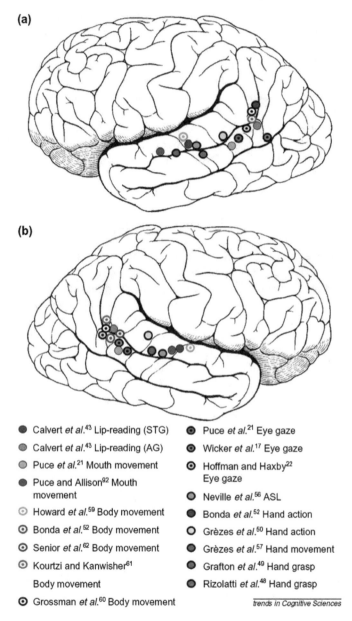

FIGURE 1–1. Activation of the Superior Temporal Sulcus (STS) region in the left hemisphere (a) and in the right hemisphere (b) during the perception of biological motion. (The references cited in the figure can be found in Allison et al., 2000. Reprinted with permission from Elsevier.)

mouths, or movements of checker-board patterns. The results of this study showed that while all three conditions activated the motion area MT/V5, only moving eyes and mouths activated the STS. These results suggest that the STS is preferentially involved in the perception of gaze direction and mouth movements, but not to non-biological motion. A study by Watanabe, Kakigi, and Puce (2001) using a magnetoencephalography system (MEG) found similar results.

Since eyes always occur within the context of a face, another issue is the extent of overlap between the brain basis of eye gaze perception and the regions activated by face processing in general. To address this question, Wicker, Michel, Henaff, and Decety (1998) used the Positron Emission Tomography (PET) to study the pattern of cortical activation resulting from direct (mutual) eye gaze. They contrasted four experimental conditions: a face with neutral gaze, a face with averted gaze (to the right or left), a face with direction of gaze not visible, and a control condition in which participants kept their own eyes closed. The results were that in all three experimental conditions, regardless of direction of gaze, areas related to face processing were activated. These areas included the occipital pole (striate and extrastriate visual cortex) and the occipito-temporal areas, particularly in the right hemisphere. In addition to these regions, other brain regions were activated by processing direction of gaze, including the occipital part of the fusiform gyrus, the right parietal lobule, the right inferior temporal gyrus, and the middle temporal gyrus in both hemispheres. At the subcortical level there was activation in the right amygdala, the right pulvinar, and bilaterally in the middle dorsal thalamic nucleus. However, in this study no conclusive evidence for specific mutual gaze processing areas was described. This result suggests the processing of eye gaze is controlled by a distributed network of brain areas not completely independent of general face processing.

In summary, results reviewed so far indicate substantial overlap between the network of regions involved in gaze processing and those activated by motion and face processing. Table 1.1 illustrates that while eye gaze processing engages some of the same structures as general face processing and motion

TABLE 1.1.
Illustration of the Regions Activated by Gaze Processing, Motion and Face Processing in Adults

	Fusiform gyrus	MT/V5	STS
Face	✔	✗	✗
Movement	✗	✔	✗
Eye gaze	✔	✔	✔

The ticks shows the regions that are activated and the crosses show the non-activated regions.

processing, the particular combination of regions activated may be specific to this task.

THE DEVELOPMENT OF EYE GAZE PROCESSING

By the end of their first year of life, infants appear to know that the looking behavior of others conveys significant information. It is commonly agreed that eye gaze perception is important for mother–infant interaction, and that it provides a vital foundation for social development (e.g. Jaffe, Stern, & Peery, 1973). The two questions we address in this section are: first, at what age are infants first able to detect eye gaze direction (i.e., perceiving eye gaze); and second, when are infants able to use direction of eye gaze to influence their own behavior (i.e. acting on eye gaze).

It is already known that human newborns have a visual preference for face-like stimuli (Johnson, Dziurawiec, Bartrip, & Morton, 1992; Valenza, Simion, Cassia, & Umilta, 1996), prefer faces with eyes opened (Batki, Baron-Cohen, Wheelwright, Connellan, & Ahluwalia, 2000), and tend to imitate certain facial gestures (Meltzoff & Moore, 1977). The significance of mutual gaze in the development of human relationships has been shown in many studies, revealing its function to provide information, to regulate adult-infant interaction, to exercise social control, and to facilitate task goals (Kleinke, 1986; Blass & Camp, 2001). Preferential attention to faces with direct gaze would provide the most compelling evidence to date that human newborns are born prepared to detect socially relevant information. For this reason, we recently investigated eye gaze detection in humans from birth. We (Farroni, Csibra, Simion, & Johnson, 2002) tested healthy human newborn infants by presenting them with a pair of stimuli, one a face with eye gaze directed straight at the newborns, and the other with averted gaze (see Figure 1–2). Videotapes of the babies' eye movements throughout the trial were analyzed by the two recorders.

Mutual Gaze   **Averted Gaze**

FIGURE 1–2. Experimental stimuli used in Farroni et al. (2002). Stimuli were color photographic images of female faces directing their gaze straight-on to the viewers (Direct Gaze) or averted to one side (Averted Gaze).

The dependent variables we used were the total fixation time and the number of orienting responses. Results showed that the fixation times were significantly longer for the face with the straight gaze (106 seconds vs. 63 seconds for the averted gaze). Further, the number of orientations was higher with the straight gaze than with the averted gaze. These results demonstrate preferential orienting to direct eye gaze from birth. The preference is probably a result of a fast and approximate analysis of the visual input, dedicated to find socially relevant stimuli for further processing.

In order to examine the specificity of this newborn preference, we recently conducted two further experiments. The goal of the first experiment was to ascertain whether inverting faces has any effect on gaze perception in newborns. If the preference for direct gaze is not found under conditions of inversion, then we may conclude that low-level aspects of the faces, such as symmetry or local spatial frequency, are not the basis for the newborn preference for direct gaze in upright faces previously observed. Further, an absence of the effect with inversion would indicate that the factors responsible for the preference require the eyes to be situated within the configuration of an upright face. Newborns did not show significant difference in total looking time at the straight gaze (mean 68.5 sec) and at the averted gaze (mean 53.7 sec), and they did not orient more frequently to the direct gaze inverted face (mean 17.8) than to the other (mean 14.61). These results allow us to rule out symmetry and local spatial frequency as possible explanations of the newborn effect. At least two possible types of underlying mechanisms for this behavioral phenomenon remain possible. By one account, even newborns have sophisticated face processing abilities sufficient to extract gaze direction when presented in the context of a face. By an alternative account, the preferences of newborns are based on a primitive "Conspec" mechanism that responds to an optimal configuration of high-contrast elements. Straight-on faces with direct gaze better fit this simple template than do faces with averted gaze (see Farroni et al., 2002; Farroni, Mansfield, Lai, & Johnson, 2003). To test between these hypotheses, we conducted a second experiment which involved similar face stimuli, but with averted head angles. We reasoned that a sophisticated face processing system would be able to extract gaze direction even when head angle varied. In contrast, a simple Conspec mechanism may only produce a preference for direct gaze under conditions where the spacing between eyes and mouth is optimal. Changing head angle will alter the relative spacing of the two eyes and mouth, and thus may disrupt the preference seen with a straight head. In this experiment newborns did not show significant differences in total looking time at the direct gaze (mean 80.3 sec) and at the averted gaze (mean 73.5 sec), and they did not orient more frequently to the direct gaze face (mean 14.2) than to the other (mean 13.9). The results of these experiments show that the strong preference for faces with direct gaze is dependent on the eyes being situated within the context of an upright straight-ahead face. This finding simultaneously rules out many low-level explanations of the original result and the suggestion that newborns may have sophisticated eye gaze perception abilities. Rather, the view that newborns orient to direct gaze due to a primitive configuration detection system (such as Conspec) gains some credence.

In a second line of experiments, we attempted to gain converging evidence for the differential processing of direct gaze in infants, by recording event related potentials (ERPs) from the scalp as infants viewed faces. We studied 4-month-old babies with the same stimuli as those used in the previous experiment with newborns and found a difference between the two gaze directions at the time and scalp location of a known face-sensitive component of the infant ERP ("infant N170," deHaan, Pascalis, & Johnson, 2002). This component of the infant ERP is thought to be the equivalent of a well-studied adult face-sensitive component and in infants is sensitive to changes in the orientation and species of a face, at least by 12 months of age (Halit, de Haan, & Johnson, 2003). Thus, our conclusion from these studies is that direct eye contact enhances the perceptual processing of faces in 4-month-old infants. This suggests a fast mechanism of gaze direction analysis that may precede the full processing of faces (see Figure 1–3a and b). This hypothesis is also supported by adults' data. An fMRI study by George, Driver, & Dolan (2001) investigated how gaze direction (direct or averted) influences face processing using a gender recognition task. They presented a face with direct or averted gaze, and the face was either a frontal view or tilted at 45°. They observed that specific regions of the fusiform gyrus yielded stronger responses to faces when these looked directly at the subject (regardless of the orientation of the head). This suggests that there may be deeper encoding of faces when gaze is directed at the observer.

In order to examine further the specificity of these eye gaze processing effects, we conducted two more ERP experiments with 4-month-olds. As in the newborn experiments, it remains possible that low-level aspects of the stimuli, such as symmetry or local spatial frequency differences, could have contributed to the effects observed. Further, the importance of an upright face configuration is unknown. For these reasons we conducted a high-density ERP experiment with a group of 4 month olds, using the same inverted faces stimuli as employed in the earlier newborn study. No modulation of the "Infant N170" was observed in this experiment, showing that under conditions of face inversion gaze direction does not modulate face processing. The clear difference in ERP results obtained in the two experiments with 4-month-olds also allows us to rule out symmetry and local spatial frequency as contributors to the gaze effect with upright faces. A further question is whether the cortical processing of faces is modulated by gaze direction in the context of an averted head. The ability to extract gaze direction under these circumstances would

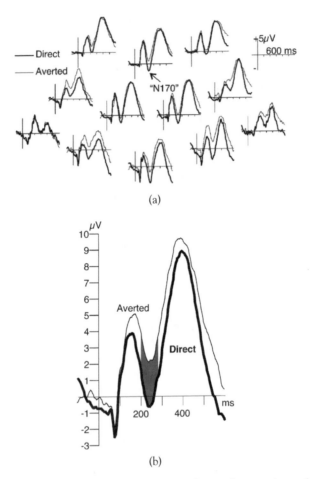

(a)

(b)

FIGURE 1–3.   ERPs recorded to faces with direct and averted gaze in 4-month-old infants in Farroni et al. (2002). (a) All but one of the electrodes over the occipital cortex recorded an enhanced N170 response (peaking at 240 msec post-stimulus) to the faces with direct gaze compared to the faces with averted gaze. (b) ERPs to the two kinds of stimuli averaged across all occipital electrode sites.

suggest a more sophisticated mechanism of processing than that which we observed in newborns. The results of this experiment were more complicated, but showed an effect of direct gaze on face processing when the head was angled to the left. This effect of head angle on gaze processing is remarkably consistent with reports from adults indicating that there is a left visual field (right hemisphere) bias for various aspects of face processing, including gaze cueing (Ricciardelli, Ro, & Driver, 2002).

Another issue that we investigated is the ability of infants to act on eye gaze. Several studies have demonstrated that gaze cues are able to trigger an automatic and rapid shifting of the focus of the viewer's visual attention (Langton & Bruce, 1999; Driver et al., 1999; Friesen & Kingstone, 1998). All these studies used variants of Posner's (1980) "spatial cueing" paradigm, where a central or peripheral cue directs the attention to one of the peripheral locations. When the target appears in the same location where the cue is directed (the congruent position), the participant is faster to look at that target compared to another target at an incongruent position relative to the previous cue. Using this paradigm, Schuller and Rossion (2001) presented a face on the screen that was first looking to the subject and then either to the right or the left. Then a target appeared which could be in the same position where the face was looking, or in the opposite position. The results with adults were that facilitation of visual processing by spatial attention is reflected in enhanced early visual evoked potentials (P1 and N1). Reflexive attention increases visual activity and speeds up the processing of visual attention. Probably, in addition to the areas discussed before, eye gaze tasks activate regions involved in covert attention such as parts of parietal cortex.

When does the ability to use eye gaze direction as an attentional cue start? Human infants start to discriminate and follow adults' direction of attention at the age of 3 or 4 months (Hood, Willen, & Driver, 1998; Vecera & Johnson, 1995). Hood et al. (1998), showed in a group of infants varying in ages from 10 to 28 weeks that the perception of an adult's deviated gaze induces shifts of attention in infants in the corresponding direction. In their experiments they modified the standard Posner cueing paradigm (Posner, 1980), using as a central cue the direction of gaze of a woman's face, thus creating a computer-generated eye gaze shift. The reaction time to make a saccade to a peripheral target was measured under conditions in which the location of the target was either congruent or incongruent with the direction of gaze of a centrally presented face. In our studies we examined further the visual properties of the eyes that enable infants to follow the direction of the gaze. We tested 4-month-olds using a cueing paradigm adapted from Hood et al. (1998). Each trial begins with the stimulus face eyes blinking (to attract attention), before the pupils shift to either the right or the left for a period of 1,500 ms (see Figure 1–4). A target stimulus was then presented either in the same position where the stimulus face eyes were looking (congruent position) or in a location incongruent with the direction of gaze. By measuring the saccadic reaction time of infants to orient to the target, we demonstrated that the infants were faster to look at the location congruent with the direction of gaze of the face.

In the second experiment of this series, we manipulated the stimulus face so that the whole face was shifted to one side (right or left) while the pupils remained fixed (see Figure 1–5). In this case, the infants were faster to look

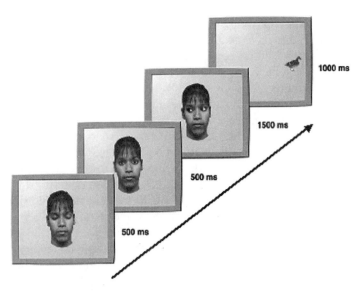

FIGURE 1–4.   Example of the edited video image illustrating the stimulus sequence for Experiment 1 in Farroni et al. (2000). In this trial the stimulus target (the duck) appears on an incongruent side.

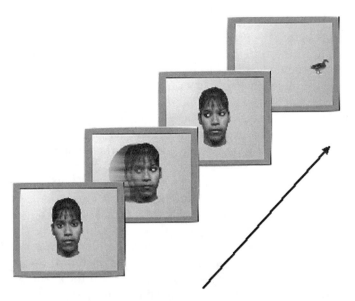

FIGURE 1–5.   Example of the edited video image illustrating the stimulus sequence for Experiment 3 in Farroni et al. (2000). In this trial the stimulus face shifted to one side, while the eyes appeared to move in the opposite side.

in the direction in which the whole face was shifted and not the direction where the pupils were directed. Therefore, the infants actually followed the biggest object with lateral motion (i.e., the face) and not the eyes.

In a third experiment, we used the same paradigm as in the first experiment, but this time when the eyes were opened the pupils were already oriented to the left or right, and the infants were not able to perceive the movement of the pupils. In this case, the cueing effect disappeared. Up to this point, the results suggested that the critical feature for eye gaze cue in infants is the movement of the pupils, and not the final direction of the pupils.

To try to understand this cueing effect better, we did three further variants of the same procedure (Farroni et al., 2002). In the first experiment in this paper, we examined the effect of inverting the face on cueing. If infants are merely cued by motion, then an inverted face should produce the same cueing as an upright one. To our surprise, the results showed that there was no significant cueing effect, suggesting that the context of an upright face may be important. In Experiment 2 we presented infants with a face that was initially presented with averted gaze, but that then shifted to the center (see Figure 1–6). If infants are responding just to the motion of elements, they

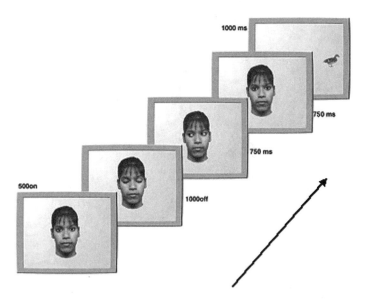

FIGURE 1–6. Example of the edited video image illustrating the stimulus sequence for Experiment 2 in Farroni et al. (2003). In this trial the eyes opened already oriented either to the right or to the left where they remained for 750 ms before shifting back to a central position for the next 750 ms.

should be cued in the direction opposite to that initially presented. Again, no cueing effect was observed. These results did not support the hypothesis that directed motion of elements is the only determining factor for the cueing effects.

In the last experiment with 4-month-olds (Experiment 3), a more complex gaze shift sequence allowed us to analyze the importance of beginning with a period of mutual gaze: the eyes shifted from center to averted, and then back to center (see Figure 1–7). Here we did observe a significant cueing effect. Taken together, these results suggest that it is only following a period of mutual gaze with an upright face that cueing effects are observed. In other words, mutual gaze with an upright face may engage mechanisms of attention such that the viewer is more likely to be cued by subsequent motion. In summary, the critical features for eye gaze cueing in infants are (1) lateral motion, and (2) at least a brief preceding period of eye contact with an upright face.

Recently, we have examined three further aspects of the neurodevelopment of eye gaze processing. In the first of these, we have assessed whether, like

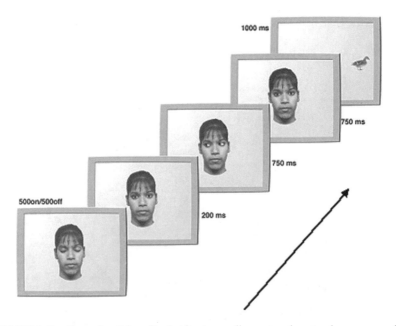

FIGURE 1–7.   Example of the edited video image illustrating the stimulus sequence for Experiment 3 in Farroni et al. (2003). Trials began with the eyes facing the baby for 200 ms and then a movement either right or left where they remained for 750 ms, giving the impression that the face was averting its eyes before going back to the central position for the following 750 ms.

older children and adults (see Hood chapter), the deeper encoding of faces when accompanied by direct gaze leads to better individual recognition (Farroni et al., In prep). Specifically, we habituated groups of 4-month-old infants to individual faces with either direct gaze or averted gaze. We then assessed the extent of novelty preferences in a paired comparison test between the habituated face and a novel one. Infants that had been exposed to the face with direct gaze subsequently showed a stronger novelty preference in the test, providing evidence that they had encoded the habituation face more deeply. Time to habituation did not predict novelty preference, allowing us to rule out the simpler explanation that it is the longer looking time to faces with direct gaze that determines better processing. Rather, it seems that increased covert attention to, or deeper processing of, faces with direct gaze is the likely explanation.

Since most of our research on gaze cueing has been with 4-month-olds, in a second line of recent research we have begun to investigate whether such abilities might exist in newborns. To maximize our likelihood of success, we used large schematic faces with targets located close to the stimulus head. Under such conditions, we observed that even newborns oriented preferentially to targets cued by the direction of gaze. While this study requires replication, together with our previous results on the detection of direct (mutual) gaze, it suggests that newborns may possess the same mechanisms we have identified at 4 months of age.

A third aspect of the neurodevelopment of gaze perception that we have been studying concerns atypical development. Specifically, we have examined the ERP correlates of direct and averted gaze in young children with autism (Grice et al., 2005). A striking observation was that the ERP responses of our autistic group looked similar to those we had earlier observed in infants. A group of typically developing controls, however, showed a different pattern of results. While preliminary, these findings suggest that in autism the processing of eye gaze remains at the stage achieved by typical young infants. The exact implications of this finding require further exploration.

DISCUSSION

We have reviewed evidence from functional neuroimaging indicating that a network of cortical and subcortical regions is engaged in eye gaze processing in adults. This network of structures overlaps with, but does not completely duplicate, the patterns of activation seen in the perception of motion, and the perception of faces in general. While it may be important to activate the whole network for eye gaze processing, one region in particular, the "eye area" of the superior temporal sulcus, appears to be critical. How does this specialization arise?

The empirical evidence we and others have gathered on the development and neural basis of eye gaze processing in infants is consistent with an "interactive specialization" perspective on functional brain development (Johnson & de Haan, 1999). Contrary to the view that there is an innate Eye Direction Detector (EDD; Baron-Cohen, 1995), interactive specialization emphasizes the importance of (1) initial biases to "bootstrap" later developing systems, and (2) the gradual specialization of individual regions through their emerging role within brain networks (see Johnson 1999 for further details). Focusing on the first of these aspects of interactive specialization, we (Farroni et al., 2002) suggest that a primitive representation of high-contrast elements (such as Johnson & Morton's "Conspec") would be sufficient to direct orienting in newborns toward faces with eye contact. Therefore, the more frequent orienting to the direct gaze in newborns could be mediated by the same mechanism that underlies newborns' tendency to orient to faces in general. Specifically, Morton and Johnson (1991) hypothesized that subcortical circuits supported a primitive representation of high-contrast elements relating to the location of the eyes and mouth. A face with direct gaze would better fit the spatial relation of elements in this template than one with gaze averted, suggesting that the functional role of this putative mechanism is more general than previously supposed. This primitive bias ensures a biased input of human faces with direct gaze to the infant over the first days and weeks of life.

According to the interactive specialization view, a network as a whole becomes specialized for a particular function. Therefore, we suggest that the "eye region" of the STS does not develop in isolation, or in a modular fashion, but that its functionality emerges within the context of interacting regions involved in either general face processing or in motion detection. Viewed from this perspective, STS may be a region that integrates motion information with the processing of faces (and other body parts). While STS may be active in infants, we propose that it is not yet efficiently integrating motion and face information. In other words, while the 4-month-old has good face processing and general motion perception, it has not yet integrated these two aspects of perception together into adult eye-gaze perception. By this account, making eye contact with an upright face fully engages face processing, which then facilitates the orienting of attention by lateral motion. At older ages, eye gaze perception becomes a fully integrated function where even static presentations of averted eyes are sufficient to facilitate gaze.

REFERENCES

Allison, T., Puce, A., & McCarthy, G. (2000). Social perception from visual cues: Role of STS region. *Trends in Cognitive Sciences, 4,* 267–278.

Baron-Cohen, S. (1995). *Mindblindness: An essay on autism and theory of mind.* Cambridge, MA: MIT Press.

Batki, A., Baron-Cohen, S., Wheelwright, S., Connellan, J., & Ahluwalia, J. (2000). Is there an innate module? Evidence from human neonates. *Infant Behavior & Development, 23,* 223–229.

Blass, E. M., & Camp, C. A. (2001). The ontogeny of face recognition: Eye contact and sweet taste induce face preference in 9- and 12-week-old human infants. *Developmental Psychology, 37,* 762–774.

Butterworth, G., & Jarrett, N. (1991). What minds have in common is space: Spatial mechanisms serving joint visual attention in infancy. *British Journal of Developmental Psychology, 9,* 55–72.

de Haan, M., Pascalis, O., & Johnson, M. H. (2002). Specialization of neural mechanisms underlying face recognition in human infants. *Journal of Cognitive Neuroscience, 14,* 199–209.

Driver, J., Davis, G., Ricciardelli, P., Kidd, P., Maxwell, E., & Baron-Cohen, S. (1999). Gaze perception triggers reflexive visuospatial orienting. *Visual Cognition, 6,* 509–540.

Farroni, T., Csibra, G., Simion, F., & Johnson, M. H. (2002). Eye contact detection in humans from birth. *Proceedings of the National Academy of Sciences USA, 99,* 9602–9605.

Farroni, T., Johnson, M. H., Brockbank, M., & Simion, F. (2000). Infant's use of gaze direction to cue attention: The importance of perceived motion. *Visual Cognition, 7*(6), 705–718.

Farroni, T., Massaccesi, S., Menon, E., Johnson H. M. (2006). Direct gaze modulates face recognition in young infants. *Cognition*

Farroni, T., Mansfield, E. M. Lai C., & Johnson M. H., (2003). Motion and mutual gaze in directing infants' spatial attention. *Journal of Experimental Child Psychology, 85,* 199–212.

Friesen, C. K., & Kingstone, A. (1998). The eyes have it! Reflexive orienting is triggered by nonpredictive gaze. *Psychonomic Bulletin & Review, 5,* 490–495.

George, N., Driver, J., & Dolan, R. J. (2001). Seen gaze-direction modulates fusiform activity and its coupling with other brain areas during face processing. *NeuroImage, 13,* 1102–1112.

Grice, S. J., Halit, H., Farroni, T., Baron-Cohen, S., Bolton, P., & Johnson, M. H. (2005). Neural correlates of eye-gaze detection in young children with autism. *Cortex, 3,* 277–281.

Halit, H., de Haan, M., & Johnson, M. H. (2003). Cortical specialization for face processing: Face-sensitive eve-related potential components in 3 and 12 month old infants. *NeuroImage, 1,* 1180–1193.

Haxby, J. V., Hoffman, E. A., & Gobbini, M. I. (2002). Human neural systems for face recognition and social communication. *Biological Psychiatry, 51,* 59–67.

Hood, B. M., Willen, J. D., & Driver, J. (1998). Adult's eyes trigger shifts of visual attention in human infants. *Psychological Science, 9,* 131–134.

Jaffe, J., Stern, D. N., & Peery, J. C. (1973). "Conversational" coupling of gaze behavior in prelinguistic human development. *Journal of Psycholinguistic Research, 2,* 321–329.

Johnson, M. H. (1999). Cortical plasticity: Implications for normal and abnormal cognitive development. *Development and Psychopathology, 11,* 419–437.

Johnson, M. H., & de Haan, M. (1999). Developing cortical specialization for visual-cognitive function: The case of face recognition. In J. L. McClelland & R. S. Seigler (Eds.), *Mechanisms of Cognitive Development: Behavioural and Neural Perspectives.* Mahwah, NJ: Lawrence Erlbaum Associates.

Johnson, M. H., & Morton J. (1991). Biology and cognitive development: The Case of face recognition. UK: Basic Blackwell.

Johnson, M. H., Dziurawiec, S., Bartrip, J., & Morton J. (1992). The effects of movement of internal features on infants' preferences for face-like stimuli. *Infant Behavior and Development, 15*, 129–136.

Kleinke, C. L. (1986). Gaze and eye contact: A research review. *Psychological Bulletin, 100*, 78–100.

Langton, S. R. H., & Bruce, V. (1999). Reflexive visual orienting in response to the social attention of others. *Visual Cognition, 6*, 541–567.

Meltzoff, A. N., & Moore, M. K. (1977). Imitation of facial and manual gestures by human neonates. *Science, 198*, 74–78.

Morton, J., & Johnson, M. H. (1991). CONSPEC and CONLERN: A two-process theory of infant face recognition. *Psychological Review, 98*, 164–181.

Perrett, D. I., Hietanen, J. K., Oram, M. W., & Benson, P. J. (1992). Organization and functions of cells responsive to faces in the temporal cortex. In V. Bruce, A. Cowey, A. Ellis, & D. Perrett (Eds.), *Processing the facial image: Philosophical Transactions of the Royal Society of London, 335*, 1–128. London: Oxford University Press.

Perrett, D. I., Rolls, E. T., & Caan, W. (1982). Visual neurones responsive to faces in the monkey temporal cortex. *Experimental Brain Research, 47*, 229–238.

Perrett, D. I., Smith, P. A., Potter, D. D., Mistlin, A. J., Head, A. S., Milner, A. D., & Jeeves, M. A. (1985). Visual cells in the temporal cortex sensitive to face view and gaze direction. *Processing of the Royal Society of London, 223*, 293–317.

Posner, M. I. (1980). Orienting of attention. *Quarterly Journal of Experimental Psychology, 32*, 3–25.

Puce, A., Allison, T., Bentin, S., Gore, J. C., & McCarthy, G. (1998). Temporal cortex activation in humans viewing eye and mouth movements. *Journal of Neuroscience, 18*, 2188–2199.

Ricciardelli, P., Ro, T., Driver, J. (2002). A left visual field advantage in perception of gaze direction. *Neuropsychologia, 40*, 769–777.

Schuller, A. M., & Rossion, B. (2001). Spatial attention triggered by eye gaze increases and speeds up early visual activity. *Neuroreport, 12*, 2381–2386.

Symons, L. A., Hains, S. M. J., & Muir, D. W. (1998). Look at me: Five-month-old infants' sensitivity to very small deviations in eye-gaze during social interactions. *Infant Behavior and Development, 21*, 531–536.

Valenza, E., Simion, F., Cassia, V. M., & Umiltà, C. (1996). Face preference at birth. *Journal of Experimental Psychology: Human Perception and Performance, 22*, 892–903.

Vecera, S. P., & Johnson, M. H. (1995). Eye gaze detection and the cortical processing of faces: Evidence from infants and adults. *Visual Cognition, 2*, 101–129.

Watanabe, S., Kakigi, R., & Puce, A. (2001). Occipitotemporal activity elicited by viewing eye movements: A magnetoencephalographic study. *NeuroImage, 13*, 351–363.

Wicker, B., Michel, F., Henaff, M. A., & Decety, J. (1998). Brain regions involved in the perception of gaze: A PET study. *NeuroImage, 8*, 221–227.

2

Neural Systems and the Development of Gaze-Following and Related Joint Attention Skills

Amy Vaughan Van Hecke
University of Illinois at Chicago

Peter Mundy
University of Miami

In a 1975 paper in *Nature*, Bruner and Scaife reported that infants increasingly display the ability to follow the direction of gaze of a social partner between the ages of 6 and 18 months. This observation was groundbreaking, in part because it was inconsistent with the prevailing Piagetian egocentric view of early cognitive development. To refer to this newly observed domain of development, Bruner (1975) adopted the general term *joint attention*. This term, though, was not only applied to gaze-following skills, but to the development of related abilities, as well, such as the tendency of infants to initiate episodes of social attention coordination with gestures (e.g., pointing, showing) and alternating eye contact. Subsequently, the study of gaze-following and related joint attention skills has become a major subdiscipline within the field of developmental psychology.

Our own interest in the development of gaze-following and joint attention has followed along several paths. In common with much of the field, we have been intrigued by the long-standing hypothesis that gaze-following and joint attention reflect the development of a social-cognitive foundation for subsequent language development in typically and atypically developing children (e.g., Bretherton, 1991; Carpenter, Nagell, & Tomasello, 1998). Beyond social-cognition theory, we have also begun to consider the links between joint attention and the early development of self-monitoring, attention-regulation, and social-motivation (Mundy, 2003; Sheinkopf, Mundy, Claussen, & Willoughby, 2004; Vaughan et al., 2003). Lastly, our research group has had an abiding interest in understanding the deficits in gaze-following and joint attention that characterize the early development of children affected by autism (e.g., Mundy, 1995; Mundy & Sigman, 1989).

Each of these lines of research has recently motivated us to begin to consider the neural systems and neurodevelopmental processes that may be involved in the ontogeny of gaze-following and joint attention. Our previous work in this regard, however, has primarily focused on the nature of the systems that may be involved in the capacity of infants to initiate joint attention bids with others (Mundy, 2003; Mundy, Card, & Fox, 2000). In this chapter, we address what is known about the neural systems that are associated with gaze-following and related abilities. To begin this discussion, we first present a brief overview of our perspective on the nature and importance of gaze-following and joint attention development. This is followed by discussions of the functional neuroanatomy of gaze-following, as well as other forms of joint attention. This leads to a consideration of a dual process theory of attention development (Posner & Peterson, 1990; Rothbart & Posner, 2001) and social-cognitive development (Frith & Frith, 1999, 2001) in order to develop a sense of the possible common, as well as unique, neuropsychological processes that may be involved in gaze-following and initiating forms of joint attention. Finally, a preliminary sketch of the important features of an integrative neuro-developmental model of gaze-following and joint attention is provided.

THE NATURE OF GAZE-FOLLOWING AND JOINT ATTENTION IN EARLY DEVELOPMENT

Joint attention refers to processes and behaviors involved in the capacity of infants to coordinate their attention with a social partner. One type of joint attention skill involves infants' ability to follow the direction of another person's gaze (Butterworth & Jarrett, 1991; Scaife & Bruner, 1975). In studies of this domain, children or adults are presented with a real or analogue social partner (e.g., a picture of a face). The gaze of the social partner is directed to the left, right, behind, or below the observing child/adult, and their behavioral or neurophysiological response to the direction of the social partner's gaze is observed. Many of these studies control for and eliminate behaviors that may naturally occur when people use gaze shifting to redirect the attention of a social partner, such as head turning, pointing, and vocalizing. Alternatively, these multi-modal stimuli may be more ecologically valid and more powerful elicitors of attention following, at least in infants (see Flom & Pick, 2003). Therefore, several studies (e.g., Mundy et al., 2000; Ulvund & Smith, 1996) have observed infants' responses to gaze shifting accompanied by head turns, vocalization, and/or pointing in a social interaction (Responds to Joint Attention [RJA]; Seibert, Hogan, & Mundy, 1982). Another dimension of joint attention that arises in the first year involves the infant's use of eye contact and/or deictic gestures (e.g., a pointing or showing) to spontaneously initiate coordinated or shared attention with a social partner. This latter type of proto-declarative act (Bates, 1976) will be referred to as Initiating Joint Attention skill (IJA; Seibert et al., 1982).

Both types of joint attention skills are critical milestones of early development and social learning. For example, much of early vocabulary acquisition in the second year takes place in unstructured or incidental social-learning situations where: a) parents provide learning opportunities by referring to new objects or events, but b) the infant may need to sort through a number of stimuli in order to focus on the correct object/event and to acquire the appropriate new word association. In this situation, infants are confronted with the possibility of "referential mapping errors" (Baldwin, 1995). To deal with this problem, infants utilize the direction of gaze of the parent to limit the number of potential stimuli to which to attend and, therefore, increase the likelihood of a correct word learning experience (Baldwin, 1995). Similarly, when infants initiate bids for joint attention, the responsive caregiver may follow the child's line of regard and take advantage of the child's focus of attention to provide a new word in a context that maximizes the opportunity to learn (cf. Tomasello, 1995). Hence, both gaze-following and IJA are early developing self-organizing facilities that are critical for much of subsequent language development (Baldwin, 1995; Mundy & Neal, 2001).

As previously noted, gaze-following/RJA and IJA may reflect social-cognitive development, or an awareness that others have perspectives and intentions (e.g., Bretherton, 1991; Carpenter et al., 1998). However, this may only be the case in the later stages of development of these skills, in the second year of life (Brooks & Meltzoff, 2002). The rudiments of joint attention and, especially, gaze-following, may emerge as early as 3 months (D'Entremont, Hains, & Muir, 1997; Hood, Willen, & Driver, 1998), and, thus, well before theory suggests that social-cognitive processes affect or organize behavior (Mundy & Sigman, 1989). Indeed, recent research suggests that, in particular, gaze-following/RJA prior to the second year of life is not necessarily complete evidence of social-cognitive development (Brooks & Meltzoff, 2002; Moore, 1996; Woodward, 2003). What other processes may be involved? Candidates here include processes associated with imitation (Meltzoff & Decety,

2003; Pomares, Mundy, Vaughan, Block, & Delgado, 2003), attention-regulation and/or social-motivation processes (Mundy et al., 2000; Sheinkopf et al., 2004), early operant learning processes (Corkum & Moore, 1998), spatial analytic processes (Butterworth & Jarrett, 1991), and inter-sensory integration processes (Flom & Pick, 2003). It may well be the case, though, that gaze-following and RJA behavior in the first year of life provides a critical source of social information that contributes to the development of later emerging social-cognitive facilities (e.g., Baron-Cohen, 1995; Meltzoff & Decety, 2003; Mundy & Neal, 2001). A more complete discussion of this hypothesis will be provided in the concluding section of this chapter.

One infrequently considered aspect of theory and research alluded to previously is that gaze-following and joint attention may involve executive functions and social-motivation processes. For example, to engage in successful gaze-following, infants need to attend to people, process social cues, and then inhibit looking to their social partner and flexibly redirect their attention based on social cues that provide spatial orientation information. Thus, gaze-following may provide a unique and valid measure of the early development of attention regulation skills in infancy. Indeed, Morales et al. (2000b) have observed that RJA at six months is associated with mothers' ratings of individual differences in attention regulation on the Infant Behavior Questionnaire (IBQ; Rothbart, 1981). This observation may be especially important since attention regulation is one of the fundamental building blocks for the development of social-competence (Matsen & Coatsworth, 1998). Therefore, above and beyond its links to language and social cognition, gaze-following may reflect aspects of executive development that are important for the subsequent regulation of social behaviors (Mundy & Sigman, in press; Sheinkopf et al., 2004; Vaughan Van Hecke et al., in press).

Individual differences in the development of gaze-following, RJA, and IJA also reflect factors associated with social-emotional and motivation processes (Mundy, 1995). This, though, may be a more prominent feature of IJA than gaze-following and RJA. Research suggests that IJA, but not RJA, is associated with temperament measures of emotional reactivity (Vaughan et al., 2003) and with the direct observation of the display of positive affect (e.g., Mundy, Kasari, & Sigman, 1992). Moreover, the self-initiation of joint attention behaviors (i.e., IJA) may more clearly reflect social motivation processes than behaviors involving the response to cues, such as gaze-following and RJA (Mundy, 1995). Indeed, it may be that these differences in social-emotional and motivation processes contribute to divergent patterns of growth and associations across observations of IJA and RJA (Block et al., 2003; Mundy, Sigman, & Kasari, 1994; Mundy & Gomes, 1998; Mundy et al., 2000). These observations are not consistent with the notion that gaze-following/RJA and IJA measure the same processes involved in the early development of social-cognition (Baron-Cohen, 1995; Tomasello, 1995; Carpenter et al., 1998). Thus, there is a need to better understand the degree to which the development of gaze-following/RJA and IJA reflect common and/or unique sets of processes. To address this issue, it is useful to compare and contrast the development of gaze-following and IJA in terms of behavioral, psychological, and neurophysiological processes. Much of our own work, including this chapter, has adopted this perspective.

THE IMPORTANCE OF GAZE-FOLLOWING AND JOINT ATTENTION IN EARLY DEVELOPMENT

One of the more important tests of theory on the importance of joint attention development involves examining the longitudinal continuity between infant gaze-following, or related joint attention skills, and later childhood developmental outcomes. A consistent observation from this type of research has been that individual differences in infant gaze-following and RJA are related to subsequent language development.

Robust correlations between RJA measures in the second year and subsequent language acquisition have been observed in both typically and atypically developing children, even after controlling for individual differences in general aspects of cognitive development (Mundy & Gomes, 1998; Mundy, Kasari, Sigman, & Ruskin, 1995). Indeed, recent data indicate that infant RJA measures have long-term predictive validity. RJA measures at 12 and 18 months have been observed to significantly correlate with language development at 3 to 7 years in typical and at-risk samples (Acra, Mundy, Claussen, Scott & Bono, 2003; Block et al., 2003; Neal et al., 2003). Moreover, there is evidence that individual differences in RJA skills may be observed as early as 6 months of age, and that these differences predict language outcomes at 12, 24, and 30 months (Morales, Mundy, & Rojas, 1998; Morales et al., 2000a, b).

IJA skills also appear to be related to language outcomes (Carpenter et al., 1998; Mundy & Gomes, 1998), but some evidence suggests that RJA measures may be the more consistent or robust correlates of early language outcomes (Mundy et al., 1995; Mundy & Gomes, 1998). However, others have reported that IJA, rather than RJA, appears to be the strongest correlate of 5 to 6-year-old verbal and performance IQ outcomes in at-risk infants (Ulvund & Smith, 1996). Obviously, more research is needed to understand the relative contributions of processes tapped by both of these dimensions of joint attention vis-à-vis language development.

There have been surprisingly few empirical reports on the longitudinal links between infant joint attention development and social cognitive development. Indeed, there currently may be only one empirical study on this issue.

Charman et al. (2000) followed a sample of 13 typically developing infants from 20 to 44 months. At 20 months, observations were recorded of toddlers spontaneously alternating eye contact between a tester and an interesting toy spectacle. This type of "alternating gaze" measure is an early index of IJA (e.g., Mundy, Sigman, Ungerer, & Sherman, 1986; Tomasello, 1995). After controlling for differences in IQ and language development, the 20-month IJA alternating gaze measure was a significant predictor of 44 month Theory of Mind (ToM) performance. No data, though, were presented on gaze-following or RJA in this study. The paucity of information on this topic is a significant gap. Nevertheless, research on the neural systems involved in gaze-following/RJA, IJA, and attention, to be described later in this chapter, provides an intriguing, albeit indirect, empirical bridge to social-cognitive development.

Recent theory and research also suggests that there may be important links between gaze-following, joint attention, and social-emotional processes that may be associated with the development of social competence (Mundy & Sigman, in press). RJA skill, assessed with caregivers at 6 months of age, was related to toddlers' adaptive emotion and attention regulatory behaviors on a delay of gratification task at 24 months (Morales, Mundy, Crowson, Neal, & Delgado, 2005). Vaughan Van Hecke and colleagues (in press) have reported that infant-tester interaction measures of both RJA and IJA at 12 months are negatively related to parent reports of externalizing behaviors at 30 months in a sample of typically developing infants. Similarly, Sheinkopf and colleagues (2004) reported that 12, 15, and 18 month average IJA and RJA scores were significantly associated with preschool teacher reports of classroom externalizing behavior at 36 months in cocaine-exposed infants. Multiple regression data in this study indicated that both joint attention measures made unique contributions to the prediction of externalizing behavior. Furthermore, infant RJA was also a significant negative predictor of teacher reports of withdrawn behavior, but a positive predictor of teacher reports of social competence. In a longer-term follow-up of this sample, though, Acra and colleagues (2003) have observed that IJA, but not RJA, was negatively related to parent and teacher observations of externalizing, but positively associated with observations of social competence at seven years of age. These studies are interesting, but much more work needs to be done to delineate and understand these possible lines of developmental continuity.

In summary, recent longitudinal data are consistent with theory that suggests that there are important points of bio-behavioral continuity between joint attention processes and later language, cognitive, and social development. One implication of this literature is that research on infant gaze-following and joint attention measures has much to contribute to understanding the processes that contribute to problems in social and cognitive outcome among "at-risk" and developmentally disordered children. Nowhere has this potential been more evident than in the study of autism.

JOINT ATTENTION IMPAIRMENTS IN AUTISM

Autism is a biologically based disorder that may be more prevalent than once thought, with the spectrum of autism-related disorders occurring at a rate of 2–6 per thousand (Fombonne, 2003). Pathognomic features of this syndrome include impaired social and communication development. One important characteristic of these social impairments is a robust early disturbance of joint attention development (Mundy et al., 1986; Mundy & Sigman, 1989). Observations of joint attention deficits are extremely well replicated and appear to be universal among young children with autism (Filipek et al., 1999). Moreover, the joint attention domain appears to be sensitive to early individual differences in the development of children with autism that are related to language and social outcomes (Bono, Daley, & Sigman, 2004; Mundy et al., 1994; Sigman & Ruskin, 1999).

Young children with autism display deficits in both IJA and RJA skills. However, with development, there is evidence of dissociation in correlates and course of these joint attention impairments. For example, although some studies suggested that children with autism may not use RJA in language development (Baron-Cohen, Baldwin, & Crowson, 1997), other research has suggested that RJA is significantly related to language development (Carpenter, Pennington, & Rogers, 2002; Sigman & Ruskin, 1999), and may even may moderate the effectiveness of early intervention on language development with these children (Bono et al., 2004). The relation of IJA to language development, though, has been less clear in these studies. Research has also suggested that RJA may be more sensitive to parent-child interaction effects associated with attachment among children with autism (Capps, Sigman, & Mundy, 1994). In contrast to RJA, observations have suggested that IJA deficits may be more highly associated with impairments in positive affective expression in autism (Kasari, Sigman, Mundy, & Yirmiya, 1990), parent reports of symptoms of social impairments (Mundy et al., 1994; see also Rogers, Hepburn, Stackhouse, & Wehner, 2003), and long-term social outcomes (Lord, Floody, Anderson, & Pickles, 2003; Sigman & Ruskin, 1999).

Of course, these observations were derived from studies with modest sample sizes; hence they may be prone to Type II error. However, several studies now indicate that, although delayed in development, children with autism display basic gaze-following ability by 2 years of age (Charwarska, Klin, & Volkmar, 2003), and problems in RJA may remit among older children with autism or those with higher mental ages (Mundy et al., 1994; Leekam & Moore, 2001; Sigman & Ruskin, 1999). However, IJA deficits remain robust. As alluded to earlier, this difference in course of joint attention skills development in autism may be explained by the basic difference between gaze-following/RJA and IJA skills. The latter reflects spontaneously generated social attention coordination behavior, whereas gaze-following/RJA involves the perception and response to the social cues of another person. IJA, then, may be more affected by executive and social-motivation processes involved in the generation and self-initiation of behavioral goals than RJA (Mundy, 1995; Mundy et al., 2000). In particular, IJA deficits in autism appear to reflect an impairment in the tendency to spontaneously initiate episodes of shared affective experience concerning an object or an event with a social partner, and this process does not appear to be involved to as great an extent in RJA (Kasari et al., 1990).

To review, gaze-following and related joint attention skills not only reflect early social cognitive development, but, also, contribute to self-organizing systems that facilitate early social learning. They also provide developmental markers of aspects of the development of attention regulation, and emotional and motivation processes that play a role in subsequent individual differences in social competence. Furthermore, deficits in gaze-following/RJA, and, especially, IJA, are cardinal symptoms of autism, a complex developmental disorder that results in a pernicious attenuation of social competencies. Therefore, it seems likely that understanding and comparing the brain systems involved in various types of joint attention skill development may provide clues with respect to critical aspects of the neurobiology of social development, as well as the neural systems that may be central to autism. In this regard, we first consider the emergent literature on the neurobiology of gaze-following and RJA.

GAZE-FOLLOWING, RJA, AND THE VENTRAL "SOCIAL BRAIN"

Social perception appears to be supported by a complex ventromedial "social brain" circuit involving the orbito-frontal cortex, temporal cortical areas, including the superior temporal sulcus (STS) as well as superior temporal gyrus (STG), and ventral subcortical areas such as the amygdala (Adolphs, 2001; Brothers, 1990). With respect to gaze-following, research using a variety of methods (electrophysiological methods, imaging, and comparative) has converged to indicate that gaze monitoring and following is mediated by part of this social brain circuit contained within the superior temporal sulcus (STS) and gyrus (STG), adjacent parietal areas (e.g., Brodmann's area 40), and the amygdala. The temporal and parietal areas of the brain are thought to contain neural networks that respond preferentially to faces, animate movement, and spatial orientation, including head, eye, and body orientation (e.g., Emery, 2000; Calder et al., 2002), while the amygdala, in conjunction with the orbito-frontal cortex, is thought to be involved in evaluating the valence or reward value of stimuli (e.g., Adolphs, 2001; Dawson et al., 2002).

Wicker, Michel, Henaff, and Decety (2002) observed that neural groups in the posterior STS were activated in response to faces with direct or horizon-tally averted eye gaze, but not to faces with downward eye gaze. Wicker et al., however, did not observe differences between direct and averted eye gaze con-ditions. Alternatively, Puce, Allison, Bentin, Gore, and McCarthy (1998) re-ported that videos of face stimuli with gaze moving horizontally from forward to averted elicited greater posterior STS activation compared to faces with sta-tic forward gaze. Face matching on the basis of direction of gaze also elicited activation of neurons in the left posterior STS, while identity-based face matching elicited bilateral activation from the fusiform and inferior occipital gyri (Hoffman and Haxby, 2000). Similarly, George, Driver, and Dolan (2001) reported that direct gaze stimuli elicited more fusiform activation than averted gaze stimuli. Finally, Kingstone, Friesen, and Gazzaniga (2000) reported data on gaze-following in two split brain patients that was consistent with the notion that parietal, as well as temporal, subsystems specialized for face processing and processing of information relevant to spatial orientation combine to support the development of gaze-following.

Mundy et al. (2000) have also reported observations linking gaze-following/RJA to parietal processes. These authors examined the longitudinal relations between baseline EEG at 14 months and RJA at 18 months in 32 typically de-veloping infants as measured on the Early Social Communication Scales (ESCS; Seibert et al., 1982; Mundy, Hogan, & Doehring, 1996). The EEG data were collected with electrodes placed bilaterally at dorso-frontal, cen-tral, temporal, parietal, and occipital sites. RJA at 18 months was predicted by EEG indices of left-parietal activation and right parietal deactivation at 14 months. These data were quite consistent with previous research (Emery, 2000) that suggested that parietal areas specialized for spatial orienting and attention, along with temporal systems specialized for processing gaze, may contribute to gaze-following or related RJA skill development.

Dawson et al. (2002) have reported a neuropsychological study of joint attention ability in young children with autism that is also indicative of rela-tions between gaze-following and temporal social brain activity. Dawson et al. observed that performance on a type of delayed non-match to sample (DNMS) measure, that has previously been associated with functions of a temporal-ventromedial-frontal circuit, was significantly associated with performance on a combined measure of RJA/IJA in children with autism and typical devel-opment. Although the joint attention measure reflected both RJA and IJA skills, it was constructed in such a fashion as to likely be biased to the former.

The DNMS measure was thought to provide an index of processes associated with rule learning that depends on the orbito-frontal and amygdala-mediated capacity to associate novel stimuli with reward value. Hence, the authors suggested that this ventral brain function plays a role in the social learning that contributes to gaze-following/RJA development. However, the results of this study did not indicate that processes tapped by the DNMS data played a major role in the nature of autism.

The results of these human imaging, electrophysiology, and neuropsychological studies are consistent with earlier reports from comparative research that provide experimental evidence of temporal (i.e., STS) and parietal involvement in gaze-following (Emery, 2000). In two studies, pre-surgical monkeys demonstrated a clear ability to discriminate face stimuli on the basis of direction of gaze. After resection of the STS, however, the gaze discrimination abilities of the monkeys fell to chance (Cambell, Heywood, Cowey, Regard, & Landis, 1990; Heyward & Cowey, 1992). Eacott, Heywood, Gross, & Cowey (1993) compared two groups of monkeys: those with and without STS surgically induced lesions, on a task of discriminating pairs of eyes directed straight ahead or averted 5° or more. The results indicated that the nonlesioned monkeys were capable of discriminating targets involving horizontal eye gaze shifts of greater than 5°, but the STS lesioned animals were not. Eacott et al. also reported that the lesioned animals performed worse than the nonlesioned animals on a non-social task involving the discrimination between stimuli formed from ASCII characters.

The latter observation reminds us that, although research is beginning to pinpoint the systems involved in gaze-following and social perception, the specificity of these systems for social versus non-social processing has still to be definitively examined. One recent study, though, has addressed a related issue in imaging research on human gaze-following. Hooker (2002) used whole brain functional magnetic resonance imaging to compare neural activity in response to: 1) horizontal eye movement stimuli that provided directional information about where a visual stimulus would appear, or 2) arrow stimuli that provided equivalent directional information, or 3) eye movements that did not provide directional information. Hooker (2002) observed more activity in the STS in the first condition compared to either of the other conditions. Alternatively, Hooker reported more activity in the fusiform gyrus and prefrontal cortex in the eye-motion control condition (Condition 3) compared to the other conditions. These data were consistent with the notion that the STS may develop a specialization for processing gaze related, social-spatial orientation information.

Activity in other areas of the social brain has also been observed to be involved in gaze-following. In one study, Kawashima et al. (1999) reported that the left amygdala displayed activation to faces with horizontal gaze aversion, but that right amygdala activation increased with presentation of direct gaze pictures of faces. It may be important to note, though, that the subjects in this study were eight righted-handed men from the Imuyama region of Japan, and the stimuli involved digitized cinematic images of an attractive Japanese woman's face (see Figure 1 in Kawashima et al., 1999). The relative attractiveness of face stimuli, however, may affect the pattern of brain activity observed in response to gaze stimuli (Kampe, Frith, Dolan, & Frith, 2001).

Specifically, the Kampe et al. (2001) study revealed increased activity in the ventral striatum in response to more attractive faces with direct gaze and decreased activity to less attractive faces with averted gaze. The ventral striatum is part of the input system of the basal ganglia and plays a specific role in the "limbic loop" that receives information from the medial and lateral temporal lobes (e.g., amygdala) and passes it on to thalamic nuclei and, ultimately, to the anterior cingulate and orbito-frontal cortex (Martin, 1996). Based on this, Kampe et al. (2001) suggested that the ventral striatum and associated neural groups may be involved in processing the relative reward value associated with eye contact and gaze aversion. This observation is not only consistent with Dawson et al. (2002), but also suggests that variability of stimulus characteristics (e.g., their representation of reward value) may both inform and complicate research on the complex neural systems involved in processing gaze and gaze direction.

One puzzling aspect of the imaging research on gaze-following has recently been noted by Calder et al. (2002). Theoretically, gaze-following behavior reflects aspects of social-cognitive processes (e.g., Baron-Cohen, 1995). In this regard, recent imaging studies have suggested that, in addition to ventral social brain activation, social-cognition is associated with activation of the dorsal medial frontal cortex (Brodmann's areas 8/9) and the anterior cingulate (Frith & Frith, 1999, 2001; Mundy, 2003). So why have studies of gaze-following not observed a link with frontal, dorsal medial activation? Calder et al. (2002) suggested that task difficulty needs to be considered in this regard. Most studies have examined passive gaze-following on tasks that did not require the perception or inference of intentions on the basis of eye gaze. These authors suggested that more complex presentations of sequences of stimuli involving gaze directed toward and away from participants may elicit this type of processing, and evidence of more dorsal contributions to the neural substrate of gaze-following. To this end, Calder et al. (2002) used Positron Emission Tomography (PET) to examine the neural responses of nine female volunteers to a relatively complex sequence of faces with gaze averted, gaze direct, and gaze down orientations. It was not completely clear from the methods described in this paper how these stimuli might have elicited more processing of intentionality than in previous studies. Nevertheless, the results provided evidence of activation in the dorsal medial frontal cortex (BA 8/9) and medial frontal cortex proximal to the anterior cingulate (BA 32), as well as areas of the STS, in response to horizontal gaze aversion. This study, though, unlike most others, employed a sample of women rather than men. So, it is unclear whether an as yet unrecognized gender effect may have also played in a role in these observations.

This caveat notwithstanding, it is clearly the case that when the interpretation of intentions is an overt feature of the demands of a gaze processing task, activation of the dorsal medial frontal cortex appears to be involved. In an fMRI study, Baron-Cohen et al. (1999) presented six individuals with Asperger disorder and 12 typical controls with the "eyes test," which requires inferring of people's emotional states or gender from pictures of their eyes. The results of this study indicated that, in addition to activity in the orbito-frontal cortex, amygdala, and STS of the social brain, activation of the left and right dorsal medial-frontal cortex was also a specific correlate of performance on this task in the typical sample. Interestingly, the autism groups failed to display amygdala activation and may not have shown as much right dorsal medial activation. Russell et al. (2000) have also employed the eyes test (Baron-Cohen et al., 1999) in an fMRI study of the neural characteristics of individuals affected by schizophrenia. The control sample displayed relatively more activity in the medial-frontal lobe (Brodmann's areas 9/45) in association with performance on this task, relative to the individuals with schizophrenia. In addition, more ventral social brain components of the left inferior frontal gyrus (Brodmann's areas 44/45/47) and the left middle and superior temporal gyri (Brodmann's areas 21/22) contributed to clinical group differences on performance on this task.

In summary, the emerging literature on gaze-following indicates that the most consistent correlates of gaze-following and RJA appear to involve ventral social brain neural clusters in the STS. However, there is also evidence that parietal, orbito-frontal, and amygdala processes may play a role in gaze-following. Moreover, when and if tasks involve inference of intentions (i.e., social cognition), more dorsal medial cortical systems may be brought to bear in processing gaze related stimuli. This pattern of results is interesting in that is consistent with developmental studies that suggest that gaze-following may initially not reflect social cognitive activity per se, but that it comes to do so over time and experience (Brooks & Meltzoff, 2002; Moore, 1996; Woodward, 2003). We will return to this issue after considering the neural correlates of other forms of joint attention, especially IJA.

IJA, SOCIAL-COGNITION, AND THE DORSAL "SOCIAL BRAIN"

In addition to the work of Dawson et al. (2002), two other studies examined the neuropsychological correlates of joint attention in children with autism and controls (Griffith, Pennington, Wehner, & Rogers, 1999; McEvoy, Rogers,

& Pennington, 1993). Unlike Dawson et al.'s research, though, these studies used separate IJA and RJA measures from the ESCS. Both of these studies observed that performance on a spatial reversal task, that presumably taps into dorsolateral frontal response inhibition, memory, and planning processes, was related to both IJA and RJA in young typically developing children and children with autism. Hence, these studies provided data that were consistent with the notion that common executive functions may play a role in RJA and IJA development.

In addition to common processes, though, Mundy (2003) has observed that the input or perception of social behaviors, such as gaze-following/RJA, is very different from the output or spontaneous organization and initiation of social behaviors, such as in initiating joint attention bids. Therefore, there may be differences, as well as similarities, in the neural systems that contribute to these types of joint attention behaviors. One aspect of these differences was observed in a study of the behavioral outcome of 13 infants who underwent hemispherectomies in an attempt to treat their intractable seizure disorders (Caplan et al., 1993). PET data were gathered prior to surgical intervention with the infants, and the ESCS was used to assess the post-surgical development of IJA and RJA, as well as the tendency for infants to Initiate Behavior Requests (IBR). In addition to comparing IJA and RJA, IBR may also be important to consider in research on joint attention. Whereas IJA reflects the social use of attention directing behavior (e.g., directing attention to show or share interest in an object), IBR involves the instrumental use of attention directing behavior (e.g., directing attention to elicit aid in obtaining an object or event). Hence, by comparing IJA behaviors (e.g., showing a jar containing toys) with IBR behaviors (e.g., giving a jar containing toys to request aid in opening the jar) brain systems associated with the spontaneous initiation of "social" joint attention bids versus "instrumental" joint attention bids may be examined. The results indicated that metabolic activity in the frontal hemispheres, and especially the left frontal hemisphere, predicted the development of Initiating Joint Attention (IJA) skill in this sample. However, the post-surgical development of the capacity of children to respond to the joint attention bids (RJA), or initiate requesting bids (IBR), was not observed to relate to any of the PET indexes of cortical activity. Moreover, metabolic activity recorded from other brain regions, including ventral social brains regions of the orbital, temporal, parietal, and occipital cortex, were not significantly associated with IJA or other social-communication skills in this study. Thus, frontal activity appeared to be specifically related to the development of the tendency to spontaneously initiate social joint attention bids to share experiences with others.

Mundy et al. (2000) followed up on these observations with a study of the links between EEG activity and joint attention development between 14 and

18 months. As previously noted, one result of this study was the observation that 14-month parietal activity predicted differences in RJA skill development at 18 months. Alternatively, individual differences in 18-month IJA were predicted by a different and complex pattern of 14-month EEG activity at left medial-frontal electrodes sites, as well as indices of right central deactivation, left occipital activation, and right occipital deactivation. Although the source location of the EEG data could not be definitively determined in this study, the frontal correlates of IJA reflected activity only from electrode F3 of the 10/20 placement system. This electrode was positioned above a point of confluence of Brodmann's areas 8 and 9 of the medial-frontal cortex of the left hemisphere (Martin, 1996). This area includes aspects of the frontal eye fields and supplementary motor cortex commonly observed to be involved in an anterior system of attention control (Posner & Peterson, 1990).

This study suggested that a dual process, or multiple systems, neurodevelopmental, model of joint attention development might be useful to consider (Mundy et al., 2000). In particular, activity of ventral and parietal systems may be a common correlate of gaze-following/RJA, while more dorsal activation may be a relatively stronger component of IJA. However, even with the combined data from Caplan et al. (1993) and Mundy et al. (2000), the evidence for frontal IJA connections was far more tenuous that the evidence for temporal-parietal RJA connections. Thus, the recent contribution of Henderson, Yoder, Yale, & McDuffie (2002) becomes even more important.

Henderson et al. (2002) also employed the ESCS to examine baseline EEG at 14 months as a predictor of 18-month joint attention development in 27 typically developing infants. However, to improve the spatial resolution of their data, they used a higher-density array of 64 electrodes. Moreover, they reasoned that, since the total ESCS scores for measures of IJA and other domains used in Mundy et al. (2000) were composites of several behaviors, the exact nature of the associations with EEG activity were unclear. Therefore, Henderson et al. (2002) compared the EEG correlates of only two types of behaviors, self-initiated pointing to share attention with respect to an active mechanical toy (IJA pointing) and self-initiated pointing to elicit aid in obtaining an out-of-reach object (IBR pointing). In the ESCS, the former involves pointing to a toy that is within easy reach, and the latter involves pointing to a toy that is out of reach.

In this study, no significant correlations were observed between any of the 14-month EEG data and IBR pointing at 18 months. However, in the 3–6 Hz band, 14-month EEG data indicative of greater brain activity over the medial frontal cortex was strongly associated with more IJA pointing at 18 months. These correlations involved electrodes that were placed above cortical regions corresponding to Brodmann's areas 8, 9, and 6. Henderson et al. (2002) also analyzed data from the 6–9 Hz band, which revealed 15 significant correlations between 14-month EEG data and 18-month IJA pointing. Again, higher bilateral activity corresponding to the previously identified medial-frontal sites was a strong predictor of IJA pointing at 18 months. In addition, IJA pointing at 18 months was also predicted by activity in this bandwidth from regions of the orbito-frontal, temporal, and dorsolateral frontal cortical regions. Thus, this study suggested that that IJA development might reflect an integration of dorsal cortical functions (Mundy et al., 2000) with the ventral social brain and dorso-lateral functions identified in other studies (Dawson et al., 2002; Griffith et al., 1999). However, there was little evidence for parietal involvement in IJA.

The study of Henderson et al. (2002) also provided information about the social specificity of the link between IJA and dorsal cortical brain activity. As previously noted, the specific medial frontal cortical areas of involvement suggested by data from Mundy et al. (2000) and some of the data from Henderson et al. (2002) correspond to aspects of both the frontal eye fields and supplementary motor cortex associated with the control of saccadic eye movement and motor planning (Martin, 1996). Therefore, these associations could simply reflect the motor control of the eye movements and/or gestural behaviors that are intrinsic to joint attention behavior. However, the Henderson et al. study controls for this possible interpretation. The gross motor topography of IJA pointing and IBR pointing is virtually identical on the ESCS. Therefore, a neuro-motor explanation of the different cortical correlates of IJA and IBR appears unlikely. Instead, since IJA pointing and IBR pointing appear to serve different social-communicative functions, it is reasonable to assume that the difference in EEG correlates of these infant behaviors also reflects differences in the neurodevelopmental substrates of these social-communicative functions.

Of course, even data from three studies (Caplan et al., 1993; Henderson et al., 2002; Mundy et al., 2000) are not sufficient to draw strong conclusions about frontal cortical associations with IJA. Recall, though, that joint attention skills, and especially IJA (Swettenham et al., 1998), may reflect an incipient aspect of social-cognitive and, specifically, theory of mind (ToM) development. If this is true, then the neural correlates of ToM-related task performance may provide information about the neural systems involved in IJA. Indeed, recent imaging research indicates that brain activity in the dorsal medial cortex (Brodmann's areas 8/9) and adjacent subcortical areas of the anterior cingulate is the most consistent correlate of ToM task performance (Frith & Frith, 1999, 2001). This is true for both verbal and nonverbal measures of social cognition, though, in the latter, areas of the right inferior-frontal cortex, right cerebellum, and right and left temporal cortices may also be involved in solving social-cognitive tasks (see Mundy, 2003, for a review). This literature provides evidence of a potentially significant neuro-functional linkage that lends credence to observations of a dorsal medial-frontal contribution to IJA.

Thus, recent research suggests that the most consistent brain process correlates of IJA, ToM, and social-cognitive performance appears to involve activity in the dorsal medial frontal cortex (DMFC), although more ventral-temporal social brain processes may also be involved (Frith & Frith, 1999, 2001; Mundy, 2003). Alternatively, current research suggests that ventral brain and parietal processes are the most consistent correlates of gaze-following and RJA, but some evidence of DMFC involvement has also been presented. Little evidence of parietal involvement in IJA has been presented. Hence, the literature reviewed so far suggests that multiple neural systems contribute to joint attention and social cognitive development.

Research and theory on attention development, which describes the initial contribution of parietal systems to less volitional attention control followed by the advent of more medial frontal contributions to volitional attention control (e.g., Rothbart, Posner, & Rosicky, 1994), may assist in understanding the function of these multiple neural systems. Similarly, social cognitive theory that describes the integration of ventral brain processes associated with the perception of others' social behavior and self-monitoring related to more dorsal medial cortical systems (Frith & Frith, 1999, 2001) might also be useful to consider. In the next section, the implications of these perspectives for a more coherent view of the neuropsychological processes involved in the development of gaze-following and other aspects of joint attention are examined.

THE POSTERIOR ATTENTION SYSTEM AND GAZE-FOLLOWING/RJA

Posner, Rothbart, and colleagues (e.g., Posner & Peterson, 1990; Rothbart et al., 1994) have described the development of mechanisms of attention in the first years of life in terms of an early developing posterior system and a later developing anterior system. The details of the posterior system may help to elucidate an understanding of the neurodevelopmental processes involved in the emergence of gaze-following/RJA (Mundy et al., 2000).

The posterior system is thought to begin to come on-line between birth and 4 months of age, and it regulates reflexive or non-volitional shifts of attention. Research suggests that aspects of this network develop in the first 4 months of life and that they are localized to the superior parietal lobe, the pulvinar and reticular nuclei of the thalamus, and the midbrain superior colliculus (Rothbart & Posner, 2001). Specifically, the parietal lobe allows the disengagement of attention from a current focus, the superior colliculus allows the shift of attention to a new location, and the pulvinar and reticular nuclei allow increased processing of information gathered from the new focus. The behavioral concomitants of this pattern of cortical and subcortical control are strikingly similar to the behavioral mechanisms involved in gaze-following and responding to joint attention (Mundy et al., 2000). Moreover, other research has begun to provide a more detailed picture of the neurodevelopment of this posterior attention system.

First, between 1 and 2 months of age, infants often engage in periods of extended gaze, also called "obligatory looking" or "sticky fixation" (Hood, 1995), controlled by a pathway from the retina through the basal ganglia, which then inhibits the superior colliculus from ending this period of fixation (Johnson, 1990; Rothbart et al., 1994). Second, infants are able to track moving stimuli at this age, but their tracking involves following a target while in their central visual field, reorienting when it moves out of the central field, and following it again. Research has shown that this type of "choppy" tracking is indicative of collicular control of eye movements (Johnson, 1990). Third, it has been suggested that the superior colliculus derives most of its input from stimuli in the temporal, versus nasal, visual field. Indeed, it has been shown that newborns orient more readily to stimuli in the temporal visual field (Simion, Valenza, & Umilta, 1998).

Evidence of more cortical control of eye movements in infants has been observed by about 3 months of age, when a pathway from the frontal eye fields (BA 8/9) that releases the superior colliculus from inhibition begins to provide additional input to structures controlling visual attention (Johnson, 1990). The function of this pathway may underlie 4-month-old infants' ability to suppress automatic visual saccades in order to respond to a second, more attractive stimulus (Johnson, 1995), and 6-month-olds' ability to respond to a peripheral target when central, competing stimuli are present (Atkinson, Hood, Wattam-Bell, & Braddick, 1992). These observations are of interest for two reasons. First, it is reasonable to speculate that the functions of this pathway also contribute to the capacity for gaze-following that also begins to manifest itself in the 3- to 6-month period (D'Entremont et al., 1997; Hood et al., 1998; Morales et al., 1998). Second, this pathway is associated with dorsal-medial cortical areas (BA 8/9) that have also been associated with social cognitive development.

The ability to make saccades to targets may also recruit the capacity to disengage attention, and this is a primary function of the parietal lobe, which develops rapidly in the 3rd and 4th months of life (Johnson, Posner, & Rothbart, 1991). Furthermore, PET studies have shown that the metabolism of the parietal lobe is at adult levels by 4 months of age (Chugani, Phelps, & Mazziotta, 1987), perhaps also coinciding with the development of infants' ability to anticipate visual shifts of attention based upon previous information (Clohessy, Posner, & Rothbart, 2001) and smoothly track moving stimuli

(Johnson, 1990). Together, these data suggest that multiple structures subserving reflexive shifts of attention are coming on-line in the first six months of life, at a time when gaze-following begins to emerge.

One aspect of this model of the posterior attention system is the supposition that it regulates reflexive attention in response to biologically significant stimuli (Rothbart et al., 1994). In this regard, research suggests that human faces are one of the most salient features of infants' early visual experience, and that there may be an innate tendency to orient toward face or face-like stimuli shortly after birth (Bard, Platzman, Lester, & Suomi, 1992). Newborn infants preferentially track schematic pictures of faces versus non-face and blank pictures (Johnson, Dziurawiec, Ellis, & Morton, 1991). In addition, Simion et al. (1998) found that infants preferentially visually fixate on head-shaped pictures with solid, black squares placed appropriately for the eyes and mouth versus head-shaped pictures where the eyes and mouth blocks are reversed (eyes where the mouth should be and vice versa). This finding remained even when infants were presented with pictures which varied in visual saliency— that is, when the blocks representing the internal features were striped, instead of solid. In this instance, infants still preferred the more naturalistic of the pictures, where solid blocks represented the internal features of the face. Infants also preferred face-like patterns with an outside contour, once again pointing to a specific inclination toward face-like stimuli that are relatively more naturalistic. Moreover, newborn infants prefer normal schematic faces to scrambled faces, and their mother's face to a stranger's, which may suggest a rapid environmental learning effect on face preference (Pascalis & de Schonen, 1994; Valenza, Simion, Cassia, & Umilta, 1996; Webb & Nelson, 2001). A preference for familiar faces contrasts with newborn processing of non-social stimuli, where novelty is preferred (Fantz, Fagan, & Miranda, 1975).

The exact nature of the mechanisms that lead to an early tendency to relegate attention to faces is not clear at this time. Theory and research has suggested the possibility of a modular system for face processing (Farah, Rabinowitz, Quinn, & Grant, 2000). Other research suggests that there may be mechanisms that lead to an initial bias to face processing because of stimulus characteristics or motivational parameters. For example, research has long suggested that an initial attention bias may occur because the human face presents general stimulus contour and contrast features that infants prefer (Fantz et al., 1975). Recent research also raises the distinct possibility that the synchronous multi-modal nature of faces (i.e., they frequently present combinations of eye, mouth, and facial muscle movement with vocal sounds) may be a pre-potent stimulus for early face attention and information processing (Bahrick & Lickliter, 2002). Alternatively, some models of early development raise the possibility of an innate affective motivation system that promotes infants' attention to the faces of their caregivers (Trevarthen & Aitken, 2001).

Subsequent to initial biases, though, experience and social learning may make a major contribution to a preference for attention to faces relative to other stimuli because of social learning (Johnson & Morton, 1991). In any event, it may well be that a proclivity for visual face processing early in infancy leads to a species-typical flow of social interaction that interacts with the developing posterior spatial orientation attention system of children to give rise to a specific facility for gaze-following.

THE ANTERIOR ATTENTION SYSTEM
AND INITIATING JOINT ATTENTION

In addition and in conjunction with this posterior system, attention is also regulated by an anterior system involving the dorsal medial frontal cortex (BA 8/9) and the anterior cingulate (BA 24). This anterior network may become functional after the posterior parietal system and is thought to make numerous contributions to the planning, self-initiation, and self-monitoring of goal-directed behaviors, including visual orienting (Rothbart et al., 1994). One important component process here is the role the anterior system plays in the capacity to share attention across dual tasks, or foci of attention (Stuss, Shallice, Alexander, & Picton, 1995), especially with respect to the capacity to maintain and flexibly switch between goal representations in working memory (e.g., Birrell & Brown, 2000; Rushworth, Hadland, Paus, & Siplia, 2002). This anterior capacity may play a role in infants' ability to maintain representations of self, a social partner, and an interesting object spectacle while flexibly switching attention between these foci in initiating joint attention behaviors (Mundy et al., 2000).

The attention switching facility of the anterior system plays a critical role in the contribution to the supervisory attention system (SAS; Norman & Shallice, 1986) that functions to guide behavior, especially attention deployment, depending on the motivational context of the task (e.g., Amador, Schlag-Rey, & Schlag, 2000; Bush, Luu, & Posner, 2000). In this regard, this system ultimately comes to participate in monitoring and representing the self, and directing attention to internal and external events (Faw, 2003).

With respect to self-representation, Craik et al. (1999) and Johnson et al. (2002) have reported studies that reveal that self-referenced memory processes preferentially activate the DMFC component of this anterior system. With respect to self-monitoring, research has led to the observation that, when people make erroneous saccadic responses in an attention deployment task, there is a negative deflection in the stimulus and response locked ERP called the error related negativity, or ERN (Luu, Flaisch, & Tucker, 2000; Bush et al., 2000). Source localization suggests the ERN emanates from an area of the

DMFC proximal to the anterior cingulate cortex (Luu et al., 2000). Observations of the ERN suggest that there are specific cell groups within the DMFC/AC that are not only active in initiating a behavioral act, such as orienting to a stimulus, but, also, distinct cell groups involved in the processing of the positive or negative outcome of the response behavior (i.e., accuracy and reward or reinforcement information; e.g., Amador et al., 2000; Holroyd & Coles, 2002).

Finally, with respect to directing attention to external and internal events, Frith and Frith (1999, 2001) have argued that the DMFC/AC integrates proprioceptive information from the self (e.g., emotions or intentions) with exteroceptive perceptions, processed by the STS, about the goal-directed behaviors and emotions of others. This integrative activity may be facilitated by the abundance of connections between the DMFC/AC and the STS (Morecraft, Guela, & Mesulam, 1993). Indeed, cell groups in and around BA 8/9 may be especially well connected to the STS (Ban, Shiwa, & Kawamura, 1991). We have described this putative facility for the integration of proprioceptive self-information with exteroceptive social perceptions as a social executive function (SEF) of the dorsal medial frontal cortex and anterior cingulate system (Mundy, 2003). Hypothetically, this SEF utilizes the DMFC/AC facility for the maintenance of representation of multiple goals in working memory to compare and integrate the actions of self and others. This integration gives rise to the capacity to infer the intentions of others by matching them with representations of self-initiated actions or intentions (Stich & Nichols, 1992). Once this integration begins to occur in the DMFC/AC, a fully functional, adaptive, human social-cognitive system emerges with experience (Frith & Frith, 1999, 2001).

A DEVELOPMENTAL INTEGRATION

There is now a substantial and growing corpus of information on the biobehavioral processes involved in the development of gaze-following, RJA, and other joint attention skills. Nevertheless, the current status of this literature may be best characterized as raising as many questions as it has answered. For example, some behavioral research suggests that initiating joint attention emerges before gaze-following and RJA (Carpenter et al., 1998). Alternatively, the hypothesis that gaze-following may be associated with an early arising posterier/parietal attention system and observations of rudimentary aspects of gaze-following in the first 3–6 months of life (e.g., Hood et al., 1998; Morales et al., 1998; 2000) suggests that this aspect of joint attention may emerge before IJA (e.g., Mundy et al., 2000a). It seems likely that such basic developmental issues will need to be resolved before we can hope to understand the full complexity of the ontogeny of joint attention. Another significant set of questions pertains to the nature and nurture of joint attention development. Is it sufficient, for example, to ascribe the development of joint attention to an innately determined unfolding of a modular system of neural components that are specific to social information processing and social behavior (Adolphs, 2001; Baron-Cohen, 1995; Emery, 2000; Farah et al., 2000)? Or, do more general transactional and learning processes also play a vital role in joint attention development (Corkum & Moore, 1998; Karmaloff-Smith, 1992)? Are these truly divergent views or do they provide complementary perspectives that offer useful information on different aspects of development in this domain?

There is currently insufficient information to resolve these questions and to build a truly veridical model of the development of gaze-following and joint attention development in infancy. Nevertheless, the ultimate description of such a model is an important goal for both basic and applied developmental research. To contribute to this goal, we outline some of the assumptions and questions that guide our own thinking and research in this area.

To start, we assume that initial perceptual biases organize attention and behavior to insure that neonates actively engage in face and social information processing (Mundy & Neal, 2001). Then, in an experience dependent fashion (Greenough, Black, & Wallace, 1987), neural systems begin to organize in response to the relative preponderance of social information input in the first months of life. The nature of the mechanisms that give rise to these initial biases and how these initial biases interact with neural development is one of the essential issues that remain to be resolved in the study of early development (Karmaloff-Smith, 1992). Nevertheless, at present, we assume that initial perceptual biases need not necessarily be specifically social in nature. Neonates preferentially orient to certain stimulus contours (e.g., curved lines) and stimulus contrasts that abound in faces (Fantz et al., 1975). Perhaps even more importantly, people, and, especially, their faces, tend to be rich and consistent sources of synchronous sound and movement information, and this type of inter-sensory redundancy is a powerful elicitor of attention and information processing in young infants (Bahrick & Lickliter, 2002). Moreover, there is some evidence that inter-sensory redundancy may facilitate gaze-following-related task performance (e.g., Flom & Pick, 2003). Of course, it may be that there are also early predilections for social stimuli. The human voice itself may be a prepotent stimulus for infant orienting (Alegria & Noirot, 1978), and there may be intrinsic affective motivation factors that tend to predispose neonates to social information processing (Trevarthen & Aitken, 2001). Related to this, it also important to recognize that parents' activity is presented to infants in a fashion that may promote and reward social information processing as part of their nurturing behaviors. Certainly, in relatively short order, social learning during nurturing interactions is likely to make social information processing of parents a preferred activity for many infants. All of this seems quite reasonable, but we have nowhere enough information as yet to know how, or if, any of these mechanisms play a fundamental role in organizing early social information processing.

Be that as it may, our model holds that in the next step of development, social information, motivation, and learning begin to interact with parietal attention regulation and spatial orienting processes to begin to bootstrap the gaze-following system by approximately 3 months of age. In particular, the ability to disengage attention, shift attention, and determine the relative spatial orientation of stimuli are all parietal functions that likely contribute to the initial phases of infants' ability to follow gaze. However, while parietal attention regulation mechanisms involve processes that may be necessary for gaze-following to emerge, these mechanisms may not be sufficient. Another important mechanism that may be necessary for the early emergence of gaze-following is imitation.

Neonates and infants have the propensity to imitate facial movements (see Meltzoff & Moore, 1997). Meltzoff and Decety (2003) also have suggested that imitation involves the types of integrated coding between perception of self and perception of others that Frith and Frith (1999, 2001) have suggested is critical to the development of social cognition. Moreover, Meltzoff and Decety (2003) have presented an important research review concerning the neural activity associated with imitation clusters in the STS and parietal lobes, as well as the dorsal cortical supplementary motor areas (BA 8/9). In particular, they note that the abundance of mirror neurons in STS and parietal lobes may potentiate the role of these cortical regions in the mediation of imitation. Mirror neurons are a specific class of motor neurons that are involved both when an individual performs a particular action and when an individual observes the same action performed by another person (Gallese & Goldman, 1998). Thus, the proposed cortical location of the neural mediators of imitation overlaps with the systems that are thought to mediate the development of gaze-following and RJA. Indeed, from a behavioral-task analytic point of view, this makes a great deal of sense.

Gaze-following and RJA basically involve copying the eye movements and/or head turn of a social partner. Alternatively, initiating joint attention behaviors do not appear to involve a discernable social copying component. Indeed, RJA development has been observed to display a significant path of association with imitation development in a longitudinal study of typically developing infants. However, in that study there were no observations of significant associations between the development of IJA and imitation (Pomares et al., 2003). Thus, it may be useful to better understand the degree to which gaze-following/RJA and imitation reflect common and unique bio-behavioral processes in early development. Indeed, the importance of this issue has long been recognized in research on autism because this syndrome involves deficits in imitation as well as joint attention skill development (e.g., Rogers & Pennington, 1991).

In the meantime, though, we assume that gaze-following and RJA, but not necessarily IJA, are special forms of imitation. Temporal/parietal processes involved in imitation, as well as attention regulation, may play a role in the initial phase of development of this behavior. This initial phase of development may be followed by two "learning" phases. In one phase, infants learn to improve the accuracy and consistency of their gaze-following/RJA. For example, the contingent reward of seeing something interesting or receiving social praise after gaze-following/RJA may increase the accuracy and efficiency of this behavior (Corkum & Moore, 1998). The course of development here, though, may be better characterized as a reduction in error trials (head or eye turns in a direction opposite to the social partner), rather than an increase in correct gaze-following/RJA trials between 6 and 10 months of age. Although 6-month-olds display evidence of gaze-following ability (Morales et al., 1998), they certainly display incremental improvements in the accuracy of this behavior from 6 to 8, 10, 12, and 15 months (Morales et al., 2000a). In unpublished observations of this longitudinal progression, it appeared, though, that the initial rates of accurate head turns remained constant over these ages, but the number of inaccurate head turns significantly decreased. This progression may be viewed as a shift in balance from imitative control systems to more control by systems that integrate accurate spatial interpretation of the direction of gaze (see Butterworth & Jarrett, 1991). Initial imitative control may not ensure accurate gaze-following responses, but does ensure the expression of a pattern of behavior that can be culled or shaped through experience to yield a more useful pattern. This "learning to" process may be mediated by parietal spatial orienting systems, perhaps in accord with dorsal error detection systems. Those interested in this possibility may find it useful to refer to Holroyd and Coles (2002) to understand how the anterior cingulate, dorsal medial cortex, and parietal cortex may be integrated in the learning of this critical motor action sequence. Of course, we should also be aware of the possibility that, in addition to being mediated by neural systems, this learning process serves to organize a subset of social brain processes through experience-expectant mechanisms (Greenough et al., 1987). Only well-designed neuro-developmental studies of the emergence of gaze-following behavior will be able to address this possibility.

Related to the experience-expectant hypothesis outline above is the possibility that infants not only learn to control gaze-following/RJA, but that they also learn from engagement in this pattern of motor behavior. That is, infants' own behavior becomes a critical source of information for subsequent executive and conceptual development (e.g., Piaget, 1952). In this regard, consider the heuristic set of observations from comparative research reviewed by Calder et al. (2002). Different sets of cells in the STS of macaque monkeys appear to contribute to the processing of gaze direction versus the processing of the direction and orientation of limb movements (Perrett, Heitenen, Oram, & Benson, 1992). However, a subset of limb movement cells appears to be modulated by activity of the gaze-following system (Jellema, Baker, Wicker, & Perrett, 2000). Jellema et al. (2000) interpret these data to suggest that the combined analysis of direction of visual attention and body movements of others provides an important source of information that gives rise to the capacity to detect intentionality in others. Translated to human development, this suggests that gaze-following does not occur in isolation, but rather as an integrated element of processing of additional dimensions of social behavioral information about others. This is consistent with the observation that, in addition to its social information processing specialization, the STS may also include polysensory areas involved in the attending to and processing of information synchronously from multiple modalities (Hikosaka, 1993). The integrated processing of others' direction of gaze, limb/postural direction, and vocal behavior ultimately may be an important, if not critical, source of information that enables the infant to learn about self, others, and social intentions. For example, with respect to gaze-following, Jellema et al. (2000) suggested that one major lesson learned from gaze-following is, "Where the eyes go, behavior follows."

It is important to understand, though, that this type of epistemological development, social or non-social, may only emerge after extensive repetitive experience with motor actions and behaviors, as well as with maturation of cognitive and executive systems (Piaget, 1952; see Karmaloff-Smith, 1992 for related arguments). That is, first the infant must master the behavior skill. Then, once this behavior pattern becomes routinized, the behavior pattern, itself, becomes fodder for higher-order processing and epistemological development. This hypothesis is consistent with recent observations that suggest that the social-cognitive component associated with gaze-following may only be evident several months after the onset of this behavior (Brooks & Meltzoff, 2002; Woodward, 2003).

Putting all of these assumptions together yields the following preliminary developmental model. Gaze-following/RJA emerges between 3 and 6 months of age as a special form of imitation that is regulated to a significant degree by an early developing parietal attention system with contributions from social perception systems of the STS. Learning, with respect to this skill, occurs between 3 and 10 months so that parietal spatial and attention regulation processes increasingly regulate imitative responses, in order to yield a reduction in incorrect responses and more consistently correct spatially directed responses. With practice and cognitive maturation (Case, 1987), a lower ratio of available processing capacity needs to be allocated by the child to support accurate gaze-following/RJA. As increased processing capacity becomes available, new potentials for integrative cognition arise. This aspect of our model leads to the testable prediction that speed of information processing in gaze-following tasks increases with age. Specifically, the latency between observing a gaze or head turn stimulus and a correct response should decrease significantly in the second 6 months of life.

With the increase in processing capacity (Case, 1987), infants begin to become increasingly capable of integrating their own proprioceptive sense of self as perceiver and actor with exteroceptive information about a related pattern of behaviors of an external agent in the immediate context of displaying gaze-following/RJA behavior. This integrated processing of information from self and other would involve processes currently ascribed to a more anterior dorsal medial cortical system (Frith & Frith, 1999, 2001; Mundy, 2003). Although the developmental period of this integrative processing phase is not clear, our current conjecture is that this occurs in the 6- to 15-month period of development. That is, the "learning from" phase overlaps considerably with the "learning to" phase of development. In the "learning from" phase, the integrated self and other processing provides information uniquely well suited to the simulation of the intentions of other through the experience of coordinated self-other triadic social interactions.

"Simulation Theory" suggests that individuals use their awareness (i.e., representations) of their own mental processes to simulate and analyze the intentions of others (Stich & Nichols, 1992). That is, with development people learn to use self-knowledge, derived from self-monitoring, to extrapolate and make inferences about the covert psychological processes that contribute to the behaviors of other people. Several lines of research suggest that the dorsal-medial frontal cortical facility for self-monitoring (see Mundy, 2003, for a review), and information input from the temporal/parietal systems for processing the behavior of others, may be integrated to yield the information that potentiates social cognitive simulation (Frith & Frith, 1999, 2001). Theoretically, beginning in infancy, this occurs in vivo in a variety of social interactive contexts. Moreover, the context of triadic social attention coordination interactions that involve the perception of self and other vis-à-vis a common object or event is thought to provide an especially powerful context for simulating the common psychological experience of self and other (Mundy, Sigman, & Kasari, 1993).

One unique aspect of the foregoing account of the nature and role of gaze-following in early development is the suggestion that processing capacity and processing speed may affect development within this domain. This assumption is derived from the repeated observation that the increasing capacity to process two or more pieces of information rapidly contributes to general aspects of social, intellectual, and language development in infancy (e.g., Case, 1991; Benasich, Thomas, Choudhury, & Leppaene, 2002; Rose & Feldman, 1997). An illustration of the importance of processing speed in development may be gleaned from considering the history of personal computing. In the early 1980s, when personal computers (PCs) began to be widely available, they had relatively slow processing speeds so that the computer could display activity derived from one piece of software at a time. With increases in processing speed, though, computers were increasingly able to rapidly switch back and forth between software applications so that, on the monitor, it appeared as though several programs (sets of information) were running at one time. This enabled the development of the types of multi-tasking operating systems (e.g., Windows) that now allow us to rapidly hold vast numbers of digital representations in computer memory so that we can compare and contrast vast amounts of information on our computer displays. It is not too much of an extrapolation from this illustration to suggest that an analogous increase in the human processing speed in the first years of life plays a role in the ability to compare and contrast self and other information in a fashion that contributes to new social-cognitive, conceptual structures.

We assume that similar "learning to" and "learning from" phases of development occur for IJA, as well. However, here imitative processes may not play as primary a role in the early "learning to" phase. Instead, infants may initially be entrained to engage in basic IJA behaviors, such as alternating gaze, when the vocalizations and positive affect of their caregivers stimulate social orienting in passive or supported joint engagement interactions. It may also be the case that "learning from" gaze-following has already begun to establish a rudimentary social-cognitive foundation by 6 to 8 months that facilitates the development of this behavior. As we have noted, though, unlike gaze-following and its relatively reflexive control systems, true initiating joint attention involves the spontaneous generation of a pattern of behavior. Spontaneous visual orienting behavior, like IJA, may be more demanding than reflexive orienting behaviors because they involve the executive integration of motivation processes, memory (e.g., representations of others), and attention switching processes perhaps regulated by a more anterior cortical system (Rothbart & Posner, 2001). Thus, this domain of behavior may develop later than gaze-following/RJA. Nevertheless, in the "learning from" phase of IJA there may be a return for the greater processing demands of this type of behavior, in that infants and children may learn something different from behaviors they initiate versus those they copy. In the internal simulation environment concurrent with IJA behaviors, infants may learn that their behavior changes the behavior of others and that they can direct the attention of others to objects. They may also learn that when they express interest or affect regarding some object or event, others take note of this and they may share or react to their expression of behavior (Bates, 1976).

Thus, self-generated IJA behavior may provide information about the self in interaction with others that is different than the information provided by patterns of responsive gaze-following/RJA behavior. This self-generated action may also be regulated to a greater degree by anterior systems such as the dorsal medial frontal cortex. However, like gaze-following/RJA, the social simulations that occur in the context of IJA may be mediated, in part, by mirror neurons. In addition to the STS and parietal cortex, the supplementary motor cortex, which overlaps with the DMFC areas implicated in IJA and social cognition, is rich in mirror neurons (Rizzolatti & Arbib, 1998). Moreover, as previously noted, that DMFC is richly interconnected with the STS and parietal cortices (e.g., Morecraft et al., 1993). These observations suggest that, although somewhat different neural systems and social learning may be involved in gaze-following/RJA and IJA, there is considerable potential for bio-behavioral integrations across the development of these joint attention skills. Understanding the details of integrated neurodevelopment of these important domains of early social behavior remains a substantial goal for developmental science. In addition, information provided by the development of both types of joint attention skills makes a significant contribution to our understanding of the bio-behavioral expression and development of social engagement and cognition.

ACKNOWLEDGMENTS

The preparation of this chapter was supported by NIH grants HD38052 and MH071273 (P. Mundy, P.I., and NIMH grant MH722072 CA Vaughan Van Hecke, P.I.).

REFERENCES

Acra, F., Mundy, P., Claussen, A., Scott, K., & Bono, K. (2003, April). Infant joint attention and social outcomes in 6- to 7-year-old at-risk children. Paper presented at the Society for Research in Child Development, Tampa, FL.

Adolphs, R. (2001). The neurobiology of social cognition. *Current Opinion in Neurobiology, 11*, 231–239.

Alegria, J., & Noirot, E. (1978). Neonate orientation behavior towards human voice. *International Journal of Behavior Development, 1*, 292–312.

Amador, N., Schlag-Rey, M., & Schlag, J. (2000). Reward predicting and reward detecting neuronal activity in the primate supplementary eye field. *Journal of Neurophysiology, 84*, 2166–2170.

Atkinson, J., Hood, B., Wattam-Bell, J., & Braddick, O. (1992). Changes in infants' ability to switch attention in the first three months of life. *Perception, 21*, 643–653.

Bahrick, L., & Lickliter, R. (2002). Intersensory redundancy guides early perceptual and cognitive development. *Advances in Child Development and Behavior, 30,* 153–187.

Baldwin, D. A. (1995). Understanding the link between joint attention and language. In C. Moore & P. J. Dunham (Eds.), *Joint Attention: Its origins and role in development* (pp. 131–158). Hillsdale, NJ: Lawrence Erlbaum Associates.

Ban, T., Shiwa, T., & Kawamura, K. (1991). Cortico-cortical projections from the prefrontal cortex to the superior temporal sulcal area (STS) in the monkey studied by means of HRP method. *Archives of Italian Biology, 129,* 259–72.

Bard, K., Platzman, K., Lester, B., & Suomi, S. (1992). Orientation to social and non-social stimuli in neonatal chimpanzees and humans. *Infant Behavior and Development, 15,* 43–56.

Baron-Cohen, S. (1995). *Mindblindness.* Cambridge, MA: MIT Press.

Baron-Cohen, S., Baldwin, D., & Crowson, M. (1997). Do children with autism use the speaker's direction of gaze strategy to crack the code of language? *Child Development, 68,* 48–57.

Baron-Cohen, Ring, H., Wheelwright, S., Bullmore, E., Brammer, M., Simmons, A., & Williams, S. (1999). Social intelligence in the normal and autistic brain: An fMRI study. *European Journal of Neuroscience, 11,* 1891–1898.

Bates, E. (1976). *Language and context: The acquisition of performatives.* New York, NY: Academic Press.

Benasich, A., Thomas, J., Choudhury, N., & Leppaene, P. (2002). The importance of rapid auditory processing abilities to early language development: Evidence form converging methodologies. *Developmental Psychobiology, 40,* 278–292.

Birrell, J., & Brown, V. (2000). Medial-frontal cortex mediates perceptual attention set shifting in the rat. *Journal of Neuroscience, 20,* 4320–4324.

Block, J. Mundy, P., Pomares, Y., Vaughan, A., Delgado, C., & Gomez, Y. (2003, April). Different developmental profiles of joint attention skills from 9 to 18 months. Paper presented at the Society for Research in Child Development, Tampa, FL.

Bono, M., Daley, T., & Sigman, M. (2004). Joint attention moderates the relation between intervention and language development in young children with autism. *Journal of Autism and Related Disorders, 34,* 495–505.

Bretherton, I. (1991). Intentional communication and the development of an understanding of mind. In D. Frye & C. Moore (Eds.), *Children's theories of mind: Mental states and social understanding* (pp. 49–75). Hillsdale, NJ: Lawrence Erlbaum Associates.

Brooks, R., & Meltzoff, A. (2002). The importance of eyes: How infants interpret adult looking behavior. *Developmental Psychology, 38,* 958–966.

Brothers, L. (1990). The social brain: A project for integrating primate behavior and neurophysiology in a new domain. *Concepts in Neuroscience, 1,* 27–51.

Bruner, J. S. (1975). From communication to language: A psychological perspective. *Cognition, 3,* 255–287.

Bush, G., Luu, P., & Posner, M. (2000). Cognitive and emotional influences in the anterior cingulate cortex. *Trends in Cognitive Science, 4,* 214–222.

Butterworth, G., & Jarrett, N. (1991). What minds have in common is space: Spatial mechanisms in serving joint visual attention in infancy. *British Journal of Developmental Psychology, 9,* 55–72.

Calder, A., Lawrence, A., Keane, J., Scott, S., Owen, A., Christoffels, I., & Young, A. (2002). Reading the mind from eye gaze. *Neuropsychologia, 40,* 1129–1138.

Cambell, R., Heywood, C., Cowey, A., Regard, M., & Landis, T. (1990). Sensitivity to eye gaze in prosopagnosic patients and monkeys with superior temporal sulcus ablation. *Neuropsychologia, 28,* 1123–1142.

Caplan, R., Chugani, H., Messa, C., Guthrie, D., Sigman, M., Traversay, J., & Mundy, P. (1993). Hemispherectomy for early onset intractable seizures: Presurgical cerebral glucose metabolism and postsurgical nonverbal communication patterns. *Developmental Medicine and Child Neurology, 35,* 582–592.

Capps, L., Sigman, M., & Mundy, P. (1994). Attachment security in children with autism. *Development and Psychopathology, 6,* 249–261.

Carpenter, M., Nagell, K., & Tomasello, M. (1998). Social cognition, joint attention, and communicative competence from 9 to 15 months of age. *Monographs of the Society for Research in Child Development, 63,* (No. 4, Serial No. 255).

Carpenter, M., Pennington, B., & Rogers, S. (2002). Interrelations among social-cognitive skills in young children with autism. *Journal of Autism and Developmental Disorders, 32,* 91–106.

Case, R. (1987). The structure and process of intellectual development. *International Journal of Psychology, 22,* 571–607.

Case, R. (1991). Stages in the development of young children's first sense of self. *Developmental Review, 11,* 210–230.

Charman, T., Baron-Cohen, S., Swettenham, J., Baird, G., Cox, A., & Drew, A. (2000). Testing joint attention, imitation, and play infancy precursors to language and theory of mind. *Cognitive Development, 15,* 481–498.

Charwarska, K., Klin, A., & Volkmar, F. (2003). Automatic attention cuing through eye movement in 2-year-old children with autism. *Child Development, 74,* 1108–1123.

Chugani, H., Phelps, M., & Mazziotta, J. (1987). Positron emission tomography study of human brain functional development. *Annals of Neurology, 22,* 487–497.

Clohessy, A., Posner, M., & Rothbart, M. (2001). Development of the functional visual field. *Acta Psychologia, 106,* 51–68.

Corkum, V., & Moore, C. (1998). The origins of joint visual attention in infants. *Developmental Psychology, 34,* 28–38.

Craik, F., Moroz, T., Moscovich, M., Stuss, D., Winocur, G., Tulving, E., & Kapur, S. (1999). In search of the self: A positron emission tomography study. *Psychological Science, 10,* 26–34.

Dawson, G., Munson, J., Estes, A., Osterling, J., McPartland, J., Toth, K., Carver, L., & Abbott, R. (2002). Neurocognitive function and joint attention ability in young children with autism spectrum disorder versus developmental delay. *Child Development, 73,* 345–358.

D'Entremont, B., Hains, S., & Muir, D. (1997). A demonstration of gaze-following in 3- to 6-month-olds. *Infant Behavior and Development, 20,* 569–572.

Eacott, M., Heywood, C., Gross, C., & Cowey, A. (1993). Visual discrimination impairments following lesions of the superior temporal sulcus are not specific for facial stimuli. *Neuropsychologia, 31,* 609–619.

Emery, N. (2000). The eyes have it: The neuroethology, function, and evolution of social gaze. *Neuroscience and Biobehavioral Reviews, 24,* 581–604.

Fantz, R., Fagan, J., & Miranda, S. (1975). Early visual selectivity. In L. Cohen & P. Slap-ateck (Eds.). *Infant perception from sensation to cognition: Vol. 1 Basic Visual Processes* (pp. 249–341). New York, NY: Academic Press.

Farah, M., Rabinowitz, C., Quinn, G., & Grant, L. (2000). Early commitment of neural sub-strates for face recognition. *Cognitive Neuropsychology, 17,* 117–123.

Faw, B. (2003). Prefrontal executive committee for perception, working memory, atten-tion, long-term memory, motor control and thinking: A tutorial review. *Consciousness & Cognition, 12,* 83–139.

Filipek, P., Accardo, P., Baranek, G., Cook, E., Dawson, G., Gordon, B., Gravel, J., John-son, C., Kallen, R., Levy, S., Minshew, N., Ozonoff, S., Prizant, B., Rapin I., Rogers, S., Stone, W., Teplin, S., Tuchman, R., & Volkmar, F. (1999). The screening and diag-nosis of autism spectrum disorders. *Journal of Autism and Developmental Disorders, 29,* 439–484.

Flom, R., & Pick, A. (2003). Verbal encouragement and joint attention in 18-month-old infants. *Infant Behavior and Development, 26,* 121–134.

Fombonne, E. (2003). The prevalence of autism. *Journal of the American Medical Association, 289,* 87–79.

Frith, C., & Frith, U. (1999). Interacting minds: A biological basis. *Science, 286,* 1692–1695.

Frith, U., & Frith, C. (2001). The biological basis of social interaction. *Current Directions in Psychological Science, 10,* 151–155.

Gallese, V., & Goldman, A. (1998). Mirror neurons and the simulation theory of mind-reading. *Trends in Cognitive Science, 2,* 493–501.

George, N., Driver, J., & Dolan, R. (2001). Seen gaze direction modulates fusiform ac-tivity and its coupling with other brain areas during face processing. *NeuroImage, 13,* 1102–1112.

Goren, C., Sarty, M., & Wu, P. (1975). Visual following and pattern discrimination of face-like stimuli by newborn infants. *Pediatrics, 56,* 544–549.

Greenough, W., Black, J., & Wallace, C. (1987). Experience and brain development. *Child Development, 58,* 539–559.

Griffith, E., Pennington, B., Wehner, E., & Rogers, S. (1999). Executive functions in young children with autism. *Child Development, 70,* 817–832.

Henderson, L., Yoder, P., Yale, M., & McDuffie, A. (2002). Getting the point: Electrophys-iological correlates of protodeclarative pointing. *International Journal of Developmental Neuroscience, 20,* 449–458.

Heyward, C., & Cowey, A. (1992). The role of the "face cell" area in the discrimination and recognition of faces by monkeys. *Philosophical Transactions of the Royal Society of London, 335,* 31–38.

Hikosaka, K. (1993). The polysensory region in the anterior bank of the caudal superior temporal sulcus of the macaque monkey. *Biomedical Research Tokyo, 14,* 41–45.

Hoffman, E., & Haxby, J. (2000). Distinct representation of eye gaze and identity in the dis-tributed human neural system for face perception. *Nature Neuroscience, 3,* 80–84.

Holroyd, C., & Coles, M. (2002). The neural basis of human error processing: Reinforce-ment learning, dopamine and the error related negativity. *Psychological Review, 109,* 679–709.

Hood, B. (1995). Shifts of visual attention in the human infant: A neuroscientific approach. In C. Rovee-Collier & L. Lipsitt (Eds.), *Advances in Infancy Research.* Norwood, NJ: Ablex.

Hood, B., Willen, J., & Driver, J. (1998). Adult's eyes trigger shifts of visual attention in human infants. *Psychological Science, 9,* 131–134.

Hooker, C. (2002). The neurocognitive basis of gaze perception: A model of social signal processing. *Dissertation Abstracts International: Science and Engineering, 63,* 2058.

Jellema, T., Baker, C., Wicker, B., & Perrett, D. (2000). Neural representation for the perception of intentionality of actions. *Brain and Cognition, 44,* 280–302.

Johnson, M. (1990). Cortical maturation and the development of visual attention in early infancy. *Journal of Cognitive Neuroscience, 2,* 81–95.

Johnson, M. (1995). The inhibition of automatic saccades in early infancy. *Developmental Psychobiology, 28,* 281–291.

Johnson, S., Baxter, L., Wilder, L., Pipe, J., Heiserman, J., & Prigatano, G. (2002). Neural correlates of self-reflection. *Brain, 125,* 1808–1814.

Johnson, M., Dziurawiec, S., Ellis, H., & Morton, J. (1991). Newborns' preferential tracking of face-like stimuli and its subsequent decline. *Cognition, 40,* 1–19.

Johnson, M., & Morton, J. (1991). *Biology and cognitive development: The case of face recognition.* Oxford: Blackwell.

Johnson, M., Posner, M., & Rothbart, M. (1991). Components of visual orienting in early infancy: Contingency learning, anticipatory looking, and disengaging. *Journal of Cognitive Neuroscience, 3,* 335–344.

Kampe, K., Frith, C., Dolan, R., & Frith, U. (2001). Reward value of attractiveness and gaze. *Nature, 413,* 589.

Karmaloff-Smith, A. (1992). *Beyond modularity: A developmental perspective on cognitive science.* Cambridge, MA: MIT Press.

Kasari, C., Sigman, M., Mundy, P., & Yirmiya, N. (1990). Affective sharing in the context of joint attention interactions of normal, autistic, and mentally retarded children. *Journal of Autism and Developmental Disorders, 20,* 87–100.

Kawashima, R., Sugiura, M., Kato, T., Nakamura, A., Hatano, K., Ito, K., Fuguda, H., Kojima, S., & Nakamura, K. (1999). The human amygdala plays an important role in gaze monitoring: A PET Study. *Brain, 122,* 779–783.

Kingstone, A., Friesen, C-K., & Gazzaniga, M. (2000). Reflexive joint attention depends on lateralized cortical functions. *Psychological Science, 11,* 159–166.

Leekam, S., & Moore, C. (2001). The development of joint attention in children with autism. In J. Barack, T. Charman, N. Yirmiya, & P. Zelazo (Eds.), *The development of autism: Perspectives from theory and research* (pp. 105–130). Mahwah, NJ: Lawrence Erlbaum Associates.

Lord, C., Floody, H., Anderson, D., & Pickles, A. (2003, April). Social engagement in very young children with autism: Differences across contexts. Paper presented at the Society for Research in Child Development, Tampa, FL.

Luu, P., Flaisch, T., & Tucker, D. (2000). Medial-frontal cortex in action monitoring. *Journal of Neuroscience, 20,* 464–469.

Martin, J. (1996). *Neuroanatomy: Text and Atlas,* 2nd Ed. New York, NY: McGraw-Hill.

Masten, A., & Coatsworth, D. (1998). The development of competence in favorable and unfavorable environments: Lessons from research on successful children. *American Psychologist, 53*, 205–220.

McEvoy, R., Rogers, S., & Pennington, R. (1993). Executive function and social communication deficits in young autistic children. *Journal of Child Psychology and Psychiatry, 34*, 563–578.

Meltzoff, A., & Decety, J. (2003). What imitation tells us about social cognition: A rapprochement between developmental psychology and cognitive neuroscience. *Philosophical Transactions of the Royal Society of London, 358*, 491–500.

Meltzoff, A., & Moore, M. (1997). Explaining facial imitation: A theoretical model. *Early Development and Parenting, 6*, 179–192.

Moore, C. (1996). Theories of mind in infancy. *British Journal of Developmental Psychology, 14*, 19–40.

Morales, M., Mundy, P., Crowson, M., Neal, R., & Delgado, C. (2005). Individual differences in infant attention skills, joint attention and emotion regulation. *International Journal of Behavioral Development, 29*, 259–263.

Morales, M., Mundy, P., Delgado, C., Yale, M., Messinger, D., Neal, R., & Schwartz, H. (2000a). Responding to joint attention across the 6- through 24-month age period and early language acquisition. *Journal of Applied Developmental Psychology, 21*, 283–298.

Morales, M., Mundy, P., Delgado, C., Yale, M., Neal, R., & Schwartz, H. (2000b). Gaze-following, temperament, and language development in 6 month olds: A replication and extension. *Infant Behavior and Development, 23*, 231–236.

Morales, M., Mundy, P., & Rojas, J. (1998). Following the direction of gaze and language development in 6-month-olds. *Infant Behavior and Development, 21*, 373–377.

Morecraft, R., Geula, C., & Mesulam, M. (1993). Architecture of connectivity within a cingula-fronto-parietal neurocognitive network for directed attention. *Archives of Neurology, 50*, 279–284.

Mundy, P. (1995). Joint attention and social-emotional approach behavior in children with autism. *Development and Psychopathology, 7*, 63–82.

Mundy, P. (2003). The neural basis of social impairments in autism: The role of the dorsal medial-frontal cortex and anterior cingulate system. *Journal of Child Psychology and Psychiatry, 44*, 793–809.

Mundy, P., Card, J., & Fox, N. (2000). EEG correlates of the development of infant joint attention skills. *Developmental Psychobiology, 36*, 325–338.

Mundy, P., & Gomes, A. (1998). Individual differences in joint attention skills in the second year. *Infant Behavior and Development, 21*, 469–482.

Mundy, P., Hogan, A., & Doehring, P. (1996). *A preliminary manual for the abridged Early Social-Communication Scales*. Coral Gables, FL: University of Miami, www.psy.miami.edu/faculty/pmundy

Mundy, P., Kasari, C., & Sigman, M. (1992). Joint attention, affective sharing, and intersubjectivity. *Infant Behavior and Development, 15*, 377–381.

Mundy, P., Kasari, C., Sigman, M., & Ruskin, E. (1995). Nonverbal communication and early language in Down syndrome and in normally developing children. *Journal of Speech and Hearing Research, 38*, 157–167.

Mundy, P., & Neal, R. (2001). Neural plasticity, joint attention and a transactional social-orienting model of autism. *International Review of Mental Retardation, 23*, 139–168.

Mundy, P., & Sigman, M. (1989). Specifying the nature of the social impairment in autism. In G. Dawson (Ed.), *Autism: New perspectives on diagnosis, nature, and treatment* (pp. 3–21). New York: Guilford Publications.

Mundy, P., & Sigman, M. (in press). Joint attention, social competence, and developmental psychopathology. To appear in D. Cicchetti and D. Cohen (Eds.) *Developmental Psychopathology, 2nd Edition, Volume One: Theory and Methods.* Hoboken, NJ: Wiley Publications.

Mundy, P., Sigman, M., & Kasari, C. (1993). The theory of mind and joint attention deficits in autism. In S. Baron-Cohen, H. Tager-Flusberg, & D. Cohen (Eds.), *Understanding other minds: Perspectives from autism* (pp. 181–203). Oxford, UK: Oxford University.

Mundy, P., Sigman, M., & Kasari, C. (1994). Joint attention, developmental level, and symptom presentation in young children with autism. *Development and Psychopathology, 6*, 389–401.

Mundy, P., Sigman, M., Ungerer, J., & Sherman, T. (1986). Defining the social deficits of autism: The contribution of nonverbal communication measures. *Journal of Child Psychology and Psychiatry, 27*, 657–669.

Neal, R., Mundy, P., Claussen, A., Mallik, S., Scott, K., & Acra, F. (2003). *The relations between infant joint attention skill and cognitive and language outcome in at-risk children.* Manuscript submitted for publication.

Norman, D., & Shallice, T. (1986). Attention to action: Willed and automatic control of behavior. In R. Davidson, G. Schwartz, & D. Shapiro, (Eds.), *Consciousness and self-regulation* (pp. 1–18). New York, NY: Plenum.

Pascalis, O., & de Schonen, S. (1994). Recognition memory in 3- to 4-day-old human neonates. *Neuroreport, 5*, 1721–1724.

Perrett, D., Heitenen, J., Oram, M., & Benson, P. (1992). Organization and functions of cells responsive to faces in the temporal cortex. *Philosophical Transactions of the Royal Society of London, 335*, 23–30.

Piaget, J. (1952). *The origins of intelligence in children.* New York, NY: Norton. Pomares, Y., Mundy, P., Vaughan, A., Block, J. & Delgado, C. (2003, April). *On the relations between infant joint attention, imitation, and language.* Paper presented at the Society for Research in Child Development, Tampa, FL.

Posner, M., & Peterson, S. (1990). The attention system of the human brain. *Annual Review of Neuroscience, 13*, 25–42.

Puce, A., Allison, T., Bentin, S., Gore, J., & McCarthy, G. (1998) Temporal cortex activation in humans viewing eye and mouth movements. *Journal of Neuroscience, 18*, 2188–2199.

Rizzolatti, G., & Arbib, M. (1998). Language within our grasp. *Trends in Neuroscience, 21*, 188–194.

Rogers, S., Hepburn, S., Stackhouse, T., & Wehner, E. (2003). Imitation performance in toddlers with autism and those with other developmental disorders. *Journal of Child Psychology and Psychiatry, 44*, 763–781.

Rogers, S., & Pennington, B. (1991). A theoretical approach to the deficits in infantile autism. *Developmental Psychopathology, 6,* 635–652.

Rose, S., & Feldman, J. (1997). Memory and speed: Their role in the relation of infant information processing to later IQ. *Child Development, 68,* 630–641.

Rothbart, M. (1981). Measurement of temperament in infancy. *Child Development, 52,* 569–578.

Rothbart, M., & Posner, M. (2001). Mechanism and variation in the development of attention networks. In C. Nelson, & M. Luciana (Eds.), *The handbook of developmental cognitive neuroscience* (pp. 353–363). Cambridge, MA: The MIT Press.

Rothbart, M., Posner, M., & Rosicky, J. (1994). Orienting in normal and pathological development. *Development and Psychopathology, 6,* 635–652.

Rushworth, M., Hadland, K., Paus, T., & Siplia, P. (2002). Role of the human medial frontal cortex in task switching: A combined fMRI and TMS study. *Journal of Neurophysiology, 87,* 2577–2592.

Russell, T., Rubia, K., Bullmore, E., Soni, W., Suckling, J., Brammer, M., Simmons, A., & Sharma,T. (2000). Exploring the social brain in schizophrenia: Left prefrontal underactivation during mental state attribution. *American Journal of Psychiatry, 157,* 2040–2042.

Scaife, M., & Bruner, J. (1975). The capacity for joint visual attention in the infant. *Nature, 253,* 265–266.

Seibert, J. M., Hogan, A. E., & Mundy, P. C. (1982). Assessing interactional competencies: The Early Social Communication Scales. *Infant Mental Health Journal, 3,* 244–245.

Sheinkopf, S., Mundy, P., Claussen, A., & Willoughby, J. (2004). Infant joint attention skills and preschool behavior outcomes in at risk children. *Development and Psychopathology, 16,* 273–291.

Sigman, M., & Ruskin, E. (1999). Continuity and change in the social competence of children with autism, Down syndrome, and developmental delay. *Monographs of the Society for Research in Child Development, 64*(Serial No. 256), 1–108.

Simion, F., Valenza, E., & Umilta, C. (1998). Mechanisms underlying face preference at birth. In F. Simion & G. Butterworth (Eds.), *The Development of Sensory, Motor, and Cognitive Capacities in Early Infancy.* East Sussex, UK: Psychological Press.

Stich, S., & Nichols, S. (1992). Folk psychology: Simulation versus tacit theory. *Mind and Language, 7,* 29–65.

Stuss, D., Shallice, T., Alexander, M., & Picton, T. (1995). A multidimensional approach to anterior attention functions. In J. Grafman, K. Holyoak, et al. (Eds.), *Structure and function of the human prefrontal cortex. Annals of the New York Academy of science: Vol. 769* (pp. 191–211). New York, NY: New York Academy of Sciences.

Swettenham, J., Baron-Cohen, S., Charman, T., Cox, A., Baird, G., Drew, A., Rees, L., & Wheelwright, S. (1998). The frequency and distribution of spontaneous attention shifts between social and nonsocial stimuli in autistic, typically developing, and nonautistic developmentally delayed infants. *Journal of Child Psychology and Psychiatry, 39,* 747–753.

Tomasello, M. (1995). Joint attention as social cognition. In C. Moore & P. Dunham (Eds.), *Joint attention: Its origins and role in development* (pp. 103–130). Hillsdale, NJ: Lawrence Erlbaum Associates.

Trevarthen, C., & Aitken, K. (2001). Infant intersubjectivity: Research, theory and clinical applications. *Journal of Psychology and Psychiatry, 42,* 3–48.

Ulvund, S., & Smith, L. (1996). The predictive validity of nonverbal communicative skills in infants with perinatal hazards. *Infant Behavior and Development, 19,* 441–449.

Valenza, E., Simion, F., Cassia, V., & Umilta, C. (1996). Face preference at birth. *Journal of Experimental Psychology–Human Perception and Performance, 22,* 892–903.

Vaughan, A., Mundy, P., Block, J., Burnette, C., Delgado, C., Gomez, Y., Meyer, J., Neal, R., & Pomares, Y. (2003). Child, caregiver, and temperament contributions to infant joint attention. *Infancy, 4,* 603–616.

Vaughan Van Hecke, A., Mundy, P., Acra, C. F., Block, J., Delgado, C., Parlade, M., Meyer, J., Neal, R., & Pomares, Y. (in press). *Infant joint attention, temperament, and social competence in preschool children. Child Development.*

Webb, S., & Nelson, C. (2001). Perceptual priming for upright and inverted faces in infants and adults. *Journal of Experimental Child Psychology, 79,* 1–22.

Wicker, B., Michel, F., Henaff, M., & Decety, J. (2002). Brain regions involved in the perception of gaze. *Neuroimage, 8,* 221–227.

Woodward, A. (2003). Infants' developing understanding of the link between looker and object. *Developmental Science, 6,* 297–311.

3

Attentional Control by Gaze Cues in Infancy

Amy C. MacPherson
Dalhousie University

Chris Moore
University of Toronto

In infant development, joint visual attention, or the capacity to look where someone else is looking, is an early type of triadic interaction, in which an infant and adult simultaneously attend to some third object (Moore, 1999b). This type of interaction is fundamental to normal human relations, which rely on the sharing of experiences and knowledge (Corkum & Moore, 1998; Moore, 1999b). Further, joint visual attention is significant in that it provides a context in which the infant can acquire new information about the world in general, the object of shared attention in particular, and about other people including the social partner (Corkum & Moore, 1998). Thus, joint visual attention is a critical tool for the acquisition of human knowledge in its various forms.

In experimental settings, joint visual attention is generally achieved when the infant follows the gaze of an adult, with whom she has been interacting, to an object of mutual interest (Butterworth & Cochran, 1980; Butterworth & Jarrett, 1991; Caron, Butler, & Brooks, 2002; Corkum & Moore, 1995, 1998; D'Entremont, 2000; D'Entremont, Hains, & Muir, 1997; Morissette, Ricard, & Gouin-Decarie, 1995). The now standard paradigm in which an experimenter or parent attempts to elicit gaze-following by presenting head turns in the context of face-to-face social interaction was introduced by Scaife and Bruner (1975). In their initial experiment, they examined 2- to 14-month-olds' responses to head turns toward hidden targets and found that the majority of infants 8 months and older followed the gaze of an adult social partner on at least one of the two trials. This result was taken as evidence that infants are capable of joint visual attention (Scaife & Bruner, 1975).

Through a substantial body of subsequent research, much has been discovered about the nature and development of infants' capacity to follow gaze under various conditions. For instance, when targets are immediately present in the infant's visual field, there is evidence of gaze-following in response to adult head turns from as early as 3 months of age (D'Entremont, 2000; D'Entremont et al., 1997). Further, when there are potential targets, not immediately available in the visual field but visible when an infant head turn is made, gaze-following in response to adult head turns occurs from about 9 months (Corkum & Moore, 1998). By 14 months, infants begin to show sensitivity to eye direction by following gaze more reliably, both to potential targets and in the absence of targets, when adult head turns are accompanied by corresponding eye turns than when the eyes are closed or remain stationary (Caron et al., 2002). Finally, when adult eye turns are presented in the absence of head turns, gaze-following to potential targets occurs reliably beginning in the second year of life (Moore & Corkum, 1998; for a review, see Moore, 1999a).

One proposed explanation for the developmental progression of gaze-following is that it is controlled by different attentional mechanisms at different ages (Butterworth & Jarrett, 1991; Moore, 1999a). According to Butterworth and Jarrett (1991) there are three mechanisms underlying the development of joint visual attention in infancy. The first of these is the "ecological mechanism" in which the 6-month-old infant gains basic information from the mother's head and eye movements about whether to look to the left or the right. When this mechanism is at work, the mother's head turn, although not providing the exact target location, "triggers a search within the infant's visual field" (Butterworth & Jarrett, 1991, p. 69). The more sophisticated "geometric mechanism" evident from about 12 months goes beyond general direction to specify target location in relation to the relative positions of infant and adult. Finally, around 18 months the infant develops a representation of space that goes beyond the limits of immediate perception and allows joint attention outside of those limits (Butterworth & Jarrett, 1991).

In view of Butterworth's ecological mechanism, Moore (1999a) proposed that early gaze-following is governed by a perceptual-attentional system. Moore also explained the different forms in the developmental progression of gaze-following in terms of exogenous and endogenous orienting, which make up one of two important distinctions in the literature and terminology of visual attention (Klein, Kingstone, & Pontefract, 1992). Exogenous orienting is reflexive or automatic, occurs quickly, and tends to depend on patterns of stimulation (Klein et al., 1992; Jonides, 1981). Thus, because gaze-following to visible targets depends on a reflexive search, as well as the presence of stimulation in the periphery of the visual field, it can be viewed as exogenously controlled (Moore, 1999a). Endogenous orienting is under conscious or strategic control, takes more time, and depends on the intentions and expectancies of the observer (Klein et al., 1992; Jonides, 1981). Gaze-following in response to head turns toward potential targets seems to reflect a more endogenous, or expectation-based, type of orienting in which the infant's attention is cued by the adult's head turn or eye turn, while their response depends on their understanding of the meaning of that cue and their expectation of locating a target (Moore, 1999a). Despite their early sensitivity to gaze direction (Hains & Muir, 1996; Vecera & Johnson, 1995), infants' understanding of the meaning of eye turns and their ability to use that information for the endogenous control of visual attention develop much more slowly than for head turns (Moore, 1999a).

Conceptualizing gaze-following in terms of the capacity of adult gaze direction to control attention has prompted the development of computerized paradigms for examining attentional cueing by gaze direction. Parallel lines of research with adults (e.g., Friesen & Kingstone, 1998) and infants (e.g., Hood, Willen, & Driver, 1998) have employed similar paradigms in which central face stimuli were used to present gaze cues that were "nonpredictive" in the sense that subsequent peripheral targets were equally likely to appear on the cued side or on the uncued side. In an experiment with adult participants, Friesen and Kingstone (1998) presented nonpredictive gaze cues from a schematic face and examined participants' key press responses to target letters in each of three counterbalanced response conditions: detection, localization, and identification. The face stimulus in this within-subjects experiment consisted of black circles and lines on a white background. It was round and contained round eyes, a small round nose as a fixation point, and a straight mouth. Participants were asked to fixate the nose on the face and were informed that gaze direction did not predict the location of subsequent targets. On each trial the schematic face appeared with blank eyes, and after a delay of 680 msec, pupils (black filled circles) appeared looking to the right, to the left, or straight ahead. This cue was presented for an interval or SOA (cue-target stimulus onset asynchrony) of 105, 300, 600, or 1005 msec, before the onset of a peripheral target (capital letter "F" or "T") appearing to the left or the right of the face. Trials were defined as "cued," "uncued," or "neutral" depending on the combination of gaze direction and target location.

Friesen and Kingstone (1998) found that RTs (reaction times) were significantly faster on cued than uncued trials in all three response conditions, with no significant difference between uncued and neutral trials. This gaze cueing effect appeared at the 105-msec SOA in the detection and localization conditions and was evident at SOAs of 105, 300, and 600 msec when collapsing across response conditions, but disappeared by 1005 msec.

Although central cues are generally used to examine endogenous orienting, Friesen and Kingstone (1998) offered several reasons for classifying their gaze cueing effect as an example of exogenous or reflexive orienting: it emerged rapidly, occurred even though cues were known to be nonpredictive, had a short timecourse (effect disappeared by 1005 msec), and showed an RT benefit at the cued location without an RT cost at the uncued location. They suggested that this difference in types of orienting might stem from brain mechanisms in the parietal cortex specialized for the processing of gaze direction. The proposed network for triggering reflexive shifts of attention in response to gaze processing includes the parietal cortex and the amygdala which are associated through mutual connections with the superior temporal sulcus (STS) of the temporal cortex (Friesen & Kingstone, 1998).

In a subsequent experiment, Ristic, Friesen, and Kingstone (2002) replicated their gaze cueing effect with adults and 4- and 5-year-old children using a schematic happy face to present gaze cues in a target detection task. The cueing paradigm varied slightly from the one used by Friesen and Kingstone (1998) in that the schematic face had a smile rather than a straight mouth, the targets were black and white line drawings of a cat and a snowman, and the SOAs were 195, 600, and 1005 msec. Although they had been informed that the cues did not predict target location, both adults and children showed significantly faster responding on cued than uncued trials, a decrease in RT as SOA increased, and a decreased difference in RT between cued and uncued locations as SOA increased. In addition, the gaze cueing effect was more pronounced in children than in adults, which, according to Ristic et al. (2002), lends further support to the case for reflexive orienting to gaze cues because volitional orienting effects are known to be weaker in young children than in adults. These two studies provide solid evidence for a gaze cueing effect in response to schematic faces, and evidence is available for a similar effect in response to cues presented by digitized photographs of human faces (Driver et al., 1999; Langton & Bruce, 1999).

In the experiments previously described, attention to a particular location was inferred from an RT benefit (facilitation) for key presses at that location relative to other locations. In infant studies, the same inferences are made except that RT for eye movements, rather than key presses, serves as the dependent variable. This difference in dependent measures also reflects a distinction in the type of orienting examined at each age group. In experiments requiring key-press responses, participants are generally asked to maintain fixation at a particular point; thus, their shifts of attention toward peripheral targets are "covert" in that they are made in the absence of eye movements (see Klein et al., 1992). Infant experiments in which attention is inferred from eye movements necessarily involve "overt" shifts of attention. In one such study, Hood et al. (1998) examined 3- to 7-month-olds' saccadic responses to peripheral targets following eye turns from a digitized photograph of a woman's face. The choice of age range in that study was based in part on the findings that although gaze-following in response to eye direction occurs only later in standard joint attention paradigms (e.g., Corkum & Moore, 1995), infants can discriminate gaze direction (Vecera & Johnson, 1995) and are sensitive to adult eye direction in the context of face-to-face interaction from as early as 3 months of age (Hains & Muir, 1996). Although the computerized gaze cueing procedure used by Hood and his colleagues to test infants bore many similarities to that typically used with adults, it differed in the following ways: (1) the face appeared with eyes blinking (alternately closed for 500 msec or looking straight ahead for 500 msec) as a fixation stimulus, (2) a single SOA of 1,000 msec was used, and (3) the face disappeared immediately before target presentation.

Thus, in Experiment 1 by Hood et al., each trial began with the appearance of the face with blinking eyes. Upon fixation, and immediately following an "eyes closed" part of the blinking cycle, the eyes opened and looked toward the left or the right. After 1,000 msec of averted gaze, the face disappeared and was replaced by a peripheral probe (a phase-reversing rectangle) either on the same side of the screen as where the eyes had looked (congruent trials) or on the opposite side (incongruent trials). The probe remained activated until the infant made a saccadic response to the right or to the left (maximum of 5,000 msec). Reaction time and direction of the first eye movement on each trial were scored from video. Hood and his colleagues found that the infants' saccadic responses toward the probe were significantly faster on congruent than on incongruent trials. In addition, infants were more likely to orient away from the target when it was spatially incongruent with the cue. These results indicate that under certain circumstances, shifts in adult eye direction can act as cues to produce corresponding shifts of attention in infants as young as 3 months (Hood et al., 1998).

To further examine this cueing effect, Hood et al. (1998) conducted a second experiment, which was identical to the first except that on half of the trials the digitized face with averted gaze remained on the screen while the probe was presented. Because it is difficult for young infants to disengage their attention from salient central stimuli (Hood, 1995), it was expected that infants would make fewer eye movements toward the probe on trials in which the face remained visible (face-on) than on trials when it disappeared (face-off). As expected, they found that there was far less orienting to the probe on face-on trials (26% compared to 87% on face-off trials) because many infants continued to fixate the face on the majority of these trials. In terms of the gaze cueing effect, there was a nonsignificant trend for infants to respond more rapidly on congruent face-off trials than on incongruent face-off trials. This experiment is notable in that it highlights an important procedural difference between adult research and infant research on the phenomenon of gaze cueing. In addition, the finding that on face-on trials most infants remained focused on the face stimulus more often than not suggests that the traditional joint attention paradigm (in which head or eye turns are presented by a physically present person) may not give a complete picture of how infant attention functions in response to gaze cues. According to Hood and his colleagues, "These experiments provide the first unequivocal support for Baron-Cohen's (1995) hypothesis that an EDD (Eye Direction Detector) mechanism is present fairly early in development and influences joint attention, in the sense of producing a corresponding shift of the infant's own attention" (Hood et al., 1998, p. 55).

Farroni, Johnson, Brockbank, and Simion (2000) acknowledged the possibility that the gaze cueing effect could be explained in terms of a mechanism similar to Baron-Cohen's EDD; however, they also proposed the alternative hypothesis that infants in the study by Hood et al. (1998) were cued by the direction of motion of the pupils rather than by gaze direction per se. In the first of three experiments, Farroni and her colleagues sought to replicate the gaze cueing effect using the same face stimuli and the same basic procedure as in Experiment 1 by Hood and his colleagues. Blinking occurred at a rate of 500 msec on and 500 msec off until fixation (as in Hood et al.); however, the eyes remained open for 200 msec immediately prior to the shift in gaze direction, thus increasing the potential influence of apparent motion. In addition, the face with eyes looking left or right remained activated for an SOA of 1,500 msec before disappearing and being immediately replaced with a peripheral target. Farroni et al. found a cueing effect similar to that of Hood et al., with significantly faster orienting to the target on congruent trials than on incongruent trials. In addition, the effect found by Farroni et al. was the stronger of the two, a finding they attributed to the narrower age range, the larger number of trials, and the modifications to the event sequence in their Experiment 1 compared to Experiment 1 by Hood et al.

In Experiment 2, Farroni and her colleagues addressed the possibility that infant attention was being cued by direction of motion rather than by the final direction of averted gaze. To test this hypothesis, they presented the same basic experiment with one modification—rather than the pupils shifting to one side, the entire face was displaced an equivalent lateral distance of 0.5° of visual angle. The end result of this shift was a face with gaze averted to one side (as in Experiment 1); however, the final direction of gaze was opposite to the direction of motion of the face. Their rationale was that more rapid orienting to the congruent (gazed at) side would indicate cueing by gaze, while more rapid orienting to the incongruent side would indicate cueing by motion. In this case, Farroni et al. found significantly faster orienting to the incongruent side (i.e., the side toward which the face had shifted). Although they favored the interpretation that cueing by direction of displacement could account for the results of both Experiments 1 and 2, they acknowledged the possibility that an effect of cueing by gaze in Experiment 2 may have been missed due to the more salient displacement of the face (Farroni et al., 2000). In addition, the unnatural lateral displacement of the entire face may have been distracting to the infants.

To provide further support for their lateral displacement hypothesis, Farroni et al. conducted a third experiment in which they modified Experiment 1 to minimize the possibility of apparent motion of the pupils. Specifically, they decreased the speed of blinking from 500 msec on and 500 msec off to 1,000 msec on and 1,000 msec off. In addition, as in the experiments by Hood et al. (1998), they presented the averted gaze after the closed eyes part of the blinking cycle. Under these conditions, the time lag between the final image with eyes looking straight ahead and the image with averted gaze was a full second, allowing little possibility of apparent motion of the pupils. As they had expected, Farroni et al. found no significant RT difference between congruent and incongruent trials. Further, a MANOVA comparing Experiments 1 and 3 revealed a significant main effect of condition (congruent vs. incongruent) that was qualified by a significant interaction between condition and experiment, meaning that subtle variations in the order and timings of stimulus events led to a significant difference in the cueing effect across experiments. Farroni and her colleagues concluded that in young infants, cueing does not occur in response to static images of averted gaze.

By way of a direct comparison between cueing by gaze in adults and infants, Mansfield, Farroni, and Johnson (2003) measured adult eye movements in a procedure similar to Experiment 3 by Farroni et al. (2002). They found that unlike the infants tested by Farroni et al., adults made significantly faster saccadic responses on congruent trials compared to incongruent trials. Thus, Mansfield et al. concluded that the gaze cueing effects observed in adults and infants result from different underlying mechanisms. Of interest here is the fact that the shifts of gaze in this study were considered to be static even though the eyes blinked at a rate of 500 msec on and 500 msec off, and thus, were closed for only 500 msec immediately before presentation of averted gaze. This blinking rate is identical to that used in the experiments by Hood et al. (1998) in which they obtained cueing effects that were later attributed to apparent motion due to the rapid blinking rate (Farroni et al., 2002). Thus, some confusion remains about the role of apparent motion in the cueing of attention by gaze and the particular blinking rates that allow or eliminate this apparent motion.

ISSUES ADDRESSED BY THE PRESENT RESEARCH

Unilateral vs. Bilateral Target Presentation

In comparing the traditional gaze-following paradigm with the more recent gaze cueing paradigm, the most obvious difference is that the former involves face-to-face interaction with an experimenter and the latter involves viewing and reacting to stimuli on a computer screen. Another potentially important difference is the number of targets used in each procedure. Whereas computerized gaze cueing paradigms to date have featured a single peripheral target on each trial (e.g., Friesen & Kingstone, 1998; Hood et al., 1998), joint attention experiments typically involve following gaze in the presence of identical targets on either side of the experimenter (e.g., Corkum & Moore, 1998; D'Entremont, 2000). The use of identical bilateral targets is also common in other visual attention research with infants (e.g., Clohessy, Posner, Rothbart, & Vecera, 1991; Johnson, 1994; Valenza, Simion, & Umiltà, 1994). The present research extends this strategy to the study of attentional cueing by gaze in computerized experiments by including identical bilateral targets in some experiments in place of the typical unilateral targets. The advantage of bilateral target presentation is that on each trial, infants have a choice between looking at a cued target and an uncued target. Moore (1999a) proposed that in the presence of bilateral peripheral targets the direction of a participant's gaze shift is controlled by a reflexive response to characteristics of the central cue. Comparing the number of looks to cued and uncued targets will help to test this proposal.

Although unilateral and bilateral target presentations are sufficiently different to preclude direct statistical comparison, the use of both procedures provides two angles from which to view a single effect. When target presentation is unilateral, cueing by gaze would only be evident if infants responded more rapidly when the cue and target were spatially congruent than when they were incongruent. When target presentation is bilateral, more frequent looking at targets on the cued side than on the uncued side would provide evidence of cueing by gaze, as would more rapid responding to targets on the cued side. Thus, the use of bilateral targets provides an additional dependent measure that is more directly observable from infant behavior and may provide more robust evidence of the gaze cueing effect.

Static vs. Animated Gaze Cues

In the present research, gaze cues preceded by closed eyes are labeled "static" and those preceded by open eyes are labeled "animated." Taken together, the results from Experiment 1 by Farroni et al. (2000) and Experiment 1 by Hood et al. (1998) provide a comparison of static and animated gaze cues at a common blinking rate of 500 msec on and 500 msec off. The gaze cueing effect, although evident in both experiments, was strongest following the animated gaze cue (Farroni et al., 2000). Further, the static gaze cue in Hood et al. (1998) was criticized for allowing some degree of apparent motion due to the rapid blinking (Farroni et al., 2000). In addition, these two experiments are not directly comparable due to subtle differences including the duration of cue and target presentations. Across Experiments 1 and 3, Farroni and her colleagues (2000) used animated and static gaze cues, respectively, at different blinking rates, and found the cueing effect with animated, but not with static, gaze cues. To further examine this issue, we included experiments in the present research that provide a direct comparison of static and animated gaze cues at a common blinking rate of 1,000 msec on and 1,000 msec off (as in Farroni et al., 2000; Experiment 3).

Timecourse

Whereas studies of gaze cueing in adults and older children typically include two or more SOAs to examine the timecourse of the effect (Driver et al., 1999; Friesen & Kingstone, 1998; Langton & Bruce, 1999; Ristic et al., 2002), the infancy studies by Hood et al. (1998) and Farroni et al. (2000) each used only one long SOA (1,000 msec and 1,500 msec, respectively) to examine this effect. In the present research, we included the three SOAs used by Ristic et al. (2002) to study gaze cueing in preschoolers and adults: 195, 600, and 1,005 msec. The purpose of including multiple SOAs was to provide a map of the timecourse of the gaze cueing effect and to compare this timecourse across different ages and conditions. We also wanted to address the possibility that the gaze cueing effect might be stronger at short SOAs in infants, as is the case in adults and preschoolers (e.g., Ristic et al., 2002). Such findings would suggest that in infants, as in other age groups, orienting to gaze cues is exogenous or reflexive.

GENERAL METHOD

Participants

Participants in the present research included a combined total of 157 infants (seventy 6-month-olds and eighty-seven 14-month-olds) across a series of experiments. The names of these infants and their parents were obtained from birth announcements in a local newspaper. Infants were then recruited through scripted telephone calls from the primary experimenter to their parents.

We chose to include 14-month-olds in the present research in order to examine gaze cueing at an age when infants demonstrate understanding of the significance of eye direction in the context of joint-visual attention (e.g., Caron et al., 2002). Six-month-olds were included because infants at this age are known to show the gaze cueing effect under certain conditions (Hood et al., 1998).

Apparatus

All experimental sessions for the present research took place in a cubicle enclosed with plain brown curtains to minimize distractions. Dim lighting was provided by a single light fixture (120 watts) mounted on the ceiling directly above the infant. The experimenter sat on a rolling chair, 50 cm in height, with the infant seated on her lap. A PowerMac 7500 or 8500[1] computer in an adjacent control room was used to run the VScope experiments, while a 17 in. (33 cm × 24.7 cm) ViewSonic 17GS Plug & Play + computer monitor, set to 256 colors, was used to display the stimuli. This monitor was located on a rolling cart, 79 cm in height, at a lateral distance of 70 cm from the infant's face, slightly above eye level. Directly behind the monitor was a tripod holding a Samsung SCF710 video camera. This camera provided a close-up view of the baby's eyes. Mounted on the wall above the experimenter's head was a Hitachi CCTV black-and-white video camera. This camera provided a full view of the computer monitor. The images from these two cameras were combined and simultaneously recorded using a split-screen generator, such that the computerized stimuli occupied the top half of the television screen and the baby's face occupied the bottom half.

Stimuli

All stimuli were presented on a white background. Our initial intention was to use black-and-white schematic face stimuli modified from those used by Ristic and colleagues (2002); however preliminary experiments with both 6- and 14-month-olds suggested that these stimuli were not sufficiently interesting or attractive for use with infants at these ages. Thus, the schematic, line-drawn face was replaced with the bright-red face of the Sesame Street character, Elmo.[2] From the reactions of infants in a previous study to an "Elmo's World"

---

[1]A PowerMac 8500 was used for about half of the participants in the first experiment, and was subsequently replaced by a PowerMac 7500 with specifications identical to those of the 8500.

[2]Although we intended to include a figure illustrating the stimuli in our experiments, we were unable to obtain copyright permission to do so.

video and to pictures of Elmo used to decorate the lab, it was concluded that Elmo is a character that is both familiar and interesting to 14-month-olds. The Elmo face used in our experiments occupied a width of 8.2° of visual angle and a height of 7.4°, including the large, round eyes (2.3° in diameter) situated on top of Elmo's head. The right eye overlapped the left eye by about 0.1°. The pupils were 0.8° in diameter, and were equivalent in size and vertical position (approximately 1° from the top edge of each eye). When Elmo's gaze was averted, the pupils remained at the same vertical position, but their horizontal position was altered. For looks toward the left side of the screen, the near pupil and the far pupil were displaced by 0.7° and 0.2°, respectively, while for looks toward the right, the near and far pupils were displaced by 0.8° and 0.3°, respectively. The slight discrepancies between left and right measurements stem from the effect of the overlap of Elmo's eyes on the placement of pupils. The target was a 3.6 × 3.9° image of the Sesame Street character, Cookie Monster, eating spaghetti. The targets were presented at a horizontal distance of 8.5° from the eyes, as measured from the center of the target to the place where the center of the nearest eye had been before the face disappeared.

Design

Across the different experiments, both the type of gaze shift and the type of target presentation varied between conditions such that each condition included either animated or static gaze shifts and either unilateral or bilateral targets, but never both. The distinction between animated and static conditions was whether the eyes were closed or open immediately before the gaze shift. On each trial in an animated condition, the eyes were open (pupils centered) in the last display before the pupils shifted. On each trial in a static condition, the eyes were closed in the last display before the pupils shifted.

Each condition was composed of four blocks of 12 randomly ordered trials, for a total of 48 trials. In conditions with unilateral target presentation, the 12 trials represented all possible combinations of three within-subjects variables: spatial congruency (congruent or incongruent), target location (right or left), and SOA (195, 600, or 1,005 msec). Spatial congruency refers to whether or not the cue accurately predicted the location of the subsequent target. Since the cues were nonpredictive, congruent and incongruent cues occurred equally often. Stimulus onset asynchrony (SOA) refers to the amount of time that passed between the onset of the cue and the onset of the target (which coincided with the offset of the cue). In conditions with bilateral target presentation, the same three SOAs were used; however, the only other within-subjects variable was cue direction (left or right). Thus, each block of 12 trials included two each of six distinct trial types.

The dependent measure for conditions with unilateral target presentation was the reaction time (RT) for saccadic responses to the target, while the dependent measures for conditions with bilateral target presentation were both RT and number of saccadic responses to the cued and uncued targets (target choice).

Procedure

When the experimenter had positioned the infant on her lap in front of the computer monitor, an assistant in an adjacent control room initiated the experiment. In cases when the infant became restless or fussy, the experimenter traded places with the infant's parent; whenever possible these changes took place between blocks.

Each trial began with a fixation stimulus consisting of two images of Elmo's face: one with open eyes and one with either squinted or closed eyes (depending on the experiment). These images were displayed in an alternating sequence at a rate of 1,000 msec each, which created the illusion of blinking. The pupils in the blinking eyes were centered to create the effect of looking straight ahead. Verbal encouragement to look at Elmo and pointing to the center of the screen below Elmo's face were used as necessary to encourage infant attention to the stimuli during the fixation interval, but not during trials.

Elmo's eyes continued to blink until an assistant monitoring the infants' eye movements from the control room judged that the infant had fixated Elmo's face. At that time, the assistant pressed a key that caused the eyes to stop blinking and the pupils to shift to the left or to the right. These shifts served as gaze cues. After an SOA of 195, 600, or 1,005 msec, Elmo's face disappeared and the target or targets (depending on the condition) appeared and remained activated for 1,000 msec. Following the disappearance of the target(s), the screen remained blank for 30 msec before beginning the next trial.

Scoring of Unilateral Trials

The experimenter viewed the videotapes of the infants' eye movements, noting which trials were usable for each participant. Trials were deemed unusable if infants blinked, turned away from the screen, moved excessively, yawned, or looked up or down during the trial. The lists of usable and unusable trials for each participant were provided to a coder who was unaware of the hypotheses of the experiment. The coder for each experiment scored all usable trials frame-by-frame (30 or 60 frames per second[3] depending on the experi-

---

[3]Videotaped footage of infants' responses was downloaded to an iMac and de-interlaced using JES De-interlacer to separate each frame into its two fields, thus allowing scoring at 60 fps rather than the usual 30 fps.

ment), noting the direction (same side as target or opposite) and RT of the first eye movement on each trial for each infant. RT was determined by counting the number of frames between the appearance of the target and the first evidence of eye movement on the part of the infant.

The experimenter then used information from VScope to determine the trial type for each usable trial. Scored trials were subsequently sorted by type and median RTs were calculated for each of the 12 trial types. When collapsing across trial types, medians were recalculated accordingly.

Scoring of Bilateral Trials

The scoring for bilateral trials was slightly different in that the direction of first eye movement was scored as either left or right depending on which of the two targets had been fixated. The experimenter then determined whether each response was to the cued or uncued side by matching the six trial types with information about which target had been fixated. All analyses of infant choice behavior on bilateral trials were based on the number of responses to meet particular criteria (e.g., number of responses to the cued side at a given SOA). RTs were scored using the same method as for unilateral trials.

RESULTS AND DISCUSSION

Data Analysis

In individual conditions with unilateral target presentation, RT data were analyzed using 2×3 Repeated Measures ANOVAs with cue-target spatial congruency (congruent or incongruent) and SOA (195, 600, or 1,005 msec) as within-subjects variables, collapsing across target location. In individual conditions with bilateral target presentation, choice data (measured in number of responses) were analyzed using 2×3 Repeated Measures ANOVAs with target choice (cued target or uncued target) and SOA (195, 600, or 1,005 msec) as within-subjects variables, while RT data (for looks to the chosen target) were analyzed using 2×3 Repeated Measures ANOVAs with choice RT (cued target or uncued target) and SOA as within-subjects variables. For all comparisons across conditions, data were analyzed using $2 \times 2 \times 3$ Repeated Measures ANOVAs with condition (static or animated) as the between-subjects variable along with the appropriate pair of within-subjects variables as described above. Planned comparisons in the form of one-tailed paired t-tests were used to examine cueing effects at individual SOAs.

Unilateral vs. Bilateral Target Presentation

In the present research, significant cueing effects were confined to conditions with bilateral target presentation. Analyses of the RT data revealed no significant cueing effects for any of the conditions with unilateral target presentation, including an animated condition with 14-month-olds, F (1, 14) = .001, p = .972, n.s., and both animated and static conditions with 6-month-olds, F (1, 27) = .400, p = .533, n.s. The latter experiment was even scored at 60 fps (as in Farroni et al., 2000) in order to improve precision of measurement, but to no avail. Given the results obtained by Hood et al. (1998) and Farroni et al. (2000) under similar conditions, our failure to find significant cueing by gaze was unexpected. One possible explanation is that because of their similarity to the social stimuli that infants encounter in everyday life, photographs of a human face provide more salient gaze information than images of an animated character's face. Although infants are known to be sensitive to the direction of gaze portrayed in line drawings of faces (Vecera & Johnson, 1995), this sensitivity may not be as strong as when gaze is portrayed in photographs of human faces and thus may not be sufficient to produce the type of orienting required to give cued trials an RT advantage over uncued trials.

In conditions with bilateral target presentation, every trial has a cued and an uncued target and both the choice of target and the RT of the response to the chosen target provide information about whether or not cueing by gaze has occurred. In a condition with animated gaze cues, 14-month-olds looked significantly more often at targets appearing on the cued side of the screen than the uncued side, F (1, 15) = 12.62, p = .003. When 6-month-olds were examined across static and animated conditions, they also looked significantly more often at cued than uncued targets, F (1, 28) = 9.21, p = .005. However, in a follow-up study with static and animated conditions, 14-month-olds showed no preference for cued targets over uncued targets, F (1, 26) = .019, p = .890, n.s.

Analyses of the RT data indicated that for 14-month-olds there was a marginally significant RT benefit when they chose to look at cued targets compared to uncued targets, both in the initial animated condition, F (1, 14) = 4.02, p = .065, and in the follow-up study across static and animated conditions, F (1, 26) = 4.19, p = .051. For 6-month-olds, the RT benefit for looks to cued targets compared to uncued targets was significant across conditions, F (1, 26) = 5.28, p = .030.

Whereas there was no evidence of cueing in the unilateral experiments, both of the dependent measures in the bilateral experiments provided at least some evidence of attentional cueing by gaze. However, as shown in this pattern of results, the two dependent measures do not always provide congruent information. For instance, 14-month-olds in the experiment with both static and animated conditions tended to look equally often at cued and un-cued targets, but still showed a marginally significant RT benefit for responses to cued targets. One possible explanation for this lack of cueing as measured by choice behavior is the tendency for some infants to show a preference or bias toward a particular side of the screen, and thus to look to that side on the majority of trials. Because these side biases tend to attenuate cueing effects, they present a limitation that should be considered when using bilateral target presentation.

Static vs. Animated Gaze Cues

The bilateral experiments in the present research provide evidence for both sides of the debate over the role of apparent motion in gaze cues. When ex-amining each condition individually, the data on infants' choices between cued and uncued targets indicate that cued targets were chosen preferentially only in conditions with animated gaze cues. More specifically, the cueing effect as measured from choice data occurred only when the blinking sequence during the fixation interval involved squinting, which was the case with the original group of 14-month-olds, $F (1, 14) = 4.02, p = .065$ (as noted above), as well as the animated condition for 6-month-olds, $F (1, 14) = 7.89, p = .014$. In these experiments, the round black pupils in Elmo's large white eyes were simply re-placed with curved black lines that were slightly wider than the pupils. Because this fixation stimulus involved motion at the precise location of the pupils, it is likely that infant attention was focused directly on the pupils, making the subsequent motion of those pupils particularly salient. In order to allow realis-tic static shifts of gaze in further experiments, including a comparison of static and animated conditions at 14 months and a static condition at 6 months, the blinking sequence was changed to an alternation between eyes with black pupils on a white background and eyes completely occluded by full red eye-lids. Because this fixation stimulus involved motion across the entire eye re-gion, there was probably less attention focused directly on the pupils during the fixation interval and upon presentation of the cue than in previous experi-ments, both in the present research and in other infancy work (i.e., Farroni et al., 2000; Hood et al., 1998). In other words, the occlusion of Elmo's large eyes by full red eyelids may have been distracting, which may explain the high incidence of preferential orienting toward a particular side of the screen (as de-scribed above), which in turn could help to explain why 14-month-olds showed no preference between cued and uncued targets in either animated or static conditions when the blinking sequence involved closed eyes.

It is worth noting, however, that 6-month-olds in the static condition (who showed little evidence of side bias) did choose the cued target more often than the uncued target, a trend which, when combined with data from

6-month-olds in the animated condition, resulted in a significant cueing effect, F (1, 28) = 9.21, p = .005 (as noted above), that was not qualified by any interaction with condition. This finding suggests that 6-month-olds behave similarly across the two conditions, despite differences both in the fixation stimulus and in the nature of the gaze cues. Likewise, 6-month-olds' RT data is consistent across conditions, as indicated by a significant overall cueing effect, F (1, 26) = 5.28, p = .030 (as noted above), that was not qualified by any interaction with condition, as well as trends of similar magnitude (animated: p = .078, static: p = .088) in the two conditions when analyzed separately. This evidence of consistency across static and animated conditions, from both choice and RT data, suggests that motion of the pupils is not a necessary condition for attentional cueing by gaze in 6-month-old infants, as suggested by Farroni et al. (2000).

For 14-month-olds, the cueing effect as measured by RT was marginally significant across static and animated conditions in the overall analysis, F (1, 26) = 4.19, p = .051 (as noted above), and although the interaction with condition did not reach significance (p = .085), separate analyses of the individual conditions indicated significant cueing by gaze in the static condition, F (1, 14) = 5.65, p = .032, but not in the animated condition, F (1, 12) = .057, p = .816, n.s. While the RT effect in the static condition provides further support for attentional cueing by static images of averted gaze in infants, the unexpected lack of cueing in the animated condition warrants further examination at individual SOAs, as described in the next section. Thus, these results illustrate that while the effect of attentional cueing by gaze can be elusive, this effect is not specific to animated gaze cues.

Timecourse

The inclusion of multiple SOAs in the present research was intended to allow exploration and comparison of the timecourse of cueing by gaze in 6-month-olds and in 14-month-olds. The present results provide some evidence of consistency in the timecourse of gaze cueing between 6-month-olds and 14-month-olds and other evidence to suggest a developmental progression in timecourse across this age range. One example of consistency across ages comes from RT data in the two experiments that compared static and animated gaze cues. Specifically, planned comparisons revealed that the RT cueing effects across conditions were specific to the 600-msec SOA, in both 6-month-olds, t (29) = −1.90, p = .030, and 14-month-olds, t (27) = −2.58, p = .008. In the 14-month-olds, this pattern represented a significant interaction between choice RT and SOA, F (2, 25) = 3.74, p = .038. This pattern of results suggests that between the ages of 6 and 14 months, the effect of cueing by gaze in the presence of bilateral targets appears at an SOA between 195 and 600 msec and disappears before 1,005 msec.

It is important to note, however, that planned comparisons at individual SOAs provide a less coherent picture when the static and animated conditions are examined separately. As described above, for instance, for 14-month-olds in the animated condition with closed eyes, RT data provided no evidence of significant cueing. Planned comparisons revealed that this result was due to a significant cueing effect at the 600-msec SOA, t (12) $= -2.12, p = .028$, being cancelled out by an opposite effect of similar magnitude at the 195-msec SOA, t (12) $= 2.26$, n.s. ($p = .022$ in unpredicted tail of 1-tailed test). In other words, infants in this condition made faster responses to targets on the uncued side at 195 msec, but to targets on the cued side at 600 msec. Further, although there was RT evidence of significant cueing for 14-month-olds in the static condition, planned comparisons revealed that this effect was not significant at any individual SOAs. Thus, although there were trends toward cueing at all three SOAs, we have no basis for drawing conclusions about timecourse in this specific condition. In the overall analysis, the conflicting effects at 195 msec cancelled each other out, while the complementary effects at 600 msec indicated significant cueing at this SOA.

The overall effect in 6-month-olds was the result of trends in the individual conditions. Planned comparisons at the individual SOAs indicated that there was cueing at 1,005 msec in the animated condition, t (13) $= -1.78, p = .050$, (consistent with Hood et al., 1998), and at 600 msec in the static condition, t (14) $= -2.03, p = .031$. Thus, the timecourse of cueing by gaze in 6-month-olds and the degree of consistency in timecourse across ages are unclear from these RT data.

Further evidence of timecourse consistency across age groups comes from choice behavior data in the original animated conditions (with squinting) at each age (see upper panel of Figure 3–1). Specifically, planned comparisons revealed that in 6- and 14-month-olds, respectively, there was significant cueing at the 600-msec, t (14) $= 2.09, p = .028$ and t (15) $= 2.42, p = .015$, and 1,005-msec SOAs, t (14) $= 2.33, p = .018$ and t (15) $= 2.39, p = .015$. Yet, when comparing the RT data for the same conditions, there was evidence of a developmental progression of timecourse (see lower panel of Figure 3–1), with significant cueing in 6-month-olds only at the 1,005-msec SOA, t (13) $= -1.78, p = .050$ (as noted above), and in 14-month-olds at the 195-msec, t (14) $= -2.18, p = .025$, and 600-msec SOAs, t (14) $= -1.88, p = .041$. In the 14-month-olds, this pattern represented a marginally significant interaction between choice RT and SOA, F (2, 13) $= 3.79, p = .051$.

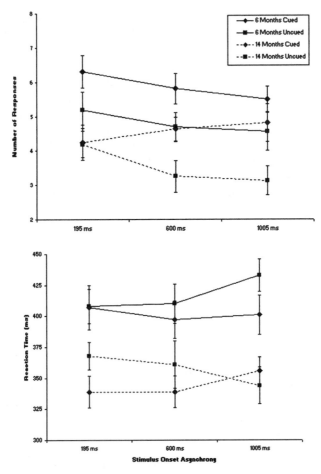

FIGURE 3–1.   Mean number (upper panel) and mean reaction time (lower panel) of responses to cued and uncued targets by 6- and 14-month-olds in the original animated condition with bilateral target presentation. Error bars represent standard error of the mean.

SUMMARY AND CONCLUSIONS

The present research included a series of experiments examining the cueing of attention by gaze under various conditions. Unique features of these experiments included the use of identical bilateral targets, the direct comparison of static and animated gaze cues within an experiment, and the inclusion of multiple SOAs to explore the timecourse of the gaze cueing effect.

The replacement of unilateral peripheral targets with bilateral targets in some experiments added an additional degree of similarity between the computerized attention-cueing paradigm and the standard joint-attention paradigm. This modification allowed for a comparison of the number of looks to cued and uncued targets, a measure similar to the difference scores used to assess joint attention by gaze-following (e.g., Moore & Corkum, 1998). Further, in bilateral (but not unilateral) experiments, the choice between cued and uncued targets was reflected in the RT data. Rather than simply measuring how rapidly infants looked to the cued side on congruent trials and the uncued side on incongruent trials, these data indicate how rapidly infants looked to the target they chose to look to on a series of trials where they had the choice between a cued target and an uncued target. These modifications worked to our advantage in that the effect of cueing by gaze, which eluded us in the unilateral experiments, was evident from one or both of the dependent measures in the bilateral experiments. The main disadvantage of bilateral target presentation was that the cueing effects were attenuated in some cases by a tendency for infants to orient preferentially to a particular side of the screen, rather than orienting in the direction of the cue.

The direct comparison of static and animated gaze cues was intended to address the issue of the distinction between sensitivity to apparent motion and sensitivity to gaze direction raised by Farroni and her colleagues (2000). Using the same blinking rate as Farroni et al. (2000, Experiment 3) in conditions with animated and static shifts of gaze, we found evidence of more rapid responding to cued targets than to uncued targets in both 6- and 14-month-olds across conditions. Of particular interest is the finding of cueing in the static condition at each of these ages. These results suggest that the cueing effect should not be attributed solely to the influence of motion, but also to infants' sensitivity to the direction of gaze. This sensitivity may be acquired through the development of expectancies based on observed contingencies between gaze direction and interesting sights. A recent study comparing 2-year-olds with autism and typically developing 2-year-olds provides additional evidence that attentional cueing by gaze early in development cannot be completely accounted for by a general sensitivity to motion (Chawarska, Klin, & Volkmar, 2003). Specifically, Chawarska and her colleagues found that 2-year-olds in both groups showed faster responding on congruent than incongruent trials when an animated gaze cue was presented by a human face, but not when an equivalent cue was presented by a non-face control stimulus. Thus, they argued that the cueing effect was specific to biological motion rather than to motion in general. Interestingly, although the children with autism showed cueing by gaze, they also showed the characteristic delay in joint attention, by not following head or gaze direction when interacting with an adult social partner. This discrepancy was attributed to a difficulty in disengaging from salient central stimuli

(Chawarska et al., 2003), much like the explanation provided for a similar discrepancy in infants (Hood et al., 1998). Overcoming this limitation of the standard paradigm is one of the key strengths of the attentional cueing method for examining infant sensitivity to gaze direction.

Exploring the timecourse of attentional effects is helpful in determining whether they result from exogenous or endogenous orienting. The effect of cueing by gaze found in adults by Friesen and Kingstone (1998) is considered to be exogenous, partially on the basis of its timecourse, including its emergence at an SOA of 105 msec and its disappearance by 1,005 msec. In the present research, whereas the RT comparisons across static and animated conditions indicated cueing only at the 600 msec SOA at both ages, the RT data in the original animated condition at the two ages suggested a developmental progression in the timecourse of cueing by gaze, with the effect occurring at the shorter SOAs in 14-month-olds and the longest SOA in 6-month-olds. Although no such progression was evident from these infants' choice data, which indicated cueing at the longer SOAs in both age groups, these data are consistent with timecourse information available in the literature. The adult-like timecourse of cueing by gaze (e.g., Friesen & Kingstone, 1998, Ristic et al., 2002) in 14-month-olds suggests that by this age infants are responding exogenously, while the later onset in 6-month-olds (which is consistent with the findings of Farroni et al., 2000 and Hood et al., 1998 who only used long SOAs) suggests that their responding may be more endogenous. If this is the case, the early cueing in our 14-month-olds and the reflexive orienting observed in adults (e.g., Friesen & Kingstone, 1998), and children (e.g., Ristic et al., 2002), may be governed by a common mechanism resulting from "overlearning" of an initially endogenous effect. Our proposal, then, is that the apparently automatic capacity of gaze direction to cue attention is actually acquired through experiences in infancy, including the observation of contingencies between gaze direction and interesting sights, the development of expectancies about the predictive value of gaze direction, and, eventually, the appreciation of the significance of gaze direction as it relates to attention. Thus, at 6 months, infants have enough experience with gaze direction to use it as an endogenous cue, and although the exact age at which exogenous control takes over is unclear in the absence of research at intervening ages, the present data suggest that such a mechanism is in place by 14 months. This account is partially consistent with the conclusion by Mansfield et al. (2003) that the gaze cueing effects observed in adults and infants are controlled by different mechanisms; however, we propose that the transition between mechanisms occurs much earlier in development.

To summarize, we have introduced bilateral target presentation to the study of attentional cueing by gaze, provided some evidence of cueing with and without visible motion of the pupils, explored the timecourse of this attentional effect in 6- and 14-month-olds, and suggested a preliminary account of a shift during the infancy period from endogenous to exogenous orienting in response to gaze direction. We anticipate that these contributions will provide some interesting directions for future research on the cueing of attention by gaze.

ACKNOWLEDGMENTS

This research was made possible by an Izaak Walton Killam Memorial Scholarship to Amy (Carr) MacPherson and through generous support from the Natural Sciences and Engineering Research Council of Canada (NSERC), including a Postgraduate Scholarship to Amy (Carr) MacPherson, an Operating Grant to Chris Moore, and an Undergraduate Student Research Award to David Quinn. We would like to thank David for his hard work and innovation and gratefully acknowledge the many other undergraduate students who helped with data collection and coding for these experiments. In addition, we would like to thank John Christie and Chris Wright for sharing their technical expertise. We also want to express our appreciation to the infant participants and parents who volunteered their time to help us with this research. Finally, Amy would like to thank her husband, Ryan MacPherson, and her parents, Terry and Jeannine Carr, whose continued love and support were essential to the completion of this chapter.

REFERENCES

Baron-Cohen, S. (1995). *Mindblindness: An essay on autism and theory of mind*. Cambridge, MA: MIT Press.

Butterworth, G., & Cochran, E. (1980). Towards a mechanism of joint visual attention in human infancy. *International Journal of Behavioral Development, 3*, 253–272.

Butterworth, G., & Jarrett, N. (1991). What minds have in common is space: Spatial mechanisms serving joint visual attention in infancy. *British Journal of Developmental Psychology, 9*, 55–72.

Caron, A. J., Butler, S., & Brooks, R. (2002) Gaze-following at 12 and 14 months: Do the eyes matter? *British Journal of Developmental Psychology, 20*, 225–239.

Chawarska, K., Klin, A., & Volkmar, F. (2003). Automatic attention cueing through eye movement in 2-year-old children with autism. *Child Development, 74*, 1108–1122.

Clohessy, A. B., Posner, M. I., Rothbart, M. K., & Vecera, S. P. (1991). The development of inhibition of return in early infancy. *Journal of Cognitive Neuroscience, 3*, 345–350.

Corkum, V., & Moore, C. (1995). Development of joint visual attention in infants. In C. Moore & P. Dunham (Eds.), *Joint attention: Its origins and role in development* (pp. 61–84). Hillsdale, NJ: Lawrence Erlbaum Associates.

Corkum, V., & Moore, C. (1998). The origins of joint visual attention in infants. *Developmental Psychology, 34,* 28–38.

D'Entremont, B. (2000). A perceptual-attentional explanation of gaze-following in 3- and 6-month-olds. *Developmental Science, 3,* 302–311.

D'Entremont, B., Hains, S. M. J., & Muir, D. W. (1997). A demonstration of gaze-following in 3- to 6-months-olds. *Infant Behaviour and Development, 20,* 569–572.

Driver, J., Davis, G., Ricciardelli, P., Kidd, P., Maxwell, E., & Baron-Cohen, S. (1999). Gaze perception triggers reflexive visuospatial orienting. *Visual Cognition, 6*(5), 509–540.

Farroni, T., Johnson, M. H., Brockbank, M., & Simion, F. (2000). Infants' use of gaze direction to cue attention: The importance of perceived motion. *Visual Cognition, 7*(6), 705–718.

Friesen, C. K., & Kingstone, A. (1998). The eyes have it! Reflexive orienting is triggered by nonpredictive gaze. *Psychonomic Bulletin & Review, 5,* 490–495.

Hains, S. M. J., & Muir, D. W. (1996). Infant sensitivity to adult eye direction. *Child Development, 67,* 1940–1950.

Hood, B. M. (1995). Shifts of visual attention in the human infant: A neuroscientific approach. In C. Rovee-Collier & L. Lipsitt (Eds.), *Advances in Infancy Research* (Vol. 9, pp. 163–216). New Jersey, Ablex.

Hood, B. M., Willen, J. D., & Driver, J. (1998). Adult's eyes trigger shifts of visual attention in human infants. *Psychological Science, 9,* 53–56.

Johnson, M. H. (1994). Visual attention and the control of eye movements in early infancy. In C. Umilta & M. Moscovitch (Eds.), *Attention and Performance, XV.* Cambridge, MA: MIT Press.

Jonides, J. (1981). Voluntary versus automatic control over the mind's eye movements. In J. Long & A. Baddeley (Eds.), *Attention and Performance, IX.* Hillsdale, NJ: Lawrence Erlbaum Associates.

Klein, R. M., Kingstone, A., & Pontefract, A. (1992). Orienting of visual attention. In K. Rayner (Ed.), *Eye movements and visual cognition.* (pp. 46–65). New York: Springer-Verlag.

Langton, S., & Bruce, V. (1999). Reflexive visual orienting in response to the social attention of others. *Visual Cognition, 6*(5), 541–567.

Mansfield, E. M., Farroni, T., & Johnson, M. H. (2003). Does gaze perception facilitate overt orienting? *Visual Cognition, 10*(1), 7–14.

Moore, C. (1999a). Gaze-following and the control of attention. In P. Rochat (Ed.), *Early social cognition: Understanding others in the first months of life* (pp. 241–256). Mahwah, NJ: Lawrence Erlbaum Associates.

Moore, C. (1999b). Intentional relations and triadic interactions. In P. D. Zelazo & J. W. Astington, (Eds.), *Developing theories of intention: Social understanding and self-control* (pp. 43–61). Mahwah, NJ: Lawrence Erlbaum Associates.

Moore, C., & Corkum, V. (1998). Infant gaze-following based on eye direction. *British Journal of Developmental Psychology, 16*(4), 495–503.

Morissette, P., Ricard, M., & Gouin-Decarie, T. (1995). Joint visual attention and pointing in infancy. A longitudinal study of comprehension. *British Journal of Developmental Psychology, 13,* 163–175.

Ristic, J., Friesen, C. K., & Kingstone, A. (2002). Are eyes special? It depends on how you look at it. *Psychological Bulletin and Review, 9*, 507–513.

Scaife, M., & Bruner, J. S. (1975). The capacity for joint visual attention in the infant. *Nature, 253*, 265–266.

Valenza, E., Simion, F., & Umiltà, C. (1994). Inhibition of return in newborn infants. *Infant Behavior and Development, 17*, 293–302.

Vecera, S., & Johnson, M. (1995). Eye gaze detection and the cortical processing of faces: Evidence from infants and adults. *Visual Cognition, 2*, 101–129.

4

Early Gaze-Following and the Understanding of Others

Barbara D'Entremont, Aimée Yazbek,
Amanda Morgan, and Sarah MacAulay
University of New Brunswick

Gaze-following is a term that has been used in the literature to denote when an infant turns to look in the same direction in which an adult is looking. The behavior has important empirical and theoretical links to key aspects of social cognition; hence, we must have a solid understanding of its emergence and developmental sequelae. From a practical viewpoint, it is important to understand its onset and developmental progression because of its links to language and cognitive abilities. For example, individual differences in gaze-following at 6 months of age have been related to individual differences in later language ability (Morales, Mundy, & Rojas, 1998; Morales et al., 2000). Studies also reveal that children use gaze direction to map words to objects (Baldwin, 1991, 1993, 1995) and appear to understand the adult's referential intent when looking at, and labelling, a novel object (Moore, Angelopoulos, & Bennet, 1999). In contrast, Baron-Cohen (1995) has found that children with autism are "blind" to the mentalistic significance of the eyes. Indeed, children with autism have been found to frequently lack the ability to use gaze direction as a cue to word comprehension and speaker's intent (Baron-Cohen, Baldwin, & Crowson, 1997).

From a theoretical viewpoint, gaze-following is important because it has been used to operationalize joint attention. Joint attention is said to occur when two individuals simultaneously pay attention to each other and some object of interest. In addition to gaze-following, some of the outward manifestations of joint attention include alternating looks between an adult and objects, the use of communicative gestures to redirect adult attention, and referential language (Carpenter, Nagell, & Tomasello, 1998). These behavioral manifestations are considered by some to emerge as the result of the infant acquiring an understanding of others as intentional beings (Carpenter et al., 1998; Tomasello, 1995). That is, when infants understand that others have goals, intentions, and attentional states, they become able to enter into, and direct, others' attention (sometimes called the intentional stance; Rochat & Striano, 1999). This is the rich interpretation of joint attention. With respect to gaze-following, under the rich interpretation, there is an assumption that the infant has understood that the adult has intentionally turned to look at something and the infant has turned to look at what the adult is looking at. This is the mentalistic interpretation of gaze-following (Bretherton, 1991; Baron-Cohen, 1994; Caron, Kiel, Dayton, & Butler, 2002).

A great deal of energy has gone into validating (or invalidating) the mentalistic interpretation of gaze-following. To this end, most research on the emergence of gaze-following has focussed on two questions: when infants first begin to follow the gaze of others, and when this behavior reflects an understanding of the referential nature of gaze. In this chapter we review the literature germane to these points and argue that there is incongruence in the answers to these two questions. We raise the question of how to interpret the gaze-following ability of infants who do not yet understand the referential nature of looking. To answer this question, we present evidence regarding how early gaze-following relates to later joint attention and language. This evidence, along with previous research, is then used to argue that gaze-following taps into a lower level detection of intentional agents, whereas other, infant initiated, measures of joint attention tap into a higher-level understanding of others' intentions towards outside objects. We further argue that early gaze (i.e., from about 3 months of age until about 9–12 months of age) reflects the former, not the latter, form of social understanding.

EMERGENCE OF GAZE-FOLLOWING

The earliest report of gaze-following comes from Scaife and Bruner (1975). These authors established what has now become the standard procedure for examining gaze-following ability in infants. In general, infants sit facing an adult who turns to fixate on a target, or location off to the side. Gaze-following is said to occur if the infant turns to look in the same direction as the adult. Variations on this general paradigm include combinations of adult head and eye turns, with or without accompanying speech or gestures, presence or absence of targets, placement and number of targets, and placement of adult and infant. It is this general paradigm and variations that we will concentrate on in our review.

Scaife and Bruner (1975) used a procedure where the adult turned his head 90° to fixate on a target not visible to the infants. They found that some infants as young as 2–4 months would follow the adult's gaze with the number increasing with age, so that by 11–14 months almost all infants were following gaze. Unfortunately, Scaife and Bruner included chance performance in their criterion leading to the question of whether the youngest infants were actually able to follow gaze. To rectify this problem, more recent researchers have begun to take incorrect turns into account. For example, by examining difference scores between correct and incorrect responses and by ensuring these were above chance performance, Corkum and Moore (1995) found no evidence of spontaneous gaze-following before 10–12 months of age. This would seem to suggest that the gaze-following of the youngest infants in the Scaife and Bruner procedure was due to chance responding. However, Corkum and Moore did not employ targets in their procedure.

The late onset of gaze-following reported by Corkum and Moore (1995) is in contrast with those who have used targets in their procedures. For example, D'Entremont, Hains, and Muir (1997) conducted a gaze-following study with infants ranging in age from 3–6 months. In their procedure, highly visible targets were present very close to the experimenter, within the infant's peripheral vision. The experimenter interacted with the infant until eye contact had been established and then turned her head 90° to fixate one of the targets. The direction of the first infant eye turn following an adult head turn was recorded. Their results showed that infants at both ages made significantly more correct than incorrect turns. Butterworth and colleagues conducted a number of studies of infant gaze-following with 6–18 month-olds (Butterworth & Cochran, 1980; Butterworth & Grover, 1990; Butterworth & Jarrett, 1991). In their studies, multiple targets were present from 25° to 150° on either side of the infant's midline. They found that at 6 months of age, infants would turn to look in the same direction as the adult when targets were in the infants' visual field, but they did not localize the correct target. At 12 months of age, infants would localize the correct target, as long as the target was in front of them, and by 18 months of age infants would follow gaze to targets behind them (Butterworth & Cochran, 1980; Butterworth & Grover, 1990; Butterworth & Jarrett, 1991). There were two exceptions where the studies included targets and where gaze-following was reported to emerge later than 6 months; however, these studies both used a more stringent criterion for "success." These two papers reported an onset of 12 months for gaze-following (Lempers, 1979; Morissette, Ricard, & Gouin-Decarie, 1995).

D'Entremont (2000) examined the effects of motion and placement of targets on 3- and 6-month-olds' gaze-following. In her study, targets were either moving or stationary and were placed at angles ranging from 15° to 40° from the infant's midline. This study was an improvement over previous work because distance of the target from the infant remained the same while the visual angle changed. In previous work, visual angle was always positively correlated with distance from the infant. Gaze-following was also evaluated with different criteria. Thus, this study allowed for an examination of both environmental supports for gaze-following as well as an evaluation of the issue of different ages of onset due to different criteria. Results of this study revealed no significant age differences; both 3- and 6-month-olds were equally successful in following gaze. Results further revealed that distance and motion showed no significant effects on gaze-following; however, infants did show the most gaze-following to 15° stationary targets and only turns to the 15° stationary targets were significantly different from chance. Thus, infants between 3 to 6 months of age can gaze follow to targets within their visual field, but whether this behavior corresponds to a referential understanding of gaze is another issue.

DEVELOPMENT OF REFERENTIAL UNDERSTANDING

To be credited with understanding the referential nature of gaze, infants must demonstrate the following: 1) a recognition that looking is intentional behavior directed to external objects and events; 2) an understanding that looking results in the mental experience of seeing; 3) a recognition that eyes are responsible for seeing; and 4) that both self and other share in the capacity to see things (Caron, Kiel, et al., 2002).

With regards to understanding looking as intentional, object-directed, behavior, previous authors have argued that infants younger than 12 months do not likely have the cognitive and representational abilities to understand the referential and intentional aspect of looking (D'Entremont, 2000; Corkum & Moore, 1995). Specifically, infants at this age are not able to reason simultaneously about self and other with regard to objects, nor can they reason simultaneously about agents and objects during causal events (e.g., Cohen & Oakes, 1993; Perner, 1991). A recent study by Woodward (2003) supports this. Woodward habituated infants to an adult turning to look at one of two objects. She then provided test events where the adult either turned to the same side as during habituation but looked at a different toy, or turned to the other side to look at the same toy as during habituation. Twelve-month-olds, but not 7- or 9-month-olds, dishabituated to the change in relation between the actor and the object. Thus, the younger infants did not understand the relation between the gazer and the object.

It is also not likely that infants younger than 12 months understand about the mental experience of seeing or the role of the eyes in this process. Corkum and Moore carried out a number of studies with infants ranging in age from 6 to 19 months in which they systematically varied the head and eye cues available to infants, including cases where head and eyes moved in opposite directions. Their studies consistently show that it is only at 18–19 months that infants begin to selectively use the eyes as a cue for which direction to turn (Corkum & Moore, 1995, 1998; Moore & Corkum, 1998). Before that age, infants seem more inclined to follow the head direction than the eye direction. For example, 15- to 16-month-olds were equally likely to follow the head alone (with eyes frontal) as they were to follow when both head and eyes turn (Corkum & Moore, 1995). Further, only 18- to 19-month-olds could be conditioned to follow eyes alone (when the head remained frontal); younger infants performed at chance levels in this condition (Moore & Corkum, 1998). Finally, since young infants do not understand the referential and mental aspects of seeing, nor do they understand about the role of eyes in this process, it is logical to assume that they cannot reason that self and other share in these processes.

While 6-month-olds' understanding of gaze direction is arguably non-referential, the status of 12- to 14-month-olds' recognition of gaze is less clear. Corkum and Moore's research seemed to suggest that infants did not understand the referential nature of gaze until they were 18–19 months of age; however, as noted by Brooks and Meltzoff (2002), Corkum and Moore's designs either excluded targets or they involved conflict between the head and eye cues (e.g., head and eyes turning in different directions or head turning while eyes remained frontal), which may have reduced the performance of the younger infants. To overcome this problem, several authors have employed targets in their experimental design and have used either external visual occluders (i.e., screens or blindfolds) or had the adult close her eyes when turning her head (e.g., Brooks & Meltzoff, 2002; Butler, Caron, & Brooks, 2000; Caron, Butler, Brooks, 2002, Caron, Kiel, et al., 2002; D'Entremont & Morgan, in press). This research has produced mixed results.

Both Butler et al. (2000) and Caron, Kiel, et al. (2002) compared infants' tendency to follow an adult's gaze in screen, window, or no-screen conditions. In the screen condition, an opaque screen was set up between the adult and infant such that the adult was not able to see the placement of the targets, though the infants could see the targets. In the window condition, a hole was cut in the screen so that both adult and infant could see the targets. The no-screen condition was the typical gaze-following set-up, where the windows and screens were pushed completely away from the testing area. In their studies, 18-month-olds followed the gaze of the adult much less when the screen was blocking her view and followed equally well to window and no-screen conditions. The 12- and 14-month-olds showed an ambiguous pattern of results, following less to the screen than the no-screen condition, but following least in the window condition (Butler et al., 2000). When the adult added a pointing gesture, along with her head and eye turn, the 14-month-olds' performance improved so that they followed more in the window than the screen condition (Caron, Kiel, et al., 2002). More recently, Dunphy-Lelii and Welman (2004) altered the barrier arrangement to make it less unusual than the set-up used by both Butler and Caron. Their results confirmed that both 14- and 18-month-olds gaze followed less in opaque barrier than either clear barrier or no barrier conditions.

Two studies have examined infants' gaze-following when the adult made a head turn with eyes closed. Brooks and Meltzoff (2002) found that infants at 12, 14, and 18 months of age looked more when the adult turned his or her head with eyes open than eyes closed. Caron, Butler, et al., (2002) found similar results for 14- but not 12-month-olds. Brooks and Meltzoff (2002) also compared infants' gaze-following when the adult wore a blindfold over her eyes versus a headband. In that study, 14- and 18-month-olds, but not 12-month-olds, followed less in the blindfold than the headband condition. In contrast, D'Entremont and Morgan (in press) found that 12- to 13-month-olds did follow less in a blindfold than headband condition. Finally, using a slightly different approach, Moll and Tomasello (2004) found that 12-month-olds would relocate past a barrier to follow an adult's gaze to a target that was visible to the adult but not the child. Thus, while earlier studies suggested that 12- to 14-month-olds do not have a referential understanding of seeing, more recent studies have suggested otherwise.

In summary, the findings suggest a developmental progression in the understanding of how physical occluders block one's view. At the younger ages (12–14 months), infants may recognize that looking is object-directed, but they may not realize that looking results in the mental state of "seeing" (Brooks & Meltzoff, 2002; Woodward, 2003). At the older ages (14–18 months), infants begin to recognize the importance of eyes for seeing and that physical objects can block sight (Butler et al., 2000; Caron, Kiel, et al., 2002). Finally, by 18 months infants seem to have a more solid grasp on the intentional, referential, nature of looking, the mentalistic experience of seeing, and the role of eyes (Butler et al., 2000; Corkum & Moore, 1995; Moore & Corkum, 1998).

PERCEPTUAL-ATTENTIONAL EXPLANATION OF GAZE-FOLLOWING

If 6-month-olds do not understand the referential nature of gaze, then an alternative explanation is necessary where infants follow the gaze of others without attributing referential or visual experience to others. For infants younger than 12 months, several theories exist and have been collectively labelled attentional/ecological (Caron, Kiel, et al., 2002). Under this group of theories, infants have some inborn priming to follow the gaze of others. As infants begin to follow others' gaze, they see interesting events or objects which reinforce their gaze-following behavior (Corkum & Moore, 1995, 1998). Over time, discriminative learning takes place whereby infants learn the discriminative cue of eyes. Butterworth and Jarrett (1991) used the term "ecological mechanism" to refer to the gaze-following at this age in that, while the adult head turn serves as a cue for the infant to shift attention, certain environmental conditions must be present for the infant to gaze follow (e.g., salient targets within the visual field). Moore (1999) offered a more parsimonious view by linking the results to more general information processing systems. He suggested that the earliest instances of gaze-following are an obligatory or reflexive shift of attention in response to the external cue provided by the adult's head turn. Once attention is shifted by this exogenous cue, the presence of targets then captures the infants' attention. He further argues that the later developing gaze-following to absent targets would be consistent with an endogenous (internally or voluntarily regulated) shift of attention.

The results of D'Entremont (2000) are consistent with Moore's (1999) perceptual-attentional explanation of 3- to 6-month-olds' gaze-following. Recall, she varied both placement and motion of targets in her design. She found that the percentage of no-turn trials increased substantially as targets moved further away. This was especially true for 3-month-olds. She argued that infants require the presence of a peripheral stimulus to attract their attention and that when that peripheral stimulus is absent (or far away), infants have difficulty disengaging their attention from the adult's face. She also speculated that the 3-month-olds, when they do disengage their attention, may be more prone to tracking the adult's head movement. This explanation is consistent with Moore's account and with what is known about 3- to 6-month-olds' ability to disengage attention and their ability to initiate voluntary saccadic movements (Johnson, Posner, & Rothbart, 1991; Haith, 1993; Hood, 1995).

D'Entremont (2000) concluded that the ecological mechanism (Butterworth & Grover, 1990; Butterworth & Jarrett, 1991) is strongly influenced by the infants' perceptual-attentional skills. Here we modify our view somewhat by proposing that the perceptual-attentional explanation serves as an alternative to the ecological mechanism. We believe this explanation is more parsimonious (as noted by Moore, 1999) in that by appealing to a more general information processing system, it does not require a separate gaze-following specific mechanism. Under this explanation, the adult's head turn serves to shift the infant's attention to one side (Hood, 1995; Hood, Willen, & Driver, 1998), but whether the infants complete the turn depends on their ability to disengage attention from a central stimulus, their ability to initiate saccadic movements, and whether there are peripheral cues to help pull their attention away from central stimulus.

RECONCILING THE PERCEPTUAL-ATTENTIONAL EXPLANATION WITH THE RICH INTERPRETATION OF JOINT ATTENTION

If the gaze-following of infants younger than 9–12 months of age does not re-flect an understanding of others' intentions to outside objects, the next task is to understand its function in the development of joint attention. Under the rich interpretation, all joint attention behaviors are interconnected through the infant's emergent understanding of others as intentional beings, yet early gaze-following does not appear to meet this criterion. One possibility is that early gaze-following is an unrelated skill controlled by reflexive orienting of attention which just happens to have the same outward appearance as later endogenously controlled gaze-following. Another possibility is that it is an in-tricate part in a process that culminates in the infants' understanding of others and self as intentional beings. One way to help distinguish between these al-ternatives is to examine how early gaze-following relates to later gaze-following, measures of joint attention, and language.

If all joint attention behaviors are a result of an emergent understanding of others as intentional beings, one would expect strong intercorrelations be-tween gaze-following and measures of joint attention, since all would be tapping into the same general construct (Slaughter & McConnell, 2003). If early gaze-following is somehow part of this process, it, too, should relate to other forms of joint attention. One might also expect a reasonable amount of stability in both gaze-following and measures of joint attention. In support of the rich in-terpretation, Carpenter et al. (1998) report an orderly sequence of emergence among joint attention behaviors. Specifically, they report that joint engagement (defined as alternating looks between toys and social partners) emerges first, fol-lowed by communicative gestures, gaze-following, imitative learning, and, fi-nally, referential language. However, a number of findings challenge the rich interpretation.

Contrary to Carpenter et al. (1998), Slaughter and McConnell (2003) found no relationship between gaze-following and other measures of joint at-tention such as social referencing and imitative learning in 8- to14-month-olds. Carpenter et al. themselves failed to find a correlation between age of on-set of gaze-following and gaze/point following. In contrast, Morissette et al. (1995) found a correlation between age of onset of gaze-following and gaze/point following when they used the ability to localize which one of several targets an adult was attending to as the criterion. Similarly, two studies which reported on stability of gaze-following reported conflicting results. Morales et al. (2000) found some evidence for stability of gaze-following with a num-ber of significant correlations between 8 to 24 months of age, while Markus, Mundy, Morales, Delgado, and Yale (2000) found little evidence of stability in infants between 12 and 18 months of age. Thus, there seems to be less co-hesion than one might expect of a unified joint attention construct.

Along this line, a growing body of research suggests that gaze-following may be one of two distinct forms of joint attention (Claussen, Mundy, & Mallik, 2002; Mundy & Gomes, 1998, Mundy & Willoughby, 1996). When an infant responds to an adult's cues by looking in the direction of the adult's gaze or point, the adult has provided the framework to elicit an orienting behavior from the child. In contrast, if a child initiates joint attention (for example, by making eye contact with the adult when both are engaged in joint play, or by pointing to communicate with the adult), the act is more volitional and self-organizing (Claussen et al., 2002). Recent neurological data supports this distinction. In particular, gaze-following was associated with activity in the posterior parietal attention system thought to reflect orienting behavior. By comparison, the latter infant initiated measures of joint attention were associated with activity in the frontal anterior attention system, thought to reflect cognitive, executive, and motivational processes (Mundy, Card, & Fox, 2000). Even if both forms of joint attention are enabled by an understanding of intentionality in others, they appear to have different social-motivational underpinnings.

The most consistent evidence that joint attention behaviors reflect the emergence of an understanding of intentionality in others comes from their associations with language. Numerous reports have documented the relations between joint attention (including gaze-following) and language (Carpenter et al., 1998; Dunham, Dunham, & Curwin, 1993; Morales et al., 1998; Morales et al., 2000; Mundy & Gomes, 1998; Slaughter & McConnell, 2003; Tomasello & Farrar, 1986). The rich interpretation holds that word production represents the infant's intentional attempts to affect the listener's attentional or intentional state (Bates, Camaioni, & Volterra, 1975; Carpenter et al., 1998). Word comprehension reflects the infant's understanding of the speaker's referential intention (Baldwin, 1991, 1993, 1995; Moore, et al., 1999). Hence, under the rich interpretation both joint attention and language rest on the infant's understanding of others as intentional beings. However, even this literature suggests different joint attention abilities exist. For example, Mundy and Gomes (1998) found that measures of infant initiated joint attention were predictive of expressive language while gaze-following measures were predictive of receptive language.

While it appears that gaze-following may be a unique aspect of joint attention, not all of the abovementioned studies addressed the gaze-following of infants younger than 12 months. In addition, much of the research citing evidence of two separate joint attention processes comes from one research group (i.e., Mundy and his colleagues) and involves small sample sizes. The field would benefit from replication from a separate lab group which included gaze-following in infants both younger and older than 12 months. To this end, we decided to report on (as yet unpublished) data available from a longitudinal study in our own lab.

We tested 57 infants at 6, 12, 18, and 24 months using two measures of gaze-following and two measures of infant initiated joint attention. In the first gaze-following procedure, the experimenter used head and eye turns to turn to look at targets, while in the second gaze-following procedure she used head and eye turns along with pointing gestures when she turned to the target. She also vocalized in the second procedure but did not vocalize in the first procedure. Henceforth, we will refer to the first gaze-following procedure as gaze-following and the second as gaze/point following. When we refer to the collective procedures, we will use the more general term of "attention following" used by Carpenter et al. (1998). In the first infant initiated joint attention procedure we measured the extent to which the infant used communicative behaviors (such as eye contact, pointing, and showing) directed towards the tester. We refer to this as initiating joint attention (Mundy, Hogan, & Doehring, 1996). In the second infant initiated joint engagement procedure we counted the number of times the infant alternated gaze between toys and the mother during a free play session. We refer to this as coordinated joint attention (Bakeman & Adamson, 1984). We also assessed language.

We expected reasonable stability within our measures of joint attention and significant intercorrelations between our different joint attention measures. We also predicted significant relations between attention following and language. Assuming two distinct forms of joint attention, we expected our two attention following measures to be more strongly related to each other and less strongly related to our two infant initiated joint attention measures. Conversely, we expected the two infant initiated joint attention measures to be more strongly related to each other than to the two attention following measures. We also expected attention following to be related to language comprehension but not expressive language (Mundy & Gomes, 1998). If early gaze-following is part of the developmental process of understanding others' intentions and acquiring joint attention, then gaze-following at 6 months should also be related to measures of joint attention and language. If early gaze-following is a separate, unrelated process, then we would expect gaze-following at 6 months to show a divergent pattern of results compared to later developing attention following measures.

In fact, the findings from our longitudinal study revealed little evidence of stability of gaze-following but more evidence of stability for gaze/point following. There are two possible explanations for this. First, our gaze-following task included near and far targets. It is possible that developmental differences in infants' ability to follow to near versus far targets obscured intercorrelations in the gaze-following data. We believe this is unlikely; informal observations of the responding to near versus far targets did not yield differing results. Alternatively, at least two papers reported increased gaze-following ability in infants 12 to 14 months of age when pointing gestures were added to the head/eye turn (Caron, Kiel, et al., 2002; Deak, Flom, & Pick., 2000). It may be that the addition of gesture and vocalizations served to make the adult's cues more salient, increasing the robustness of the gaze/point following data in comparison to the gaze-following data. Turning to the correlations amongst the joint attention measures, several significant correlations were observed both within and across the two types of joint attention (i.e., attention following and infant initiated joint attention). There was some tendency to see more correlations within, rather than across, the two types. However, many correlations were weak and failed to reach significance.

In contrast to the sparse correlations within the attention following measures and between attention following and the infant initiated joint attention measures, a number of the attention following measures were related to language. In general, there were more relationships between gaze/point following and language than gaze-following and language. This may be because, as already mentioned, gaze/point following may be more robust than gaze-following. In addition, our measure of gaze/point following included behind trials. These two factors may have increased the amount of meaningful variance in the gaze/point following measure.

One hypothesis we had was that attention following measures would be related to receptive but not expressive language. Earlier research had indicated that attention following was related to receptive but not expressive vocabulary (Markus et al., 2000; Mundy & Gomes, 1998). Morales et al. (2000) speculated that, at the younger ages, this might be due to the fact that language measures at 12 months are not likely to show meaningful individual differences in expressive language. Our findings suggest otherwise. Attention following measures at 6 and 12 months were related to both vocabulary production and words understood at 12 months. These discrepancies may be due to differences in procedure (e.g., increased variance in the attention following measure due to the inclusion of behind trials, use of brief language measures in previous research versus full language measures in current research), or they may be random fluctuations due to the small sample sizes in each of the studies. Regardless, our findings refute the notion that attention following is an especially good predictor of receptive (as opposed to expressive) language, at least at 12 months of age.

In summary, while we found some intercorrelations among our four joint attention measures, the overall evidence for stability in joint attention was weak, with the best evidence for stability in gaze/point following. Further, only weak evidence was provided that gaze-following was one of a group of measures all tapping into the same underlying measure of joint attention. If that were the case, we would have expected more intercorrelations among the four joint attention measures. Nor did the 6-month gaze-following measure stand out as being any less related to the other measures than the 12- through 24-month gaze-following data. In contrast, even though the attention following measures showed only sparse correlations with each other, they were fairly consistently related to language. This was also the case for the 6-month gaze-following.

CONCLUSIONS

If one combines the data from our longitudinal study with previous studies that have examined multiple measures of joint attention, the overall picture is more consistent with the idea of two forms of joint attention as reviewed herein. Rather than a singular understanding of intentionality, we believe that the different social-motivational processes evidenced in the two forms of joint attention reflect different levels of social understanding. The less voluntary attention following, we argue, reflects a lower-level detection and response to intentional agents, whereas the more voluntary initiated and coordinated joint attention reflects a higher-level understanding of an adult's intention towards an outside entity. This argument was recently made by Yazbek and D'Entremont (in press). They found that a 6-month measure of infant sensitivity to adult intentionality cues was related to attention following but not initiating joint attention at 12 months. Because 6-month-olds do not likely have a mentalistic understanding of others, they argued that their 6-month measure and attention following were related because both tapped into the infant's responsiveness to intentional agents, without necessarily tapping into a higher-level understanding of agents' intentions towards outside objects. In contrast, two studies which examined joint attention and attachment showed opposite results (Claussen et al., 2002; Hartung & D'Entremont, 2002). These authors argued that social processes involved in the attachment system affect infants' motivation to share attention with others. Both these studies found that attachment was related to the more voluntary initiating joint attention but not attention following. The argument that there are different levels of understanding intentional agents is consistent with several theorists who suggest infants can detect intentional agents without necessarily understanding or attributing mental states to those agents (Baron-Cohen, 1994; Gergely, Nádasdy, Csibra, & Bíró, 1995; Leslie, 1994; Premack & Premack, 1997). This argument also fits nicely with Slaughter and McConnell's (2003) suggestion that the understanding of agents is necessary, but not sufficient, for the emergence of joint attention.

Assuming that there are different levels of understanding intentional agents and that some level of understanding is necessary for joint attention would suggest that early gaze-following reflects the lower-level detection of agents described by Yazbek and D'Entremont (in press). Consequently, it should have been related to later gaze-following; however, this was not what we found. It is not unreasonable to propose that early gaze-following does tap into some lower level detection of agents: young infants do appear to know much about agents. Before their first birthdays, infants are able to detect agents, attend selectively to behaviors that are relevant to agents' intentions, they can analyze and parse intentional action, and they expect agents to act in certain ways (Amano, Kezuka, & Yamamoto, 2004; Baldwin, Baird, Saylor, & Clark, 2001; Cohen & Oakes, 1993; Legerstee, Barna, & DiAdamo, 2000; Woodward, 1998, 1999). Moore (2006) recently suggested that infants' understanding of intentionality is acquired piecemeal. Our results are more in line with this argument. This would explain why early gaze-following does not relate well with later joint attention measures, why joint attention abilities are only sometimes related and can also accommodate the perceptual-attentional explanation of early gaze-following. For example, early gaze-following could be enabled by a representational system that detects and categorizes agents (Johnson, 2003), but individual differences in perceptual-attentional and sensorimotor abilities or differences in methodology (such as presence or absence of targets) may introduce certain limitations on infants' performance, reducing the robustness of any interrelations. One could test our proposal, as did Yazbek and D'Entremont (in press), by determining whether these tasks thought to tap into lower level detection of agents selectively related to attention following but not initiating or coordinated joint attention, or whether 6-month-olds selectively follow the gaze of agents (see Johnson, 2003). Finally, it may be that understanding of intentions in different domains (such as epistemic, emotive, or connotative; Moore, 2006) or goal directed versus referential actions (Csibra, 2003) develops at different rates; indeed there is already evidence to support this (Woodward, 1998, 2003; Woodward & Guajardo, 2002). Thus, we end by suggesting that researchers attend carefully to the type of tasks used and the task demands, as well as to variations in results across types of task. We believe this information processing approach will be more fruitful than simply searching for a single underlying "intentional revolution."

REFERENCES

Amano, S., Kezuka, E., & Yamamoto, A. (2004). Infant shifting attention from an adult's face to an adult's hand: A precursor of joint attention. *Infant Behavior & Development*, 27, 64–80.
Bakeman, R., & Adamson, L. (1984). Coordinating attention to people and objects in mother-infant and peer-infant interactions. *Child Development*, 55, 1278–1289.

Baldwin, D. A. (1991). Infants' contributions to the achievement of joint referencing. *Child Development, 62,* 872–890.

Baldwin, D. A. (1993). Infants' ability to consult the speaker for clues to word reference. *Journal of Child Language, 20,* 395–418.

Baldwin, D. A. (1995). Understanding the link between joint attention and language. In C. Moore & P. J. Dunham (Eds.), *Joint attention: Its origin and role in development.* Hillsdale, NJ: Lawrence Erlbaum Associates.

Baldwin, D. A., Baird, J. A., Saylor, M. M., & Clark, M. A. (2001). Infants parse dynamic action. *Child Development, 72,* 708–717.

Baldwin, D. A., & Moses, L. J. (1996). The ontogeny of social information gathering. *Child Development, 67,* 1915–1939.

Baron-Cohen, S. (1994). How to build a baby that can read minds: Cognitive mechanisms in mindreading. *Cahiers de Psychologie Cognitive, 13,* 513–552.

Baron-Cohen, S. (1995). *Mindblindness: An Essay on Autism and Theory of Mind.* Cambridge, MA: The MIT Press.

Baron-Cohen, S., Baldwin, D. A., & Crowson, M. (1997). Do children with autism use the speaker's direction of gaze strategy to crack the code of language? *Child Development, 68*(1), 48–57.

Bates, E., Camaioni, L., & Volterra, V. (1975). The acquisition of performatives prior to speech. *Merrill-Palmer Quarterly, 21,* 205–226.

Bretherton, I. (1991). Intentional communication and the development of mind. In D. Frye & C. Moore (Eds.), *Children's theories of mind. mental states and social understanding* (pp. 49–76). Hillsdale, NJ: Lawrence Erlbaum Associates.

Brooks, R., & Meltzoff, A. N. (2002). The importance of eyes: How infants interpret adult looking behavior. *Developmental Psychology, 38*(6), 958–966.

Butler, S. C., Caron, A. J., & Brooks, R. (2000). Infant understanding of the referential nature of looking. *Journal of Cognition and Development, 1*(4), 359–377.

Butterworth, G., & Cochran, E. (1980). Towards a mechanism of joint visual attention in human infancy. In L. Weiskrantz (Ed.), *Thought without language* (pp. 5–25). Oxford: Oxford University Press.

Butterworth, G., & Grover, L. (1990). Joint visual attention, manual pointing, and preverbal communication in human infancy. In M. Jeannerod (Ed.), *Attention and performance XIII* (pp. 605–624). Hillsdale, NJ: Lawrence Erlbaum Associates.

Butterworth, G., & Jarrett, N. (1991). What minds have in common is space: Spatial mechanisms serving joint attention in infancy. *British Journal of Developmental Psychology, 9*(Special Issue), 55–72.

Caron, A. J., Butler, S., & Brooks, R. (2002). Gaze-following at 12 and 14 months: Do the eyes matter? *British Journal of Developmental Psychology, 20,* 255–239.

Caron, A. J., Kiel, E. J., Dayton, M., & Butler, S. C. (2002). Comprehension of the referential intent of looking and pointing between 12 and 15 months. *Journal of Cognition and Development, 3*(4), 445–464.

Carpenter, M., Nagell, K., & Tomasello, M. (1998). Social cognition, joint attention, and communicative competence from 9 to 15 months of age. *Monographs of the Society for Research in Child Development.*

Claussen, A. H., Mundy, P. C., & Mallik, S. A. (2002). Joint attention and disorganized attachment status in infants at risk. *Development and Psychopathology, 14*, 279–291.

Cohen, L. B., & Oakes, L. M. (1993). How infants perceive a simple causal event. *Developmental Psychology, 29*, 421–433.

Corkum, V., & Moore, C. (1995). Development of joint visual attention in infants. In C. Moore & P. J. Dunham (Eds.), *Joint Attention: Its origin and role in development*. Hillsdale, NJ: Lawrence Erlbaum Associates.

Corkum, V., & Moore, C. (1998). The origins of joint visual attention. *Developmental Psychology, 34*, 28–38.

Csibra, G. (2003). Teleological and referential understanding of action in infancy. *Philosophical Transactions of the Royal Society of London, 358*, 447–458.

Deak, G. O., Flom, R. A., & Pick, A. D. (2000). Effects of gesture and target on 12- and 18-month-olds' joint visual attention to objects in front of or behind them. *Developmental Psychology, 36*(4), 511–523.

D'Entremont, B. (2000). A perceptual-attention explanation of gaze-following in 3- and 6-month-olds. *Developmental Science, 3*(3), 302–311.

D'Entremont, B., Hains, S., & Muir, D. (1997). A demonstration of gaze-following in 3- and 6-month-olds. *Infant Behavior and Development, 20*, 569–572.

D'Entremont, B., & Morgan, R. (in press). Experience with visual barriers and its effects on subsequent gaze-following in 12- to 13-month-olds. *British Journal of Developmental Psychology*.

Dunham, P., Dunham, F., & Curwin, A. (1993). Joint attentional states and lexical acquisition at 18 months. *Developmental Psychology, 29*, 827–831.

Dunphy-Lelii, S., & Wellman, H. M. (2004). Infants' understanding of occlusion of others' line-of-sight: Implications for an emerging theory of mind. *European Journal of Developmental Psychology, 1*, 49–66.

Gergely, G., Nádasdy, Z., Csibra, G., & Bíró, S. (1995). Taking the intentional stance at 12 months of age. *Cognition, 56*, 165–193.

Haith, M. M. (1993). Future-oriented processes in infancy: The case of visual expectations. In C. E. Granud (Ed.), *Visual perception and cognition in infancy* (pp. 235–264). Hillsdale, NJ: Lawrence Erlbaum Associates.

Hartung, C. L., & D'Entremont, B. (2002, April). *The relationship between attachment security, affect sharing and joint attention at 14–17 months of age.* Paper presented at the XIII Biennial International Conference on Infant Studies, Toronto, Canada.

Hood, B. M. (1995). Visual selective attention in infants: A neuroscientific approach. In L. Lipsitt & C. Rovee-Collier (Eds.), *Advances in Infancy Research* (Vol. 9, pp. 163–216). Norwood, NJ: Ablex.

Hood, B. M., Willen, D., & Driver, J. (1998). Adult's eyes trigger shifts of visual attention in human infants. *Psychological Science, 9*, 53–56.

Johnson, M. H., Posner, M. I., & Rothbart, M. K. (1991). Components of visual orienting in early infancy: Contingency learning, anticipatory looking, and disengaging. *Journal of Cognitive Neuroscience, 3*, 335–344.

Johnson, S. C. (2003). Detecting agents. *Philosophical Transactions of the Royal Society of London, 358*, 549–559.

Legerstee, M., Barna, J., & DiAdamo, C. (2000). Precursors to the development of intention at 6 months: Understanding people and their actions. *Developmental Psychology,*
36, 627–634.

Lempers, J. D. (1979). Young children's production and comprehension of nonverbal deictic behaviors. *Journal of Genetic Psychology, 135*, 93–102.

Leslie, A. M. (1994). ToMM, ToBy, and Agency: Core architecture and domain specificity.
In L. Hirschfeld & S. Gleman (Eds.), *Mapping the mind: Domain specificity in cognition*
and culture (pp. 119–148). New York: Cambridge University Press.

Markus, J., Mundy, P., Morales, M., Delgado, C., & Yale, M. (2000). Individual differences
in infant skills as predictors of child-caregiver joint attention and language. *Social De-*
velopment, 9, 302–315.

Moll, H., & Tomasello, M. (2004). 12- and 18-month-old infants follow gaze to spaces behind barriers. *Developmental Science, 7*, 1–9.

Moore, C. (1999). Gaze-following and the control of attention. In P. Rochat (Ed.), *Early*
social cognition: Understanding others in the first months of life (pp. 241–256). Mahwah,
NJ: Lawrence Erlbaum Associates.

Moore, C. (2006). Representing intentional relations and acting intentionally in infancy:
Current insights and open questions. In G. Knoblich, I. Thornton, M. Grosjean, &
M. Shiffrar (Eds.), *Human body perception from the inside out* (pp. 427–442). New York:
Oxford University Press.

Moore, C., Angelopoulos, M., & Bennet, P. (1999). Word learning in the context of referential and salience cues. *Developmental Psychology, 35*, 60–68.

Morales, M., Mundy, P., Delgado, C. E. F., Yale, M., Messinger, D., Neal, R., Schwartz, H. K.
(2000). Responding to joint attention across the 6- through 24-month age period and
early language acquisition. *Journal of Applied Developmental Psychology, 21*(3), 283–298.

Morales, M., Mundy, P., & Rojas, J. (1998). Following the direction of gaze and language development in 6-month-olds. *Infant Behavior and Development, 21*, 373–377.

Morissette, P., Ricard, M., & Gouin-Decarie, T. (1995). Joint visual attention and pointing
in infancy: A longitudinal study of comprehension. *British Journal of Developmental Psy-*
chology, 13, 163–175.

Mundy, P., Card, J., & Fox, N. (2000). EEG correlates of the development of infant joint
attention skills. *Developmental Psychobiology, 36*, 325–338.

Mundy, P., & Gomes, A. (1998). Individual differences in joint attention skill development in the second year. *Infant Behavior and Development, 21*, 469–482.

Mundy, P., Hogan, A., & Doehring, P. (1996). *A preliminary manual for the abridged Early*
Social-Communication Scales. Coral Gables, FL: University of Miami, www.psy.miami.
edu/faculty/pmundy

Mundy, P., & Willoughby, J. (1996). Nonverbal communication, joint attention, and social
emotional development. In M. Lewis & M. Sullivan (Eds.), *Emotional development in*
atypical children (pp. 65–87). New York: Wiley.

Perner, J. (1991). *Understanding the representational mind.* Cambridge, MA, US: The MIT
Press.

Premack, D., & Premack, A. J. (1997). Motor competence as integral to attribution of
goal. *Cognition, 63*, 235–242.

Rochat, P., & Striano, T. (1999). Social-cognitive development in the first year. In P. Rochat (Ed.), *Early Social Cognition* (pp. 3–34). Mahwah, NJ: Lawrence Erlbaum Associates.

Scaife, M., & Bruner, J. S. (1975). The capacity for joint attention in the infant. *Nature, 253*, 265–266.

Slaughter, V., & McConnell, D. (2003). Emergence of joint attention: Relationships between gaze-following, social referencing, imitation, and naming in infancy. *The Journal of Genetic Psychology, 164*(1), 54–71.

Tomasello, M. (1995). Joint attention as social cognition. In C. Moore & P. J. Dunham (Eds.), *Joint attention: Its origins and role in development* (pp. 103–130). Hillsdale, NJ: Lawrence Erlbaum Associates.

Tomasello, M., & Farrar, M. J. (1986). Joint attention and early language. *Child Development, 57*, 1451–1463.

Woodward, A. L. (1998). Infants selectively encode the goal object of an actor's reach. *Cognition, 69*, 1–34.

Woodward, A. L. (1999). Infants' ability to distinguish between purposeful and non-purposeful behaviors. *Infant Behavior and Development, 22*, 145–160.

Woodward, A. L. (2003). Infants' developing understanding of the link between looker and object. *Developmental Science, 6*(3), 297–311.

Woodward, A. L., & Guajardo, J. J. (2002). Infants' understanding of the point gesture as an object-directed action. *Cognitive Development, 17*(1), 1061–1084.

Yazbek, A. & D'Entremont, B. (in press). A longitudinal investigation of the still-face effect at 6 months and joint attention at 12 months. *British Journal of Developmental Psychology*.

5

Increasing Specificity and the Development of Joint Visual Attention

Ross Flom
Brigham Young University

Anne D. Pick
University of Minnesota

Human newborns are socially active and communicative from birth. They have already begun the process of learning, including learning about communication. While still in utero, they hear various extrauterine sounds including their mother's voice (Querleu, Renard, Boutteville, & Crepin, 1989), and by one day of age infants can discriminate their mother's voice from another woman's voice (DeCasper & Fifer, 1980). Newborns also communicate through their level of arousal as well as by means of various coos and cries (Adamson, 1996). Even during the first few hours of postnatal life, infants prefer to look at schematic faces compared to other patterned stimuli (Fantz 1963; Johnson & Morton 1991), and there is some evidence that infants can recognize their mothers' faces within hours of birth (Bushnell, Sai, & Mullin, 1989; Field, Cohen, Garcia, & Greenberg, 1984; Walton, Bower, & Bower, 1992). Infants come into the world with a readiness to engage in early communicative exchanges and to learn about their world (Gibson & Pick, 2000).

Given their readiness, how do infants learn about their world? Clearly the context of much early learning is in interacting with others. One form of early interactions involves coordinating visual attention among the infant, adult, and some object or event. Initially, the responsibility for coordinating attention rests primarily with the adult caregivers as they strive to direct babies to look at a rattle or bottle, or they themselves look at the object momentarily capturing babies' attention. Such instances of shared visual attention and communication provide babies opportunities to learn about their world, and they also provide a setting for babies to learn how to participate in and establish joint visual attention. Thus, infants' guided participation in social exchanges promotes their learning about objects and events and also about how to engage others in social communication. We seek to understand how participating in joint visual attention promotes learning about objects and events. We also seek to understand how infants learn to participate in such social-communicative exchanges. In this chapter, we focus on the second question: how infants learn to engage in joint visual attention.

THE EMERGENCE OF JOINT VISUAL ATTENTION:
A BRIEF REVIEW

Newborns' visual acuity and contrast sensitivity is not fully developed. However, as we noted, they can orient visually to some aspects of faces. By 2.5 months of age they can perceive various features of another's face (Banks & Crowell, 1993; Banks & Dannemiller, 1987). For example, infants as young as 2 months of age prefer to look toward a static face display with the gaze directed toward themselves rather than a display with the gaze directed away from themselves (Farroni, Csibra, Simion, & Johnson, 2002; Hood & Macrae, this volume; Johnson & Farroni, this volume). Similarly, Vecera and Johnson (1995) found that 4-month-olds are able to discriminate direct eye gaze from averted eye gaze, but only if the eyes were presented within the "context" of an upright and colored photograph of a face. Newborns also look longer toward a photograph of a woman with her eyes open than toward a photograph of the same woman with her eyes closed (Batki, Baron-Cohen, Wheelwright, Connellan, & Ahluwalia, 2000). Other research has found that 5-month-olds' smiling and visual attention toward a live actress decreased when the actress averted her gaze to the side of the infant (Symons, Hains, & Muir, 1998). Similarly, when Hains and Muir (1996) had adults alternate their focus of attention between looking at or away from a 5-month-old, 5-month-olds smiled more frequently and looked longer toward the adult when the adult maintained eye contact. Thus, between 2 and 5 months of age infants are sensitive to changes in an adult's direction of gaze, both in static and in dynamic displays, and prefer faces that direct their gaze toward the infant rather than away from the infant.

The ability to follow another's direction of gaze emerges between 3- and 6-months of age. Hood, Willen, and Driver (1998), using a Posner (1980) cueing procedure where a central cue (pair of schematic eyes) is presented and infants' visual orienting response latency is assessed, found that 3-month-olds more rapidly looked toward a target when the cue was oriented in the same direction as the peripheral target compared to an event where the cue and the peripheral target were oriented in opposite directions. In other research, D'Entremont and her colleagues (D'Entremont 2000; D'Entremont, Hains, & Muir, 1997) found that 3-month-olds will follow an adult's direction of gaze (i.e., head and eye orientation) toward an oscillating puppet placed on the experimenter's hand located 90° to the infant's left or right side.

Between 6 and 9 months of age infants will look where an adult is looking as long as the object of shared attention remains within the infants' visual field, and it is the first object encountered along the infants' scan path (Butterworth & Cochran, 1980; Butterworth & Jarrett, 1991; Morales, Mundy, & Rojas, 1998). In other words, by 6 months of age infants are able to establish joint visual attention, yet they can only do so as long as they are not distracted by some other object. Butterworth (1995) described this in terms of an ecological mechanism as follows "what initially attracts the mother's attention and leads her to turn is also likely, in the natural environment, to capture the attention of the infant" (see Butterworth, 1995 p. 32). From Butterworth's perspective, the various attention directing behaviors of an adult, e.g., the mother, serve as a type of general orientating cue that initiates a change in the infant's direction of gaze, and the first interesting object visually encountered by the infant becomes the new focus of the infant's visual attention.

According to Butterworth, by 12 months of age infants are able to ignore an intermediate object in establishing joint visual attention; however, they fail to look toward an object that is placed outside their immediate visual field (Butterworth & Cochran, 1980; Butterworth & Jarrett, 1991). From about 12 to 18 months of age, infants begin to use what Butterworth referred to as a "geometric mechanism." According to Butterworth (1995), infants are now extrapolating an invisible vector between the adult and the object of shared visual attention; because of this mechanism's increased precision, infants are no longer distracted by intermediate objects or events, and they will frequently alternate their gaze between the object of shared visual attention and the adult. However, according to Butterworth, 12- to 18-month-old infants are still not able to establish joint visual attention toward an object that is located outside their immediate visual field. The ability to establish joint visual attention toward an object that is not immediately visible is said to require the development of a representational mechanism that emerges around 18 months of age (Butterworth, 1995; Butterworth & Jarrett, 1991). Thus, by 18 months of age infants comprehend the referential nature of joint visual attention and also possess an increased representational understanding of the spatial layout of their environment such that they are able to establish joint visual attention to objects outside their immediate visual field.

Although Butterworth's account has been challenged (e.g., Corkum & Moore, 1998; Deák, Flom, & Pick, 2000; Moll & Tomasello, 2004), it was the first relatively comprehensive portrayal of the development of joint visual attention. In addition, his perspective pointed to the interconnections of joint visual attention with other developmental achievements such as spatial representation, the development of language, theory of mind, and children's understanding of others' intentions including the use of deception. These linkages between language, theory of mind, and the like with joint visual attention are the focus of other chapters in this volume (e.g., Graham, Nilsen, & Nayer; Meltzoff & Brooks; Poulin-Dubois, Demke, & Olineck; Sabbagh, Henderson, & Baldwin). In these chapters, joint visual attention is examined as it informs our understanding of behaviors such as language, theory of mind, understanding other's intentions and children's knowledge of deception. Historically, much of the research examining the significance of joint visual attention has focused on how an infant's ability to look where another is looking sets the stage for these later cognitive achievements. Less frequently examined or discussed, however, is how infants' early social exchanges, perceptual abilities, and the like promote infants' development of joint visual attention.

One goal, for the remainder of this chapter, is to examine how the emergence of joint visual attention is related to earlier developmental achievements such as the development of perception of affective expressions. A second goal is to describe how factors such as adults' attention-directing actions, the nature of the target object, and its placement in the visual field promote or inhibit infants' participation in joint visual attention. Important in this discussion is our assumption that perceiving is an active process involving the pickup of information about objects and events in the world including others' faces and voices.

PERCEIVING AFFECT, FACES, AND VOICES

The earliest dyadic communications between an infant and adult involve the sharing of affective information, and by the time infants are beginning to follow another's direction of gaze they are adept perceivers of faces and voices. The significance of these behaviors is that they promote and help maintain dyadic exchanges and subsequently infants' learning about the nature of social partners.

A considerable literature exists regarding infants' *discrimination* of affective expressions and reveals that between 4 and 7 months of age infants are able to discriminate dynamic, bimodally specified, affective expressions such as happy, sad, and angry (e.g.,Caron, Caron, & MacLean, 1988; Flom & Bahrick, in press; Walker-Andrews & Lennon, 1985). By 5 months of age infants are able to discriminate changes in affect based on vocal expressions alone (Walker-Andrews & Grolnick, 1983; Walker-Andrews & Lennon, 1991), and by 7 months of age infants are able to discriminate static facial expressions on the basis of affect (Caron, Caron, & Myers, 1985; Kestenbaum & Nelson, 1990; Ludemann & Nelson, 1988; see Walker-Andrews, 1997 for a review).

Researchers examining infants' ability to *recognize* face-voice expressions of affect reveals that by 7 months of age infants are able to match happy, sad, neutral, and angry voices to an appropriate face (Walker-Andrews 1986, 1988). Soken and Pick (1992; 1999) found that 7-month-olds can perceive the correspondences between facial and vocal expressions of affect, even when the facial and vocal information is produced by different people, and when the facial information is conveyed in the form of a point-light display. Thus, at about the same time infants discriminate as well as recognize various affective expressions (i.e., 5–7 months), they are also beginning to follow another's direction of gaze (i.e., 6 months). While the ability to recognize and discriminate affect is important in terms of dyadic communication, this ability is also important within the context of exploring, communicating about, and in general learning about other objects and events.

Researchers investigating infants' use of others' affective expression in guiding their own exploratory behavior, i.e., social referencing, have observed somewhat older infants. For example Mumme, Fernald and Herra (1996) found that 1-year-olds looked longer toward their mother, spent less time near an unfamiliar toy, and displayed more negative affect when the infant's mother provided only negative verbalizations and when her back was turned away from the infant and the novel object. Sorce, Emde, Campos, and Klinnert (1985) placed 12-month-olds at the edge of a visual cliff whose depth was ambiguous as to whether it easily afforded crawling over. The infants more frequently crossed the cliff if their mother posed a positive or happy affective expression than when she posed a negative or fearful expression. More recently, Vaish and Striano (2004), using a similar apparatus, found that 12-month-olds more rapidly crossed the visual cliff when their mother provided positive verbalizations even though the infants' view of her was occluded. Finally, Hornik, Risenhoover, and Gunnar (1987), found that 12-month-olds decreased their frequency of reaching toward, or willingness to play with, a particular toy if it was the focus of their mother's negative affective expression.

Studying 10- to 12-month-olds' participation in circumstances involving social referencing is important for understanding how they learn about various objects and events. However, given that younger infants also recognize and discriminate various affective expressions, one might ask whether there are circumstances when these expressions can also guide younger infants' exploratory behavior, for example, in the context of joint visual attention. Implicit in much of the social referencing literature is the assumption that infants must understand, at least to a degree, the referential nature of another's expression of affect. Since referential understanding as been assumed not to emerge until sometime during the second 12 months of life (e.g., Butterworth & Jarrett, 1991; Butterworth, 1995), there has been investigation of the role of adult affective expression in infant gaze-following prior to 1 year of age.

For young infants, in fact from the beginning, the affective expressiveness of caregivers and others has important communicative meaning. An adult's happy face and voice affords soothing and comfort, whereas sad or angry expressions may portend avoidance or distress. During their first year, infants learn to perceive other meanings conveyed by the affective expressions of others. As discussed above, by the end of the first year, they can use such expressions to guide their own behavior, e.g., as warnings or encouragement. The context of this learning is dyadic social communicative exchanges, and the course of the learning may involve discovering multiple meanings of various affective expressions and gestures. An example of one such meaning, conveyed by a smiling as well as a neutral face, accompanied by turning of the head or pointing, is where to look to see something interesting. Dyadic social communicative exchanges provide opportunities, among other things, for infants to learn how to establish joint visual attention. Participating in these exchanges, infants are learning to develop control and flexibility as they learn to selectively and differentially respond to multiple features of an ongoing communicative event. Still, little is known how affective expressions affect younger infants' exploratory behaviors, including their proclivity for early gaze-following.

EFFECTS OF EXPERIMENTER AFFECTIVE EXPRESSION AND GAZE-FOLLOWING

Given that infants begin to establish joint visual attention about the same time they begin to recognize various affective expressions (see Walker-Andrews, 1997, for a review) we have begun to examine how different affective expressions might influence infants' following of another's direction of gaze to establish joint visual attention (Flom & Pick, 2005). We chose 7-month-olds for the first experiment because infants of this age can discriminate as well as recognize various affective expressions and can follow the gaze of another person. In our experiment, an unfamiliar adult female posed a dynamic (though silent) happy, sad, or neutral affective expression while alternating her gaze between the infant and a multicolored Styrofoam object located 60° to the infant's right or left side. We found that 7-month-olds looked longer and more frequently toward the object when the experimenter posed a neutral affective expression compared to either a sad or happy affective expression. Although the adult's affective expression influenced the infants' gaze-following, the pattern of influence was somewhat unexpected. Based on the social referencing literature, we thought that the 7-month-olds' frequency of establishing shared visual attention would be greatest when the adult posed a positive or happy affective expression compared to either a neutral or sad affective expression. We expected that the adult's negative, or sad affective expression, would reduce infants' looking toward the experimenter, as well as their frequency of looking toward the target object; we were surprised that the adult's happy, expressions also reduced infants' frequency of looking toward the object.

One possible explanation regarding why 7-month-olds failed to look more frequently toward the correct target object when the adult posed a happy expression is that infants of this age fail to understand the referential nature of an affective expression. The fact that the adult's happy expression did not increase the infants' frequency of gaze-following is congruent with such an explanation and other findings that 10-month-olds also fail to link emotional cues with an object of another's visual interest (e.g., Mumme & Fernald, 2003, Mumme, Bushnell, DiCorica, & Lariviere, this volume). Another possibility, however, is that the adult's happy expression was more interesting or more compelling for the infant than the information specifying where the adult was looking. Infants in both the happy and neutral conditions looked longer toward the experimenter (and equally so) than did infants in the sad condition. Perhaps 7-month-olds lack the attentional flexibility required to attend to the adult's affective expression and, as well, that information specifying where the adult is looking. Therefore, infants in the happy condition attended to the adult's affective expression and ignored where the adult was looking, whereas infants in the neutral condition (absent any compelling affective information) attended to where the adult was looking and subsequently followed their direction of gaze.

INCREASING SPECIFICITY
AND JOINT VISUAL ATTENTION

We argue that the course of infants' learning to follow others' gaze to participate in episodes of joint visual attention reflects increasing specificity of perceiving in development. Historically in psychology, this perspective can be traced to James and Eleanor Gibson (Gibson & Gibson, 1955) who offered a specificity theory of perceptual learning. They argued that, in the course of development, perception changes toward closer correspondence with the environment as infants and children obtain more and more previously unnoticed information about the world and themselves. Exploratory activity is an important means for obtaining information. As infants explore and interact with the objects and events of their world, their tasks, e.g., looking, reaching, inter-

acting become more differentiated and their behavior becomes more controlled (Gibson & Pick, 2000). There is a good deal of evidence supporting an
increasing specificity perspective as a way to understand the development of infants' perception of objects (Bahrick, 2001), visual-tactile relations (Hernandez-
Reif & Bahrick, 2001), and both children's and adults' faces and voices
(Bahrick, Hernandez-Reif, & Flom, 2005; Bahrick, Netto, & Hernandez-Reif,
1998). We believe that the emergence of joint visual attention is also consistent with an increasing specificity perspective.

We propose that infants' participation in face-to-face interactions promotes their detecting previously unnoticed features of others' faces, including where they are looking, thus promoting learning to follow another's gaze
direction. With experience, infants become increasingly adept perceivers of
where another is looking and perhaps require less ostensive attention-directing
behaviors to successfully look where another is looking. The 7-month-olds in
our experiment focused their behavior on the adults' facial expressions—gazing
at the happy faces and averting their gaze from the sad faces—rather than on
where the adult was looking. The infants in the neutral condition more frequently and more easily followed the adult's direction of gaze in the absence
of competing information about the adult's affective expression. Consistent
with an increasing specificity perspective, and congruent with other research,
with experience infants should come to perceive the adult's attention directing
action and her affective expression in relation to the object or event of shared
visual attention (Moses, Baldwin, Rosicky, & Tidball, 2001; Mumme & Fernald,
2003; Repacholi, 1998).

INCREASING SPECIFICITY AND THE DEVELOPMENT
OF JOINT VISUAL ATTENTION

We expect that the emergence of joint visual attention will follow a course
such that the effectiveness of an adult's gesture for engaging infants in joint
visual attention will depend on the infant's ease of noticing the gesture, the
nature of the object or event of interest, and the location of that object or event
relative to the infant. This perspective on increasing specificity is illustrated
in a recent study (Deák, Flom, & Pick, 2000). We compared 12- and 18-month-
olds' frequency of joint visual attention as a function of adults' attention directing action—looking (with head turn), looking and pointing, and looking,
pointing, and verbally encouraging—as well as the placement of the object of
shared visual attention (in front of, behind, and within the infants' peripheral
field of view). Each experimental session began by having one of the infant's
parents (typically the mother) recruit the infant's visual attention and establish face-to-face eye contact. After eye-contact was established, the parent
then turned and gestured toward a particular object for 15 seconds.

While each trial was 15 s in length, we analyzed the data separately for each of the three 5 s blocks. Within the first 5 s block we found that older infants (18-month-olds) engaged in more episodes of joint visual attention than younger infants (12-month-olds). Important to our increasing specificity hypothesis was the prediction that an effect of age would reflect older infants' capability to use less noticeable gestures compared to younger infants. The results confirmed this prediction. Within the first 5 s of the trial for the looking alone condition, 18-month-olds engaged in more joint visual attention than did the 12-month-olds. Thus, older infants were initially more adept at following another's direction of gaze than younger infants given a relatively more subtle gesture (looking alone). However, no difference was found between older and younger infants' gaze in response to the more explicit gestures either during the first 5 s of the trial or during the entire 15 s trial.

According to an increasing specificity perspective, infants become increasingly flexible in their attention and can detect a wider array of information. While the results just described are consistent with this perspective, it is important to recall that the effect of age is based on 1) infants' frequency of joint visual attention *for the first 5 seconds of the trial* which lasted a total of 15 s and 2) a more subtle gesture (i.e., head turn and looking unaccompanied by any other indicator). Subsequent analyses of the infants' frequency of joint visual attention across the full trial (all 15 s) revealed that the older and younger infants did not reliably differ for any of the three gesture conditions. Importantly, the analyses demonstrate that the nonsignificant difference in 12- and 18-month-olds' joint visual attention across the full 15 s trial is the result of an *increase* in 12-month-olds' joint visual attention and not a *decrease* in 18-month-olds' frequency of joint visual attention. In general, these data demonstrate that with an increase in opportunity for exploratory behavior (i.e., an additional 10 s) 12- and 18-month-olds become similar in their frequency of joint visual attention. In turn, that suggests that younger infants require more time/experience to perceive where another is looking and subsequently follow their attention directing behavior when provided a less obvious or explicit gesture.

The finding that 12- and 18-month-olds' frequency of joint visual attention differed within the first 5 s of a 15 s trial, but not across the entire length of the trial, is significant for at least two reasons. First, it demonstrates that initially, younger infants require a more elaborate attention directing action, relative to older infants, and that over time, in this case an additional 10 s, younger infants are able to perceive and use the adults' attention directing action in establishing joint visual attention. Second, much of the literature regarding the development of joint visual attention documents a reliable difference between 12- and 18-month-olds' participation in joint visual attention when the trial length is around 7 s (Butterworth & Cochran, 1980; Butterworth & Itakura, 2000; Butterworth & Jarrett, 1991; Moore & Corkum, 1998; Morissette, Ricard,

& Gouin-Décarie, 1995). In other words, in those studies where the trial
length is 10 s or less, significant age differences are often reported. We also
replicated this result when 1) we examine the first 5 s of the trial and 2) the
gesture involves the parent merely turning the head and looking toward the
target object.

In a subsequent experiment we also examined whether the placement or
position of the target object relative to the infant and the adult contributes to
the ease with which parental gestures promote infants engaging in joint visual
attention (Deák, Flom, & Pick, 2000). In this experiment we varied the seating orientation of the parent to their infant. In the typical experimental
arrangement the adult and infant are situated face-to-face. With this arrangement there is variation in the magnitude of the adults' gestures toward objects
in different locations relative to the infant. For example, when the infant and
adult are seated face-to-face the adult makes a larger change in their head and
eye gaze to look toward objects located in front of the infant than toward objects located behind the infant (see panel A in Figure 5–1). This issue is impor-

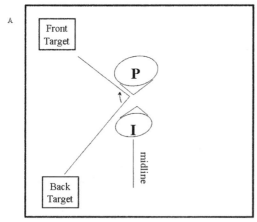

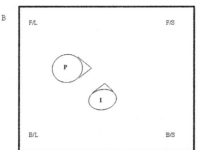

FIGURE 5–1. Schematic dia-
gram of the room showing traditional seating arrangement (panel
1A) and the modified seating
arrangement (panel 1B). P = parent; I = infant; F = target placed
within the infant's visual field;
B = target placed outside the infant's immediate visual field; L =
larger head turn required of the
parent to visually fixate the target,
S = smaller head turn required of
the parent to visually fixate the
target. (From Flom, Deák, Pick, &
Phill, 2004. Reprinted with permission from Elsevier.)

tant to the claim that young infants cannot establish joint visual attention to objects outside their field of view. In this follow-up experiment (Deák, Flom, & Pick, 2000) we rotated the parent 90° to their infant's left or right side. This modified and the traditional seating arrangements are shown in Figure 5–1.

With the parents situated 90° to their infants' right or left side, the magnitude of the adults' head and eye gaze gestures are no longer confounded with the position of the target objects within or outside of the infants' visual field. Specifically, adults need to make a *larger* gesture (i.e., head turn) toward one object located within and one object located outside the infants' visual field (see positions F/L and B/L in Figure 5–1). Likewise, adults make a *smaller* gesture toward one object located within and one object located outside the infants' visual field (see positions F/S and B/S in Figure 5–1). We predicted that the magnitude of the parents' gesture would affect the ease with which infants detect or notice it and thus respond to it.

Twelve and 18-month-olds and their parents were again recruited for participation. Half of the parents were situated to their infant's right side and half were situated to their infant's left. Each infant-parent dyad completed 12 trials, with 3 trials occurring at each of the four object locations shown in Figure 5–1b. Half of the parents attempted to establish joint visual attention with their infant by looking and pointing toward the target object, and the other half only turned their heads and looked toward the object.

With this modified seating arrangement, 12- and 18-month-olds did not reliably differ in terms of their frequency of establishing joint visual attention toward objects located within their visual field. However, for the two targets placed outside the infants' visual field 12-month-olds engaged in fewer instances of joint visual attention than 18-month-olds. In addition, 12-month-olds engaged in more joint visual attention to objects outside their visual field when their parents looked and pointed than when the parents just turned their heads and looked toward the target object. In contrast, 18-month-olds' frequency of joint visual attention toward objects located either outside or within their visual field did not vary depending on their parents' gesture.

The significance of these results is the demonstration that the 12-month-olds were in fact able to establish joint visual attention to a previously unseen object, whereas others, all using the typical seating arrangement, (Butterworth, 1995; Butterworth & Cochran 1980; Butterworth & Jarrett, 1991) have claimed this behavior does not emerge until approximately 18 months of age. The results also replicate our first experiment (Deák, Flom, & Pick, 2000) because the more noticeable (looking and pointing) and larger gesture (modifying the seating arrangement) promoted younger, but not older, infants' participation in joint visual attention to previously unseen objects.

In both experiments we found that 12- and 18-month-olds engaged in more episodes of joint visual attention when their parents looked and pointed than when they just turned their heads and looked to the target object. Parents' additional verbal encouragement, e.g., describing the object of attention, did not promote further increase in infants' frequency of joint visual attention. This is not surprising since the objects used in these experiments (multi-colored cutouts of various abstract shapes) did not have obvious names or labels.

We further explored the effects of parental verbal encouragement in an experiment with 18-month-olds using common everyday objects that could be described and named (Flom & Pick, 2003). In this experiment, the parents either verbally encouraged their infant to look toward the target object, or they turned and silently pointed toward the object, or they turned, pointed, and provided verbal encouragement. The condition in which there was only verbal encouragement to look toward the object (without turning and looking toward it) is a bit contrived compared to the normal circumstance in which verbal exhortation to look toward an object would ordinarily be accompanied by looking at it and pointing toward it. However, we wanted to get some indication of the influence of verbal encouragement by itself.

The significance of adults' verbalizations for promoting joint visual attention may be to enhance the information provided by gestures of looking and pointing. Looking and pointing direct and guide attention to where one is looking, but verbalizations can elaborate and specify precisely what can be jointly perceived and conceived (Harris, Barlow-Brown, & Chasin, 1995). In addition to labeling or naming the object of joint visual attention, verbalizations can specify particular features or properties of an object or event and can also be used to query children about what they know or comprehend regarding the object or event, thus promoting further communication.

In this experiment (Flom & Pick, 2003), we recorded the number of episodes of joint visual attention as well as the proportion of time 18-month-olds engaged in joint visual attention. Our rationale for assessing the proportion of time infants engaged in joint visual attention is that previous researchers (e.g., Baldwin & Markman, 1989) have found that infants between 10 and 20 months of age looked longer at the object of shared visual attention when parents' attention-directing actions included verbalizations than when the gestures did not include verbal encouragements.

As in earlier experiments, the parent and child sat facing each other. The parent established eye-contact with the child and the adult then engaged in one of the three attention-directing actions to redirect the child's visual attention to one of four objects. In this experiment all four objects (two familiar and two unfamiliar) were located within the child's field of view. The children had had experience with and understood the labels for the familiar objects (e.g., book, ball, cup, etc.). Unfamiliar objects were those with which the child had had limited experience and did not know their labels (e.g., pliers, snorkel, sponge, etc.). Familiarity and unfamiliarity were assessed for each child individually.

In general, the results of this experiment replicate previous demonstrations that parents' actions accompanied by verbalizations promote longer episodes of joint visual attention (i.e., Baldwin & Markman, 1989). More specifically, we found that the 18-month-olds spent proportionately more time engaging in joint visual attention toward an unfamiliar but not toward a familiar object when their parents' actions were accompanied by verbalization. Labeling or naming the object without other gestures facilitated joint attention to familiar but not to unfamiliar objects—an unsurprising result since the label alone is uninformative if one doesn't know the name of an object. Other gestures (looking and pointing, looking, pointing and verbalizing) did not influence the number of episodes of joint visual attention either to familiar or to unfamiliar objects.

Verbalizations accompanying behavior gestures for where to look are useful in maintaining joint visual attention with 18-month-olds, when the object is unfamiliar to the child (Flom & Pick, 2003). From the perspective of increasing specificity, the fact that verbal encouragement promotes longer episodes of joint visual attention to unfamiliar objects may reflect the children's flexibility in responding to the adults' actions. The adults' attention-directing actions become relevant for learning about the object or event, not just specifying where to look to engage in joint visual attention looking. Indeed, there is much evidence that such learning occurs in the context of joint visual attention. For example, Newland, Roggman, and Boyce (2001) conducted a longitudinal study of mothers playing with toys with their infants who ranged in age from 11 to 17 months. Within this context of shared attention to the same object, they observed mothers using and encouraging their infants to use words. They also found that mothers' labeling of toys at 11 months was related to measures of their infants' language at 17 months. Adamson, Bakeman and Deckner (2004) similarly observed infants longitudinally from 18 to 30 months of age during joint engagement with their mothers and found that communication during these episodes of joint engagement promoted the children's word production, comprehension, and emerging knowledge of symbols.

CONCLUSIONS

Development makes no compunctions about its complexity; the emergence of joint visual attention provides one example of this complexity. We have discussed how various factors influence infants' participation in episodes of triadic communication. In particular, our research demonstrates (1) how the relative perspectives of adult and infant affect the ease with which infants can look toward a previously unseen target object, (2) how adults' verbalizations and infants' familiarity with an object influence how long the infants engage in joint visual attention, and (3) how the presence or absence of adults' affective facial expressions influences infants' ease of following adults' gaze direction.

Certainly the readers of this volume are well acquainted with the complexity of coordinated attention and acknowledge that many questions remain unanswered concerning the interconnections of social, cognitive, and perceptual development and the emergence of joint visual attention. From a theoretical perspective we have described the emergence of joint visual attention as reflecting an increasing specificity in perceiving another person (Gibson, 1969; Gibson & Pick, 2000). While this perspective has it roots in explaining infants' learning to perceive objects and events, we believe it also provides insights and hypotheses for understanding infants' learning to engage in socially coordinated attention with other people.

ACKNOWLEDGMENTS

This research was supported by the Brigham Young University Family Studies Center and a BYU undergraduate mentoring grant awarded to the first author.

REFERENCES

Adamson, L. B. (1996). *Communication development during infancy* (pp. 121–159). Boulder, CO: Westview Press.

Adamson, L. B., Bakeman, R., & Deckner, D. F. (2004). The development of symbol-infused joint engagement. *Child Development, 75,* 1171–1187.

Bahrick, L. E. (2001). Increasing specificity in perceptual development: Infants' detection of nested levels of multimodal stimulation. *Journal of Experimental Child Psychology, 79,* 253–270.

Bahrick, L. E., Hernandez-Reif, M. R., & Flom, R, (2005). The development of infant learning about specific face-voice relations. *Developmental Psychology, 41,* 541–552.

Bahrick, L. E., Netto, D., and Hernandez-Reif, M. (1998). Intermodal perception of adult and child faces and voices by infants. *Child Development, 69,* 1263–1275.

Baldwin, D. A., & Markman, E. M. (1989), Establishing word-object relations: A first step. *Child Development, 60,* 381–398.

Banks, M. S., & Crowell, J. A., (1993). Front-end limitations to infant spatial vision: Examinations of two analyses. In K. Simins (Ed.), *Early visual development: Normal and abnormal* (pp. 91–116). New York: Oxford University Press.

Banks, M. S., & Dannemiller, J. L. (1987). Infant visual pyschophysics. In P. Salapatek & L. Cohen (Eds.), *Handbook of infant perception. Vol. 1. From sensation to perception* (pp. 115–184). Orlando, FL: Academic Press.

Batki, A., Baron-Cohen, S., Wheelwright, S., Connellan, J., & Ahluwalia, J. (2000). Is there an innate gaze module? Evidence from human neonates. *Infant Behavior and Development, 23,* 223–229.

Bushnell, I., Sai, F., & Mullin, J. (1989). Neonatal recognition of the mother's face. *British Journal of Developmental Psychology, 7,* 3–15.

Butterworth, G. E. (1995). Origins of mind in perception and action. In C. Moore & P. Dunham (Eds.), *Joint attention: Its origins and role in development.* Hillsdale, NJ: Lawrence Erlbaum Associates.

Butterworth, G. E., & Cochran, E. (1980). Towards a mechanism of joint visual attention in human infancy. *International Journal of Behavioral Development, 3,* 253–272.

Butterworth, G. E., & Itakura, S. (2000). How the eyes, head and hand serve definite reference. *British Journal of Developmental Psychology, 18,* 25–50.

Butterworth, G. E., & Jarrett, N. (1991). What minds have in common is space: Spatial mechanisms serving joint visual attention in infancy. *British Journal of Developmental Psychology, 9,* 55–72.

Caron, A. J., Caron, R. F., & MacLean, D. J. (1998). Infant discrimination of naturalistic emotional expressions: The role of face and voice. *Child Development, 59,* 604–616.

Caron, R. F., Caron, A. J., & Myers, R. S. (1985). Do infants see emotional expressions in static faces? *Child Development, 56,* 1552–1560.

Corkum, V., & Moore, C. (1998). The origins of joint visual attention in infants. *Developmental Psychology, 34,* 28–38.

D'Entremont, B. (2000). A perceptual-attentional explanation of gaze-following in 3- and 6-month-olds. *Developmental Science, 3,* 302–311.

D'Entremont, B., Hanis, S. M. J., & Muir, D. (1997). A demonstration of gaze-following in 3- to 6-month-olds. *Infant Behavior and Development, 20,* 569–572.

Deák, G., Flom, R., & Pick, A. D. (2000). Effects of gesture and target on 12- and 18-month-olds' joint visual attention to objects in front of or behind them. *Developmental Psychology, 36,* 511–523.

DeCasper, A. J., & Fifer, W. (1980). Of human bonding: Newborns prefer their mothers' voices. *Science, 208,* 1174–1176.

Fantz, R. (1963). Pattern vision in newborn infants. *Science, 140,* 296–297.

Farroni, T., Csibra, G., Simion, F., & Johnson, M. (2002). Eye contact detection in humans from birth. *Proceedings of the National Academy of Sciences, 99,* 9602–9605.

Field, T., Cohen, D., Garcia, R., & Greenberg, R. (1984). Mother-stranger face discrimination by their newborn. *Infant Behavior and Development, 7,* 19–25.

Flom, R., & Bahrick, L. (in press). The effects of multimodal stimulation on infants' discrimination of affect: An examination of the intersensory redundancy hypothesis. *Developmental Psychology.*

Flom, R., Deák, G., Pick, A. D., & Phill, C. (2004). 9-Month-olds' shared visual attention as a function of gesture and object location. *Infant Behavior and Development, 27,* 181–194.

Flom, R., & Pick, A. D. (2003). Verbal encouragement and joint attention in 18-month-olds. *Infant Behavior and Development, 26,* 121–134.

Flom, R., & Pick, A. D. (2005). Experimenter affective expression and gaze-following in 7-month-olds. *Infancy, 7,* 207–218.

Gibson, E. J. (1969). *Principles of perceptual learning and development.* New York, NY: Appleton Century Crofts.

Gibson, E. J., & Pick, A. (2000). *An Ecological Approach to Perceptual Learning and Development.* New York, NY: Oxford University Press.

Gibson, J. J., & Gibson, E. J. (1955). Perceptual learning: Differentiation or enrichment? *Psychological Review, 62,* 32–41.

Gogate, L., Bahrick, L. E., & Watson, J. D. (2000). A study of multimodal motherese: The role of temporal synchrony between verbal labels and gestures. *Child Development, 71,* 878–894.

Hains, S. M. J., & Muir, D. W. (1996). Effects of stimulus contingency in infant-adult interactions. *Infant Behavior and Development, 19,* 49–61.

Harris, M., Barlow-Brown, F., & Chasin, J. (1995). The emergence of referential understanding: Pointing and the comprehension of object names. *First Language, 15,* 19–34.

Hernandez-Reif, M., & Bahrick, L. E. (2001). The development of visual-tactual perception of objects: Amodal relations provide the basis for learning arbitrary relations. *Infancy, 2,* 51–72.

Hood, B. M., & Macrae, N. (2006). Look into my eyes: The effect of direct gaze on face processing in children and adults. In R. Flom, K. Lee, & D. Muir (Eds.) *The ontogeny of gaze processing.* Mahwah, NJ: Lawrence Erlbaum Associates.

Hood, B. M., Willen, J. D., & Driver, J. (1998). An eye direction detector triggers shifts in visual attention in human infants. *Psychological Science, 9,* 53–56.

Hornik, R., Risenhoover, N., & Gunnar, M. (1987). The effects of maternal positive, neutral, and negative affective communications on infant responses to new toys. *Child Development, 58*(4), 937–944.

Johnson, M. H., & Farroni, T. (2006). The neurodevelopmental origins of eye gaze perception. In R. Flom, K. Lee, & D. Muir (Eds.), *The ontogeny of gaze* processing. Mahwah, NJ: Lawrence Erlbaum Associates.

Johnson, M., & Morton, J. (1991). Biology and cognitive development: The case of face recognition. Blackwell, Oxford: UK.

Kestenbaum, R., & Nelson, C. A. (1990). The recognition and categorization of upright and inverted emotional expressions by 7-month-old infants. *Infant Behavior and Development, 13,* 497–511.

Ludemann, P., & Nelson, C. A. (1988). Categorical representation of facial expressions by 7-month-old infants. *Developmental Psychology, 24,* 492–501.

Moll, H., & Tomasello, M. (2004). 12- and 18-month-old infants follow gaze to space behind barriers. *Developmental Science, 7,* 1–9.

Moore, C., & Corkum, V. (1998). Infant gaze-following based on eye direction. *British Journal of Developmental Psychology, 16,* 495–503.

Morales, M., Mundy, P., & Rojas, J. (1998). Following the direction of gaze and language development in 6-month-olds. *Infant Behavior and Development, 21,* 373–377.

Morissette, P., Ricard, M., & Gouin-Décarie, T. (1995). Joint visual attention and pointing in infancy: A longitudinal study of comprehension. *British Journal of Developmental Psychology, 13,* 163–175.

Moses, L. J., Baldwin, D., Rosicky, J. G., & Tidball, G. (2001). Evidence for referential understanding in the emotions domain at 12 and 18 months. *Child Development, 72,* 718–735.

Mumme, D. L., & Fernald, A. (2003). The infant as an onlooker: Learning from emotional reactions observed in a television scenario. *Child Development, 74,* 221–237.

Mumme, D. L., Bushnell, E. W., DiCorica, J. A., & Lariviere, L. A. (2006). Infants' use of gaze cues to interpret others' actions and emotional reactions. In R. Flom, K. Lee, & D. Muir (Eds.) *The ontogeny of gaze processing.* Mahwah, NJ: Lawrence Erlbaum Associates.

Mumme, D. L., Fernald A., & Herrera, C. (1996). Infants' responses to facial and vocal emotional signals in a social referencing paradigm. *Child Development, 67*, 3219–3237.

Newland, L. A., Roggman, L. A., & Boyce, L. K. (2001). The development of social toy play and language in infancy. *Infant Behavior and Development, 24*, 1–25.

Posner, M. (1980). Orienting of attention. *Quarterly Journal of Experimental Psychology, 32*, 3–25.

Querleu, D., Renard, X., Boutteville, C., & Crepin, G. (1989). Hearing by the human fetus? *Seminars in Perinatology, 13*, 409–420.

Repacholi, B. M. (1998). Infants' use of attentional cues to identify the referent of another person's emotional expression. *Developmental Psychology, 34*, 1017–1025.

Soken N. H., & Pick, A. D. (1999). Infants' perception of dynamic affective expressions: Do infants distinguish specific expressions? *Child Development, 70*, 1275–1282.

Soken N. H., & Pick, A. D. (1992). Intermodal perception of happy and angry expressive behaviors by seven-month-old infants. *Child Development, 63*, 787–795.

Sorce, J. F., Emde, R. N., Campos, J., & Klinnert, M. D. (1985). Maternal emotional signaling: Its effect on the visual cliff behavior of 1-year-olds. *Developmental Psychology, 21*, 195–200.

Symons, L. A., Hains, S. M. J., & Muir, D. W. (1998). Look at me: Five-month-old infants' sensitivity to very small deviations in eye-gaze during social interactions. *Infant Behavior and Development, 21*, 531–536.

Vaish, A., & Striano, T. (2004). Is visual reference necessary? Contributions of facial versus vocal cues in 12-month-olds' social referencing behavior. *Developmental Science, 7*, 261–269.

Vecera, S., & Johnson, M. (1995). Gaze detection and cortical processing of faces: Evidence from infants and adults. *Visual Cognition, 2*, 59–87.

Walker-Andrews, A. (1997). Infants' perception of expressive behaviors: Differentiation of multimodal information. *Psychological Bulletin, 121*, 437–456.

Walker-Andrews, A. S., & Grolnick, W. (1983). Discrimination of vocal expressions by young infants. *Infant Behavior and Development, 6*, 491–498.

Walker-Andrews, A. S., & Lennon, E. (1991). Infants' discrimination of vocal expressions: Contributions of auditory and visual information. *Infant Behavior and Development, 14*, 131–142.

Walker-Andrews, A. S., & Lennon, E. (1985). Auditory-visual perception of changing distance by human infants. *Child Development, 56*, 544–548.

Walton, G., Bower, N., & Bower, T. G. R. (1992). Recognition of familiar faces by newborns. *Infant Behavior and Development, 15*, 265–269.

6

Influence of Mutual Gaze on Human Infant Affect

Elliott M. Blass, Julie Lumeng,
and Namrata Patil

University of Massachusetts, Amherst

This chapter is concerned with gaze as a social motivator in human infants. As other chapters in this volume attest, infant gaze has been studied largely from the perspective of cognitive domains that have ranged from face learning and recognition, to the ontogeny of language, to mutual gaze in joint attention. Another facet of gaze that has been more recently explored is gaze as a motivational entity. This interest has gained traction through the pioneering studies and theory of Baron-Cohen and colleagues (Baron-Cohen, 1989). Gaze, in general, and its special case of mutual eye engagement, provides a potential linkage between cognitive and motivational domains in face preference. Moreover, infant reactions to different faces, based on their experiences with the individual behind the face (Blass & Camp, 2001, 2003a), can now be studied as can the neural mechanisms that mediate affective reaction to and preference for particular faces. The newly explored interest in affect also helps illuminate how value is bestowed upon particular objects. This is exemplified by the chapters by Mumme et al. (2004) and Poulin-Dubois (2004) in the current volume.

In our view, cognitive facets of mutual gaze and shared attention to objects must be rooted in social precedents that sustain gaze between infant and adult. Eye-to-eye engagement precedes directional gaze by months. Indeed, despite limits in visual acuity (Banks, 1980), newborns look considerably longer at a photo of a woman staring full face with eyes "looking" at the subject than at the identical photo with eyes averted (Farroni, Csibra, Simon, & Johnson, 2002). Moreover, newborns prefer the face of their mother within hours after birth, thereby speaking to the immediate ontogenetic availability of positive affect as a determinant of choice (Waldron, Bower, & Bower, 1992; Bushnell, 1982; Bushnell, Sai, & Mullen, 1983). Positive affective reaction in newborn humans is an evolutionarily conserved feature, which, presumably, helps establish the mother-infant bond. It parallels findings in newborn rats that also interact uniquely with their mother based on very limited experience (Pedersen & Blass, 1982; Teicher & Blass, 1977).

In order to understand how mutual gaze controls affect, we have chosen to study eye engagement and its consequences at the time of its first stable manifestation in infants starting at about 4 weeks of age (Wolff, 1963,1987). If we could identify the determinants of this readily available behavior, then we could more confidently study its less accessible origins and its function. We have focused on three aspects of gaze and human infant social affect. The first aspect determines how mutual gaze between infant and adult *calms* and *conserves energy* in 4- to 12-week old infants. Distressed infants actively seek eye contact, which, in conjunction with sucrose administration, arrests crying.

The second affective quality of mutual gaze is manifest in the behavior of 6 to 12-week-olds during their initial encounter with a stranger. Seeking and maintaining eye contact is one facet of a series of social overtures through which infants engage adults to help rapidly establish a face preference based on adult behavior towards the infant. Mutual gaze is necessary, although not sufficient, for preference induction. It must be accompanied by a concomitant change in energy balance or stimulation of the central nervous system (CNS).

The third aspect focuses on how mutual gaze modulates nursing-suckling exchanges. We will demonstrate that eye and social engagement causes a 44% increase in milk intake from a bottle. In addition, we will provide evidence for two distinct classes of nutritive suckling. One is under the control of physiological events related to energy balance and growth. The other class of suckling is not controlled by metabolic or growth needs; it is apparently driven by social factors, broadly defined, and becomes manifest when the infant visually engages the feeder's face, especially the eyes.

Eye engagement during infancy was first systematically documented through the heroic studies of Peter Wolff (1987), who visited homes of newborns for 3 hours daily during the early postnatal months. Wolff reported an abrupt change in social engagement patterns at about 4 weeks of age, when mother and infant became visually engaged for prolonged periods. Remarkably, mothers were not aware of this qualitative change in social interaction. In general, they reported that their infants felt more "human" and interactive, but the mothers were at a loss as to the genesis of change. In fact, according to

Wolff, infants both initiated and controlled eye-to-eye contact. From an evolutionary perspective, this type of behavior could be favored even if it only elicited more attentive maternal behavior. Greater attentiveness, in principle, would have the benefit of sustaining maternal contact and reducing the possibility of infant neglect and possibly abuse.

GAZE AND CRYING REDUCTION

Zeifman, Delany, and Blass (1996), extended these findings; more was involved beyond capturing maternal attention. Starting at about 4 weeks of age eye engagement was needed to calm crying infants who were not being held and comforted through contact. According to Zeifman et al. (1996), sucrose could continue serving as a quieting agent (Smith, Fillion, & Blass, 1990) only if delivered by adults who were in eye contact with the crying infant. Failure to maintain eye contact resulted in protracted crying even when up to 4 ml of sucrose were taken by infants in the course of minutes. In one study in which the experimenter fastened her gaze on the infants' forehead, most infants actively sought to catch the experimenter's gaze by turning their heads upward and extending their torso in these obvious efforts. This is particularly impressive when considering that the infants could easily see the experimenter's full face, including her eyes; eye engagement was the issue. The necessity of eye engagement in these 4-week-olds is also noteworthy because as little as 0.1 ml of sucrose calms crying newborns, even when the deliverer could not be seen.

Eye contact was necessary but not sufficient to stop crying in 4-week-olds. Crying persisted in infants who were in eye contact and in those who received sucrose alone, but was arrested in infants who received the combination treatment. Quieting can not be attributed to additivity of the individual contributions of the two treatments; quieting emerged from the unity of the two afferents. Moreover, the effect persisted after sucrose delivery was suspended but gaze continued. This suggests that central neurochemical changes, presumably opioid in nature (Blass, Fitzgerald, & Kehoe, 1987; Blass & Ciaramitaro, 1994), linked with eye contact to calm infants. Cardiac changes paralleled behavioral ones. Crying induced tachycardia was immediately reduced and normal heart rate levels were sustained during crying cessation (Zeifman et. al., 1996). Thus, eye contact in conjunction with sucrose taste contributed significantly to energy conservation (Rao, Blass, Brignol, Marino, & Glass, 1997).

These affective consequences were developmentally transient. Although sucrose curtailed crying in 4- and 6-week-olds, 9-week-old infants differed. They, too, stopped crying when tasting sucrose alone (Blass, 1998), but crying almost immediately resumed upon termination of sucrose delivery. By 12 weeks, crying continued through sucrose delivery in visually engaged infants, although sucking a sweet pacifier arrested crying (Blass & Camp, 2003b). It should be noted that these older infants cry rather little spontaneously (Brazelton, 1962); they appear to cry with "cause" (Barr, 1998). Efforts to arrest crying in older infants will be more successful when they match the crying source.

We believe that these progressive affective changes starting at 4 weeks of age reflect central and not peripheral changes, e.g., lower taste threshold, in motivational systems. At birth, humans (Steiner, 1979) and other mammals taste and savor sweet solutions (Blass & Smith,1992), and sweet taste can serve as a basis for conditioning in both rat (Shide & Blass, 1991) and human infants (Blass, Ganchrow, & Steiner, 1984). In fact, the gain from relatively low levels of taste and flavor stimulation is such (Kehoe & Blass, 1986) to cause actual analgesia (Blass & Hoffmeyer, 1991; Blass & Watt, 1999) and preference for the associated individual or odor in both neonatal rats and humans. The mechanisms are well conserved.

The advent of eye contact starting at Week 4 and its necessity with sucrose to arrest crying might be better understood within the context of infants starting to learn about their immediate caretakers and their more extended social surround. Infants actively engage adult strangers in what appears to be efforts to elicit particular behaviors from them. Eye contact and smiling are not sufficient (Blass & Camp, 2001). We propose that these behavioral interactions, with their concomitant changes in infant state, form a basis for the infant's initial preference of an adult. It is a process of information seeking, conceptually comparable to processes of seeking information about the properties of objects in other situations. The social process can be subtle. Its expression reflects infant age, energetic demands and central nervous system development. The bases for infant face preference and their putative underlying mechanisms are now addressed.

THE ONTOGENY OF INFANT PREFERENCE

A hallmark of mammalian infant development is the rapidity and apparent ease with which maternal recognition and preference can be induced at birth. Human newborns exhibit a preference for their mother's voice and material that she had read out loud during pregnancy (DeCasper & Spence, 1986). Fathers' voices are not preferred, nor is material that had been read to the fetus for at least the same length of time. Bone conduction is a reasonable candidate for transmission. Newborns prefer to look at their mothers within hours of birth (Field, Cohen, Garcia, & Greenberg, 1984), although the bases of the preferences have not been established (Bushnell, 1982). Human maternal olfactory preferences have been documented as early as Day 3 (MacFarlane, 1975; Schaal, 1988). Early affect availability is not unique to human infants.

Rat newborns are attracted to and suckle their mother's nipples based on the agreement between the olfactory properties of the amniotic fluid, sampled prenatally, and the fluid that anoints the mother at the time of initial suckling (the mother guarantees the match by spreading amniotic fluid over her nipple region after delivering and cleaning each pup; Pedersen & Blass, 1982). The availability and potency of a capacity to learn about and prefer certain parental features and the role of the parent to educate infants of a variety of species during the nest period is impressive. It helps ensure that infants acquire knowledge about the structure of the world that they will ultimately enter independently, without learning through trial and error (Blass, 1990). The centrality of an unencumbered transition from nest to world and then dependence upon parental tutorial led us to seek the rules through which human infants establish preferences for adults upon first brief exposure. Our assumption is that the preferred individual will be the preferentially followed one.

Blass and Camp (2001, 2003a) have started to show that human infant preference formation and expression reflect a confluence of infant age, state, eye contact, and the particular experience provided by a stranger during brief (3.5 min) interactions with the infant. Central to the decision-making process is infants seeking information from adults about the quality of the interaction that the adult is willing to provide. Establishing eye contact is integral to this process. The quality of the interactions is gauged by the infants and may provide a basis for infant preference and future interactions.

Blass and Camp's paradigm was founded on the established properties of animal and human infant preference formation. First, because even newborn humans can form very strong preferences for their own mothers within hours of birth (Waldron et al., 1992) over identically attired women of similar visage (Field et. al., 1984; Pascalis, deSchonen, Morton, Deruelle, & Fabre-Grenet, 1995), we assumed that brief exposure of older infants to adults under felicitous circumstances would induce preference. Second, we assumed that preference formation would have accessible material bases. Accordingly, infants tasted sucrose, alone or on a pacifier, or were simply exposed to adults with eye contact. Once the basis for preference was established at each age, the critical condition was replicated, but absent eye contact. To determine whether infants had to undergo a change in state for preference induction, half of the infants entered the study crying and half were studied when calm.

Infants, 6 to 12 weeks of age, were exposed to undergraduate females for 3.5 min, during which time half of the infants received 1.0 ml of a 12% sucrose solution per minute over the course of 30 sec during mutual gaze. The remaining infants continuously sucked a sweetened pacifier. Although the sweetness probably wore off within 20–25 sec, the pacifier was not replaced except on the rare occasion when it fell out of an infant's mouth. After the 3.5 min exposure, the experimenter left the room for 1 min to return with an identically garbed confederate. They sat in front of, and equidistantly, to either side of the infant for a total of 3 min, changing places every 30 sec to prevent expression of a side preference. The metric for preference expression was simply the percentage of time that the infant looked at the experimenter versus looking time to the stranger. Control conditions will be further detailed after presentation of these findings.

A number of in-principle predictions are presented as alternative unifying hypotheses for the basis of preference formation in infants 6 to 12 weeks of age:

- *Chemosensory basis*: If sweet taste per se induces a preference, as it does in rat pups (Shide & Blass 1991), then infants who received the sucrose solution should prefer the experimenter to the identically garbed confederate. Note that state is irrelevant here.

- If the basis for preference was *suckling per se*, then only infants who sucked the pacifier should form a preference for the person who supplied the pacifier.

- If preference was determined by a *change in state* caused by either sucrose or by pacifier sucking, then only crying infants who were calmed by sweet taste or the pacifier should form a preference. This also helps evaluate whether individuals who *conserved infant energy* (through crying cessation) would also be preferred (Rao et. al., 1997). According to this hypothesis, calm infants should not exhibit a preference.

- Regardless of the motivational source(s) of change, preference should not obtain unless the infant was in *visual contact* with the experimenter. This hypothesis predicts that infants presented with the identical set of conditions that induced preference, except for eye-to-eye contact, should not prefer the experimenter, even though the infant could fully see her face.

The paradigm is silent on the interactive behaviors of infants in the different experimental situations. For example, there were no a priori predictions about infant behavior when infants were in visual contact with adults and receiving sucrose versus when they were not in visual contact or not receiving sucrose. Likewise, no predictions were made on the basis of infant putative states at a particular age and preference for the interacting experimenter. As will be shown next, both of these were important issues.

Only 3 of the 12 conditions supported preference formation, one per age, and they are highlighted at each age. The successful conditions each yielded substantial preferences of almost 2:1 in favor of looking at the familiar experimenter. Infants in the remaining 9 conditions were essentially evenly divided in their looking times between experimenter and stranger. In particular, of the Week 6 infants in this study, only those who were crying and sucked a pacifier preferred the experimenter. Remarkably, calm Week 6 infants did not prefer their experimenters regardless of whether sucrose or a sweetened pacifier were offered the infants (and accepted).

Crying 9-week-olds did not prefer their experimenters, even when sucrose or the pacifier reduced crying. Calm Week 9 infants, however, expressed a very strong preference for adults who provided them with sweet pacifiers to suck during eye contact. They did not prefer experimenters who gave them sucrose, even though sucrose was avidly accepted.

Finally, 12-week-old infants differed from both groups of younger infants. Only calm Week 12 infants who received sucrose alone preferred the experimenter who had delivered the sucrose. Neither group of crying infants preferred their familiar experimenter. Likewise, Week 12 infants who sucked a pacifier while in eye contact with their experimenter did not prefer her over the identically garbed stranger.

These findings do not support any unitary hypothesis concerning the ontogeny of infant preference across the restricted age range of 6 to12 weeks. Preference does not rely on change of state or energy conservation per se because only one of the six crying groups manifested a preference for the experimenter. In this regard sucking a sweetened pacifier cannot account for this pattern of findings. Only two of the six groups, one calm and one crying, exhibited a preference; four did not. The data do not support the hypothesis of sweet taste inducing a preference for the person who delivered it because only one of the six groups who received sucrose from a syringe preferred the experimenter. It is also worth noting that only one group at a given age established a preference. This precludes statements concerning different sets of overarching rules for each age that change with age.

In seeking a basis for this unanticipated data set, Blass and Camp (2003a) were drawn by the parallels between their findings and human infant daily crying during the first 12 weeks. Daily crying peaks at about 6 weeks of age. Crying in Week 6 infants is paradoxical. On the one hand, it does not necessarily abate to "appropriate" attention. On the other hand, it can be mollified by "nonspecific" forms of stimulation, sucrose and fat for example. Crying then declines till it reaches a nadir at about 12 weeks, remaining low thereafter (Barr, 1998; Brazelton, 1962). Crying is thought to be triggered by specific events at that point (Barr, 1998), and infants can be comforted by the appropriate change of the offending stimulation, be it a soiled diaper, hunger, temperature changes, etc. Nonspecific stimulation, holding a possible exception, loses its potency by then or shortly thereafter (although infants who have taken a pacifier routinely since birth continue to be soothed). Although the shape of the crying curve is constant across cultures, absolute daily values vary inversely with level of maternal interaction. At the extremes are infants in industrialized western societies who, at 6 weeks of age, cry about 2 hours daily. In contrast, infants in the !Kung San society, who are essentially in constant contact with their mothers, are nursed frequently and are socially stimulated through interactions with adults, children and other infants during daily communal activities, average about 1 hour of crying daily (Barr, Bakeman, Konner, & Adomson, 1991; Konner, 1976).

The confluence of 1) the stable inverted "U" shape of the crying function across cultures, 2) the range of spontaneous crying, and 3) the inverse relationship between stimulation provided by adults and infant crying raises the following possibility. Differential age-related crying may reflect changing ideal levels of requisite central stimulation. Self-stimulation produced by crying may help meet those needs. We will return to this issue from a clinical perspective, but first want to explore how the crying hypothesis as an organizing principle squares with the current data set. The hypothesis predicts that adults who either caused or were associated with a state of high activation should be preferred by 6-week-olds, a state of intermediate activation by Week 9 infants and a state of very low activation by 12-week-old infants.

Figure 6–1 is consonant with this view. The inverted "U" function delimited by the shaded area represents daily crying. Data point couplings represent hypothesized starting and ending central activity levels for each condition at each age. A uniform, high starting level for infants in the crying condition is reasonable because all infants who cried met the same inclusion criterion of crying for 30 sec/min. The differing levels of crying reduction are empirical. Thus, sucking a sweet pacifier reduced crying in Week 6 infants by more than 90%. Sucrose or pacification treatments at the other ages did not cause this level of reduction. Thus, for the purpose of exposition, the Week 6 preference data point is placed at the apex of the daily crying curve; the other data points fall above the function, considerably so in 9- and 12-week-olds for whom sucrose was no longer an effective calming agent (Blass & Camp, 2003b).

Our assumption of initial equality for infants in the calm starting condition is on shakier grounds. None of the infants cried. They were awake, calm, and alert throughout, accepted the sucrose or the pacifier, and interacted with the experimenter. Based on newborn heart-rate data, we assume that sucking a pacifier increases heart rate (Nelson, Clifton, Dowd, & Field, 1978) and possibly central activity. Furthermore, heart rate in newborns who taste sucrose decreases (Blass & Ciaramitaro, 1994). Whether either of these changes occurs in infants in the current studies is an open question that will be evaluated empirically. We assumed uniformity in response to the various classes of stimulation—in particular, increased central activity in calm infants who sucked a pacifier and a uniform decrease in infants who tasted sucrose. These assumptions and findings yield the portrait presented in Figure 6–1. The pu-

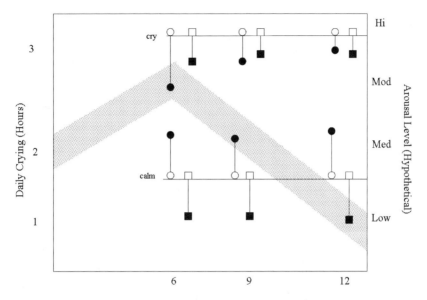

FIGURE 6–1.   Relationship between preference, change in putative central activation and mean daily crying (shaded area) in 6-, 9-, and 12-week-old infants. (From Blass & Camp, 2003a. Reprinted with permission of Blackwell Publishing.)

tative increase in central activity in calm Week 9 infants who sucked a pacifier placed them in the "preferred" activity range. Likewise, calm Week 12 infants preferred their experimenter only when they had tasted sucrose, which presumably lowered their central activity levels into the "preferred" range.

This orientation has all of the limitations that we specified at the outset. There are strengths that should be attended to, however. First, the hypothesis is consonant with the obtained data. That is not trivial because if any of the remaining 9 conditions had yielded a preference, then the theory as stated would have to be discounted immediately. Second, first-approximations to the underlying assumptions can be obtained at each age through heart rate recordings and, slightly more directly, through recording of brain activity, although at this point the critical portion(s) of the brain and the change(s) that occur therein can only be speculated upon (see below). Third, a priori predictions are made as to the behavioral patterns of infants to the left of the 6-week data point. Newborns and 2-week-olds should *not* prefer adults who interact with them while the infants are crying. Only calm newborns should prefer adults who provide sweet taste alone. Two-week-olds who had sucked a pacifier should exhibit a preference for the person who had provided it. Four-week-olds may be at a transitional point. More mature ones may act like Week 6 infants;

less mature ones may be closer to 2-week-olds in their determinants. The be-havior of these infants would be predicted by their individual daily crying levels. Indeed, the current studies should be replicated with each subject's daily crying record (Hunziker & Barr, 1986) in hand to determine how indi-vidual preferences align with individual crying functions.

This orientation is founded upon extensive rat and human infant litera-tures that point to two broad determinants of infant affect. One is linked to *energy conservation* and is manifest in preferences for individuals who provide contact, warmth (Alberts & Cramer, 1988; Alberts & May, 1984) and nutrient (Shide & Blass, 1991). The other source of preference is *punctate activation*. This has been established through convergent series of rat studies Coopersmith & Leon (1988); Hall (1979); Camp & Rudy (1988); Moran, Lew & Blass (1981). Each preference source is vital for normal growth and development, especially of brain (Gonzalez, Lovic, Ward, Wainwright, & Fleming, 2001; Meany, Aitken, Sharma, Viau, & Sarrieau, 1996). The first, energy acquisition and retention, is self-evident. All studies in human and rat infants have demonstrated preferences for individuals or substances that have been associ-ated with energy enhancement (Alberts & Cramer, 1988; Shide & Blass, 1991; MacFarlane, 1975; Field et al., 1984; Bushnell et al., 1983).

Exogenous stimulation provided by dams during ongoing interactions highlights the importance of natural kinds of activating stimulation. Both lab-oratory and, especially, clinical reports have revealed the consequences of withholding activating stimulation on behavioral and neural development. In-fants born to and raised by depressed women have poor social affect, even when interacting with high-affect laboratory personnel (Teicher, Glod, Surrey, & Swett, 1993). Lack of early parental stimulation is also revealed materially through decreased EEG activity. Rat studies point in the same direction. The offspring of mothers that provide very little stimulation by way of anogenital stroking have reduced hippocampal development relative to control animals (Meaney et al., 1996). This was validated by Gonzalez and his colleagues (2001) who experimentally controlled the frequency of highly activating anogenital stimulation in rats fed intragastrically in the absence of maternal or sibling contact.

Interestingly for both human and rat infants, excessive stimulation, i.e., beyond the norm provided by most mothers may actually be beneficial. The hippocampus of rats that had received more stimulation from their mothers was more developed than in rats whose levels of stimulation was reduced (Meaney, et. al., 1996). This was also true in the Gonzalez studies. In a fascinat-ing prospective report on children who had sustained at least one febrile seizure during infancy and childhood, Chang, Guo, Wang, Huang, and Tsai (2001) found that performance on a number of standardized cognitive tests was 2 SD above the mean. Other, possibly harmful effects of febrile seizures have been extensively evaluated. Remarkably, none of the seven reports on this issue have observed adverse sequellae to early febrile seizures (Nelson & Ellenberg, 1976, 1978, 1981; Roos, Peckham, West, & Butler, 1980; Verity, Butler, & Colding, 1985; Verity & Golding, 1991; Annegers, Hauser, Shirts, & Kurland, 1987).

Anogenital stimulation provided by rat dams prior to nursing also causes important short- and long-term central changes as documented by Johnson and Leon (2001). Anogenital stimulation activates the locus coreleus (LC) in the brainstem. The LC is the source of the brain adrenergic system that synthesizes and releases central norepinephrine (NE). The NE system targets both affective and Hebbian types of neural networks that may establish the linkage between anogenital stimulation and its associated novel odors. These new odors, in turn, come to elicit nipple attachment (Blass, Williams, & Pedersen, 1982), preferences for the dam (Coopersmith & Leon, 1988), possibly siblings (Holmes, 2001), and, possibly milk-borne flavors (Galef & Beck, 1990). These flavors may signify food safety and induce initial preferences for the "safe" foods. Blocking noradrenergic transmission interferes with these processes (Leon, 1992). Striking an ideal level of arousal through the judicious combination of stroking and amphetamine injection facilitates both behavioral and neuroanatomical change (Leon, 1992).

Additional studies in rats draw our attention to the contribution of punctate arousal to affective development. For example, Moran et al. (1981) reported that rats from Day 3 through to Day 12 worked for high levels of stimulation of the medial forebrain bundle, provided that such stimulation elicited considerable motor activity. According to Camp and Rudy (1988) and Roth and Sullivan (2001) shock to the feet in Day 6 rats, that caused extensive motor activity, also caused a strong preference for the odors associated with the shock. Preference was obtained, therefore whether activation was induced directly via electrical stimulation of the medial forebrain bundle (MFB), or indirectly by applying mild shock to the forepaws or by infusing liquid diet into the mouths of rats that had been deprived of maternal contact and suckling for 24 hours (Hall, 1979). In each case the rat pups *had to be visibly activated* by their respective classes of stimulation in order for conditioning and preference to occur. Note that activation-induced preference in rats has a limited time frame, confined to about the first 10–12 postnatal days. After that, preference induction becomes more complex and subtle, taking on the properties of adult preference formation. This provides an interesting parallel with regard to the changing parameters in the human infant studies discussed already.

In summary, we have presented arguments that point to idealized levels of stimulation in infant rats, the necessity of such stimulation for normal development, and infant willingness to both work for it and to prefer its source.

This linkage in rats of source and stimulation is normally achieved through the confluence of maternal characteristics and activation that approach the laboratory-based paradigms of classical conditioning.

The human infant data are in accord. We have suggested that one function served by crying is to supplement the levels of stimulation that infants receive so *that insufficient external stimulation is compensated for by increased self-stimulation through crying.* This should not seem remote; we readily accept the idea of self-quieting and calming in infants and self-stimulation and excitement seeking in adults. The current hypothesis aligns our conceptualization of neural function between infants and adults concerning the necessity of maintaining optimal, sometimes apparently exaggerated, levels of central activation during the early developmental period. It further acknowledges the particular status of the emerging central system, its behavioral manifestations and the necessity of conceptualizing an early period of sustained change in ideal levels of central activity.

This view is also consonant with the literature of excessive crying in infants with colic, a default classification when no organic source of crying has been determined (Wessel, Cobb, Jackson, Harris, & Detwiler, 1954; Barr, 1998). The inconsolable crying of colic is transient, generally easing by about 12 weeks of age, the nadir of the crying function. It is of interest that many parents of colicky infants assuage crying by providing extra stimulation, including jiggling, rocking, singing, taking infants for car rides in the early hours, and even placing the infant on a washing machine, during the spin cycle. Perhaps, infants with colic are providing additional self-stimulation through crying. Regardless, the crying function provides direction for a material source of preference in infants from birth to 12 weeks of age.

Behavioral Engagement

If human infants strive for ideal levels of stimulation, then one basis of preferring particular adults is their ability to cause or be associated with the ideal level. Accordingly, adults will be sought after and "judged" by their ability to bring infants to their "ideal" state. This implies active engagement of adults by infants. A suggestion of this was provided by Wolff (1963), who reported that Week 4 infants actively visually engaged their mothers during feeding. We will return to the feeding aspect below, but want first to document very consistent infant behavioral patterns through which, we believe, infants seek information about adults whom they meet for the first time. Social information-seeking parallels infants seeking information about objects, we believe, in that they align knowledge about a person or object, with rules that influence how infants respond to classes of individuals or objects.

Figure 6–2 presents the incidence of positive and negative affective behaviors presented by calm 9- and 12-week-old infants in different circumstances. Of special note is the fact that 75% of these infants emitted contentment sounds (coos, for example), faces, or gestures, such as flirting, when they were in eye contact with experimenters who did *not* provide sucrose or any other form of stimulation. In this regard, infants who received sucrose or a sweet pacifier while in visual contact with the experimenter emitted very few "contentment" behaviors. Paradoxically, these were the only infants who preferred the experimenter (recall that preferences were substantial). Infants who presented the contentment expressions of cooing, smiling, and flirting did *not* prefer their experimenters over the stranger. The lack of preference in the expressive infants and the substantial preference of 9- and 12-week-old infants who did not present expressions or sounds of contentment suggest that gestures are natural behavioral tools to elicit adult social behavior. We further suggest that preferences for particular adults reflect the adult's ability to induce the proper level of central stimulation in infants in the age range under discussion.

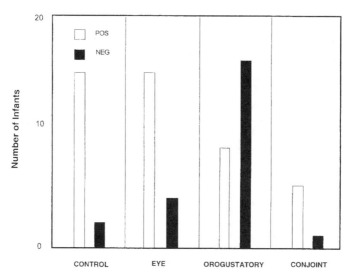

FIGURE 6–2.   Incidence of positive and negative affect in calm 9- and 12-week-old infants tested under different conditions. (From Blass & Camp, 2001. Reprinted with permission of the American Psychological Association.)

An unexpected robust finding was obtained in infants who received sucrose from adults who *avoided* eye contact with the infants. As shown in the third panel of Figure 6–2, absence of eye contact elicited considerable infant crying. This suggests an incongruity of providing an energy source while avoiding physical (e.g., holding) or social interaction, as defined by eye-to-eye contact. This was a primary animator of our subsequent research on eye contact during suckling.

SUMMARY

We have reported the outcomes of two studies on the induction of human infant preferences for adults with whom they had interacted in a constrained biosocial situation for a total of 3.5 minutes. The paradigm, although restricted in both time and range of interaction, has revealed a consistent pattern of behavior and preference that draws attention to a possible organizing principle of infant preference for new adults—namely, the level of central activity that adults induce in an infant. We suggest that this is one basis, among others, upon which infants judge adults. If valid, this paradigm holds considerable promise for the study of human infant affect and the bases of individual preference.

Gaze and the Ontogeny of Human Infant Suckling

The necessity of eye contact and energy delivery to induce adult preference led us to explore the circumstances under which eye contact might influence the expression of a natural behavior. We chose suckling/milk intake as a vital behavior that occurs with variability from meal to meal. The experimental venue was a setting in which a mother fed her infant his (her) normal formula through the infant's bottle twice in her usual manner. This bracketed the remaining four feedings which were conducted by research nurses in the General Clinical Research Center (GCRC) at the Boston University School of Medicine. Each feeding represented a combination of two factors that contribute to standard infant bottle feeding. In a 2 × 2 experimental design, infants were either held or not held by the nurse, and either received social interactions from her, with an emphasis on eye contact and verbal interaction, (e.g., calling the infant's name and other spontaneous expressions of affection), or did not receive them. In the latter condition, the nurse deliberately avoided infant eye contact by focusing on the infant's chest and refrained from any verbal interactions.

All sessions were video-recorded and scored for ingestive behavior by counting the number of sucks emitted when infants were in or out of eye contact with the feeder. This was readily achieved through the use of two cameras.

One was set up at middle range to capture eye gaze between infant and feeder. The second camera was positioned up close to provide detailed movements of the infant's cheek during the suckling act. This allowed us to evaluate bout pattern and context and to relate this to the amount of milk that the infants ingested during a session. Intake was determined simply by measuring bottle contents (in ml) before and after the session (bottles were wrapped so that the feeder could not gauge their contents, although differences in weight could certainly be detected). All 10 infants participated in all six feeding conditions. This allows within subjects comparisons and sidesteps the variability inherent among infants in basal suckling intake. These studies have generated an enormous data base. We can now report on how infant intake of a familiar formula is determined by social interactions with a novel feeder. Social factors derange the ingestive linkage between deprivation time, its putative physiological changes, and compensation through suckling. This uncoupling can even occur during a single session.

Figure 6–3 demonstrates that infants whose feeders interacted considerably with the infants during the feeding through gaze took in considerably more of their familiar formula than when social interaction was considerably more limited. The increase was substantial, on the order of a 44% increase

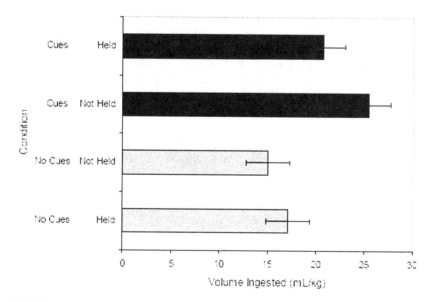

FIGURE 6–3. Formula intake (+/− SE) in ml/Kg. Body Weight of 8- to 14-week-old infants when the feeder either looked at and interacted socially with the infant and when she did not (upper histograms). The lower panels present intake when infants were either held by the feeder during the meal or fed in an infant seat and not held.

from circa 16 ml to circa 23 ml. This was verified statistically ($p < .001$). The influence of eye contact-social engagement did not depend upon whether the infant was held during feeding or was in the infant seat ($p > .10$). Moreover, total intake was not affected by whether infants were held while given the bottle or received the bottle when in an infant seat, as shown in the right-hand portion of Figure 6–3 ($p > .10$). This failure was unexpected because, although infants were accustomed to infant seats, they had not necessarily been fed in them before.

Although Figure 6–3 successfully identified the influence of social engagement on feeding, it did not address the relationship between privation and ingestion. The relationship is not necessarily obvious. For example, if ingestive behavior in human infants is geared to growth, as in rats (Blass, 1995), then intake should be independent of privation, within limits. Alternatively, human suckling, in which there is normally no competition for the mother's resources, may obey laws of adult intake and be driven by deprivation time.

As documented below, we are drawn to the conclusion of two nutritive suckling systems in human infants. One is engaged when infants are *not* looking at the feeder. This is the regulatory system and is linked to some neurophysiological concomitant of time that had elapsed between feeding bouts. The other is a social feeding system. It is engaged when held infants *look at the feeder*. It does not bear any relationship to deprivation length between meals. Figures 6–4a and 6–4b present the relationship between the period of privation and the amount of food ingested by the infants when held by the feeder, or fed in the infant seat, respectively. When infants are held during feeding, a *linear relationship is obtained with a projected intercept of near zero*, exactly what would be expected of a physiological system triggered at a modest threshold, that continues to function until either the precipitating threshold is crossed, an opposing signal arises, such as gastric distension, or a motor program triggered by the deficit has been spent (see Blass & Hall, 1976) for a more complete discussion of this issue as it pertains to water intake). When infants were not held by the feeder, however, the relationship was essentially flat, with an intercept approaching 13 ml/Kg, as shown in Figure 6–4b; intake was not reliably determined by deprivation time. This was especially noteworthy in infants who had self imposed rather brief privation times of two hours or fewer between feeding episodes. Thirteen of the 14 held infants consumed less than 15 ml formula/Kg during the meal. In contrast, 6 of the 11 infants fed in the infant seat took in more than 16 ml/Kg. Thus, a boundary condition for the manifestation of physiological control over intake is that infants be held during feeding. This condition is naturally honored during nursing. Although mean intake between seated and held conditions did not differ (see Figure 6–3), in fact, different pathways were taken to achieve equality. Intake when held was

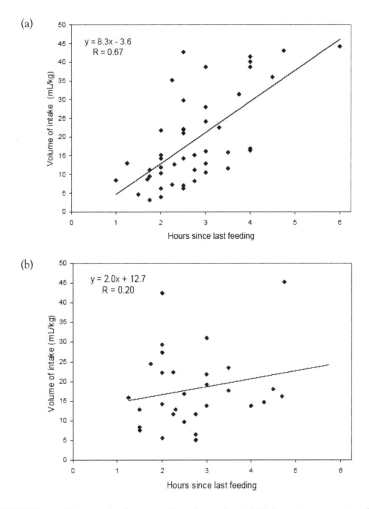

FIGURE 6–4.   Relationship between formula intake (ml/Kg.) against time since last feeding in 8- to 14-week-old infants when held during meal (left panel, a) or when not held and fed in an infant seat (b). Each data point is for an individual infant.

linked to some correlate of suckling abstinence. When these same infants were fed in the infant seat, intake was disengaged from abstinence time, despite equality in mean intake.

Even though a within-subjects design was used, thereby increasing confidence in our findings, feeding in an infant seat may have been inherently peculiar, triggering the disconnection between privation and intake. Evaluating infant behavior within a session when held by the feeder helps ease this concern and provides additional support for two independent nutritive feeding systems. Figure 6–5 demonstrates the relationship between privation and sucking frequency when infants were *not* looking at the feeder. Once again the relationship between privation length and the number of sucks is linear. (The correlation between intake and sucking incidence is strong, $r = .61$, so that, at least for now, sucking frequency can serve as an index of intake when infants are not looking at the feeder.)

In contrast, the relationship between privation and intake flattened when infants looked at the feeder. During mutual gaze, privation length did not predict sucking incidence. This suggests that engaging the social feeding system, through looking, may have inhibited or otherwise disengaged the mechanism(s) that links intake with privation length and its attendant signals. The disconnections described herein can not be attributed to a peculiarity of the test setting. Rather they seem to be manifestations of two separable nutritive suckling systems, one driven by physiological factors, yet to be identified in human infants—the other driven by social factors, also not yet determined. Further evidence for two different systems is found in a strong correlation between sucking and intake when infants did not look at the feeder and a remarkably weak correlation of sucking and intake when looking at the feeder. This suggests considerably more variability in the execution of individual sucks when infants are looking at the feeder. The weak correlation does not simply reflect that sucking while looking occurred towards the end of a meal because both

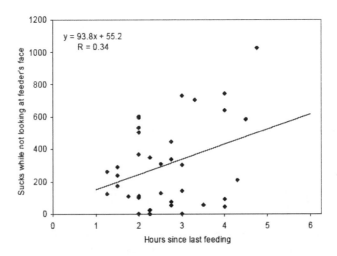

FIGURE 6–5.   The number of sucks that occurred when infants were not looking at the feeder during a given meal. Sucking frequency is plotted against time since the last meal.

forms of sucking were uniformly distributed throughout the meal. The measures are approximate and await more precise documentation, which we will obtain with a device that will measure volume/each suck.

DISCUSSION

Our studies have revealed four ways in which mutual infant-adult gaze influences infant affect, levels of arousal, preference for interactive adults, and control of milk intake via suckling. Given that large, interesting and cohesive sets of findings have emerged at each research turn, we believe that the current report, although preliminary, has exposed the surface of mutual gaze influences on the ontogeny of motivation and affect. Future studies as to the determinants of affective change, its consequences, and its underlying mechanisms will be richly rewarded. Because these findings interface naturally with much of the material in this volume, opportunities are presented to study the relationship between cognition and affect that should be seized.

AFFECT REGULATION

The conjunction of eye contact and sucrose delivery that was necessary to quiet crying 4- to 9-week-old infants was unexpected. It is a powerful, but transient phenomenon that has disappeared by Week 12. The transition presumably reflects particular central changes because sucking a sweet pacifier continued to quiet crying Week 12 infants. Had sucrose ineffectiveness reflected a unitary central affective change, then crying should have continued. Separate timetables are congruent with separate chemosensory and orotactile afferent systems in human infant comforting (Blass & Ciaramitaro, 1994) and separate neurochemical mediation of each (Blass, Brunson, Fillion, & Weller, 1990). It also seems very unlikely that loss of sucrose influence represents a diminution in peripheral afferent coding.

The basis of mutual gaze as a source of calming remains elusive. It is of interest that mutual gaze was not necessary until Week 4 and not sufficient (with sucrose) after Week 12. Within this 8-week time frame, however, establishing eye contact is clearly motivated because both crying and calm infants actively sought it. The function of eye contact is currently unknown, however, from either an emotional or cognitive perspective.

The following reflections on the influences of mutual gaze are coherent with literatures on infant face recognition, energy conservation and growth, and the increasing specificity of infant motivation, analgesic, and calming mechanisms. They may help organize and direct future research on the contribution of mutual gaze on infant coping, face representation, affect, and choice. Concerning the transience of nonspecific analgesia and stress reduction, both rat and human infants, within weeks and months of birth, respectively, move from a state in which nonspecific stimulation (e.g., sweets and fats) are calming, to one in which removing the particular discomforting source most effectively curtails crying (holding, which also comforts adults, is a possible exception to this developmental progression). The previously unopposed, and very potent, opioid mechanisms that were sufficient to induce a profound analgesia and comfort both rat and human infants through taste afferents, have come under the control of developing cortical mechanisms that, presumably, allow endogenous opioids to continue to sooth infants, but no longer block pain afferents at their point of entry in the dorsal horn of the spinal cord (Ren, Blass, Zhou, & Dubner, 1997). In ways that we do not yet understand, visual engagement is transiently needed to comfort. Because eye contact is actively sought, we find it unlikely that it acts through distraction.

Eye contact as a source of calming also provides opportunities for infants to recognize and prefer faces that are associated with crying relief, energy conservation, or attaining a putative idealized state of central activity. Eye contact therefore may become linked with opioid and nonopioid calming systems that had been sufficient in both premature and term newborns to arrest crying and provide analgesia (Smith & Blass, 1996; Smith, Fillion, & Blass, 1990; Blass & Hoffmeyer, 1991; Blass & Watt, 1999). This expansion in the motivational domain is of interest because it occurs when infants first start to spontaneously utilize eye contact to engage their mothers (Wolff, 1963, 1987), with the shift in face attention from peripheral face scanning to scanning eye features (Haith, Bergman, & Moore, 1977), and in the increasing use of configuration stability as a possible source of face identity (Bartrip, Morton, & Schonen, 2001; Blass & Camp, 2004). Thus, both systems that combat pain and those involved in face perception and preference function at levels of increasing specificity. Pain is best relieved by blocking or removing the specific source. Faces are increasingly recognized through the stable internal features and configurations that most reliably define them.

Increases in both complexity and specificity of stimulus arrays needed to maintain affective stability are consonant with the findings of Muir and his colleagues on reversing the loss of affective tone in infants suddenly confronted with a still face. The parallels between our findings in 4- to 9-week-olds and Muir's findings in older infants (Stack & Muir, 1992; D'Entremont & Muir, 1997; D'Entremont, Haines, & Muir, 1997) are striking. In both cases eye contact is necessary, but not sufficient, to achieve affective equilibrium. In Muir's studies, another domain such as touch or voice has to be added to the still face for positive affect to be reinstated. In short, mutual gaze as a motivational factor first appears in human infants towards the end of their first postnatal month. The effect is transient within the context that we have identified. Motivational and communicative gaze influences, however, endure for a lifetime in humans. We are the only species with a very rich affective visual communication system for both positive and negative affect, although see de Waal on social visual influences in Bonobo apes, as a possible addition.

GAZE AND AROUSAL

Consistent with its multiple social functions, mutual gaze also sustains infant performance. As documented in Table 1, 8- to 14-week-olds suckled for longer periods of time when in mutual gaze with the feeder, independent of holding. The effect was substantial: eye contact increased intake by 43%, an impressive figure. This implies that intake driven by physiological control constitutes a fraction of total intake by 2- to 3-month-old infants. Suspension of control through social engagement has important implications for feeding control. This suspension may be local, i.e., in the service of infants learning about the feeder. It may be a more general manifestation, however, of the effects of distraction on intake. If true, this has important implications for our understanding later manifestations of overeating and obesity.

These data alert us to the arousing and sustaining properties of eye contact and social interactions on formula feeding from a bottle. To our knowledge, this is the initial experimental manifestation of this property in a vital biosocial setting. In principle, chronic under-stimulation could produce chronic low affect. This is supported by studies on human infants born to and reared by depressed women. Affective levels were very low, even when the infants interacted with animated adults. Moreover, chronic changes in these infants' brain EEGs were also the rule. The findings of the present report may be clinically relevant. If potential neurological and behavioral problems can be identified through knowledge of parent emotional state and objectively through behavioral interactions, then appropriate interventions might be instantiated to sustain both normal affect and its underlying neurology. This may also be relevant to the depressed intake and growth of infants with poor eating behavior in the context of a suboptimal feeding interaction.

Based on the rat literature, we may expect that nonspecific arousal originating from social sources to importantly influence infant basal affect and, later, learning and performance. According to Meany et al. (1996), rats that had, as pups, received considerable anogenital stimulation from their mothers, had long-term increases in hippocampal density and performed better in a number of learning tasks. This was experimentally validated by Gonzales et. al. (2001), who actually controlled the amount of stimulation provided to rats that were reared by chronic intragastric intubation in the absence of mother or sibling interactions. More recently, Fleming and colleagues (2003) have reported that rats that had been raised in isolation showed specific deficits as adults in social learning, with their abilities to solve more cognitive tasks unimpaired. This report is somewhat at variance with others that had demonstrated cognitive impairments following isolation rearing. Resolving the differences among these laboratories will help shed light on early social and cognitive developmental processes.

Differences among studies, however, should not obscure the important fact that either withholding particular natural interactions between mother and infant, or exaggerating these interactions, leave powerful impressions on adult cognition, social learning, and behavior. These studies provide direction for research on human infants in central changes associated with changes in arousal as defined both physiologically and behaviorally (Dawson, Klinger, Panagiotides, Hill, & Spiker, 1992). Because the dawn of assessing human infant neural function through brain imaging is providing its first light, behavioral studies must be conducted in anticipation of the technical advances that will link behavioral changes and cognitive processes with their underlying neural mechanisms. The research reported herein, which has demonstrated a substantial range of affect and arousal during early mammalian development, and a vulnerability to various forms of experience, may be seen as precursors of brain analyses dedicated to the neurology of affect.

Interactions Between Physical State and Mutual Gaze in Determining Social Preferences

There are a number of relevant points. First, preference formation is very rapid. Under the present circumstances, as little as 3.5 minutes of the "appropriate" social interaction sufficed for preference formation in 6- to 12-week-old infants (Blass & Camp, 2001, 2003a). Lower limits have not been determined, nor has preference endurance. Both of these parameters must be explored in order to better understand the ontogeny of human affect.

Although preferences have been robust and easily established as early as Week 6 in our experimental paradigms, data available from other labs point to earlier capacities in the formation of affective bonds as indicated. Indeed, newborns discriminate among adults along multiple dimensions, including olfaction and audition. Maternal face preferences have been expressed during the first 24 postpartum hours, but the motivational bases of these preferences are not known. Also, the contributions of eye contact to the process and to face memory have not been evaluated. The evidence is strong that masking external facial features disrupts preference (Bartrip et. al., 2001), but the basis of the disruption is not clear. Because newborns are very sensitive to adult internal facial features (Slater, Bremner, Johnson, Hayes, & Brown, 2000; Field et. al., 1984, Meltzoff & Moore, 1977, 1984), including eye direction (Farroni et. al., 2002), failure to discriminate between the mother and another woman when their hairlines are covered requires additional evidence before concluding that external facial features are bearing the weight of the discrimination.

Blass and Camp (2004), using a habituation-dishabituation paradigm, reported that 8- to 21-week-old infants can use the internal features of the face to identify an individual. Yet, when infants were habituated to an individual with a full face and presented with that person a second time with the external features covered, there was no sign of recognition relative to presenting a stranger with features covered. The same held true for the converse situation. Infants habituated to the internal features of a person showed the same looking times when either that person or a different one, whom they had never seen before, was presented to the infant (Blass & Camp, unpublished data, 2003). Thus it appears infants can discriminate among individuals on the basis of internal features, but this capacity is diminished when there is a change in context caused by altering the frame provided by the hairline.

At present no common factor has been identified that determines choice in infants 6 to 12 weeks of age who were studied by exposing them to an experimenter who either allowed the infants to taste sucrose or suck a sweetened pacifier when in eye contact. Only 3 of the 12 conditions yielded preferences. In each case the preference was robust (circa 2:1 in favor of the experimenter). These data are unified by what we have referred to as the crying function. Putative levels of activation that were required to induce a preference for the experimenter coincided well with the amount of daily crying reported in the literature for infants of a particular age. Thus, Week 6 infants had to be in a crying state when interacting with the experimenter; Week 9 and Week 12 infants had to be calm. The former infants (i.e., Week 6 infants) preferred experimenters who had allowed them to suck on a pacifier, presumably increasing their arousal levels. The older infants preferred experimenters who had given them sucrose by syringe, presumably inducing further calm. Although these explanations are posthoc, they do make specific predictions as to preferences in younger infants. If the predicted outcomes are obtained they would support the suggestion that certain aspects of crying may be in the service of stimulating the developing brain.

AN ACTIVE ROLE FOR INFANTS
IN PREFERENCE FORMATION

We have presented these ideas in some detail (Blass & Camp, 2001; 2003a) but emphasize in the current context that both calm and crying infants sought to engage the eyes of adults who sat opposite them delivering sucrose or a pacifier. Calm 9- to 12-week-olds were also socially proactive with experimenters who engaged them visually but did not provide stimulation other than a smile. Interestingly, the quality of the interaction did not cause further infant solicitation—only the absence of an interaction did. On these grounds, we have suggested an active seeking of information, at least on the part of the 9- to 12-week-olds whom we have studied. This information is dedicated to the earliest decisions concerning individual acceptance or rejection. The bases of acceptance or rejection, beyond the initial description provided above, have not even been identified.

TWO SEPARATE NUTRITIVE SUCKLING SYSTEMS

In addition to addressing broad issues of identity and preference as they are influenced by eye gaze, we have also focused narrowly on how gaze affects suckling behavior. Our studies have revealed two separate nutritive suckling systems in infants 8 to 16 weeks of age, that are most manifest when infants are fed by strangers. One system is physiologically driven. It is expressed in the linear relationship between intake and privation time when infants are held by the feeder. The second system seems to be driven by social factors and appears when held infants look at the feeder. Intake then is not related to deprivation levels. Eye contact occurred for at least a portion of 85% of the feeding bouts when fed by a stranger, and was maintained by the infants during 30% of the feeding session. In contrast, when fed by their mothers, eye contact occurred in only 21% of all bouts and was maintained for only 17% of the session. The latter findings demonstrate a precipitous drop off from the extended eye contact reported by Wolff (1987) in 4-week-old infants fed by their mothers and suggests that both facial and emotional recognition have occurred. The high levels of looking in Week 4 infants suggest that there should be considerable spontaneous suckling variability at that age, possibly accompanied by variability in body weight gain.

The existence of two suckling systems is of considerable interest from the perspective of ingestive behavior including growth and regulation. We have discussed the possible effects of under-stimulation as it relates to established clinical manifestation. The converse of potentially inappropriate over-stimulation is a poignant health issue in contemporary western societies in which both childhood and adult obesity are epidemic. The developmental origins of the problem are not known, which makes the existence of an infant ingestive system that is disengaged from physiological control and is determined by social factors worthy of our attention (Blass, 2003). In this regard, disengagement from physiological controls can occur when flavorful foods or beverages are ingested or when attention is distracted during feeding. The connections of the infant segregation with the overeating of adults remain to be established.

Finally, the time course of social influences on ingestive behavior is not known. It may not be a developmental phenomenon that changes with age. The meal is the central, stable, enduring social relationship both within a family and among unrelated individuals. In addition to influencing intake, social factors that involve mutual gaze may significantly contribute to familial stability and learning about our and others' cultures and values (Rozin, 1976).

REFERENCES

Alberts, J. R., & Cramer, C. P. (1988). Ecology and experience: Sources of means and meaning of developmental change. In E. M. Blass (Ed.), *Handbook of behavioral neurobiology, Volume 9, Developmental psychobiology and behavioral ecology* (pp. 1–40). NY: Plenum Press.

Alberts, J. R., & May, B. (1984). Nonnutritive thermotactile induction of filial huddling in rat pups. *Developmental Psychobiology, 17,* 161–181.

Annegers J. F., Hauser, W. A., Shirts, S. B., Kurland, L. T. (1987). Factors prognostic of unprovoked seizures after febrile convulsions. *New England Journal of Medicine, 316,* 493–498.

Banks, M. S. (1980). The development of visual accommodation during early infancy. *Child Development, 51,* 646–666.

Baron-Cohen, S. (1989). Joint attention deficits in autism: Towards a cognitive analysis. *Development and Psychopathology, 1,* 185–189.

Barr, R. G. (1990). The normal crying curve: What do we really know? *Developmental Medicine & Child Neurology, 32,* 356–362.

Barr R. G. (1998). Reflections on measuring pain in infants: Dissociation in responsive systems and "honest signalling." *Archives of Disease in Childhood Fetal Neonatal Edition, 79,* F152–F156.

Barr, R. G., Bakeman, R., Konner, M., & Adomson, L. (1991). Crying in Kung infants: A test of the cultural specificity hypothesis. *Developmental Medicine and Child Neurology, 33,* 601–610.

Bartrip, J., Morton, J., & de Schonen, S. (2001). Response to mother's face in 3- week to 5-month-old infants. *British Journal of Developmental Psychology, 19,* 853–855.

Blass, E. M. (1990). Suckling: Determinants, changes, mechanisms, & lasting impressions. *Developmental Psychology, 26,* 520–533.

Blass, E. M. (1995). The ontogeny of ingestive behavior. In A. Morrison & S. Fluharty (Eds.), *Progress in Psychobiology and Physiological Psychology* (pp. 1–51). NY: Academic Press.

Blass, E. M. (1998). Changing influence of sucrose and visual engagement in 2- to 12-week-old human infants: Implications for maternal face recognition. *Infant Behavior and Development, 20,* 423–434.

Blass, E. M. (2003). Biological and environmental determinants of childhood obesity. *Nutritional and Clinical Care, 6*, 13–19.

Blass, E. M., & Camp., C. A. (2001).The ontogeny of face recognition: Eye contact and sweet taste induce face preference in 9- and 12-week-old human infants. *Developmental Psychology, 37*, 762–774.

Blass, E. M., & Camp, C. A. (2003a). Biological bases of face preference in six-week-old infants. *Developmental Science, 6*, 524–536.

Blass, E. M., & Camp, C. A. (2003b). Crying Determinants in 6–12-Week-Old Human Infants. *Developmental Psychobiology, 42*, 312–316.

Blass, E. M., & Camp, C. A. (2004). The Ontogeny of Face Identity: I. Eight to 21-week-old Infants Use Internal and External Features in Identity. *Cognition 92*, 305–327.

Blass, E. M., & Ciaramitaro, V. (1994). Oral determinants of state, affect, and action in newborn humans. *Monographs of the Society for Research in Child Development, 59*, 1–96.

Blass, E. M., Fillion, T. J., Weller, A., & Brunson, L. (1990). Separation of opioid from nonopioid mediation of affect in neonatal rats: Nonopioid mechanisms mediate maternal contact influences. *Behavioral Neuroscience, 104*, 625–636.

Blass, E.M., Fitzgerald, E., & Kehoe, P. (1987). Interactions between sucrose, pain and isolation distress. *Pharmacology Biochemistry and Behavior, 26*, 483–489.

Blass, E. M., Ganchrow, J. R., & Steiner, J. E. (1984). Classical conditioning in newborn humans 2–48 hours of age. *Infant Behavior and Development, 7*, 223–235.

Blass, E. M., & Hall, W. G. (1976). Drinking termination: Interactions among hydrational, orogastric, and behavioral controls in rats. *Psychological Review, 83*, 356–374.

Blass, E. M., & Hoffmeyer, L. B. (1991). Sucrose as an analgesic in newborn humans. *Pediatrics, 87*(2), 215–218.

Blass, E. M., & Smith, B. A. (1992). Differential effects of sucrose, fructose, glucose and lactose on crying in 1–3-day-old human infants. *Developmental Psychology, 28*, 804–810.

Blass, E. M., & Watt, L. (1999). Suckling and sucrose-induced analgesia in human newborns. *PAIN, 83*, 611–623.

Blass, E. M., Williams, C. L., & Pedersen, P. E. (1982). Activation and odor conditioning of suckling behavior in 3-day-old albino rats. *Journal of Experimental Psychology: Animal Behavioral Processes, 8*, 329–341.

Brazelton, T. B. (1962). Crying in infancy. *Pediatrics, 29*, 579–588.

Bushnell, I. W. R. (1982). Discrimination of faces by young infants. *Journal of Experimental Child Psychology, 33*, 298–308.

Bushnell, I. W. R., Sai, F., & Mullin, J. T. (1983). Neonatal recognition of mother's face. *British Journal of Developmental Psychology, 7*, 3–15.

Camp, L. L., & Rudy, J. W. (1988). Changes in the categorization of appetitive and aversive events during postnatal development of the rat. *Developmental Psychobiology, 21*, 25–42.

Chang, Y. C., Guo N. W., Wang, S. T., Huang, C. C., & Tsai, J. J. (2001). Working memory of school-aged children with a history of febrile convulsions: A population study. *Neurology, 57*, 37–42.

Coopersmith, R., & Leon, M. (1986). Enhanced neural response by adult rats to odors experienced early in life. *Brain Research, 371*, 400–403.

Dawson, G., Klinger, L. G., Panagiotides, H., Hill D., Spiker S. (1992). Frontal lobe activity and affective behavior of infants of mothers with depressive symptoms. *Child Development, 63*, 725–737.

Dawson, G., Frey K., Panagiotides, H., Yamada, E., Hessl, D., & Osterling, J. (1999). Infants of depressed mothers exhibit atypical frontal electrical brain activity during interactions with mother and with a familiar, nondepressed adult. *Child Development, 70,* 1058–1066.

D'Entremont, B., Haines, S., & Muir, D. (1997). A demonstration of gaze-following in 3- to 6-month-olds. *Infant Behavior and Development, 20,* 569–572.

D'Entremont, B., & Muir, D. (1997). Five month olds' attention and affective responses to still-faced emotional expressions. *Infant Behavior and Development, 20,* 563–568.

de Schonen, S., & Mathivet, E. (1990). Hemispheric asymmetry in a face discrimination task in infants. *Child Development, 61,* 1192–1205.

de Waal, F. B. M. (1988). The communicative repertoire of captive bonobos (Pan paniscus), compared to that of chimpanzees. *Behaviour, 106,* 183–251.

Field, T. M., Cohen, D., Garcia, R., & Greenberg, R. (1984) Mother-stranger face discrimination by the newborn. *Infant Behavior and Development, 7,* 19–25.

Galef, B. G., Jr., & Beck, M. (1990). Diet selection and poison avoidance by mammals individually and in social groups. In E. M. Stricker, *Handbook of Behavioral Neurobiology: Neurobiology of food and fluid intake* (Vol. 10, pp. 329–352). New York: Plenum Press.

Gonzalez, A., Lovic, V., Ward, G. R., Wainwright, P. E., & Fleming, A. S. (2001). Intergenerational effects of complete maternal deprivation and replacement stimulation on maternal behavior and emotionality in female rats. *Developmental Psychobiology, 38,* 11–32.

Haith, M., Bergman, T., & Moore, M. (1977). Eye contact and face scanning in early infancy. *Science, 198,* 853–855.

Hall, W. G. (1979). Feeding and behavioral activation in infant rats. *Science, 190,* 1313–1315.

Holmes, W. G. (2001). The development and the function of nepotism: Why kinship matters in social relationships. In E. M. Blass (Ed.), *Handbook of behavioral neurobiology, Volume 12. Developmental psychobiology, developmental neurobiology and behavioral ecology: Mechanisms and early principles.* New York. Plenum.

Hunziker, U. A., & Barr, R. G. (1986). Increased carrying reduces infant crying: A randomized controlled trial. *Pediatrics, 77,* 641–648.

Johnson, B. A., & Leon, M. (2001). Spatial coding in the olfactory system: The role of early experience. In E. M. Blass (Ed.), *Handbook of behavioral neurobiology, Volume 12. Developmental psychobiology, developmental neurobiology and behavioral ecology: Mechanisms and early principles.* New York, Plenum.

Kehoe, P., & Blass, E. M. (1986). Conditioned aversions and their memories in 5- day-old rats during suckling. *Journal of Experimental Psychology: Animal Behavior Processes, 12,* 40–47.

Levy, F., Melo, A. I., Galef, B. G., Madden M., & Fleming, A. S. (2003). Complete maternal deprivation affects social, but not spatial, learning in adult rats. *Developmental Psychobiology, 43,* 177–191.

Leon, M. (1992). The neurobiology of filial learning. *Annual Review of Psychology, 43,* 377–398.

Konner, N. (1976). Maternal care, infant behavior and development among the !Kung. In R. B. Lee & I. DeVore (Eds.). *Kalahari hunter gatherers of the !Kung San and their neighbors* (pp. 218–245). Cambridge, MA, Harvard University Press.

MacFarlane, A. (1975). Olfaction in the development of social preferences in the human neonate. In *Parent-infant interaction (CIBA Foundation Symposium, #33).* Amsterdam: Elsevier.

Meaney, M., Aitken, D. H., Sharma, S., Viau, V., & Sarrieau, A. (1996). Early environmental regulation of forebrain glucocorticoid receptor gene expression: Implications for adrenocortical response to stress. *Developmental Neuroscience, 18,* 49–72.

Meltzoff, A. N., & Moore, M. (1977). Imitation of facial and manual gestures by human neonates. *Science, 198,* 75–78.

Meltzoff, A. N., & Moore, M. (1984). Newborn infants imitate adult gestures. *Child Development, 54,* 702–709.

Moran, T. H., Lew, M. F., & Blass, E. M. (1981). Intra-cranial self-stimulation in 3-day-old rat pups. *Science, 214,* 1366–1368.

Mumme, D., Bushnell, E. W., Lariviere, L. A., & DiCorica, J. A. Infants' use of gaze to interpret object-directed emotional signals and action sequence. In R. Flom, K. Lee, & D. Muir (Eds.) *Gaze-following: its development and significance.* Erlbaum: Mahwah, NJ. pp. 143–170.

Nelson, M. J., Clifton, R. K., Dowd, J. M., & Field, T. M. (1978). Cardiac responding to auditory stimuli in newborn infants: Why pacifiers should not be used when heart rate is the major dependent variable. *Infant Behavior and Development, 1,* 277–290.

Nelson, K. B., & Ellenberg, J. H. (1976). Predictors of epilepsy in children who have experienced febrile seizures. *New England Journal of Medicine, 295,* 1029–33.

Nelson, K. B., & Ellenberg, J. H. (1978). Prognosis in children with febrile seizures. *Pediatrics, 61,* 720–7.

Nelson K. B., & Ellenberg, J. H. (1981). *Febrile Seizures.* New York: Raven Press.

Pascalis, O., de Schonen, S., Morton, J., Deruelle, C., & Fabre-Grenet, M (1995). Mother's face recognition by neonates: A replication and an extension. *Infant Behavior and Development, 18,* 79–86.

Pedersen, P. E., & Blass, E. M. (1982). Prenatal and postnatal determinants of the first suckling episode in albino rats. *Developmental Psychobiology, 15,* 349–355.

Poulin-Dubois, D. A fresh look at gaze: Infants' attribution of desires from peoples' behaviors towards objects. ants' use of gaze to interpret object-directed emotional signals and action sequence. In R. Flom, K. Lee, & D. Muir (Eds.) *Gaze-following: its development and significance.* Erlbaum: Mahwah, NJ. pp. 263–282.

Rao, M., Blass, E. M., Brignol, M. M., Marino, L., & Glass, L. (1997). Reduced heat loss following sucrose ingestion in premature and normal human newborns. *Early Human Development, 48,* 109–116.

Ren, K., Blass, E. M., Zhou, Q-q., & Dubner, R. (1997). Suckling and sucrose ingestion suppress persistent hyperalgesia and spinal Fos expression after forepaw inflammation in infant rats. *Proceedings of the National Academy of Sciences, 104,* 1471–1475.

Roos, E. M., Peckham, C. S., West, P. B., Butler, N. R. (1980). Epilepsy in childhood: Findings from the national child development study. *British Medical Journal, 280,* 207–210.

Roth, T. L., & Sullivan, R. M. (2001). Endogenous opioids and their role in odor preference acquisition and consolidation following odor-shock conditioning in infant rats. *Developmental Psychobiology, 39,* 188–198.

Rozin, P. (1976). The selection of foods by rats, humans and other animals. In J. Rosenblatt, R. A. Hinde, E. Shaw, & C. Beer (Eds.). *Advances in the Study of Behavior* (Vol. 6, pp. 21–76).

Schaal, B. (1988). Olfaction in infants and children: Developmental and functional perspectives. *Chemical Senses, 13*, 145–190.

Shide, D. J., & Blass, E. M. (1991). Opioid mediation of odor preferences induced by sugar and fat in 6-day-old rats. *Physiology & Behavior, 50*, 961–966.

Slater, A., Bremner, G., Johnson, S. P., Hayes, R., & Brown, E. (2000). Newborn infants' preference for attractive faces: The role of internal and external features. *Infancy, 1*, 265–274.

Smith, B. A., & Blass, E. M. (1996). Taste-mediated calming in premature, preterm, and full-term human infants. *Developmental Psychology, 32*, 1084–1089.

Smith, B. A., Fillion, T. J., & Blass, E. M. (1990). Orally-mediated sources of calming in one- to three-day-old human infants. *Developmental Psychology, 26*(5), 731–737.

Stack, D. M., & Muir, D. W. (1992). Adult tactile interaction during face-to-face interactions modulates 5-month-olds' affect and attention. *Child Development, 63*, 1509–1525.

Steiner, J. E. (1979). Human facial expressions in response to taste and smell stimulation. In H. W. Reese & L. P. Lipsitt (Eds.), *Advances in Child Development and Behavior, 13*, pp. 257–295. New York: Academic Press.

Teicher, M. H., & Blass, E. M. (1977). First suckling response of the newborn albino rat: The roles of olfaction and amniotic fluid. *Science, 198*, 635–636.

Teicher, M. H., Glod, C. A., Surrey, J., Swett, C., Jr. (1993). Early childhood abuse and limbic system ratings in adult psychiatric patients. *Journal of Neuropsychiatry & Clinical Neurosciences, 5*, 301–306.

Verity, C. M., Butler, N. R., & Colding, J. (1985). Febrile convulsions in a national cohort followed up from birth. II. Medical history and intellectual ability at 5 years of age. *British Medical Journal, 290*, 1311–1315.

Verity, C. M., & Golding, J. (1991). Risk of epilepsy after febrile convulsions: A national cohort study. *British Medical Journal, 303*, 1373–1376.

Waldron, G. E., Bower, N. J. A., & Bower, T. G. R. (1992). Recognition of familiar faces by newborns. *Infant Behavior & Development, 15*, 265–269.

Wessel, M. A., Cobb, J. C., Jackson, E. B., Harris, G. S., & Detwiler, A. C. (1954). Paroxysmal fussing in infancy, sometimes called "colic." *Pediatrics, 14*, 421–434.

Wolff, P. H. (1963). Observations on the early development of smiling. In B. Foss (Ed.) *Determinants of infant behavior* (Vol. II, pp. 113–138). London: Methuen.

Wolff, P. H. (1987). The Development of behavioral states and the expression of emotions in early infancy: New proposals for investigation. Chicago, University of Chicago Press.

Zeifman, D., Delaney, S., & Blass, E. M. (1996). Sweet taste, looking and calm in two- and four-week-old infants: The eyes have it. *Developmental Psychology, 32*, 1090–1099.

7

Infants' Use of Gaze Cues to Interpret Others' Actions and Emotional Reactions

Donna L. Mumme, Emily W. Bushnell,
Jennifer A. DiCorcia,
and Leslie Adams Lariviere
Tufts University

How do infants make sense of the continual stream of events they observe day after day? Infants may watch their parents pushing buttons on the microwave, their siblings pounding happily on colorful blocks, their babysitters recoiling as a bee buzzes by, and their televisions showing Ernie gazing fondly at his rubber ducky. How do infants know which objects are OK for play and which actions are worth repeating? In order to move sensibly from observation to action, infants have to understand at some level the goals or meaning behind what they see others doing.

How then do infants access others' intentions? One important clue that infants may rely on is gaze—where a social partner's visual attention is focused (e.g., Phillips, Wellman, & Spelke, 2002; Woodward, 2003). Gaze cues, according to Phillips et al. (2002), are only one of several behavioral cues that infants may use in combination to infer intention in action. Changes in body posture and facial and vocal displays often co-occur with changes in gaze direction when a person intends to act on an object. For example, when big sister intends to smash her hammer down on the orange block, she looks at the orange block (but not the green one); she might smile once she has her eyes on it and then hoot in triumph as she swings the hammer down. Are young infants able to pull these different pieces of information together to help them make sense of other people's behaviors and to help them make decisions about their own behaviors?

Researchers have demonstrated that one-year-olds can use a person's gaze to locate interesting objects, and slightly older infants can use gaze to learn which of two objects a person is labeling (e.g., Baldwin, 1993; Butterworth & Cochran, 1980; Corkum & Moore, 1998). Others have shown that one-year-old infants are beginning to understand gaze as behavior that connects the gazer and the object (Woodward, 2003) and to use gaze cues and emotion cues to make predictions about what a person is likely to do next (Phillips et al., 2002). The accumulation of evidence suggests that, by the end of the first year, infants are beginning to use gaze cues to make predictions about others' intentions.

The work described in this chapter extends these findings by examining how infants use gaze to acquire additional information about objects and how they then apply that information to their own actions. By paying attention to where a person is looking and to how the person appears to feel, infants may be able to draw inferences about whether to select or avoid particular objects. By paying attention to where a person is looking as the person is acting on an object, infants may be able to draw inferences about whether an action is necessary to get that object to work. In this chapter we will explore the tools infants need in order to build an understanding of other people's actions and emotional reactions, and we will examine how infants put these tools to work.

MAKING CONNECTIONS BETWEEN EMOTIONAL SIGNALS AND GAZE

Phillips et al. (2002) used a visual habituation-dishabituation procedure to show that one-year-old infants can use information from an adult's direction of gaze and emotional expression to predict action. When an adult behaved inconsistently by looking and smiling at one object and then seconds later picking up a different nearby object, 1-year-old infants looked longer than when the adult behaved consistently. Phillips et al.'s study is one example of several recent studies that have focused on how infants use others' behaviors to draw inferences about intentions or to make predictions about future behaviors (e.g., Brooks & Meltzoff, 2002; Meltzoff & Brooks, 2001; Woodward, 1999, 2003). At the same time that infants are drawing connections between actions, emotion cues, and gaze cues in order to make sense of other people, they are using this same behavioral information to make decisions about how they themselves should act.

Several laboratories have recently demonstrated that infants between the ages of 12 and 14 months appreciate the object-focused nature of emotional signals (Moses, Baldwin, Rosicky, & Tidball, 2001; Mumme & Fernald, 2003; Repacholi, 1998). Using different methodologies, these researchers have found that 12- to 14-month-old infants not only paid attention to where an adult was looking as she expressed an emotion, but also applied this information to their own actions. If the adult was looking at, for example, a red novel object and reacting negatively towards it, infants in these studies were likely to avoid that red object and instead play with another nearby novel object that had not been the target of the negative emotion. These recent studies have refined the standard infant social referencing procedure in order to show that infants are indeed making the link between the communicative signal (i.e., the emotional reaction) and its specific referent (i.e., the novel object).

During the last several years, our laboratory has been extending the work by Mumme and Fernald (2003) in order to discern the age at which infants are first capable of making this object-emotion link, the robustness of this link, and the skills or tools underlying this ability. In order to set the stage for our recent work, we will briefly describe the original work by Mumme and Fernald.

In the traditional social referencing procedure, experimenters place infants in a situation likely to elicit uncertainty or wariness (e.g., Klinnert, 1984; Sorce, Emde, Campos, & Klinnert, 1985; Walden & Ogan, 1988). For example, infants have been placed at the edge of a step-deep visual cliff or have been confronted with novel, noise-making toys. In these studies there is always another adult in the room, either the infant's parent or a friendly experimenter. Only when the infant turns toward the adult, does the adult express an emotional reaction about the ambiguous event. In contrast, the infants in Mumme and Fernald's study were passive onlookers to the events. The novel objects used in the study were unfamiliar and interesting, but not threatening (comparable to electrical outlets and oven knobs in the home). These objects were not likely to generate feelings of uncertainty or wariness. Infants were not expected to seek out information about the objects; instead, an emotional appraisal was imposed on infants. (This is also comparable to the situation at home when a father goes on full alert as his infant tries to insert a fork into the electrical outlet.) In the Mumme and Fernald study, an actor on television delivered the emotional message. Specifically, 10- and 12-month-olds were shown a video recording of an actor directing her attention to one of two novel objects and then responding in an affectively neutral, negative, or positive manner. As soon as the video clip ended, the infants were allowed to interact with the objects. Each session began with a neutral expression trial, which served as a baseline. Infants' behaviors during the neutral-baseline trial were then compared to their behaviors during the second trial, the emotional-test trial.

Mumme and Fernald (2003) presented three possible outcomes for infants' interactions with the objects. One possibility was that infants would simply ignore or be unable to use the emotional information. In this case, their behaviors during the baseline trial and after witnessing the emotional reactions would look identical. A second possibility was that infants would pick up on the emotional tenor of the scene, but ignore the attentional cues, and react to both the target and distracter objects similarly (the generalization hypothesis). For example, if the actor displayed negative emotion, infants would generalize this negative information to the two salient objects in the scene and would subsequently avoid contact with the target and the distracter, alike. A third possibility was that the infant would apply the emotional information to only the object that was the focus of the actor's attention (the referential specificity hypothesis). In this case, the infant would make the link between the emotional reaction and the object by using the attentional cues of gaze direction and head turn. The infants would then play more with the target in response to positive messages and less with the target in response to negative messages, but behavior toward the distracter object would be unaffected. We would like to propose a fourth possibility that Mumme and Fernald did not consider. It is also possible that infants might follow the attentional cues of the actor, but ignore the emotion. We will refer to this as the attention hypothesis. In this case, one would expect the infant to link the attentional cues with the target object and to interact with that object more, regardless of the emotion associated with it. Woodward (2003) has shown that gaze is a compelling attentional signal. The 12-month-olds in her study looked at the object that was the target of the actor's gaze twice as long as the other object. Similarly, in our studies combining gaze and emotion cues, the actor's gaze could be the more powerful signal. If infants were drawn to the target object by the actor's gaze and yet failed to pick up on the emotional cues, we would expect infants to interact with the target object more than the distracter, regardless of emotion condition.

Mumme and Fernald also described the emotional contagion hypothesis, which has to do with changes in the infants' mood state rather than changes in infants' interactions with the objects. If infants experience emotional contagion, they should respond to positive signals with more positive affect overall and to negative signals with more negative affect overall. It is important to note that experiencing emotional contagion does not preclude an infant from responding with referential specificity. An infant could experience a negative feeling state in response to the actor's negative emotional reaction and still pay attention to where she is looking in order to understand that the negative emotion is about the target object. This is the same kind of response as we might see in an adult, who might startle in response to a friend's scream upon seeing a mouse in the kitchen, but still understand that the scream was about the mouse. We elaborate on this point because in earlier studies of infant social referencing, researchers often conflated the ideas of "generalization" and "emotional contagion" by using the construct of mood modification or mood induction (e.g., Hornik, Risenhoover, & Gunnar, 1987; Walden & Ogan, 1988). However, these constructs are distinct. Referential specificity and generalization concern infants' ability to use another's attentional focus as a cue to reference in emotional communications. Emotional contagion involves infants' ability to pick up on and match another's emotional state.

Mumme and Fernald (2003), in fact, found evidence for both referential specificity and emotional contagion in 12-month-old infants. These infants behaved as if they were able to make the full object-emotion link and as if they were affected by the tone of the actors' emotional reaction. In response to the actor's negative emotion, 12-month-olds showed more furrowed brows and frowns and avoided the object at which the actor was looking. They did not, however, avoid the other object. Interestingly, infants did not differentiate between neutral and positive signals. They touched the target object for similar amounts of time in the neutral and positive trials. It was only during the negative trial that infants avoided the target object. This set of findings suggests that infants were able to perceive the valence of the negative emotional signal and also the direction of the actor's gaze. Most importantly, they were able to put these two pieces of information together to guide their own decisions about whether or not to play with an object.

Equally interesting, 10-month-old infants appeared to gather no information from this encounter with a person on television. They played similarly with the distracter and target objects. Their interactions with the novel objects did not change from the neutral-baseline trial to the emotion-test trial. In other words, 10-month-olds were no more likely to touch the objects after witnessing a positive emotional reaction than after witnessing a negative emotional reaction. They were also no more likely to look distressed while viewing the negative reaction than while viewing the positive reaction.

WHAT'S MISSING FROM
THE 10-MONTH-OLD'S TOOLBOX?

In order to begin to understand why the 10-month-old infants failed to show any consistent response to the emotional displays, we need to consider what lies behind an appropriate object-focused response. First, the infant has to recognize that a person's shifts in gaze and turns of the head are meaningful gestures that usually signal a change in visual focus. Second, the infant has to recognize that a person's emotional expressions also carry meaning and, at the very least, usually signal a positive or negative evaluation or experience. Finally, the infant has to draw the link between the person's attentional gestures, the emotional expressions, and the object or event that is their focus. In other words, the infant needs to realize that when someone is looking at an object and communicating, they are likely to be communicating about that object.

Given the existing evidence, Mumme and Fernald (2003) had predicted that 10-month-olds would not be able to use the actors' gaze to figure out the object-focused nature of the emotional signal. Although numerous studies have shown that infants are sensitive to shifts in gaze in the first months of life (e.g., D'Entremont, 2000; Hood, Willen, & Driver, 1998; Zeifman, Delaney, & Blass, 1996), research on infants' ability to engage in joint attention proper (e.g., their ability to use another's gaze to locate an object in space) suggests that this skill emerges around 10 months of age and gradually becomes fine-tuned during the second year (cf. Butterworth & Jarrett, 1991; Corkum & Moore, 1995). For example, Corkum and Moore (1998) report that most 10- to 11-month-old infants in their study either spontaneously followed the experimenter's gaze to a location in space or could be operationally conditioned to do so during the experimental session. Interestingly, very few infants just one month younger did so spontaneously and many were unable to learn via conditioning to follow the gaze. Similarly, Carpenter and colleagues also report shifts in infants' joint attention skills around this time (Carpenter, Nagell, & Tomasello, 1998). Their study followed children longitudinally from 9 to 15 months. Although every 9-month-old in their sample was capable of joint engagement with the experimenter, it was not until 11 months that these same children could pass a point-following task. Furthermore, it was only at 13 months that a majority of the infants passed a gaze-following task. These findings suggest that the 10-month-olds in Mumme and Fernald's work may have been just at the brink of joint attention. Was this the weak link—the faulty tool—that led to the 10-month-olds' poor performance in the task? Clearly, research that uses an age-held-constant design to compare the "emotion reading" skills of 10-month-olds who follow the gaze in a joint attention task to those who do not could answer this question.

However, the 10-month-old infants in the Mumme and Fernald (2003) study did not just fail to treat the target and distracter objects differently, which would be expected given immature gaze-following skills. These infants also failed to show any consistent responding to the emotion. They did not show more smiles and raised brows in response to the positive displays, nor did they show more frowns and furrowed brows in response to the negative displays. Were the 10-month-olds unable to pick up on the actor's emotion?

It would be surprising to find that 10-month-olds are oblivious to others' emotional reactions. Researchers have shown again and again that even very young infants differentiate among emotional expressions (for reviews see Nelson, 1987; Saarni, Mumme, & Campos, 1998; Walker-Andrews, 1997). An example of a recent study is one by Montague and Walker-Andrews (Montague & Walker-Andrews, 2001), which showed that 4-month-old infants both discriminate between emotional expressions and respond differentially to them. These researchers embedded sad, anger, and fear faces in a peekaboo game. After playing a few rounds of the standard peekaboo game using a happy face and voice, the experimenter emerged with a non-standard facial and vocal expression. The 4-month-olds responded to this change. As compared to their responses to the happy peekaboo expressions, infants responded to the sad peekaboo expressions with increased interest and surprise, more affect lability, and greater overall expressiveness. They responded to the fear peekaboo expressions with longer looks to the experimenter, increased interest and surprise, and greater overall expressiveness. Finally, infants responded to anger peekaboo expressions with longer looks to the experimenter, increased interest and surprise, and greater overall expressiveness. Although infants looked longer in both the fear and the anger conditions, their patterns of looking were distinct across the eight trials. This research demonstrates that, even at 4 months of age, infants are sensitive to others' emotions.

Thus, it seems unlikely that 6 months later, when the infants are 10-months old, they would completely lack sensitivity to emotional signals. We have now begun to take a closer look at 10-month-old infants' emotion processing skills. What tools are in the 10-month-old's emotion understanding toolbox and which ones still need to be picked up? As previously mentioned, the likely candidates are (1) the ability to follow attentional cues such as gaze shifts and head turns to specific spatial locations, (2) a sensitivity to emotional signals, and (3) the ability to put these two pieces of information together to connect an emotion with the thing that elicited it.

As a first step in answering this question, we tested whether the presentation medium influenced infants' ability to process emotional information (Mumme, DiCorcia, & Wedig, submitted). Was the failure of the 10-month-olds an artifact of Mumme and Fernald's televised procedure? In other words, is it the case that 10-month-olds are able to respond appropriately to object-focused emotional signals, but that they are simply unable to gather information from televised presentations? This seemed like a reasonable possibility given that other researchers have shown that infants' ability to imitate televised actions consistently lags behind their ability to imitate live actions (Barr & Hayne, 1999). In order to test whether this might also be true for infants' ability to process emotional information, we presented the emotional messages live, rather than on television.

As in the original work, infants began the session with a neutral-baseline trial, which was then followed by either a positive or a negative emotion-test trial. Each trial consisted of a brief presentation period (10–12 s) and a 30-second play period. The primary difference between the original study and the new study was that a female experimenter presented the emotions live, rather than via television. She sat at a table across from the infant. A tray with two objects slid from behind a curtain and rested in front of the experimenter. Once the experimenter had the infants' attention, she looked at the target object and delivered the emotional signal. The emotional display contained both facial and vocal cues. The vocalizations were simple descriptions of the novel objects, which did not contain any affect-laden words. For example, in response to a blue spiral letter holder, the experimenter said, "Hmm. Look at that. It's blue. It has four legs. Hmm. Look at that." The experimenter used the same description across emotion conditions. After delivering the neutral or emotional messages, the experimenter pushed out the tray so the objects were within the infants' reach.

We found that live presentations did not completely resolve the poor emotion processing observed in 10-month-old infants. Data from this live emotional signaling study suggested 10-month-olds' shortcomings in the earlier study resulted from a combination of limitations of the televised presentations and infants' own cognitive limitations. As shown in Figure 7–1, 10-month-olds paid attention to the live experimenter when she delivered the emotional messages, especially the negative message.

They looked at her longer during the emotion presentations than during the neutral presentations. The infants' expressions of negative affect also in-

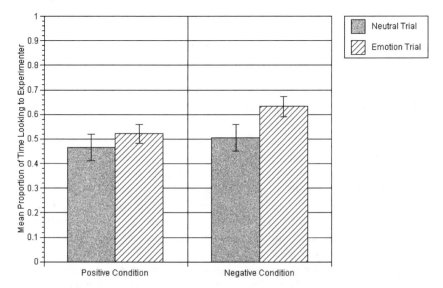

FIGURE 7–1.   Changes in time 10-month-olds spent looking at the experimenter while she delivered live neutral and emotional messages.

creased in response to the live negative messages. However, as Figure 7–2 reveals, 10-month-olds still failed to connect the experimenter's message to the object at which she was looking. Although there was a lot of variability in how much time individual infants touched the objects, overall their interactions with the target and distracter objects were similar across the neutral baseline trials and the emotion test trials. This pattern of results indicates that the 10-month-olds were sensitive to the emotional tenor of the message, but not its object-focused intent. Thus, even when the attentional and emotional information were presented live, 10-month-old infants were unable to connect the experimenter's gaze and emotion cues to a specific object.

We suspect that, at 10 months, infants still lack the skills necessary to recognize the full communicative potential of an emotional expression. They are not able to identify the referent of interest and, thus, do not regulate behavior in accordance with the information provided by the emotional message. Picking up the gaze-following tool for use in triadic interactions will certainly put 10-month-olds that much closer to making the object-emotion link in our studies. However, researchers investigating young infants' skills in other types of triadic interactions suggest that gaze-following might not be the only

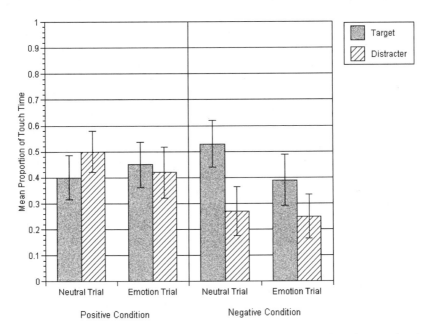

FIGURE 7–2.   Mean proportions of time 10-month-olds spent touching the stimulus objects after witnessing live neutral and emotional messages. (Note: There are no significant differences across trials or conditions.)

tool missing from the box. Woodward (2003) has shown that even though 7- and 9-month-old infants were able to follow an actor's gaze to a target toy, they failed to detect a change in the relationship between the looker and the object. In Woodward's work, infants were habituated to an actor gazing at one toy, for example, the bear on the right. During the testing phase, the toys switched sides and infants were presented either with the actor looking in the same direction but at a different toy, or with the actor looking in the opposite direction but at the same toy. The 7- to 9-month-old infants failed to notice that the object that was the target of the actor's gaze changed between habituation and test. In contrast, the 12-month-old infants in Woodward's study both followed the actor's gaze and seemed to appreciate the relation between looker and object. Twelve-month-olds showed a novelty response when, for example, the actor continued to gaze to the right, but switched from gazing at a bear to gazing at a ball. They did not show a novelty response when she switched her direction of gaze in order to continue looking at the same toy. Woodward (2003) documents not simply a change between 9 and 12 months in gaze-following skills, but rather a change in infants' attention to the relation between the person and the object of her gaze. Thus, a lack of attention to the *relationship* between the actor and the target of her gaze might be another tool missing from the 10-month-olds' toolbox.

Findings by Phillips and Wellman (Phillips & Wellman, 2002; Phillips et al., 2002; Wellman & Phillips, 2001) document a similar shift between 9 and 12 months. Their work suggests that infants' awareness of the object-directedness of human reaching emerges around 12 months of age. In their study, 12-month-olds seemed to recognize that reaching actions are goal directed, but 9-month-olds did not (Phillips & Wellman, 2002). When the older infants saw a person behave inconsistently by making an indirect reach (i.e., reach over a barrier that was no longer there), they looked longer than when they saw a person make a direct reach. However, 9-month-old infants failed to dishabituate to the inconsistent event. Phillips and Wellman (2002) suggest that 12-month-old infants may understand reaches not just in terms of arms and hands—which Woodward (1998) has shown in younger infants—but in terms of the whole person. They seem able to coordinate information about an object and information about a person's facial orientation, gaze, and emotional expression. Nine-month-old infants, in contrast, may be starting to pay attention to the whole person, but are still unable to coordinate information about bodies, faces, and objects. This inability to coordinate multiple pieces information in triadic interactions could be another tool missing from the 10-month-olds' toolbox.

At this point in our research, we do not know whether gaze-following is the critical ability that is too immature in the 10-month-old infant or whether it is a limitation at the next level—a lack of attention to the relation between the person and the object of her gaze. Clearly, infants have to be able to monitor a person's attentional focus to identify the target of the emotional display, and they have to understand the connection between where one looks and what one is looking at. However, there may be the additional demand for coordinating three pieces of information that presents its own set of challenges to young infants.

Future studies should assess how infants' gaze-following skills, their understanding of the actor-object relation, and their ability to coordinate multiple pieces of information contribute to infants' emotion processing skills. Moore and his colleagues (Barresi & Moore, 1996; Corkum & Moore, 1995) suggest it is probably repeated experiences in bouts of joint attention in multiple settings that enable infants to build up an understanding of the looker-object relation and, in our work, an understanding of emotional messages that takes into account their referential nature (see also Woodward, 2003). However, in recent work Woodward (in press) suggests that experience in one aspect of social understanding might not generalize to other aspects of social understanding and behavior. Woodward and her colleagues (reviewed in Woodward, in press) have documented relations between specific aspects of social cognition and specific social behaviors. For example, they found significant correlations between infants' understanding of gaze and their engagement in shared attention with their caregiver, but no relationship between gaze understanding and infants' skills at pointing. Thus, an interesting question is what specific kinds of experiences do infants need to understand the interconnection between referential and emotional information. Between 10 and 12 months do infants increasingly have opportunities to observe regularities in others' behavior as others react emotionally to specific events and then engage with, or disengage from, those events depending on the valence of the emotional reaction? Perhaps changes in infants' own interactions with their environments as their motor skills advance from crawling to walking increase their opportunities for witnessing coordinated emotional exchanges (cf. Campos, Kermoian, & Zumbahlen, 1992). In sum, the tools of gaze-following and sensitivity to emotions may be available to the 10-month-old, but it may be only with exposure and practice that infants are able to use them in concert and use them consistently.

A SHAKY SET OF SKILLS AT 12 MONTHS OF AGE

Other on-going work in our laboratory (DiCorcia, 2004; DiCorcia & Mumme, 2003) suggests that 12-month-olds also need more practice with their emotion processing skills. Although several different laboratories (e.g., Moses et al., 2001; Mumme & Fernald, 2003) have shown that 12-month-old infants can appropriately use a communication partner's direction of gaze and accompanying emotional expressions, we are finding that the 12-month-olds' skills are still quite fragile. At 12 months, infants are clearly able to rely on emotional information to help them form preferences for objects and to select some over others to explore. When that information is available, one-year-olds are pretty good at using it. But how robust is their understanding of emotional information? Are infants able to store it and retrieve it later, so that they can use it again when confronted with the same situation in the future?

Let's return to the example of the infant and the electrical outlet. The outlet itself looks interesting; it is a different color from the wall, it has holes in it, and grown ups are often sticking things into those holes. As the infant heads for the outlet with the fork in hand, her father shouts out, "No! Don't Touch!" in an alarmed voice. Then the father picks up the infant and places her in another room to play with toys. We would expect, given the data from recent studies (Moses et al., 2001; Mumme & Fernald, 2003; Repacholi, 1998), that the infant would make the immediate connection between the warning and the outlet and would avoid the outlet. But, what happens a little while later, when the infant is back in the living room with the electrical outlet? Will she remember her father's warning about the outlet (referential specificity hypothesis)? Will she avoid objects in the living room altogether (generalization hypothesis)? Will she not remember anything and approach the outlet again without hesitation? Or, perhaps even worse, will she remember that her father had really paid a lot of attention to that outlet and, thus, make a beeline straight for it (attention hypothesis)?

These are the questions we are attempting to answer in an ongoing series of studies. We know from research on infant memory that infants have good "procedural" memories for motor movements and action sequences they themselves perform. Infants as young as a few months old can remember an action sequence after a delay (e.g., Greco, Rovee-Collier, Hayne, Griesler, & Earley, 1986; Rovee & Fagen, 1976). Research on infant imitation has shown that 9-month-old infants remember modeled actions after a one-month delay, and 10-month-olds remember modeled actions after a 6-month delay (Carver & Bauer, 2001). Moreover, in studies of deferred imitation, in which infants do not have the opportunity to act on the object before the delay period, infants similarly show robust memories for actions (Meltzoff, 1988a, 1988b). Meltzoff showed that 14-month-olds remembered the demonstrated action for 4 months when the demonstration was live and for at least 24 hours when an actor on television presented the demonstration.

In order to test whether infants have similar lasting memories for emotional events, DiCorcia and Mumme (2003) used a passive social referencing paradigm similar to the procedure used by Mumme and Fernald (2003). Once again, during the first trial, 12-month-old infants watched a video recording of an actor reacting to one of two objects in a neutral manner. When the presentation ended, the infant had a chance to interact with the objects. The change in procedure from Mumme and Fernald's (2003) study occurred in the second (emotion-test) trial. Instead of letting infants play with the objects immediately, the experimenters introduced a 15-minute delay between the presentation and the play period. Infants watched the positive or negative emotion presentation as before, but as soon as the presentation ended, infants were removed from the testing room for a 15-minute break with their caregivers and an experimenter. After the delay, infants returned to the testing room and were then allowed to interact with the objects. Thus, similar to deferred imitation studies, infants did not interact with the objects until after the delay.

Our primary question was how infants would respond to the objects after the delay. If they remembered the emotional reaction, they should use it to guide their interactions with the objects and avoid the object that was the target of negative emotion, as infants had under the immediate conditions in the Mumme and Fernald (2003) study. However, we predicted that infants would remember only half of the situation. Specifically, we predicted the infants would remember only the actor's attention to the target object and would touch that object more despite it being the target of a negative emotional reaction.

Why did we make such a prediction? Mumme and Fernald (2003) found that infants responded with referential specificity and, at the same time, seemed to experience emotional contagion. In their study, infants in the negative condition not only touched the target less, but also showed more negative affect during the emotion trial. Mumme and Fernald proposed that infants might have avoided the negative object because it became associated with their negative affective state. In other words, the actor's attention to the target object made that object more salient, the actor's negative message created a negative affective state in the infant, and, ultimately, the salient object and the negative state became associated. This association may have led infants to avoid the object, because they were still in the negative state when the objects were presented.

In contrast, infants in the memory study would probably not be experiencing negative emotion when they interacted with the objects after the delay. During the delay period, we expected infants would experience other emotions. In particular, we encouraged infants to play happily with their caregivers in the waiting area during this break. Consequently, when infants returned to the testing room, we expected their negative state to have dissipated. This would make difficult the task of resurrecting the negative valence of the message to guide their behavior. In order to form a memory in this task, the infant must remember not only of the actor's focus of attention and the novel objects but also of the actor's emotional state. Unlike an object, one cannot touch and manipulate an emotional state. Although the emotional component of the actor's reaction is important, it is intangible, and we predicted its salience would fade during the delay and it would be forgotten. Thus, infants may fail at this task not because they lack long-term memory capabilities in general, but rather because of the complexity of remembering the objects, the actor's attentional focus, and the emotional information.

The findings from our first study of 12-month-olds were along the lines of what we originally predicted (DiCorcia & Mumme, 2003). Upon seeing the objects after the delay, infants acted as if to say, "Hmm . . . there was something special about this one" (see Figure 7–3). This pattern of results supports the attention hypothesis: infants touched the target, and only the target, more after witnessing the negative reaction. The infants' behavior suggested that they forgot the actor's emotional message and instead remembered the focus of the actor's attention. However, this result must be interpreted with some caution. As shown in Figure 7–3, the mean touch value for the baseline target object was lower than expected. (In past studies, baseline levels of target and distracter touch have been nearly identical.) On the one hand, given this low level of touching during the baseline trial, target touch may have had nowhere to go but up. On the other hand, because all objects were counterbalanced across trials, there is no obvious explanation for a floor effect, so the significant increase in infants' target touch after witnessing a negative reaction may represent a real effect.

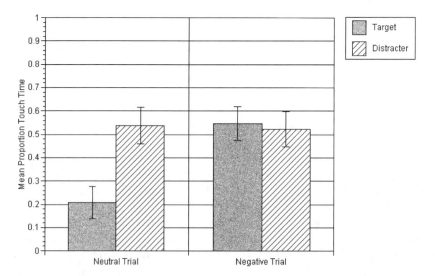

FIGURE 7–3.   Mean proportions of time 12-month-olds spent touching the stimulus objects in the first memory for emotional messages study.

The findings from this study suggest two possibilities. The first possibility is that 12-month-olds may not be able to remember emotional messages after a delay. Although infants this age are able to use another's emotions to guide their behavior, this ability may fade over a short period of time. If this is the case, it is no wonder the infant heads for the electrical outlet when given the chance. She has forgotten that it is something to avoid. The second possibility is that 12-month-olds may be able to remember emotional messages, but our paradigm posed too many other challenges. The infants needed to recognize the emotion, follow the actor's gaze, connect the emotion to the object, and finally remember everything over a short delay in which infants experienced other emotions. If the infants' skills at linking emotional messages with their intended referents are still fragile, they may need additional help to remember the information. For example, father's messages about the electrical outlet may need to be stronger and repeated many times. We will consider these possibilities.

First, do the 12-month-olds just not remember emotional messages? Data from another recent study of infants' memories for emotional messages suggest the answer could be yes (Hertenstein & Campos, 2004). Hertenstein and Campos tested 11- and 14-month-old infants and found that the older infants were able to remember an emotional message after a 1-hour delay. These infants avoided the object the experimenter had reacted to with disgust. However, the younger infants did not seem to remember. Just like the 12-month-olds in our study, the 11-month-olds in their study failed to use the emotional information to regulate their interactions with the objects. Only when the delay was very short (3 min), did 11-month-olds respond to the disgust reaction: they played less with both objects overall. On the one hand, findings from these two studies suggest that perhaps the ability to remember emotions does not develop until sometime after 12 months of age. On the other hand, this conclusion does not fit with the findings from other studies on infant memory. Infants as young as 2 months old can remember to kick a mobile after a 24-hour delay (Rovee & Fagan, 1976), and 12-month-old infants can remember an action sequence for months after the initial exposure (Hartshorn et al., 1998).

If we assume that 12-month-olds have the capacity to remember, then we need to consider other reasons for why they did not remember in our study. As suggested above, infants might need additional help to remember the information if their skills are fragile. In a second study (DiCorcia & Mumme, 2003), we tried to change the relationship between the actor and the object from being an invisible connection (gaze) to being a physical one (touch). This study was identical to the first with the exception of how the actor interacted with the objects. Instead of merely turning her head and emoting towards an object, the actor picked up the target object. Additionally, during the negative trial the actor reacted as if she touched something painful by rapidly dropping the object and withdrawing her hand. These changes were an attempt to create a physical connection between the actress, the emotion, and the object. We found, however, that we were too successful in creating such a connection. As seen in Figure 7–4, infants in both the neutral and negative trials touched the target objects more compared to the distracter objects. The simplest explanation for these findings is that infants merely imitated the actor's behavior. The actor picked up the object, so the infants picked up the object. It seemed as though touching the object led to a greater interest in the object but not to greater attunement with the emotional reaction.

Finally, perhaps the problem is not with 12-month-olds' memories, but with the kind of information we asked them to encode and retrieve. In our studies, the infants saw the emotional presentation only once. Hertenstein and Campos (2004) presented the emotion twice. However, even with two repetitions, the 11-month-olds in their study still did not remember the emotional message. Perhaps a greater number of repetitions is need to solidify younger infants' memories for emotional message. Of course, in addition to repeating the emotional message, there may be other ways to make the emotional message itself more salient.

The classic experiment by Watson and Rayner (Watson & Rayner, 1920) showed that Little Albert remembered the conditioned emotional response for months after the initial exposure. In this study, the researchers used a loud

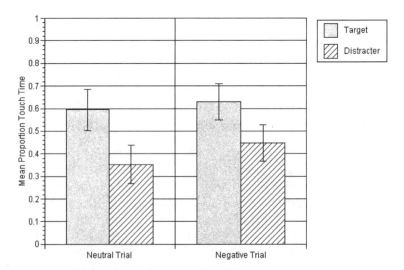

FIGURE 7–4. Mean proportions of time 12-month-olds spent touching the stimulus objects in the second memory for emotional messages study.

noise to elicit distress. During the first day of testing, when Little Albert was 11 months old, he was exposed to a white rat and loud noise pairing only twice. After a week delay, Little Albert acted timid at first sight of the white rat, as well as anything resembling the white rat. Although the data in our studies on infants' expressions of affect suggest that the infants "caught" the actor's emotion, perhaps the actor's emotional reactions were not strong enough to elicit a comparably strong emotional reaction in the infants themselves. The emotional messages in DiCorcia and Mumme (2003) were presented via video. Although Hertenstein and Campos (2004) used live, rather than videotaped presentations, their presentations were similar in intensity to ours. In neither study were the actor's emotional reactions as startling as the gong in Watson and Rayner's work. The personal experience of distress may have solidified Little Albert's memory for the negative associations with the white rat. If infants are given more information at encoding, they might succeed at our task. Stronger messages and more salient targets might be additional external supports young infants need to bolster their somewhat shaky emotion processing skills.

Some tools, such as enhancing the emotional and attentional information, we can provide to help infants remember. However, there are other skills that infants may bring to the task to help themselves. Language is another tool infants add to their toolbox around their first birthdays. Once infants begin to label objects, they have access to a new tool to help with encoding and retrieval of information. As others have suggested (Carpendale & Lewis, 2004), language facilitates development by giving children new means of engaging with others, trying out new concepts and reflecting on information, among other things. We are currently examining the role of language acquisition in infants' memory for emotional messages.

The studies discussed in this section show that the ability to follow gaze is an important tool in emotional communication. It plays a role in the emergence of social referencing and other emotion processing skills at the end of the first year. However, gaze-following is only one of many tools necessary to be a competent processor of emotional information. In addition, the ability to use others' gaze in emotional exchanges is not an all-or-nothing skill. This skill appears to emerge at around 1 year of age, but infants need experience and practice with it to become fully proficient.

As they experiment with how others' gaze works, infants undoubtedly discover that gaze-following is a tool that can be applied to many different tasks. In another series of studies, we have asked whether infants also rely on a partner's gaze and accompanying expressions to help them assign meaning to actions and select some over others to imitate (Adams Lariviere, 2003; Adams Lariviere, Sidman, Mumme, & Bushnell, 2001).

THE ROLE OF GAZE CUES IN MAKING
SENSE OF ACTION SEQUENCES

Let's return again to the example of the father, his daughter, and the electrical outlet. By now the father has discovered his daughter is just not going to mind his alarming messages about the electrical outlet, so he decides to take a different tack and distract her with some music. The father gets out the Fisher-Price tape player. He sets it next to his daughter, straightens the tape player, scratches his nose, picks up a tape, and inserts it into the player, brushes some lint off the top of the player, sneezes, and pushes the play button. Now the music starts, after which the father picks up a cup, adjusts the volume of the tape player, and carries the cup over to the counter. With such a scenario, we would not be surprised if later in the day the baby inserted a tape and started some music for herself. But given this stream of events, how did she know which actions were the crucial ones to reproduce? The baby needs to have some way of segmenting the stream of events into those that are necessary to make the tape player work and those that are not.

Infants must bring to the table an array of tools in order to determine which actions are necessary to successfully complete a task. Because it is not necessary to replicate every action they observe, such as a dog barking in the background or the father scratching his nose, infants must somehow decide which aspects of the display deserve their attention and which actions are necessary to reproduce the result. How do infants do this? There are a variety of tools infants may use to make sense of complex streams of behavior. Of course, one set of tools is likely to include skills at using various social cues. The same tools that proved useful for interpreting emotions are likely to be useful for interpreting actions, namely, gaze-following skills and sensitivity to affective reactions. However, there are additional tools that might help infants make sense of actions on objects. These include the ability to detect regularities in human goal-directed actions and the ability to reason about cause and effect (i.e., to understand which actions cause which effects). We will consider these latter tools first and then consider the role of social cues in interpreting actions.

Baldwin and her colleagues have demonstrated that infants are tuned in to the basic structure of intentional actions (Baldwin, Baird, Saylor, & Clark, 2001). When people intend to do something, there is regularity in their behavior. They typically locate with their eyes the object they intend to act on, they move toward the object and use their hands to make contact with it, and they manipulate it. Once they have achieved their goal, they usually release the object. The 10- to 11-month-old infants in Baldwin et al.'s (2001) work were familiarized with a videotaped action sequence, such as a woman picking a towel up off the floor and hanging it up. They were then tested on two different versions of the same sequence with pauses inserted into the action stream. The "completing" test videos paused just as the actor completed an intentional act (e.g., grasped the towel). The "interrupting" test videos paused in the middle of an ongoing intentional action (e.g., as the actor was bending down to grasp the towel). Infants looked longer at the interrupting test sequences, suggesting they detected the violation in the action structure. Thus, one tool available to infants before their first birthdays seems to be an ability to detect structure and organization in everyday intentional actions. The ability to detect structure in action helps put infants on the path to making sense of complex actions. This tool may help the infant eliminate her father's sneeze as being relevant to turning the tape player on. However, it may not be powerful enough to eliminate intentional but irrelevant actions, such as the father scratching his nose or picking up a cup on the floor. Some additional tools are needed to help infants sort out which actions are the important ones for reaching a goal.

One such tool may be infants' emerging understanding of physical causality. That is, infants may apply their knowledge of what actions are likely to lead to effects to the task of sorting out action streams. Brugger, Bushnell and their colleagues (Brugger, 2003; Brugger & Bushnell, 1999; Brugger, Adams Lariviere, Mumme, & Bushnell, submitted) have shown that infants use certain spatial constraints and their ability to reason about cause and effect to help them select actions to imitate. These researchers used an elicited imitation technique in which infants were shown a toy and a two-action sequence (Action 1, Action 2) that led to an interesting effect. For example, one of the toys was a box with a door, inside of which was a bouquet of silk flowers. The appearance of the flowers was an effect infants enjoyed; they were motivated to make it happen again. In Brugger and Bushnell's work, opening the door was always the second action in the action sequence demonstrated by a model. The researchers manipulated the nature and location of the first action in several ways. In some conditions, the first action involved an action directly on the toy, such as undoing a latch. Sometimes this action was necessary, and infants had to do this action in order to make the toy work. For example, they had to undo the latch (Action 1) before they could open the door (Action 2) to see the flowers. Other times, this action was unnecessary. For example, the latch that the model undid was not holding the flower box door down. Instead, it was to the side of the door and not holding down anything. In a third condition, the first action involved doing the same action, but the action was on an object separate from the flower box. And in a final condition, the first action involved the model acting on her own body. For example, the model patted her head three times before executing the second action (e.g., opening the flower box door). After watching the model demonstrate the two-action sequence, infants had an opportunity to reproduce the effect.

Brugger (2003) found that 15-month-olds and 21-month-olds almost never performed the first action if it was directed toward the body. This systematic omission suggests that the infants assumed actions directed to the body are not related to effects occurring on an object. The 15-month-olds seemed to rely on a similar constraint when the first action was on a remote object. They were also likely to omit that action, suggesting that infants tend to rule out actions on objects that are not connected to the object they intend to work. These findings suggest infants may "filter" the stream of events through their emerging knowledge of objects and causality. However, when the actions were on the objects, infants had a more difficult time. They were most likely to reproduce actions that were necessary, but about one third of the infants also imitated the unnecessary actions performed on the object.

In trying to understand why infants might have imitated unnecessary actions, other tools infants might be putting to work in this situation should be considered. Did something else take precedence over the available causal information? As we have noted throughout this chapter, the evidence suggests that infants do not just pay attention to the model's actions; they also pay attention to the model's intentions.

Meltzoff (1995) demonstrated that 18-month-old infants show sensitivity to the intention of the model. In this work, an experimenter demonstrated how to use different toys, and infants had a turn to interact with the toy after each demonstration. One group saw the demonstrator complete an intended act on each object three times. This group imitated the actions when given a turn to manipulate the toy. The other group saw the model try and fail to complete an act three times. Instead of imitating exactly what they were shown, infants in this group performed the actions that resulted in success. In other words, they enacted the model's intended actions rather than her actual actions. These findings indicate that infants are attending to features of the situation that go beyond what the model does to the object. Other aspects of the model's behavior and other aspects of the objects must have clued infants in to what the model intended to do and, thus, on what the infants were "supposed" to do.

In Brugger and Bushnell's work (Brugger, 2003), the demonstration included many clues about the model's intentions. Certainly, at the structural level, the unnecessary actions were part of an intentional action stream (cf. Baldwin et al., 2001). In addition, the model used a variety of social cues to signal to the infant that her actions were important. These social cues included alternating gaze between the infant and the action, acting enthusiastic about doing each action, and orienting her body and hands toward the actions.

Several research groups have begun to investigate the roles of these different social cues in interpreting action sequences. For example, Carpenter and her colleagues manipulated the model's vocal response to completing an action (Carpenter, Akhtar, & Tomasello, 1998). In their study, a model showed 14- and 18-month-old infants how to use several novel objects upon which two different actions could be performed. The model demonstrated how to use the objects by performing both actions each time. However, for one action, the model behaved as though her action was accidental by saying, "Woops!" after performing the action. For the other action, she behaved as though her action was intentional by saying, "There!" after performing it. Even 14-month-olds used these linguistic-affective cues to guide their interactions with the toys. Infants imitated the intentional actions (i.e., those associated with "There!") approximately twice as often as they imitated accidental ones (i.e., those associated with "Woops!"). Thus, infants responded differently when the model behaved as though she meant to do something than when the model behaved as though her action was accidental.

Another social cue that has been embedded in the studies discussed above (Baldwin et al., 2001; Carpenter et al., 1998; Meltzoff, 1995) is the direction of the model's gaze. The model looks where she intends to act. As discussed earlier, gaze direction and action are powerful cues to intention (Phillips et al., 2002). When an actor intends to do something, a shift in gaze usually signals that the action is about to commence. When the actor's gaze has settled on a location, this usually signals the place where the action is likely to occur.

We have recently conducted a pair of studies to isolate the effects of the model's gaze on infants' interpretations of the model's actions. In Brugger and Bushnell's work described earlier, the model deliberately demonstrated both actions for the infants (Brugger, 2003; Brugger & Bushnell, 1999). The model looked at and talked to the infant before modeling each action, and, if the action was on an object, she looked at the object as she acted. These bouts of eye contact and vocalization may have functioned to "frame" the sequence of critical actions for the observing child and may have led the child to assign meaning to particular actions. The model's deliberate demonstrations might have led infants to perceive, "She's doing that action on purpose, and she's doing it for me." These social cues might have signaled to the infant that the action was intentional, that it was important and that they should do it if they wanted the toy to work. Thus, infants may have imitated unnecessary actions, because they were also using their emerging social skills to make sense of the demonstration.

In order to test whether infants do indeed use such social information to interpret the model's actions, we used a variant of Brugger and Bushnell's two-action elicited imitation procedure (Adams Lariviere, 2003; Adams Lariviere et al., 2001; Brugger et al., submitted). As described above, the model showed 14- to 16-month-old infants a two-action sequence that led to an interesting effect, and then infants were given a turn to produce the interesting effect themselves. We manipulated two aspects of the task. First, we manipulated the causal relationship between the first action and the effect. As in the earlier work, for some toys the first action was necessary in order for the effect to occur and for other toys it was unnecessary. Second, we manipulated the social cues provided by the model. In the Attention Bid condition, the model highlighted the first action by looking at the infant and vocalizing toward the infant prior to performing the action. When looking at the infant, the model made statements such as, "Hey! What's this? What can we do with this?" In the No Attention Bid condition, the model looked at the wall across the room and vocalized toward the wall before doing the first action. For example, when looking at the wall, the model's vocalizations included phrases such as, "Wow! It's nice outside. Spring's almost here!" In both the Attention Bid condition and the No Attention Bid condition, the experimenter kept the emotional tone and the phrase length of the vocalization (interjection, short sentence, short sentence) equivalent whether looking at the infant or at the wall.

For three of the four toys, infants engaged in the first action more quickly when the model made a bid for the infants' attention than when she did not. One possibility is that infants were distracted by the experimenter looking at the wall during the No Attention Bid trials. In fact, in more than one quarter of these trials, infants missed seeing the demonstrations of the first action altogether. As it turns out, these infants did follow the model's gaze—they followed it right to the wall. In contrast, only one infant failed to see the first action in the Attention Bid trials. Nevertheless, even in the No Attention Bid trials, when infants did see the first action, they were not as quick to perform it as compared to when an attention bid preceded the first action.

Interestingly, when we examined whether infants looked at the experimenter prior to the demonstration of Action 1, we discovered that they did not look at her very often, even in the Attention Bid condition. More often than not, infants looked at the toy during this part of the trial. Perhaps as infants looked at the toy, they could still detect whether the experimenter was leaning in and looking toward them or whether she was sitting straight up and looking at the wall. Perhaps the experimenter's posture and proximity to the infant in the Attention Bid condition signaled to the infant that she was talking to the infant and marking her next action as something she meant to do for the infant.

Additional analyses revealed that infants were most likely to do the first action first when that action was both necessary and cued with a bid for attention. Infants were least likely to do the first action first when the action was unnecessary and had not been cued. When the model made a bid for attention before demonstrating a first action that was unnecessary, infants were mixed in their responding. About half the infants did the first action first. Responses were similarly mixed when the action was necessary, but had not been cued. Overall, this study showed that, by directing her attention toward the infant before demonstrating Action 1, the model increased the likelihood that infants would do the first action first, even though it was sometimes unnecessary. This suggests infants interpret the model's attention bid, which included directing her gaze and leaning her body toward the infant, as a signal that the subsequent action is purposeful.

In a follow-up study, we attempted to separate the effects of making a bid for attention from the effects of the model looking at what she was acting on. When intentionally demonstrating an action, a model is likely to look to the observer in order to catch his or her attention. We assume this bid for attention signals to the observer "watch this." This was part of the model's deliberate demonstration in the original work (Brugger, 2003), and this is what we asked the model to do in the Attention Bid condition of our first study. However, this bid for attention is a much more active gaze cue than the attentional cues that are used in most studies of gaze-following and social referencing. For example, in Mumme and Fernald's (2003) work, the actor simply turned her head and shifted her gaze toward the target object. She did not make an effort to grab the infants' attention.

In our follow-up study, we examined whether infants needed the bid for attention to realize the importance of the upcoming action or whether having the model simply look in the direction of her actions (e.g., look down at the toy before her hands worked the toy) was enough information to signal an intentional act. We used a similar set of two-action toys in this study. Infants were assigned to one of three conditions: Attention Bid, Gaze to Object, or No Demonstration Control. Across the two demonstration conditions, the model's vocalizations and behaviors were similar. Upon seeing the toy, she said, "Wow! What's this? What can I do with this?" She then completed the first action, followed by the second action. She did both actions with clear and deliberate movements. The only factor that varied between conditions was where the model looked before demonstrating Action 1. As in the first study, infants in the Attention Bid group experienced a bid for attention, which included an attempt to make eye contact with the infant and the vocalization, before the model did the first action. Infants in the Gaze to Object group experienced no bid for attention. Instead of looking at the infant, the model looked at the toy and vocalized at the toy. Infants in the No Demonstration Control were simply presented with the toys one by one and given 30 seconds to interact with each toy.

In this study, all infants in the demonstration conditions saw the model perform the first action. Thus, regardless of whether she made a bid for attention first or simply directed her attention to the toy, infants followed the model's gaze to the toy. In contrast to our earlier study, there were no differences between the performance of infants in the Attention Bid and Gaze to Object groups. These infants performed the first action at similar rates and had similar levels of success at operating the toys. The only thing that mattered was whether the infants had seen a demonstration. Infants in the No Demonstration Control performed the first action less frequently and more slowly than infants in the two demonstration groups. Thus, infants' success in the Gaze to Object group was not a result of the toys being so simple that infants could operate them without a demonstration. Instead, the infants' success in this condition suggests that infants did not need a specific bid for attention to recognize the model's action as intentional and worthy of imitation. This is probably because infants' gaze-following skills and their ability to recognize the relationship between the gazer and the object are pretty well established by 13 to 15 months of age (Butterworth & Jarrett, 1991; Woodward, 2003). In the simple and constrained context of this study, infants were probably able to read the intention of the model just because she was looking at the toy (and vocalizing about the toy and engaged in goal-directed actions). Undoubtedly, as activities become more complex, infants probably benefit from bids for attention at critical junctures in the action stream. A pause to make eye contact and regain the infants' attention may help infants recognize the boundaries for the critical actions, especially when these boundaries are less obvious than they were in our recent studies. For example, if the father really wants his daughter to understand that pressing the button is a key step in getting the Fisher Price tape player to work, it would not surprise any of us to observe the father pause, look at his daughter and say, "Watch this!" as he turns his attention back to the tape player button and presses it. As other work suggests, it would also help if, upon completing the button press, the father exclaimed cheerfully, "There! I did it!" or "See! It started!"

Thus, data are accumulating to suggest that infants' ability to interpret others' actions does not just depend on their cognitive skills at processing the action and its effects on an object. Rather, infants' action processing abilities also depend on their skills at using additional kinds of information, such as the inherent structure of intentional actions, the actor's appraisals of the action once it is completed, and the actor's attentional focus as she initiates actions. Infants seem to combine this social sensitivity with their own cognitive appraisals of actions in order to filter and interpret complex event sequences.

CONCLUSIONS

The work discussed here indicates that 12- to 15-month-old infants use others' direction of gaze to interpret object-directed emotional signals and action sequences. Infants appear to use gaze as an important clue to figure out which objects they should avoid and which actions they should do. Although other researchers have found that infants are sensitive to gaze shifts before their first birthdays, our research suggests that it is not until around age 1 that infants are able to put this sensitivity to use.

We have presented this work in terms of the tools infants need to acquire. These include gaze-following; sensitivity to emotional expressions, to the structure of intentional actions, and to body posture and gestures; an understanding of physical causality; an awareness of the relationship between the gazer and the object; and the ability to coordinate multiple pieces of information. There is research evidence suggesting infants have access to and can use each of these tools early in their second year of life. There are some obvious tools whose roles we have not yet examined, such as language. There are also likely to be some other tools that we have not yet discovered. Piaget emphasized the study of children's failures to understand their thinking. It seems here, too, we are likely to reach a deeper understanding of how infants make sense of other people's behaviors by investigating infants' failures. Why do 10-month-old infants not respond appropriately to emotional messages about events in their environments? Why do 12-month-old infants have a hard time remembering emotional messages? Why do 15-month-old infants imitate unnecessary actions? There are undoubtedly some skills underlying these abilities that we have not yet identified. However, having all the necessary tools in one's toolbox is not the end of the story. Just like with real tools, one needs practice to become good at coordinating and selecting among them. It is probably the case that infants need practice with these emotion-reading and action-reading tools to become proficient users. They get this practice as they watch over and over again their parents pushing buttons on the microwave, their siblings pounding happily on colorful blocks, their babysitters recoiling as a bee buzzes by, and their televisions showing Ernie gazing fondly at his rubber ducky.

REFERENCES

Adams Lariviere, L. (2003). *Infant imitation: The role of teacher cues and novel object properties*. Unpublished masters thesis, Tufts University, Medford, MA.

Adams Lariviere, L., Sidman, J., Mumme, D. L., & Bushnell, E. W. (2001). *The effect of a model's directed eye gaze and vocalization on infants' imitation*. Paper presented at the Society for Research in Child Development, Minneapolis, MN.

Baldwin, D. A. (1993). Early referential understanding: Infants' ability to recognize referential acts for what they are. *Developmental Psychology, 29*(5), 832–843.

Baldwin, D. A., Baird, J. A., Saylor, M. M., & Clark, M. (2001). Infants parse dynamic action. *Child Development, 72*(3), 708–717.

Barr, R., & Hayne, H. (1999). Developmental changes in imitation from television during infancy. *Child Development, 70*(5), 1067–1081.

Barresi, J., & Moore, C. (1996). Intentional relations and social understanding. *Behavioral & Brain Sciences, 19*(1), 107–154.

Brooks, R., & Meltzoff, A. N. (2002). The importance of eyes: How infants interpret adult looking behavior. *Developmental Psychology, 38*(6), 958–966.

Brugger, A. E. (2003). *Imitation strategies used by 15- and 21-month-old infants for learning to work novel objects.* Unpublished dissertation, Tufts University, Medford, MA.

Brugger, A. E., & Bushnell, E. W. (1999). *Imitative strategies employed by 15- and 21-month-old infants for learning to work novel objects.* Paper presented at the Society for Research in Child Development, Albuquerque, NM.

Brugger, A., Adams Lariviere, L. Mumme, D. L., & Bushnell, E. W. *Doing the right thing: Infants' selection of actions to imitate from observed event sequences.* Manuscript submitted for publication.

Butterworth, G., & Cochran, E. (1980). Towards a mechanism of joint visual attention in human infancy. *International Journal of Behavioral Development, 3*(3), 253–272.

Butterworth, G., & Jarrett, N. (1991). What minds have in common is space: Spatial mechanisms serving joint visual attention in infancy. *British Journal of Developmental Psychology, 9*(1), 55–72.

Campos, J. J., Kermoian, R., & Zumbahlen, M. R. (1992). Socioemotional transformations in the family system following infant crawling onset. In N. Eisenberg & R. A. Fabes (Eds.), *Emotion and its regulation in early development, New directions for child development, No 55: The Jossey-Bass education series* (pp. 25–40). San Francisco, CA: Jossey-Bass.

Carpendale, J. I. M., & Lewis, C. (2004). Constructing an understanding of mind: The development of children's social understanding within social interaction. *Behavioral & Brain Sciences, 27*(1), 79–151.

Carpenter, M., Akhtar, N., & Tomasello, M. (1998). Fourteen- through 18-month-old infants differentially imitate intentional and accidental actions. *Infant Behavior & Development, 21*(2), 315–330.

Carpenter, M., Nagell, K., & Tomasello, M. (1998). Social cognition, joint attention, and communicative competence from 9 to 15 months of age. *Monographs of the Society for Research in Child Development, 63*(4).

Carver, L. J., & Bauer, P. J. (2001). The dawning of the past: The emergence of long-term explicit memory in infancy. *Journal of Experimental Psychology, 130*(4), 726–745.

Corkum, V., & Moore, C. (1995). Development of joint visual attention in infants. In C. Moore & P. Dunham (Eds.), *Joint attention: Its origins and role in development.* Hillsdale, NJ: Lawrence Erlbaum Associates.

Corkum, V., & Moore, C. (1998). The origin of joint visual attention in infants. *Developmental Psychology, 34*(1), 28–38.

D'Entremont, B. (2000). A perceptual-attentional explanation of gaze-following in 3- and 6-month-olds. *Developmental Science, 3*(3), 302–311.

DiCorcia, J. A. (2004). Memory for emotion: Investigating the long-term effects of social referencing. Unpublished masters thesis. Tufts University, Medford, MA.

DiCorcia, J. A., & Mumme, D. L. (2003). *Memory for emotion: Investigating the long-term effects of social referencing.* Paper presented at the Society for Research in Child Development, Tampa, FL.

Greco, C., Rovee-Collier, C., Hayne, H., Griesler, P., & Earley L. (1986). Ontogeny of early event memory: I. Forgetting and retrieval by 2- and 3-month-olds. *Infant Behavior & Development, 9*(4), 441–460.

Hartshorn, K., Rovee-Collier, C., Gerhardstein, P., Bhatt, R. S., Klein, P J., Wondoloski, T. L., & Wurtzel, N. (1998). The ontogeny of long-term memory over the first year-and-a-half of life. *Developmental Psychobiology, 32*(2), 69–89.

Hertenstein, M. J., & Campos, J. J. (2004). The retention effects of an adult's emotional displays on infant behavior. *Child Development, 75*(2), 595–613.

Hood, B. M., Willen, J., & Driver, J. (1998). Adult's eyes trigger shifts of visual attention in human infants. *Psychological Science, 9*(2), 131–134.

Hornik, R., Risenhoover, N., & Gunnar, M. (1987). The effects of maternal positive, neutral, and negative affective communications on infant responses to new toys. *Child Development, 58*(4), 937–944.

Klinnert, M. D. (1984). The regulation of infant behavior by maternal facial expression. *Infant Behavior & Development, 7*(4), 447–465.

Meltzoff, A. N. (1988a). Imitation of televised models by infants. *Child Development, 59*(5), 1221–1229.

Meltzoff, A. N. (1988b). Infant imitation after a 1-week delay: Long-term memory for novel acts and multiple stimuli. *Developmental Psychobiology, 24*(4), 470–476.

Meltzoff, A. N. (1995). Understanding the intentions of others: Re-enactment of intended acts by 18-month-old children. *Developmental Psychology, 31*(5), 838–850.

Meltzoff, A. N., & Brooks, R. (2001). "Like me" as a building block for understanding other minds: Bodily acts, attention, and intention. In B. F. Malle, L. J. Moses & D. A. Baldwin, (Eds.) *Intentions and intentionality: Foundations of social cognition* (pp. 171–191). Cambridge, MA: The MIT Press.

Montague, D. P., & Walker-Andrews, A. S. (2001). Peekaboo: A new look at infants' perception of emotion expressions. *Developmental Psychology, 37*(6), 826–838.

Moses, L. J., Baldwin, D. A., Rosicky, J. G., & Tidball, G. (2001). Evidence for referential understanding in the emotions domain at twelve and eighteen months. *Child Development, 72*(3), 718–735.

Mumme, D. L., DiCorcia, J. A., & Wedig, M. M. Limitations in 10-month-old infants' emotion processing abilities. Manuscript submitted for publication.

Mumme, D. L., & Fernald, A. (2003). The infant as onlooker: Learning from emotional reactions observed in a television scenario. *Child Development, 74*(1), 221–237.

Nelson, L. A. (1987). The recognition of facial expressions in the first two years of life: Mechanisms of development. *Child Development, 58*(4), 889–909.

Phillips, A. T., & Wellman, H. M. (2002). *Infants' understanding of object-directed action.* Unpublished manuscript.

Phillips, A. T., Wellman, H. M., & Spelke, E. S. (2002). Infants' ability to connect gaze and emotional expression to intentional action. *Cognition, 85*(1), 53–78.

Repacholi, B. M. (1998). Infants' use of attentional cues to identify the referent of another person's emotional expression. *Developmental Psychology, 34*(5), 1017–1025.

Rovee, C., K., & Fagen, J. W. (1976). Effects of quantitative shifts in a visual reinforcer on the instrumental response of infants. *Journal of Experimental Child Psychology, 21*(2), 349–360.

Saarni, C., Mumme, D. L., & Campos, J. J. (1998). Emotional development: Action, communication, and understanding. In N. Eisenberg (Ed.), *Social, emotional and personality development. Handbook of Child Psychology* (Vol. 3). New York: John Wiley.

Sorce, J. F., Emde, R. N., Campos, J. J., & Klinnert, M. D. (1985). Maternal emotional signaling: Its effect on the visual cliff behavior of 1-year-olds. *Developmental Psychology,*
21(1), 195–200.

Walden, T. A., & Ogan, T. A. (1988). The development of social referencing. *Child Devel-*
opment, 59(5), 1230–1240.

Walker-Andrews, A. S. (1997). Infants' perception of expressive behaviors: Differentiation
of multimodal information. *Psychological Bulletin, 121*(3), 437–456.

Watson, J. B., & Rayner, R. (1920). Conditioned emotional reactions. *Journal of Experi-*
mental Psychology, 3(1), 1–14.

Wellman, H. M., & Phillips, A. T. (2001). Developing intentional understandings. In B. F.
Malle & L. J. Moses (Eds.), *Intentions and intentionality: Foundations of social cognition*
(pp. 125–148). Cambridge, MA: The MIT Press.

Woodward, A. L. (1998). Infants selectively encode the goal object of an actor's reach.
Cognition, 69(1), 1–34.

Woodward, A. L. (1999). Infants' ability to distinguish between purposeful and non-
purposeful behaviors. *Infant Behavior & Development, 22*(2), 145–160.

Woodward, A. L. (2003). Infants' developing understanding of the link between looker
and object. *Developmental Science, 6*(3), 297–311.

Woodward, A. L. (in press). The infant origins of intentional understanding. In R. V. Kail
(Ed.), *Advances in child development and behavior.* (Vol. 33). Oxford: Elsevier.

Zeifman, D., Delaney, S., & Blass, E. M. (1996). Sweet taste, looking, and calm in 2- and
4-week-old infants: The eyes have it. *Developmental Psychology, 32*(6), 1090–1099.

8

What Infants' Understanding of Referential Intentions Tells Us about the Neurocognitive Bases of Early Word Learning

Mark A. Sabbagh
and Annette M. E. Henderson
Queen's University at Kingston

Dare A. Baldwin
University of Oregon

Human infants are born ready to learn language. Neonates just hours old show preferences for listening to speech over other similarly complex stimuli (Vouloumanos & Werker, 2004). From as young as they have been tested, young children show evidence that they have tuned into the melodies and rhythms of their native language (Nazzi, Bertoncini, & Mehler, 1998). It is also apparent that these young infants can rapidly isolate meaningful speech sounds (i.e., phonemes) from the speech stream (Kuhl, Williams, Lacerda, Stevens, & Lindblom, 1992; Werker & Tees, 1984). By 8 months of age, children's developing facility with these sounds becomes fodder for powerful statistical learning skills that, along with other kinds of information, enable children to group these sounds into words (Johnson & Jusczyk, 2001; Saffran, Aslin, & Newport, 1996; Thiessen & Saffran, 2003).

The cognitive and neurocognitive bases of some of these early emerging speech-processing competencies are becoming increasingly well understood. For instance, recent innovative neuroimaging work with infants suggests that children's early sensitivities to speech sounds may be attributable to very early emerging neural specializations within the left temporal lobes (Dehaene-Lambertz, Dehaene, & Hertz-Pannier, 2002). Intriguingly, these left temporal regions appear to be isomorphic with those shown to be especially sensitive to speech processing in adults (Vouloumanos, Kiehl, Werker, & Liddle, 2001). These findings complement recent studies that have used event-related brain potential (ERP) techniques to characterize the time course and neural regions associated with discriminating speech sounds in early infancy (Cheour et al., 1998).

Infants' early abilities to extract the formal and structural characteristics of the ambient linguistic stream are absolutely critical to language learning; without these fundamental abilities, language learning would never get off the ground. Yet, these sensitivities, in and of themselves, do not bestow language with communicative power. The transition from a sensitivity to structural characteristics to appreciating meaning in language has its start with children's abilities to map words to referents. Fortunately, most children show just as much facility with this step as they do with the ones that came before. Between the ages of 18 months to 5 years, children typically acquire an average vocabulary of approximately 10,000 words—an average of 7 to 9 new words a day (Carey, 1978). Not surprisingly, this feat is attained because, as research has shown, children add words to their lexicon with remarkable ease—they require very few exposure trials (Baldwin, 1993; Carey & Bartlett, 1978; Heibeck & Markman, 1987), they do not need to be explicitly taught (Akhtar, Jipson, & Callanan, 2001), and they make few errors along the way.

Unfortunately, not all children show such facility with word learning. For instance, children with autism are severely delayed in vocabulary development (Frith & Happé, 1994). In some cases, they establish inappropriate word-referent links that are difficult to correct (Kanner, 1946). An emerging body of work suggests that the same may be true, although perhaps to a lesser extent, in children who early in infancy acquired damage to the right cerebral hemisphere (Sabbagh, 1999; Bates & Roe, 2001). In these cases of neuropathology, it seems likely that the neural systems critical for word learning are particularly affected. Yet, very little work has been carried out to characterize these neural systems in typically developing infants. The main goal of our chapter is to sketch out a framework for developing a better understanding of the neural bases of infants' word learning.

We take as our starting point a group of experiments showing that infants' early word learning may be guided by their sensitivity to speakers' referential intentions. This sensitivity is made possible, at least in part, by their skill at interpreting others' gaze direction. After briefly reviewing this literature showing that gaze direction and judgments about referential intentions are important for word learning, we turn to the question of how an understanding of the neural bases of gaze direction detection and intention attribution might inform us about the neural systems associated with word learning. Finally, we offer a proposal for understanding how children's rich appreciation of the information conferred by gaze direction may set the stage for rapid encoding of word-referent links by neural systems associated with semantic memory.

WORD LEARNING: A DIFFERENT KIND OF PROBLEM

For many aspects of language development, measurable advances are often characterized as advances in identifying structural regularities that are present in language itself. For instance, in the domain of speech processing, research suggests that from very early on, infants are predisposed to categorically discriminate the building blocks of speech (i.e., phonemes; Kuhl et al., 1992; Werker & Tees, 1984). Then infants' statistical learning skills provide them with a starting place for extracting structural regularities that provide a basis for combining phonemes into words. Importantly, the information necessary to make these linguistic advances in early infancy can be gleaned from the linguistic stream itself—although extralinguistic resources may be helpful (see Jusczyk, Hohne, & Bauman, 1999), it does not seem that they are required for infants or adults (Saffran et al., 1996; Saffran, Newport, Aslin, Tunick, & Barrueco, 1997).

In contrast, no single piece of readily available information is sufficient to drive a reliable inference about how a word is linked with a particular referent. With respect to object-label learning (to which we will confine our discussion), a speaker's use of a particular word in natural conversation (i.e., Here's an *apple*.) does not *in itself* specify a referent. The word could map onto anything including the exciting toy that currently occupies the word learner's attention, the boring piece of furniture in the corner of the room, the whimsical knick-knacks that sit on top of the furniture, or even something that is absent from the immediate scene (Baldwin, 1995). This problem cannot be solved by analyzing the linguistic stream itself. Instead, multi-modal extra-linguistic social information—information about the speaker's gaze direction, tone of voice, body posture, gestures, and so on—needs to be skillfully coordinated in order for word learning to get off the ground.

This general point has two important implications for studying the neural bases of word learning. First, the majority of the research that has investigated the neural bases of language development typically converges on the finding that language is localized to perisylvian regions of the left hemisphere even early in development. Given that this is the neural region most commonly associated with the brain's specialization for language, it seems intuitive to assume that these regions would also perform the computations necessary for word learning. However, this previous research has considered primarily the neural processing of structural characteristics of language (e.g., phonology, syntax). Because word learning cannot rely solely on structural characteristics of language, we might expect neural systems outside of the perisylvian region to be critical to this important task.

A second related implication is that we might not expect that the neural systems associated with word learning to be specific to word learning. Because word learning requires the coordination of multiple sources of information, often across modalities, we might expect that word learning would require the recruitment and coordination of several different neural systems. This point echos recent theoretical work by Bloom (2000, 2004) who argues that word learning is not likely to be a neurocognitively specialized skill, but rather one that involves decoding and coordinating information from various sources to make reliable inferences about how speakers refer to things in the world. With these considerations, we turn now to evidence showing that the coordination of gaze direction and labeling information is crucial to establishing word-referent links.

GAZE DIRECTION AND WORD LEARNING: BEHAVIORAL EVIDENCE

The claim that children have to figure out how speakers specify the referents of their utterances has a long tradition in the word-learning literature. Specifically, we and others (Baldwin, 1991; Baldwin & Tomasello, 1998; Bloom, 1997; Sabbagh & Baldwin, 2005) have argued that children's abilities to impute "referential intentions" to the speaker help them to make reliable judgments about how a word should be connected with a referent. More specifically, we believe that children implicitly assume that language is an intentional act, and that people use words to purposefully refer to things in the world. The important implication of this is that infants understand that speakers specify the targets of their referential intentions. There are several clues that speakers might provide naturalistically that can inform infants about their referential intentions, including body posture, head orientation, voice direction and gaze direction. In naturalistic face-to-face interactions, the information provided by each of these clues is highly redundant—that is, each provides converging evidence for a given referent. For the purpose of simplicity, we will refer to this highly redundant cluster of cues as "gaze direction" because there is some evidence that, although the naturalistic redundancy may be important, infants pay special attention to gaze direction when learning words (Baldwin, 1993).

There is now a large body of research showing that children as young as 16 to 19 months use speakers' gaze direction to learn new words. For instance, Baldwin (1991) presented 16- to 19-month-old infants with a novel word in one of two conditions. In the "follow-in" condition, she presented the label while looking at a novel toy on which the child was likewise focused. By contrast, in the "discrepant" condition, she presented the label while peering into an opaque bucket just as the child was focused on a different toy. Two results from this experiment are important. First, in the discrepant condition, infants did not mismap the novel label to the object on which they themselves had been focused at the time of the labeling. This finding shows that simple covariation detection (i.e., simultaneously seeing an object and hearing a word) did not lead to learning. Second, 18- to 19-month-olds consistently linked the novel word with the object that the *experimenter* was attending to when she uttered the label—even though that object was out of view at the time of labeling. In other words, on hearing a novel label, infants spontaneously disengaged their attention from their own object, actively sought information about the speaker's focus of attention, and used that information to guide the formation of a new word-object link.

Additional evidence that children appreciate the importance of gaze direction for word learning also comes from Baldwin and colleagues (Baldwin et al., 1996). In these studies, 18- to 20-month-olds were seated beside an experimenter and presented with a novel toy in one of two conditions. In one condition, an experimenter (who was seated in view of the child and jointly focused on the novel toy) uttered a novel word. In a contrasting condition, an experimenter seated behind a sound-conducting rice paper screen uttered the novel word. From the adult point of view, the novel toy is unlikely to be the target of the speaker behind the screen because the barrier prevented the speaker from seeing that toy. As in the previous studies, speakers in both conditions provided their novel word just as the child was focused on the target toy. Results showed that infants learned words only when the speaker was in view. When the speaker was behind the screen, infants responded unsystematically to comprehension questions. Again, infants respected the importance of gaze direction when learning new words.

Gaze direction is likely not the only cue that infants can use to learn new words (Werker, Cohen, Lloyd, Stager, & Cassosola, 1998). However, research has shown that around the age of 18 months, gaze direction appears to trump other compelling environmental cues in guiding children's early word-world mappings. For instance, it seems possible that "temporal contiguity," using a word and then handing the child a candidate referent, might be a particularly salient cue for word learning. Baldwin (1993b) tested 19- and 20-month-olds to de-termine what happens when gaze direction and temporal contiguity are placed in conflict. In the key "mismatch" condition, an experimenter looked into one bucket, provided a novel label for the object (e.g., "It's a modi!"), but then handed the child an object from a different bucket. Thus, the first object in-fants saw after labeling (which was the object temporally contiguous with the label) was not the object the speaker looked at during labeling. Results showed that infants were not fooled; they still reliably mapped the word to the object the speaker was looking at when she provided the novel label. Thus, gaze direction seems to be more salient to 18- and 19-month-olds than temporal contiguity.

In an equally compelling demonstration, researchers have found that a speaker's gaze direction can override the powerful cue of object salience as a cue during word learning (Baldwin, 1993; Moore, Angelopoulos, & Bennett, 1999). For example, Moore et al. (1999) created a mismatch situation similar to that of Baldwin (1993b) in which gaze direction was pitted against object salience just as a novel label was being provided. Specifically, an experimenter looked at one novel object and provided a novel label, while at the same time a second object (out of the experimenter's view) flashed brightly and moved about. Their results were intriguing. Twenty-four-month-olds showed clear evidence that they mapped the label to the referent the speaker was looking at, and not the salient toy. In contrast, 18-month-olds had more difficulty using gaze direction; they were more likely to map the word to the more salient ob-ject. These findings have been replicated by others, suggesting that children's use of gaze direction as a privileged cue for word learning may not come online until 24 months (Hollich, Hirsh-Pasek, & Golinkoff, 2000). Nonetheless, by the end of the infancy period, gaze direction appears to be the trump cue for establishing word-referent links.

Perhaps the most striking demonstration of children's reliance on gaze direction to learn words comes from a recent set of studies investigating how children establish word-referent links while overhearing adult conversations. In a preliminary set of studies, 2-year-olds were placed in an experimental sit-uation in which they sat by and overheard a conversation in which one adult, in conversation with another, provided a novel label for a novel object (Akhtar, et al., 2001). Importantly, when providing the novel label, the speaker made no explicit attempt to engage the attention of the overhearing child. Yet, when tested later, overhearing children showed clear learning of the word-referent link—impressively, learning was about as robust in the overhearing condition as it was in a control condition in which they were taught a word-referent link directly. More interesting with respect to the current discussion, how-ever, a second set of studies was conducted to investigate how children pull off this impressive feat (Akhtar, 2005). Again, children were placed in the overhearing paradigm as before, only this time, they were given an interesting toy to occupy their attention while the adults labeled objects. Detailed analyses of infants' behavior in this paradigm showed that upon hearing the novel label, children typically disengaged their attention from their interesting toy, oriented to the speaker, and followed her gaze direction to the target object. This demonstration is so impressive because it shows that even when children are not being spoken to directly, they remain sensitive to the importance of speakers' gaze direction when establishing word-world mappings.

Akhtar (2005) notes that this propensity to follow gaze direction in these overhearing situations may speak to the cross-cultural utility of this word-learning tool. Some ethnographic reports suggest that face-to-face infant-child conversations might be relatively rare in some cultures (e.g., Schieffelin & Ochs, 1986). The relative rarity of these conversations has been thought to potentially put children in other cultures at risk for relative delays in language acquisition (Tomasello, 2003). Akhtar's finding demonstrates that the motivation to follow a given speaker's gaze direction to identify the referent of an utterance is robust, even in the absence of face-to-face communication.

NEURAL BASES OF GAZE DIRECTION AND INTENTION DETECTION

Infants' word learning is clearly affected by their ability to use gaze direction to make appropriate inferences about speakers' referential intentions. These findings raise the hypothesis that whatever neural mechanisms are important for decoding gaze direction and making inferences about intentions are important constituents of the neural word-learning machinery. Fortunately, some of the groundwork has been laid with respect to understanding the neural bases of both of these skills in adult systems. We will discuss them each in turn.

Neural Bases of Gaze Direction Detection

Baron-Cohen (1994, 1995) was one of the first to suggest that humans may have a special neural region dedicated to the rapid computation of gaze direction information. Now, there are several lines of evidence suggesting that this may indeed be the case. The first comes from behavioral studies showing that seeing a picture of eyes, even for a very brief period, can trigger a shift of attention independent of conscious awareness (Driver et al., 1999; Friesen & Kingstone, 1998). In an intriguing extension of this work, research with split-brain patients suggests that the attentional shifts induced by eyes are lateralized to cortical mechanisms within the right hemisphere (Kingstone, Friesen,

& Gazzaniga, 2000). Second, neuroimaging studies of face perception that include specific experimental manipulation of eye gaze stimuli seem to suggest that the right middle temporal gyrus is a critical area for processing eyes, and possibly the social information that they carry (Kanwisher, McDermott, & Chun, 1997; Wicker, Michel, Henaff, & Decety, 1998). Finally, the right middle temporal gyrus in humans is hypothesized to be homologous to the superior temporal sulcus (STS) region in the monkey, where single cell recordings have revealed the existence of cells that are specifically sensitive to gaze direction (Perrett & Emery, 1994). When taken together, these findings suggest that there may be a fast, perception-like neurocognitive system that is dedicated to the processing of eye gaze direction in humans, and that this neural system may be located within the temporal lobe of the right hemisphere.

It is noteworthy that in these studies, researchers go to considerable lengths to ensure that neural regions are specifically sensitive to gaze direction. In particular, other kinds of information that often go together with gaze direction, such as head and body orientation, are held constant across critical experimental conditions. This kind of control stands in contrast to the word learning studies in which gaze direction is often provided as a cue to referential intentions along with several other redundant cues. This mismatch raises two interesting questions for research. First, would children learn words on the basis of gaze direction if it were presented without the naturalistically rich and redundant cues that are typically provided? Answering this question would be informative about centrality of the neural systems for gaze direction detection in word learning. Second, how would the neural systems associated with gaze direction respond if eye stimuli were presented in conjunction with information such as head orientation and body posture? It seems possible, given the high degree of naturalistic covariation, that perception and interpretation of these redundant cues may share similar neural mechanisms. We believe that both of these questions are important ones for future research.

Neural Bases of Intention Inferences

Throughout our discussion of the importance of gaze direction for word learning, we have suggested that gaze direction is an important cue that gives information about speakers' referential intentions. We have argued this because there is nothing available in the percept of gaze direction (or associated cues) that obviously signals the conceptual relation between the physical stimulus of the eyes and the psychological states of *seeing*, *attending*, or *intending* that we so readily attribute to others. Instead, these psychological attributions rely to some extent on inference. Baron-Cohen (1995) has suggested that imputing some psychological states may require minimal inference because of their tight ecological relation with gaze direction. That is, gaze direction is usually a highly reliable indicator of what object someone is seeing and the focus of their current attention. Thus, with development, or perhaps with evolution, the link between gaze direction and certain psychological states may be automatically made. In contrast, there is good reason to believe that judgments about intentions would more regularly rely on inference to a greater degree. Simply knowing that a speaker is attending to an object underconstrains any prediction of specific intentions with respect to that object. It is only once subsequent action is taken (e.g., uttering a novel word) that an inference can be made about a particular intention. We argue that this intentional inference is important for children's word learning.

Little work has examined the neural bases of judgments about others' intentions. Instead, the bulk of the work investigating the neural bases of intention has focused on reflecting on one's own intentions during motor control tasks (Blakemore & Decety, 2001). For instance, Lau, Rogers, Haggard, and Passingham (2004) found that when participants attended to their intention to move (as opposed to the motion itself), there was activity in the right dorsal prefrontal cortex and pre-supplementary motor areas. A number of researchers and theorists have suggested that judgments about one's own and others' intentions should share some aspects of neural representation (Barresi & Moore, 1996; Meltzoff & Decety, 2003). Thus, it may well be that these regions are also the critical ones implicated when making judgments about others' referential intentions.

We do know of one study that required participants to make judgments about others' intentions. Intriguingly, their results are not entirely consistent with those shown in the intentional action studies. Brunet and colleagues (Brunet, Sarfati, Hardy-Bayle, & Decety, 2000) conducted a positron emission tomography (PET) study in which regional cerebral blood flow was measured while participants reasoned about others' intentions. That activity was then compared with changes in blood flow elicited while making judgments about physical causality. On the basis of this comparison, the authors concluded that reasoning about intentions was associated with the right medial prefrontal cortex, and not the right dorsal prefrontal cortex shown in the intentional action studies. Although it is just one study, it is noteworthy that the findings of Brunet and colleagues converge well with those shown in studies that have used neuroimaging techniques to study a larger set of theory of mind tasks—tasks in which participants make inferences about a wide range of mental states, including beliefs, desires, and emotions (Frith & Frith, 2001; Gallagher & Frith, 2003; Siegal & Varley, 2002). This convergence supports the possibility that right medial prefrontal regions are important for making judgments about others' intentions.

SUMMARY

When taken together with the previous findings, then, it seems that there might be at least two neural systems associated with the ability to use gaze direction to resolve the referential intentions of a speaker. The first is the neural system located within the right superior temporal gyrus that is associated with making judgments about the attentional state of the speaker through gaze direction. The second is the system that makes judgments about others' intentions, which may be located within the right medial frontal cortex.

Links with Autism and Right-hemisphere Damage

Given that word learning capitalizes on both gaze direction detection and judgments about referential intentions, it stands to reason that if the neural systems supporting either of these skills were compromised, word-learning might be compromised as well. This may be precisely the case in autism. One of the most striking clinical features of autism is abnormal attention to others' eyes (Lord et al., 2000). Recent work using eye-tracking methodologies has shown that when scanning filmed social scenes, individuals with autism appear to systematically avoid looking at the eye-regions of the face (Pelphrey et al., 2002). Beyond this abnormal avoidance of gaze, work by Baron-Cohen and colleagues has shown that even when gaze direction is made particularly salient and clear, individuals with autism are unable to use this information to make appropriate inferences about others' intentions or desires (Baron-Cohen, 1989; Leekam, Baron-Cohen, Perrett, Milders, & Brown, 1997). These findings, and others, have led some to suggest that autism might be characterized by a fundamental neurocognitive impairment in the ability to make use of gaze direction to decode others' intentions.

There is some reason to believe that this impairment in using gaze direction to make judgments about intentions may underlie abnormal word learning in autism. Baron-Cohen, Baldwin, and Crowson (1997) tested children with autism in the discrepant labeling paradigm developed by Baldwin (1991). Recall that in this paradigm, an experimenter utters a novel label while looking at a toy in an opaque bucket just as children are looking at a toy of their own. Typically developing children tested in this paradigm use the experimenter's gaze direction as a cue and resist mapping the novel label to their own toy, and by 18 months, reliably map the novel label to the toy in the bucket. Children with autism show a very different pattern—they reliably map the novel label to their own toy, thereby failing to take into account the speaker's likely referential intentions as indicated by gaze direction. These findings show that for autism, a neuro-developmental disorder in which sensitivity to gaze direction and intentions is known to be impaired, particular kinds of word learning difficulties ensue.

Autism is a developmental disorder in which the neuropathology has not been well characterized (see Abell et al., 1999). A more direct approach to investigating whether word learning is compromised by damage to neural systems associated with gaze direction detection and intentional inference might come from a consideration of infants with acquired right-hemisphere damage. Recall that both the neural substrates for both gaze direction detection and intentional inference are lateralized to the right hemisphere. In groundbreaking work, Bates and her colleagues (Bates et al., 1997; Thal, Marchman, Stiles, & Aram, 1991, see Bates & Roe, 2001 for a review) have consistently found that more severe impairments in lexical acquisition are typically found following right, rather than left, hemisphere damage. Bates and colleagues interpret these findings as evidence that the left lateralization of language is a developmental outcome rather than a developmental starting point. We offer that by understanding the neural bases of the skills that are so important for early word learning, we gain new insight into precisely *why* right-hemisphere damage might affect word learning in particular. Specifically, we argue that pattern may arise because word learning capitalizes on gaze direction detection and intentional inference, both neural systems that are lateralized to the right hemisphere (Sabbagh, 1999).

To date, no one has tested the possibility that individuals with right-hemisphere damage have difficulty perceiving gaze direction or making judgments about others' intentions. Clearly, this research would be an important step in understanding the neural bases of early word learning. Based on the research reviewed above, we offer that one important concern in conducting this research is lesion localization. Typically, the research on language difficulties in infants with right hemisphere damage involves groups that are heterogeneous with respect to the location and extent of the lesion. Based on the data reviewed above, there is some reason to believe that different kinds of right hemisphere damage might have different effects on word learning. For instance, for infants with right-hemisphere damage localized to superior temporal regions, we might expect that there would be difficulties in following eye gaze, and possibly other cues that are informative about others' intentions. In contrast, for infants with damage to more anterior regions of the right hemisphere, we might expect a more global difficulty in making judgments about others' intentions based on any kind of information. Although it is difficult to do, we believe that this research would be a valuable first step in understanding the neural bases of early word learning.

Successful Encoding in Semantic Memory: A Role for Inferences about Intentions

The behavioral evidence establishes that gaze direction is an important cue that gives information about speakers' intentions, and that when the neural systems associated with gaze direction and intentional inference are impaired, there is some evidence that language development is affected in predictable ways. Yet, important issues still remain. One issue of particular importance concerns *how* judgments about gaze direction and intentions might lead to better word learning. That is, what are the neurocognitive mechanisms by which children's word learning is advantaged by their sensitivity to gaze direction and referential intentions? In the remainder of this chapter, we will sketch out a proposal for how this process might be characterized.

We take as our starting place one set of less obvious observations from the research investigating children's use of gaze direction when learning words. In the discrepant labeling paradigm, it is typically found that young children learn words when, and only when, the speaker's gaze direction disambiguates the referent (e.g., Baldwin et al., 1996). Recall that in these situations, the speaker provided a labeling utterance just as children were most interested in a toy of their own. Across these studies, when speakers' gaze direction was either discrepant from their own or not discernable, they did not simply map the novel word to the novel object that occupied their attention. Instead, they showed no evidence for any systematic learning at all. Another way of saying this is that when information about referential intentions was impoverished or absent, semantic encoding was less reliable.

Before proceeding with the implications of this finding, it is important to consider a challenge that has recently emerged in the literature. Specifically, Werker and colleagues (Werker et al., 1998) have shown that children will learn words even when there are no obvious physical cues regarding the speaker's intentions. In their study, 14-month-olds were habituated to a display in which two phonologically dissimilar words (e.g., *lif* and *neem*) were each associated with a distinctive novel object. In the test phase, the referents for each of the words were swapped, and looking times were measured to determine whether infants were surprised by this change. Results revealed that infants were indeed surprised, indicating that children could learn words even in this pared down paradigm that is free of obvious social cues. These findings are similar to those shown by other groups of researchers (i.e., Schafer & Plunkett, 1998; Werker et al., 1998) and provide some evidence against the notion that children require evidence for referential intentions before they establish word-referent links.

There are several reasons to doubt whether these findings truly show that intentions are unnecessary for rapid word learning. First, Baldwin and Moses

(2001) note that even though these situations lack the kinds of information that are typically included when testing infants' judgments about speakers' referential intentions, there is no evidence that these children have not made some kind of intentional inference. Specifically, in these studies, the word and the referent are presented synchronously, 12 times or more. From the adult point of view, this level of covariation over just a few minutes is not likely an accident, and as such, is likely intended by some human agent for some reason. Whether such young children are capable of making judgments based upon this kind of information has not been examined. Second, this number of utterances (or, in learning terms, "training trials") is well above that which is typically required in studies in which clear cues about speakers' intentions are provided (Woodward, Markman, & Fitzsimmons, 1994). Thus, these findings may actually provide indirect support for the importance that children's attention to intentional cues has for establishing reliable word-referent links.

Given that there is good reason to believe that gaze direction and intentional inference lead to increased efficiency in encoding words into semantic memory, an important task is to characterize the neurocognitive bases of this advantage. We argue that a consideration of the factors that lead to successful encoding in semantic memory may provide some insight into the fundamental cognitive mechanisms by which intentions aid in word learning. Furthermore, we believe that the neural bases of successful encoding should also be considered critical constituents of the word learning system, and that their development may be critical in pacing vocabulary acquisition.

Intentions, Attention, and Coherence

Attention

Perhaps one of the most robust findings in the semantic encoding literature is that attention to a stimulus greatly enhances the probability that the stimulus will be encoded into semantic memory. This raises the possibility that one way in which gaze direction could benefit word learning is by heightening infants' attention to particular objects in the world.

There is some reason to think that this might be true. For instance, Hood, Willen and Driver (1998) have shown that 4-month-olds will attend more to a target when that target is suddenly looked at by a cartoon character. Thus, from very early on, young children may be biased to attend specially to things that other people are looking at, which may in turn partially account for why gaze direction leads to superior encoding of word-referent links. This idea is similar to ideas first offered by Tomasello and colleagues (e.g., Tomasello & Farrar, 1986) who argued for the importance of parents' establishing joint attention to promote word learning. However, an important point of difference here is that Tomasello and colleagues focused on the role the parent plays in ensuring that children's attention is on the object being labeled. In contrast, the studies by Hood and colleagues (Hood et al., 1998), and several of the studies by Baldwin and colleagues reviewed herein (e.g., Baldwin, 1991) show that children themselves have the capacity to shift their attention to objects looked at by others.

It is unlikely that this attentional shift provoked by gaze direction detection completely accounts for improved word learning. This doubt comes from the fact that other ways of increasing attention to an object have not been shown to improve word learning. For instance, Baldwin et al.'s (1996) study in which a label was provided by a speaker who was obscured by a rice paper screen included a condition in which the presentation of the label covaried perfectly with the infant's attention to the object. Results showed that when there was such striking covariation, children showed increased attention to the object. Yet, they did not show evidence that they learned the word. Of course, this evidence does not rule out the possibility that attention may still partly facilitate learning novel word-referent links. Given the relative difficulty of the word learning problem, even small enhancements may be important for rapid semantic encoding of word-referent links.

Coherence

A second factor known to affect the extent to which information is encoded into semantic memory is "coherence," or "contextual coherence." Coherence is the term used to describe the extent to which the elements of a given communicative act are interrelated (Holtgraves, 2002). There are two ways in which coherence can be established. The first is from the semantic qualities of the constituents themselves. If the elements within a communicative act are interrelated, then the act is typically judged to have high coherence, and the elements are more likely to be individually remembered. The second way to establish coherence is by explicitly providing a conceptual framework that highlights the non-obvious interrelations between elements. For example, in their classic work, Bransford and Johnson (1972) showed one group of participants a text that was judged to be low in internal consistency, and the constituent propositions in the text were remembered poorly. A second group was shown the same text, but this time the passage had a title that provided a context for establishing the interrelations between elements. Participants in this second group remembered the elements in this passage with little difficulty.

An appreciation of intentions provides the same sort of coherence with respect to understanding the interrelations between actions (Baldwin & Baird,

2001). At a large-scale level, the consecutive acts of mopping a floor, shaking the crumbs out of a toaster and putting dishes in a cabinet might strike a naïve observer as fairly disjointed given that on their surface they have little in common. However, if one is able to attribute a plausible intention to the actor—in this case, cleaning the kitchen—the actions cohere and form a sensible pattern.

Could a similar process be at work to aid in children's word learning? As noted earlier, establishing word-referent links might pose infants with a difficult problem given the fact that the relevant naturalistic covariation data are likely highly noisy. Yet, the bulk of the word-learning research reviewed previously shows that, despite this noisiness, children are able to rapidly learn appropriate word-referent links, avoiding a multitude of possible errors along the way. Thus, it seems that young children have some way of filtering out the noisiness inherent in a word-learning situation and zeroing in on just those events that are most informative. Children's motivation to interpret speakers' utterances in terms of referential intentions may provide just the framework that enables them to establish islands of coherence in a sea of disjointed noise. It seems possible that this, in turn, promotes the rapid and deep encoding of word-referent links.

In some sense, some aspect of contextual coherence may be important for word learning even before 18 months. Intriguingly, it seems that at these earlier ages, coherence necessary for word learning might have a different form. As noted above, coherence can be established both from constituent elements within a given context, or from the top-down influence of a conceptual framework. Work by Hollich and colleagues (2000) shows that at 12 months old, infants learn words best when there are multiple redundant cues as to how a word maps to its referent. It could be that these multiple redundant cues are essential for establishing the coherence necessary for successful encoding at this age. In contrast, by 18 months, infants show the ability to rely solely on gaze direction to establish word-referent links. This development may reflect children's increasing ability to use information that is more selectively associated with speakers' referential intentions as a top-down framework for establishing coherence. In any case, the principle of contextual coherence may provide a way of describing the continuity in word learning from early through late infancy.

Neural Correlates of Successful Semantic Encoding

A considerable amount of research has been investigating the neural bases of successful semantic encoding in adults. One paradigm that has been particularly informative with respect to the present discussion has used event-related brain imaging techniques (such as event-related brain potentials, or event-related functional magnetic resonance imaging (fMRI) to characterize the neural activity present at stimulus encoding that predicts whether a given stimulus will be remembered later (e.g., Buckner, Kelley, & Peterson, 1999; Casasanto et al., 2002; Wagner et al., 1998). Intriguingly, in contrast to the right-lateralization that was shown for neural systems that are important for making inferences about others' referential intentions, these systems associated with memory seem to be lateralized to the left hemisphere. This network includes regions of the left prefrontal cortex, left temporoparietal cortex, and left medial temporal cortex (Buckner et al., 1999).

There are two findings from the developmental neuroscience literature that are particularly intriguing with respect to understanding how these left-lateralized frontal and temporal systems associated with semantic memory may relate to word learning. Specifically, Tucker (1992) reviewed evidence suggesting that around the age of 18 to 24 months, the left hemisphere undergoes a rapid period of growth and maturation, such that the infant begins to show a typical adult-like pattern of left cerebral dominance. Intriguingly, it is also around this time that some researchers report that children's rate of productive vocabulary acquisition accelerates through the so-called vocabulary burst (e.g., Goldfield & Reznick, 1990). It could be that these general left-hemisphere developments affect word learning via the maturation of neural systems associated with successful encoding. Second, research by Mills and colleagues (Mills, Coffey-Corina, & Neville, 1993, 1997) has shown that infant ERP responses to well-known words become more left-lateralized around 20 months. This pattern of lateralization is especially evident for children who have larger vocabularies. Although it is unclear as to whether children's increased vocabulary size is antecedent or consequent to the emergence of anatomical and functional changes, it does provide an intriguing connection between left frontal regions and early word learning.

To date, it is not clear as to the specific nature of the contribution made by left frontal areas to word learning. On the one hand, recruitment of these regions could simply reflect the computations that are required for encoding per se. On the other hand, they might be critical for establishing the conditions that are necessary for encoding. The fact that coherence and encoding tend to go hand in hand in experimental paradigms makes these two possibilities difficult to tease apart. Although it is beyond the scope of this paper to outline how this teasing apart might occur, it is intriguing to note that the timing of left frontal maturation is coincident with children's ability to put gaze direction to work for word learning. This developmental synchrony may suggest that left frontal contributions to word learning reflect the ability to use referential intentions as a top-down conceptual framework for establishing the contextual coherence necessary to promote rapid semantic encoding.

SUMMARY AND CONCLUSIONS

Word learning requires coordinating social information across modalities to make appropriate inferences about how words are associated with referents in the world. Behavioral work suggests that the goal of this coordination is making judgments about others' referential intentions, and that speakers' gaze direction is a prepotent and reliable cue in driving these judgments. Thus, the neurocognitive systems that support word learning are likely to be closely related to those that are associated with processing gaze direction and making inferences about intentions. We argue that by considering the neural bases of word learning in this way, we gain insight into the word learning impairments shown by individuals with right hemisphere damage and autism. Finally, we suggest that judgments about intentions set the stage for rapid and deep semantic encoding of word-referent links via the neural systems that are associated with long-term semantic memory.

ACKNOWLEDGMENTS

Preparation of this chapter was supported by a Discovery Grant from Natural Science and Engineering Research Council of Canada to Sabbagh, and by National Science Foundation grant no. 0214484 to Baldwin. We thank Kevin Munhall for helpful comments on a previous draft.

REFERENCES

Abell, F., Krams, M., Ashburner, J., Passingham, R., Friston, K., Frackowiak, R., Happé, F., Frith, C., & Frith, U. (1999). The neuroanatomy of autism: A voxel-based whole brain analysis of structural scans. *Neuroreport, 10,* 1647–1651.

Akhtar, N. (2005). Monitoring third-party conversations: Learning through eavesdropping. *Developmental Science, 8,* 199–209.

Akhtar, N., Jipson, J., & Callanan, M. A. (2001). Learning words through overhearing. *Child Development, 72,* 416–430.

Baldwin, D. A. (1991). Infants' contribution to the achievement of joint reference. *Child Development, 62,* 875–890.

Baldwin, D. A. (1993). Early referential understanding: Infants' ability to recognize referential acts for what they are. *Developmental Psychology, 29,* 832–843.

Baldwin, D. A. (1993b). Infants' ability to consult the speaker for clues to word reference. *Journal of Child Language, 20,* 395–418.

Baldwin, D. A. (1995). Understanding the link between joint attention and language. In C. Moore & P. J. Dunham (Eds.), *Joint attention: Its origins and role in development.* Hillsdale, NJ: Lawrence Erlbaum Associates.

Baldwin, D. A., & Baird, J. A. (2001). Discerning intentions in dynamic human action. *Trends in Cognitive Sciences, 5*, 171–178.

Baldwin, D. A., Markman, E. M., Bill, B., Desjardins, R. N., Irwin, J. M., & Tidball, G. (1996). Infants' reliance on a social criterion for establishing word-object relations. *Child Development, 67*, 3135–3153.

Baldwin, D. A., & Moses, L. J. (2001). Links between social understanding and early word learning. *Social Development, 10*, 309–329.

Baldwin, D. A., & Tomasello, M. (1998). Word learning: A window on early pragmatic understanding. In E. Clark (Ed.), *The proceedings of the twenty-ninth annual child language research forum* (pp. 3–23). Chicago: CSLI.

Baron-Cohen, S. (1989). The autistic child's theory of mind: A case of specific developmental delay. *Journal of Child Psychology and Psychiatry and Allied Disciplines, 30*, 285–298.

Baron-Cohen, S. (1994). How to build a baby that can read minds. *Current Psychology of Cognition, 13*, 513–532.

Baron-Cohen, S. (1995). *Mindblindness: An essay on autism and theory of mind.* Cambridge: The MIT Press.

Baron-Cohen, S., Baldwin, D. A., & Crowson, M. (1997). Do children with autism use the speaker's direction of gaze strategy to crack the code of language? *Child Development, 68*, 48–57.

Barresi, J., & Moore, C. (1996). Intentional relations and social understanding. *Behavioral and Brain Sciences, 19*, 107–122.

Bates, E., & Roe, K. (2001). Language development in children with unilateral brain injury. In C. A. Nelson & M. Luciana (Eds.), *Handbook of developmental cognitive neuroscience* (pp. 281–307). Cambridge, MA: MIT Press.

Bates, E., Thal, D., Trauner, D., Fenson, J., Aram, D., Eisele, J., & Nass, R. (1997). From first words to grammar in children with focal brain injury. *Developmental Neuropsychology, 13*, 275–343.

Blakemore, S., & Decety, J. (2001). From the perception of action to the understanding of intention. *Nature Reviews Neuroscience, 2*, 561–567.

Bloom, P. (1997). Intentionality and word learning. *Trends in Cognitive Sciences, 1*, 9–12.

Bloom, P. (2000). *How children learn the meanings of words.* Cambridge, MA: MIT Press.

Bloom, P. (2004). Myths on word learning. In D. G. Hall & S. R. Waxman (Eds.), *Weaving a lexicon* (pp. 205–224). Cambridge, MA: MIT Press.

Bransford, J. D., & Johnson, M. K. (1972). Contextual prerequisites for understanding: Some investigations of comprehension and recall. *Journal of Verbal Learning and Verbal Behavior, 11*, 717–726.

Brunet, E., Sarfati, Y., Hardy-Bayle, M., & Decety, J. (2000). A PET investigation of the attribution of intentions with a nonverbal task. *NeuroImage, 11*, 157–166.

Buckner, R. L., Kelley, W. M., & Peterson, S. E. (1999). Frontal cortex contributes to human memory formation. *Nature Neuroscience, 2*, 311–314.

Carey, S. (1978). The child as word-learner. In M. Halle, J. Bresnan & G. A. Miller (Eds.), *Linguistic theory and psychological reality.* Cambridge, MA: MIT Press.

Carey, S., & Bartlett, E. (1978). Acquiring a single new word. *Papers and Reports and Child Language Development, 15*, 17–29.

Casasanto, D. J., Killgore, W. D. S., Maldjian, J. A., Glosser, G., Alsop, D. C., Cooke, A. M., Grossman, M., & Detre, J. A. (2002). Neural correlates of successful and unsuccessful verbal memory encoding. *Brain and Language, 80,* 287–295.

Cheour, M., Ceponiene, R., Lehtokoski, A., Luuk, A., Allik, J., Alho, K., & Naatanen, R. (1998). Development of language-specific phoneme representations in the infant brain. *Nature Neuroscience, 1,* 351–353.

Dehaene-Lambertz, G., Dehaene, S., & Hertz-Pannier, L. (2002). Functional neuroimaging of speech perception in infants. *Science, 298,* 2013–2015.

Driver, J., Davis, G., Ricciardelli, P., Kidd, P., Maxwell, E., & Baron-Cohen, S. (1999). Gaze perception triggers reflexive visuospatial orienting. *Visual Cognition, 6,* 509–540.

Friesen, C. K., & Kingstone, A. (1998). The eyes have it! Reflexive orienting is triggered by nonpredictive gaze. *Psychonomic Bulletin & Review, 5,* 490–495.

Frith, U., & Frith, C. D. (2001). Biological basis of social interaction. *Current Directions in Psychological Science, 10,* 151–155.

Frith, U., & Happe, F. (1994). Language and communication in autistic disorders. *Transactions of the Royal Society of London, B, 346,* 97–104.

Gallagher, H. L., & Frith, C. (2003). Functional imaging of "theory of mind." *Trends in Cognitive Sciences, 7,* 77–83.

Goldfield, B. A., & Reznick, J. S. (1990). Early lexical acquisition: Rate, content, and the vocabulary spurt. *Journal of Child Language, 17,* 171–183.

Heibeck, T. H., & Markman, E. M. (1987). Word learning in children: An examination of fast mapping. *Child Development, 58,* 1021–1034.

Hollich, G., Hirsh-Pasek, K., & Golinkoff, R. M. (2000). Breaking the language barrier: An emergentist coalition model of word learning. *Monographs of the Society for Research in Child Development, 65* (Serial No. 262).

Holtgraves, T. M. (2002). *Language as social action: Social psychology and language use.* Mahwah, NJ: Lawrence Erlbaum Associates.

Hood, B. M., Willen, J. D., & Driver, J. (1998). Adult's eyes trigger shifts of visual attention in human infants. *Psychological Science, 9,* 131–134.

Johnson, E. K., & Jusczyk, P. W. (2001). Word segmentation by 8-month-olds: When speech cues count more than statistics. *Journal of Memory and Language, 44,* 548–567.

Jusczyk, P. W., Hohne, E. A., & Bauman, A. (1999). Infants' sensitivity to allophonic cues for word segmentation. *Perception & Psychophysics, 61,* 1465–1476.

Kanner, L. (1946). Irrelevant and metaphorical language in infantile autism. *American Journal of Psychiatry, 103,* 242–246.

Kanwisher, N., McDermott, J., & Chun, M. M. (1997). The fusiform face area: A module in human extrastriate cortex specialized for face perception. *Journal of Neuroscience, 17,* 4302–4311.

Kingstone, A., Friesen, C. K., & Gazzaniga, M. S. (2000). Reflexive joint attention depends on lateralized cortical connections. *Psychological Science, 11,* 159–166.

Kuhl, P. K., Williams, K. A., Lacerda, F., Stevens, K. N., & Lindblom, B. (1992). Linguistic experience alters phonetic perception in infants by 6 months of age. *Science, 255,* 606–608.

Lau, H. C., Rogers, R. D., Haggard, P., & Passingham, R. E. (2004). Attention to intention. *Science, 303,* 1144–1146.

Leekam, S. R., Baron-Cohen, S., Perrett, D. I., Milders, M., & Brown, S. (1997). Eye-direction detection: A dissociation between geometric and joint attention skills in autism. *British Journal of Developmental Psychology, 15,* 77–95.

Lord, C., Risi, S., Lambrecht, L., Cook, E. H. J., Leventhal, B. L., Dilavore, P. C., Pickles, A., & Rutter, M. (2000). The autism diagnostic observation schedule-generic: A standard measure of social and communication deficits associated with the spectrum of autism. *Journal of Autism & Developmental Disorders, 30,* 205–223.

Meltzoff, A. N., & Decety, J. (2003). What imitation tells us about social cognition: A rapprochement between developmental psychology and cognitive neuroscience. *Philosophical Transactions of the Royal Society of London, Series B, Biological Sciences, 358,* 491–500.

Mills, D. L., Coffey-Corina, S. A., & Neville, H. J. (1993). Language acquisition and cerebral specialization in 20-month-old infants. *Journal of Cognitive Neuroscience, 5,* 317–334.

Mills, D. L., Coffey-Corina, S. A., & Neville, H. J. (1997). Language comprehension and cerebral specialization from 13 to 20 months. *Developmental Neuropsychology, 13,* 397–445.

Moore, C., Angelopoulos, M., & Bennett, P. (1999). Word learning in the context of referential and salience cues. *Developmental Psychology, 35,* 60–68.

Nazzi, T., Bertoncini, J., & Mehler, J. (1998). Language discrimination by newborns: Toward an understanding of the role of rhythm. *Journal of Experimental Psychology: Human Perception and Performance, 24,* 756–766.

Pelphrey, K. A., Sasson, N. J., Reznick, J. S., Paul, G., Goldman, B. D., & Piven, J. (2002). Visual scanning of faces in autism. *Journal of Autism & Developmental Disorders, 32,* 249–261.

Perrett, D. I., & Emery, N. J. (1994). Understanding the intentions of others from visual signals: Neurophysiological evidence. *Current Psychology of Cognition, 13,* 683–694.

Sabbagh, M. A. (1999). Communicative intentions and language: Evidence from right-hemisphere damage and autism. *Brain and Language, 70,* 29–69.

Sabbagh, M. A., & Baldwin, D. A. (2005). Understanding the role of perspective taking in young children's word learning. In N. Eilan, C. Hoerl, T. McCormack, & J. Roessler (Eds.), *Joint attention: Communication and other minds.* Oxford: Oxford University Press.

Saffran, J. R., Aslin, R. N., & Newport, E. L. (1996). Statistical learning by 8-month-old infants. *Science, 274,* 1926–1928.

Saffran, J. R., Newport, E. L., Aslin, R. N., Tunick, R. A., & Barrueco, S. (1997). Incidental language learning: Listening (and learning) out of the corner of your ear. *Psychological Science, 8,* 101–105.

Schafer, G., & Plunkett, K. (1998). Word learning by 15-month-olds under tightly controlled conditions. *Child Development, 69,* 309–320.

Schieffelin, B. B., & Ochs, E. (1986). Language socialization. *Annual Reviews Anthropology, 15,* 163–191.

Siegal, M., & Varley, R. (2002). Neural systems involved in "theory of mind." *Nature Reviews, 3,* 463–471.

Thal, D. J., Marchman, V. A., Stiles, J., & Aram, D. (1991). Early lexical development in children with focal brain injury. *Brain and Language, 40,* 491–527.

Thiessen, E. D., & Saffran, J. R. (2003). When cues collide: Use of stress and statistical cues to word boundaries by 7- to 9-month-old infants. *Developmental Psychology, 39,* 706–716.

Tomasello, M. (2003). *Constructing a language: A usage-based theory of language acquisition.* Cambridge, MA: Harvard University Press.

Tomasello, M., & Farrar, M. J. (1986). Joint attention and early language. *Child Development, 57,* 1454–1463.

Tucker, D. M. (1992). Development of emotion and cortical networks. In M. Gunnar & C. Nelson (Eds.), *Minnesota Symposium on Child Development: Developmental Neuroscience* (pp. 75–128). Oxford: Oxford University Press.

Vouloumanos, A., Kiehl, K. A., Werker, J. F., & Liddle, P. F. (2001). Detection of sounds in the auditory stream: Event-related fMRI evidence for differential activation to speech and nonspeech. *Journal of Cognitive Neuroscience, 13,* 994–1005.

Vouloumanos, A., & Werker, J. F. (2004). Tuned to the signal: The privileged status of speech for young infants. *Developmental Science, 7,* 270–276.

Wagner, A. D., Schachter, D. L., Rotte, M., Koutstaal, W., Maril, A., Dale, A. M., Rosen, B. R., & Buckner, R. L. (1998). Building memories: Remembering and forgetting of verbal experiences as predicted by brain activity. *Science, 281,* 1188–1191.

Werker, J. F., Cohen, L. B., Lloyd, V., Stager, C., & Cassosola, M. (1998). Acquisition of word-object associations by 14-month-old infants. *Developmental Psychology, 34,* 1289–1309.

Werker, J. F., & Tees, R. C. (1984). Cross-language speech perception: Evidence for perceptual reorganization during the first year of life. *Infant Behavior and Development, 7,* 49–63.

Wicker, B., Michel, F., Henaff, A., & Decety, J. (1998). Brain regions involved in the perception of gaze: A PET study. *NeuroImage, 8,* 221–227.

Woodward, A. L., Markman, E. M., & Fitzsimmons, C. M. (1994). Rapid word learning in 13- and 18-month-olds. *Developmental Psychology, 30,* 553–566.

9

Following the Intentional Eye: The Role of Gaze Cues in Early Word Learning

Susan A. Graham, Elizabeth S. Nilsen, and Samantha L. Nayer
University of Calgary

Consider the following situation: a young child is in the kitchen and hears an adult utter a word that she has never heard before, the word *whisk*. How might the child determine what that new word means? To acquire a novel word, young children must successfully negotiate several steps. First, they must identify the word in the speech stream and encode a phonological representation of the word. Next, they must identify the intended referent of the novel word from amongst the many possible candidates present in the scene. For example, they must identify the whisk as the referent of that word, rather than another object (e.g., a *ladle*), a property of the object (e.g., *metal*), or the way the object is being used (e.g., *to beat an egg*). They must then generalize that word to other appropriate instances of the referent when encountered in the future (e.g., other whisks). Finally, in order to successfully use words to communicate, children must develop an understanding that words have communicative power because their meanings are conventional or shared within a linguistic community. That is, they must assume that other English-speaking individuals will also share the understanding of the meaning of the word *whisk*.

Given the complexity involved in learning a simple label like *whisk*, one might expect children to acquire new words very slowly and with a great deal of effort. Yet, young children acquire their native language at a striking pace, learning approximately five to six new words a day between 18 months and 6 years of age (Anglin, 1993). In order to explain children's prodigious word learning, researchers have examined the diverse set of strategies and abilities that young children recruit to acquire new words. To date, much progress has been made in understanding the processes that help young children identify the intended referent of a new word. That is, research has demonstrated that young word learners are highly skilled at exploiting multiple sources of information to establish appropriate mappings between words (e.g., *ball*) and objects (e.g., balls), including social cues, linguistic cues, and word learning strategies (see Akhtar & Tomasello, 2000; Baldwin & Moses, 2001; Bloom, 2000; Hollich, Hirsh-Pasek, & Golinkoff, 2000; Sabbagh & Baldwin, 2004; Woodward & Markman, 1998 for reviews).

In this chapter, we first review research documenting the role of eye gaze direction in guiding young children's formation of mappings between words and objects. Next, we discuss the intentional versus attentional explanations for the role of gaze direction in word learning. Finally, we describe two studies from our lab that have attempted to disentangle the relative contribution of attentional and intentional cues in infants' reliance on gaze cues to learn new words.

INFANTS' USE OF GAZE DIRECTION CUES
TO LEARN NOVEL WORDS

The critical role that joint attention plays in the language-learning enterprise was articulated many years ago by Bruner and his colleagues (Bruner, 1975, 1983; Scaife & Bruner, 1975). Joint attention occurs when two individuals are focused on the same aspect of their environment and are both aware of this joint attentional focus. With reference to word learning, Bruner and colleagues argued that sharing attention with another serves as a means by which children can establish correct mappings between words and the appropriate objects, events, or properties in the environment.

In support of this proposal, a large body of empirical evidence has documented that children acquire words more readily in joint attentional contexts (e.g., Akhtar, Dunham, & Dunham, 1991; Akhtar & Tomasello, 1996; Baldwin, 1991; 1993a; Baldwin et al., 1996; Carpenter, Nagell, & Tomasello, 1998; Dunham, Dunham, & Curwin, 1993; Tomasello & Barton, 1994; Tomasello & Farrar, 1986). For example, using a longitudinal design, Carpenter et al. (1998) found that the amount of time mothers and their 11- to 13-month-old infants spent in joint attention was positively correlated with infants' receptive vocabulary sizes between 11 and 15 months. Using an experimental word learning paradigm, Baldwin et al. (1996) demonstrated that 19- to 20-month-old infants linked a novel word with a novel object when an adult speaker seated beside them uttered the novel word while gazing at the object that was the focus of the infants' attention. In contrast, infants resisted establishing a word-object linkage when the novel word was uttered by a speaker who was seated out of view of the infant.

Other studies have demonstrated that naming objects that an infant is already focused on in a joint attentional episode will facilitate the task of establishing word-object mappings. In a classic study, Tomasello and Farrar (1986) demonstrated that 17-month-old infants were more likely to acquire a novel word when the novel label was introduced while the infant was focused on the intended referent versus when the infant was focused on some other aspect of the environment (see Dunham et al., 1993 for similar findings). In a significant extension of this research, Akhtar et al. (1991) examined mothers' use of two kinds of directives in interactions with their 13-month-old infants: *lead prescriptives*, wherein the parent directed the infant's attention to a new object or toy (e.g., "Let's play with the ball.") versus *follow prescriptives*, wherein the parent attends to the object the infant is focused on, but may offer some additional information about it (e.g., "It's a big truck."). Akhtar and her colleagues found that mothers' use of *follow prescriptives* with their 13-month-old infants was positively related to the size of their infants' productive vocabulary at 22 months of age. In contrast, mothers' use of *lead prescriptives* was negatively related to the size of infants' productive vocabulary at 22 months of age.

Following from this significant work on the facilitative role of joint attention in early word learning, researchers have examined the types of cues that infants may use to establish joint attention and thereby determine the intended referent of a novel label. Studies have demonstrated that young children's tendency to link a novel label with an object can be directed by a speaker's affective and/or behavioral cues (e.g., Tomasello & Barton, 1994; Tomasello, Strosberg, & Akhtar, 1996), and by the relative novelty of objects or actions in the discourse context (e.g., Akhtar, Carpenter, & Tomasello, 1996; Tomasello & Akhtar, 1995). Within this realm of study, however, it is the seminal work of Baldwin and her colleagues that has documented infants' reliance on eye gaze direction cues to learn novel words. Specifically, Baldwin has established that infants can use an adult's line of regard to identify the intended referent of a novel word in situations where there are numerous possible candidates available (i.e., when a novel label is uttered in the presence of two or more nameless objects). For example, Baldwin (1991, 1993a) demonstrated that when 18- to 19-month-old infants are presented with a novel label, they will monitor a speaker's gaze direction, follow that focus, and subsequently map the new label onto the object that is the focus of the speaker's regard. Moreover, infants in this age range can successfully use line of regard to establish correct word-referent mappings even when faced with discrepant la-beling situations—that is, when a new word is presented while an infant is fo-cusing on an incorrect referent and an adult is focusing on the target object. This suggests that infants as young as 18 months can switch their own atten-tional focus and assign the new label to the object that is the focus of the adult's attention.

Although infants as young as 18 months can rely on gaze direction to es-tablish word-object mappings, research with younger infants suggests that this ability is not present earlier in word learning. Using an interactive object-based paradigm, Baldwin (1991, 1993b) found that infants in the 14- to 17-month range appeared to use the adult's eye gaze direction to establish joint attention. They did not, however, reliably map the novel label onto the target object using gaze direction cues. Similarly, in a series of studies using an interactive in-termodal preferential looking paradigm, Hollich et al. (2000) demonstrated that 12-, 19-, and 24-month-old infants could follow an experimenter's eye gaze direction to a target object. However, only 19- and 24-month-olds could use that gaze direction to map novel words to novel objects. Twelve-month-olds were only able to establish reliable word-object mappings when the adult speaker both gazed at and pointed to the novel object while labeling it 10 times. When considered with other research on joint attention, these findings suggest that younger infants can follow adult gaze direction from the early stages of language development. However, they are less able to use a gaze direction cue to determine the precise referent that the adult is referring to with a novel label.

To summarize, the research described in this section indicates that by 18 months of age, infants possess the impressive ability to monitor an adult's gaze cues and to use these cues to map novel words to novel objects (e.g., Baldwin, 1991; 1993a; 1993b; Hollich et al., 2000). Although the majority of studies conducted on children's use of eye gaze for word mapping have focused on the acquisition of object words, recent research by Poulin-Dubois and Forbes (2002) indicates that 27-month-old infants, but not 21-month-old in-fants, are sensitive to cues such as eye gaze when learning the meanings of verbs. While often interpreted as providing evidence that infants are sensi-tive to others' intentional cues, the studies described above do not allow us to specify the motivations or mechanisms that underlie infants' reliance on eye gaze cues to learn novel words, as we will discuss in the next section.

What Processes Underlie Infants' Use of Gaze Cues to Learn Novel Words?

There are two major classes of explanation that can be offered to account for infants' use of gaze direction to identify the referent of a novel word. One ac-count emphasizes the intentional nature of eye gaze, while the second emphasizes the attentional nature of eye gaze. The differences between these two accounts parallels a larger debate within the domain of word learning, namely, the debate between those that advocate a social-pragmatic view of word learning (e.g., Akhtar & Tomasello, 2000; Baldwin & Moses, 2001) and those that advocate a more mechanistic perspective that emphasizes the role of attention and memory (e.g., Samuelson & Smith, 1998; Smith, Jones, & Landau, 1996).

Eye Gaze as a Marker of Intention

One interpretation of the findings that infants use gaze direction to establish word-object linkages suggests that infants are attuned to the intentional nature of gaze cues. That is, when an adult utters a novel word while gazing at a specific object in an array, infants appreciate that eye gaze direction is an indication of the adult's intention to refer to that particular object. Thus, they will map the novel word to the gazed-at object. This explanation implies that children possess the social-cognitive abilities necessary to understand the relevance of gaze direction as clues to another's intentions.

The social-cognitive account stems from theories that emphasize the importance of social understanding for language acquisition (e.g., Akhtar et al., 1996; Akhtar & Tomasello, 2000; Baldwin & Moses, 2001; Bruner, 1975, 1983; Sabbagh & Baldwin, 2004; Tomasello, 1992). This perspective emphasizes the fundamentally social and communicative nature of word learning and focuses on how young children's understanding of others' intentions and mental states guides their word learning. Support for this perspective comes from research demonstrating that young children can attend to an adult's intentional behaviors as a part of the word learning process (e.g., Akhtar & Tomasello, 1996; Tomasello et al., 1996; Diesendruck, Markson, Akhtar, & Reudor, 2004). For example, Tomasello and his colleagues have provided evidence indicating that word learners are able to use a speaker's statement about an impending event (e.g., "Let's find the toma.") to learn the meaning of a new word. For example, in Tomasello and Barton (1994, Study 4), an experimenter played a finding game with 24-month-olds using four novel objects. During this game, an experimenter provided a language model (e.g., "Let's find the toma.") before searching for a target object. In one group, the target object was found directly after the language model was provided, and in a second group, the experimenter visibly rejected two non-target objects (e.g., she frowned) before finding the target object. In both groups the experimenter demonstrated gleeful behavior after finding the target object. Results indicated that 24-month-olds were able to make correct word-object mappings regardless of whether the target was found directly preceding the language model, or whether two non-target objects were found prior to the target object. Thus, the infants were clearly identifying intentional actions of the experimenter and using only these actions (not accidental actions) to map a novel label to a correct referent. Tomasello and colleagues have replicated these findings with 18-month-olds, using a similar procedure (Tomasello et al., 1996).

Eye Gaze as Directing Attention to an Object

An alternative account of infants' reliance on gaze direction cues to learn novel words focuses on the salience-enhancing or the attention-getting nature of eye gaze. That is, it is possible that gaze direction facilitates word learning because it triggers a shift of visuospatial attention towards one of the novel objects, thereby enhancing the salience of that object. In other words, gazing at an object is like shining a light on one object in an array of multiple objects. Thus, infants map the word to the gazed-at object because their attention has been shifted to that object and it has been made salient, rather than because they are sensitive to a speaker's referential intentions.

The notion that eye gaze may trigger shifts in attention stems from a large body of research that has examined the attention-getting nature of eye gaze. Attentional orientation to gaze direction cues has been posited to be controlled both exogenously and endogenously. Exogenous orientation occurs when attention is shifted reflexively (e.g., Farroni, Johnson, Brockbank, & Simion, 2000; Farroni, Mansfield, Lai, & Johnson, 2003; Hood, Willen, & Driver, 1998; Kingstone, Smilek, Ristic, Friesen, & Eastwood, 2003). That is, an individual orients their attention towards a visual prompt involuntary and automatically. Endogenous orientation occurs when the attentional shift to eye gaze direction is conscious and voluntary. Differentiating between attentional orienting due to endogenous or exogenous orienting is typically based on the exploration of the time course of attentional effects. Those that occur rapidly are thought to be more reflexive, while those that occur at a slower time course are thought to be more endogenous (see Moore, 1999; MacPherson & Moore, this volume for a discussion of the distinction between endogenous and exogeneous orienting to eye gaze).

Studies have demonstrated that reflexive orientation to eye gaze shifts occur in adults, younger children, and infants (see Kingstone et al., 2003 for review). For example, adults are quickest to respond to a target's location when eye gaze is directed towards that target, even when eye gaze was deemed nonpredictive of the target's location (Friesen & Kingstone, 1998). Similarly, MacPherson and Moore (this volume) found that 14-month-old infants displayed reflexive eye gaze orientation when presented with an animated eye gaze stimulus. This reflexive orientation is not specific to eye movement, but can also be elicited by other non-biological stimuli, such as directional arrows (Ristic, Friesen, & Kingstone, 2002; Tipples, 2002).

Studies have also demonstrated that endogenous, voluntary orientation to eye gaze shifts is present in even very young infants. For example, infants as young as 3 months of age consistently orient their attention due to shifts in another's eye gaze with a computerized face (Hood et al., 1998). Around 3 to 6 months of age, infants can notice sensitive, discreet differences in eye gaze shifts (Hains & Muir, 1996; Symons, Hains, & Muir, 1998). However, it is not until 18 months of age that infants reliably follow gaze direction to predict the location of a target (Brooks & Meltzoff, 2002; Moore & Corkum, 1998), and are able to understand the intentional nature of looking behavior (Butler, Caron, & Brooks, 2000).

DISENTANGLING INTENTIONAL VERSUS ATTENTIONAL COMPONENTS OF GAZE DIRECTION IN WORD LEARNING

Disentangling the intentional versus attentional aspects of infants' reliance on gaze direction is critical to our understanding of the development of infants' understanding of intentionality and the role that gaze direction may play in early word learning. Two lines of research provide evidence relevant to this debate: research on word learning in children with autism and research contrasting the eye gaze cues with salience-enhancing cues.

Children with Autism's Use of Gaze Direction to Learn New Words

One line of research has focused on the word learning abilities of children whose social understanding is thought to be impaired, namely, children with autism. Within the realm of gaze monitoring and joint attention, research has demonstrated that children with autism do possess basic knowledge about eyes and seeing. That is, they are able to determine when someone is looking at them (Baron-Cohen, Campbell, Karmiloff-Smith, Grant, & Walker, 1995) and what object a person is looking at (Baron-Cohen, 1989). Despite this understanding, children with autism are impaired in their ability to spontaneously orient to adults' direction of attention (e.g., Carpenter, Pennington, & Rogers, 2002). For example, Leekham, Baron-Cohen, Perret, Milders, and Brown (1997) found that children with autism were less likely than typically developing children and children with Down syndrome first, to monitor an adult's head and eye movement, and second, to turn to look in a similar direction as an adult. It appears that the ability to monitor gaze is mediated by the developmental age of children. For example, Leekam and her colleagues (Leekam, Hunnisett, & Moore, 1998; Leekam, Lopez, & Moore, 2000) demonstrated that children with autism who possessed a mental age of more than 4 years were able to spontaneously follow another person's gaze and had no difficulty in determining where an individual was looking, while children with younger mental ages did not. The deficits in children with autism's ability to spontaneously follow gaze direction, however, cannot be attributed to deficits in attentional processing, as these skills have been demonstrated to be intact in this population (e.g., Chawarska, Klin, & Volkmar, 2003; Kylliäinen & Hietanen, 2004; Leekham et al., 2000). For example, Chawarska et al. (2003) demonstrated that preschool children with autism showed similar shortening of saccadic reaction times in response to an eye gaze cue as typically developing peers. Similarly, Kylliäinen and Hietanen (2004) found that the static gaze direction of another person triggered an automatic shift in attention of children with autism. Thus, despite an inability or lag in the ability to establish joint attention, children with autism do orient their attention reflexively to shifts in eye gaze direction.

If eye gaze direction in a word learning context functions as an intentional cue, then one would expect children with autism to have difficulty using gaze direction to identify the intended referent of a novel word. In contrast, if eye gaze functions to shift attention, one might expect children with autism to use this cue to identify the referent of a novel word. In keeping with an intentional account of eye gaze direction, Baron-Cohen et al. (1995, Experiment 2) demonstrated that children with autism tended not to use eye gaze when learning a new label. That is, they were less likely than typically developing children and children with a developmental delay to use the eye gaze direction of a cartoon's face to determine which object the cartoon character was referring to when he uses a new label (e.g., the experimenter says, "Charlie says, 'There's the beb!'").

In a similar vein, Baron-Cohen, Baldwin, and Crowson (1997) presented children with autism, children with a developmental delay, and typically-developing children with the discrepant labeling paradigm of Baldwin (1991, 1993a). As discussed earlier, Baldwin (1991, 1993a) demonstrated that 18- to 19-month-old infants can switch their own attentional focus and assign the new label to the object that is the focus of the adult's attention. Baron-Cohen et al.'s results, however, indicate that children with autism tended to link the novel label with the object they were attending to instead of the object that was the focus of the experimenter's regard when faced with a discrepant labeling situation. These findings could not be attributed to general cognitive deficits as the majority of children with a developmental delay (but without autism) correctly mapped the novel label to the object that was the focus of the speaker's attention.

When considered with the results of studies that demonstrated that children with autism do orient automatically to a shift in gaze direction (e.g., Chawarska et al., 2003; Kylliäinen & Hietanen, 2004; Leekham et al., 2000), the results of the word learning studies suggest that children with autism fail to appreciate the intentional significance of another's eye gaze. That is, when an adult utters a novel word while gazing at a specific object in an array, children with autism do not appear to treat that eye gaze direction as an indication of the adult's intention to refer to that particular object.

Contrasting Eye Gaze Cues with Salience-Enhancing Cues

Another line of research has focused on contrasting eye gaze with salience cues in an effort to disentangle the intentional versus attentional aspects of gaze direction. These studies compare word learning situations in which an adult's gaze direction is used to identify the referent of a novel word with word learning situations in which salient cues are used to identify the referent of the novel word. The reasoning behind these studies is as follows: If eye gaze direction serves to orient an infant's attention to an object, leading it to be more salient (as opposed to providing information regarding the speaker's referential intent), then infants should perform similarly in word learning situations where eye gaze is used and in word learning situations wherein the salience of an object is enhanced in some other way. Furthermore, contrasting these two types of cues in one word learning situation enables the examination of the priority that infants give to each cue.

In one of the first studies to examine the issue of salience versus intentionality, Baldwin (1993b) presented 19- to 20-month-olds with two novel objects that were subsequently hidden in separate containers. In Experiment 1, the adult lifted the lid, looked in one container, and introduced a novel label (e.g., "There's a *modi* in here."). In Experiment 2, the experimenter looked at the infant, while manipulating the lid of one container and introducing a novel label. The manipulation of the lid was intended to increase the salience of the toy hidden in the container. In Experiment 1, the infants linked the novel label to the object located in the container. In contrast, in Experiment 2, infants did not link the novel label systematically to any object, indicating that they did not use the enhanced salience of the object to guide their word-object mappings. As noted by Moore, Angelopoulos, and Bennett (1999), however, the lid manipulation used by Baldwin may have made the container, rather than the object contained within it, salient. Thus, these results, though promising, may not have provided a clear test of the role of salience cues and intentional cues in word learning.

In a more stringent test of this issue, Moore et al. (1999) presented 18- and 24-month-old infants with a novel word in the presence of two novel objects, accompanied by a referential cue (a shift in an adult's attention, indicated by head orientation) or a salience cue (activation of one of the objects through illumination and rotation). Across various conditions, the referential cues and the salience cues presented were either congruent (the salience cue and referential cue both designated the same object), conflicting (the salience cue and referential cue designated opposing objects), or neither (one cue was held constant while the other designated the target object). Results indicated that 24-month-olds appreciated the referential intent of the speaker—when the salient and referential cues were in competition, infants ignored the salient toy and mapped the novel word to the object that was the focus of the adult's attention. In the absence of any referential cues, 24-month-olds did rely on salience cues to map the word to the novel toy. In contrast, the 18-month-old infants were able to use the referential cues to establish a word-object mapping only when there was no conflict between the referential and salient cues. They were not able to acquire the novel word when only salience cues were present.

In a similar vein, Hollich et al. (2000; Experiments 1 to 3) examined the role of perceptual salience (i.e., attractiveness) and eye gaze direction in guiding 12-, 19-, and 24-month-olds' acquisition of novel words. The perceptual salience manipulation consisted of a contrast between an attractive object (e.g., a pink and orange clacker) and a less attractive object (e.g., a white bottle opener). The results of these studies revealed a developmental pattern in the relative reliance on eye gaze direction versus perceptual salience. At 12 months, infants relied less on eye gaze and more on perceptual salience to learn novel words (although it should be noted that their word learning was very fragile). At 19 months, infants could rely on eye gaze to acquire the novel words, but only when there was no conflict with perceptual salience, consistent with the results of Moore et al. (1999). Finally, the 24-month-olds relied on gaze direction to establish word-object mappings, even when this cue conflicted with perceptual salience.

Taken together, research to date has demonstrated that 24-month-old infants will rely on gaze direction, rather than a salient cue, to map novel words to novel objects. In particular, when there was a contrast between an eye gaze cue and the salience of an object, children as young as 24 months attended to the eye gaze cue to identify the referent of a novel word. This sensitivity to gaze direction, however, is more fragile in infants younger than 24 months in that when there is a conflict between saliency and eye gaze direction, 18- to 19-month-olds do not exhibit a clear pattern of word learning.

In sum, the studies described above provide two lines of evidence favoring an intentional interpretation of infants' reliance on eye gaze to learn novel words. First, evidence from children with autism suggests that they fail to use gaze direction to learn novel words despite having intact abilities to orient automatically to shifts in gaze direction. Second, studies have convincingly demonstrated that 24-month-old infants will rely on gaze direction, rather than on a cue that highlights the salience of an object, when establishing novel word-referent linkages.

Research to date, however, does not specifically address the possibility that eye gaze may be triggering attention to an object because of the directional nature of eye gaze itself. That is, eye gaze could lead to a shift in visuospatial attention to a particular location at the time the novel word is presented. This shift in attention would allow the infant to link the novel word with the novel object. The studies discussed herein, which contrast salience cues with gaze direction cues, do not allow us to assess this possibility as the salience cues used led the object itself to become salient, rather than the spatial location of the object. Thus, those studies do not directly address whether it is the shift in visuospatial attention that facilitates word learning.

EXAMINING THE ROLE OF VISUOSPATIAL ATTENTION IN THE ACQUISITION OF NOVEL WORDS

In a recent series of studies in our lab, we have pursued the examination of attentional orienting in word learning. In particular, we have begun to examine the possibility that triggering attention to locations might facilitate 24-month-old infants' acquisition of novel object words. In the first study to be described, we examined whether a nonreferential cue would guide 24-month-olds' attention to the location of an object in a word learning context. In a second study, we examined whether eye gaze direction would similarly lead 24-month-olds to orient to the impending location of an object. In both studies, we tested 24-month-olds, as previous research has indicated that 24-month-olds exhibit a robust reliance on gaze cues over other cues in word learning situations (e.g., Hollich et al., 2000; Moore et al., 1999).

Using Lights to Cue Object Locations and Objects

In a first step towards examining the possible role of attentional orienting in infants' use of gaze direction to learn novel words, we began by examining whether shifts in basic visuospatial attention play a role in young children's acquisition of new words for novel objects (Friesen & Graham, 2002). That is, we examined whether simply directing 24-month-olds' attention to a location using a nonreferential cue might facilitate word-object mappings.

We used a nonreferential cue to highlight the spatial location of an object, rather than using a salience manipulation that led to properties of the object itself being highlighted (e.g., by being more attractive or by lighting up and moving). That is, we first cued a particular spatial location using a ring of flashing lights, and then placed a novel object in that location. We reasoned that if shifts in visuospatial attention play a role in word learning, then infants would attach a novel label to the object appearing at an attended location.

In this study, we presented thirty 2-year-olds with a novel label ("I want to find the *kopie*."), followed by an attentional cue (flashing lights) to draw their attention to one of two locations, using a specially-designed apparatus. This apparatus consisted of a long, narrow wooden box, with two wooden disks fixed on top of the box. The two disks were each ringed by a series of colored LED lights which could be activated by means of two foot pedals placed under the table out of sight from the child. A schematic of the experimental set-up is presented in Figure 9–1.

Each trial began with the experimenter establishing eye contact with the child and saying, "I want to find the *kopie*." Keeping her gaze straight ahead, she briefly flashed either the left or the right set of lights, and then brought two objects from the set out from under the table and placed them on the disks, one on the left and one on the right, and said, "Oh!" The object that was designated in advance as the target object was always placed at the location where the lights had flashed, and the nontarget object was always placed at the location where the lights had not flashed. After a brief pause, the experimenter removed both objects from the infants' view. During each trial, no additional cues as to the possible referent of the novel word were provided. That is, the researcher looked straight ahead throughout the trials, and no properties of the

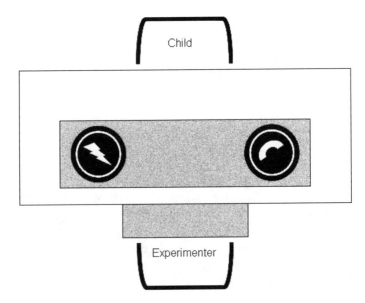

FIGURE 9–1. Schematic of the experimental set-up (Friesen & Graham, 2002).

objects themselves were made salient (i.e., the target object did not light up, become animated, nor was it handled differently from the nontarget object when the objects were presented to the children). Each toddler received a block of four trials in which the lights cue occurred equally often on the left or right and in which the same object always appeared at the location that had been cued. Thus, the lights cue was predictive of the appearance of a specific object (the target object).

After these trials were completed, infants were asked to select the referent of the novel word from a set of three objects that included the target object (the one that had appeared at the cued location), the nontarget object (the one that had appeared at the uncued location), and a distractor object. Following this comprehension trial, infants were presented with a second set of objects, differing only in color from the first set, and were asked to generalize the novel label to one of the objects. We expected that if basic visuospatial attention plays a facilitative role in the mapping of novel labels onto novel objects, then children would select the object that had appeared at the cued location (i.e., the target object) as the referent of the novel label. If infants had established a robust word-object mapping, we expected them to generalize that label to the different colored exemplar of the target object.

Videotapes of the infants' responses were coded by a researcher who was blind to the purposes of the experiment. Both the infants' looking behavior during the test trials and their responses on the comprehension and generalization trials were recorded. Specifically, the coder recorded (1) whether the child looked at the cued location in response to the lights cue, and (2) which object the child selected on the comprehension and generalization task.

In analyzing the data from this experiment, we first established that all 30 children had looked at the cued location in response to the flashing lights on every trial, indicating that the cue did indeed capture their attention. Object selection frequencies for the comprehension task and generalization task are presented in Figure 9–2.

On both the comprehension trial and the generalization trial, significantly more children selected the target object than either the nontarget or distracter objects (χ^2 (2, $n = 30$) = 9.80, $p < 0.01$; (χ^2 (2, $n = 30$) = 6.20, $p < 0.05$, respectively). We then used binomial probabilities ($p = 0.33$, $q = .66$) to calculate whether the number of infants who chose the target object on each trial differed from the level expected by chance alone. Significantly more children than expected by chance alone chose the target object on the comprehension trial ($p = .01$) and on the generalization trial ($p = .02$).

The results of this study indicate that infants did map the novel label onto the novel object that appeared at the location that was cued with the flashing lights. This process necessitated several steps on the part of the child. First, the child had to switch his or her attention from the experimenter to the location

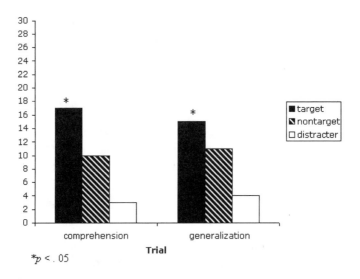

FIGURE 9–2.   Frequency of selection of the target, nontarget, and distractor objects for
the comprehension trial and generalization trial.

that was cued. Then, he or she had to make a link between the cued location
and the object that subsequently appeared at the location. Finally, he or she
had to pair the novel label (uttered by the experimenter before cueing the location) with the object that had appeared at that cued location. In a brief
follow-up study, we used the lights cue to highlight specific objects, rather than
object locations. In this study, the same procedure was followed as in the study
previously described with one exception: once the experimenter indicated
her desire to find the referent of a novel word, she immediately put the target
object and the nontarget object on the platform and flashed the lights around
the target object. Infants were presented with the same comprehension and
generalization tasks previously described. Preliminary data from this study suggest that significantly more children than expected by chance alone chose the
target object on the comprehension trial (8 out of 14; $p = .03$) and on the generalization trial (8 out of 13; $p = .02$). When considered with the previous
study, these results suggest that cueing a specific object with a nonreferential
cue and cueing an object location facilitated infants' word learning to a similar degree.

The results of these studies support the notion that attentional orienting
does play a role in facilitating word learning. These findings are consistent with
research by Moore et al., (1999) and Hollich et al. (2000) in demonstrating
that 24-month-olds can use attentional cues to learn new words. This study

adds to the current literature by demonstrating that simply shifting infants' attention to a location, rather than highlighting an object itself, can guide word learning.

These results, although provocative, do not address whether eye gaze direction functions similarly as a primary attention-getting cue in word learning. That is, simply because attentional cueing has been shown to play a role in word learning, this does not automatically imply that the role of gaze direction in word learning can be reduced to an attentional mechanism. That is, 24-month-olds might treat eye gaze differently than a nonreferential cue because they view eye gaze as a marker of another's intentionality. In the next study, we examined whether using eye direction to cue locations functioned similarly to the lights cue in facilitating 24-month-olds' establishment of word-object mappings.

Using Eye Gaze to Cue Location and Objects

In a second study, we compared cueing the location of objects versus cueing objects themselves with gaze direction (Graham, Neufeld, & Kilbreath, 2004). As discussed earlier, nonpredictive, nonreferential gaze cues can trigger an automatic shift of attention in adults (e.g., Driver et al., 1999; Friesen & Kingstone 1998; Langton & Bruce 1999), and in children and infants (e.g., Hood et al., 1998; Ristic et al., 2002; MacPherson & Moore, this volume). In this study, we examined whether a shift in gaze direction would lead to a shift in attention that would then facilitate word learning. That is, we examined word learning for novel objects when a gaze cue was provided before an object was placed in a particular location (object absent) versus word learning for novel objects when a gaze cue was provided after an object was placed in a particular location (object present). To clarify, we examined word learning in two word learning situations: for one group of infants, a novel object was placed at a location that was previously cued by the researcher's gaze; for a second group of infants, the researcher's gaze was directed at the novel object that was already at a particular location. For each group, we examined whether they would attach the novel label to the cued object and whether they would generalize the label to another object from the same category.

If eye gaze direction is interpreted by infants as marking the experimenter's intention to refer to a particular object, then cueing an empty location with eye gaze should not result in meaningful word learning. In contrast, cueing a particular object with eye gaze should lead to infants to attach the novel label to the object that is the focus of the experimenter's regard. If eye gaze simply functions as an attentional cue, then word learning in both conditions should be relatively equivalent. That is, cueing the actual object versus directing infants' attention to the location where the object will appear should not result in a word learning advantage.

Our participants included 46 infants, 24 girls and 22 boys (M = 25.49 months; SD = 1.07; range = 23.30 to 27.75). Participants were randomly assigned to one of two groups: target present or target absent. The *target present group* (n = 21) consisted of 11 girls and 10 boys (M = 25.27; SD = 1.24; range = 23.30 to 27.10), and the *target absent group* (n = 25) consisted of 13 girls and 12 boys (M = 25.45; SD = 0.91; range = 24.23 to 27.75).

Infants were brought into the testing room and placed in a booster seat next to their parent at a table. The apparatus described in Figure 9–1 was placed on the table in front of them. Just before the experiment began, infants were introduced to a black-and-white spotted dog puppet, named "Doggie," and were told that they were going to play a finding game. Each infant first received two warm-up trials. These trials were designed to familiarize infants with objects appearing on both sides of the platform and with the notion of finding referents of objects. During each of these trials, the experimenter first established eye contact with the infant and indicated that she wanted to find a particular object (e.g., "I want to find the *car*. Let's find the *car*."). The experimenter then placed a target object (e.g., a car) and a nontarget object (e.g., a stuffed bear) on their respective sides of the circular platform for 3 seconds and then removed the toys. She then presented the infant with three familiar objects (the target object, the nontarget object, and a distractor object) and asked for the referent of the target word ("Show me the *car*."). These steps were repeated for the second set of familiar objects.

TARGET ABSENT GROUP

At the beginning of each of the test trials, the experimenter established eye contact with the infant and then indicated that she wanted to find an object (e.g., "I want to find the *fep*. Let's find the *fep*."). Both the experimenter and the puppet then gazed at the specific side of the platform for 3 seconds. The experimenter then immediately placed the target object on the side of the platform where she had been gazing and the nontarget object on the other side of the platform for 3 seconds. Just before the experimenter took the objects off of the platform, she said, "OK." These steps were repeated three more times for the same objects, for a total of four repetitions. The only thing that differed for the three remaining trials was which side of the platform was gazed at and where the target object appeared. Note that the target object always appeared at the cued location. Thus, the gaze cue was perfectly predictive of the appearance of the target object.

Following the training trials, infants were asked to select the referent of the novel word from a set of three objects that included the target object (the one that had appeared at the cued location), the nontarget object (the one that had appeared at the uncued location), and a distractor object (e.g., "Show me the *fep*."). Following this comprehension trial, infants were presented with a second set of objects, differing only in color from the first set, and were asked to generalize the novel label to one of objects. After both the comprehension and generalization tasks had been completed, the entire training and testing procedure was repeated with a second set of objects. Thus, each infant completed two blocks of training (with two different object sets) and two comprehension and generalization trials.

TARGET PRESENT GROUP

The procedure for this group was identical to that for the *Target Absent* group with the following exception: rather than gazing at a target location, the experimenter gazed at the target object. That is, the experimenter first established eye contact with the infant and indicated that she wanted to find an object (e.g., "I want to find the *fep*. Let's find the *fep*."). The experimenter immediately put the target object and the nontarget object on the platform and gazed at the appropriate side of the platform for a total of 3 seconds. Just before the experimenter took the objects off of the platform, she said, "OK." These steps were repeated three more times for the same objects, for a total of four trials. The only thing that differed for the three remaining trials was the side of the platform where the target object appeared and where the experimenter directed her gaze. Infants then received the same comprehension and generalization task previously described. After both the comprehension and generalization tasks had been completed, the whole training and testing procedure was repeated with a second set of objects.

Videotapes of the infants' responses were coded by a researcher who was blind to the purposes of the experiment. For both the comprehension tasks and the generalization tasks, the coder recorded (1) which object the infant first looked at, and (2) which object they chose as the referent of the target word.

For each participant, the number of times the child chose the target object, across the four possible trials, was summed, to yield a score out of four. Independent groups t-tests indicated that infants in the target present group (M = 2.19) chose the target object as the referent of the novel word significantly more often than infants in the target absent condition (M = 1.40; $t(44) = 2.10, p < .05$). In terms of first looks, infants in the target present group also looked at the target object (M = 1.95) significantly more often than infants in the target absent group (M = 1.20) in response to the request for the referent of the target word, $t(44) = 2.10, p < .05$.

We then used binomial probabilities ($p = .33, q = .67$) to calculate whether the number of infants who chose the target object in all the test trials differed from chance (see Figure 9–3). Significantly more infants in the target present group than expected by chance chose the target object on the first comprehension trial ($p = .001$) and the second comprehension trial ($p = .03$). In contrast, the number of infants in the target absent group who chose the target object did not differ from chance on either of the comprehension trials ($p = .08$ and $p = .16$). On the generalization trials, significantly more infants in the target present group than expected by chance chose the target object on the second generalization trial ($p = .005$) but not on the first generalization trial ($p = .15$). As on the comprehension trials, the number of infants in the target absent group who chose the target object did not differ from chance on either of the generalization trials ($p = .17$ and $p = .17$).

The results of this study indicate that infants in the target present condition demonstrated significantly more word learning than infants in the target absent condition. When the infants' performance was broken down trial by trial, the results revealed that children in the target present condition chose the target object significantly more often than expected by chance on every trial (except the first generalization trial). Thus, our results are consistent with several of the studies reviewed earlier in this chapter, indicating that 24-month-olds will rely on gaze direction cues to map novel words to novel objects (e.g., Hollich et al., 2000; Moore et al., 1999).

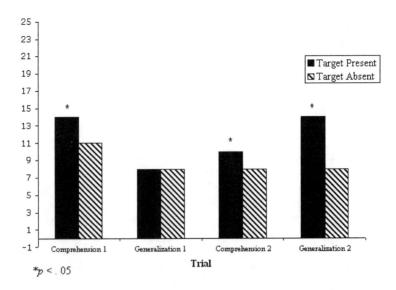

FIGURE 9–3.   Frequency of selection of the target objects as a function of group and trial.

In contrast to the results from the first study (Friesen & Graham, 2002), the present findings indicate that cueing a location with gaze direction did not facilitate infants' word-object mappings. Although infants appeared to have switched their attention from the experimenter to the location that was cued with eye gaze, they did not associate the novel label with the object that subsequently appeared at that location. This suggests that eye gaze did not function similarly to a nonreferential cue in facilitating infants' word acquisition, an issue we will discuss further in the next section.

SUMMARY AND CONCLUSIONS

In the studies just described, we have begun to examine the possibility that eye gaze may be triggering attention to an object because of the directional nature of eye gaze itself. That is, we examined whether orienting infants' attention to locations versus objects differentially affects their acquisition of novel object words. In the first study, we demonstrated that infants mapped a novel word to a novel object that had appeared at the location cued by a nonreferential cue (i.e., flashing lights). Moreover, word learning when an object location had been cued did not appear to differ from word learning when the object itself has been cued with the flashing lights. The results of this study support the notion that attentional orienting can play a role in facilitating word learning. More specifically, these findings indicate that merely shifting infants' attention to a location can lead infants to associate a novel word with a novel object.

The results of the second study, however, suggest that gaze direction cues do not operate in a similar fashion to nonreferential cues. That is, while cueing a specific object with a gaze direction cue led infants to map a novel word to that object, cueing an object location with gaze direction did not result in meaningful word learning. These findings suggest that infants do view gaze direction as a marker of intentionality. That is, upon hearing a novel word, infants treated an adult's eye-gaze direction as an indication of the experimenter's intention to refer to a particular object, in the absence of other cues. Thus, when the experimenter gazed at a specific object, infants attached the novel word to that object. However, when the experimenter gazed at a location, rather than an object, infants did not treat her gaze direction as an indication of her intent to refer to the object that subsequently appeared there.

To summarize, our studies suggest that different processes underlie the reliance on a nonreferential cue versus an eye gaze cue in word learning situations. We propose that nonreferential cues do indeed serve to shift infants' visual-spatial attention and that this shift can facilitate their word-object mappings. In contrast, eye gaze serves an intentional cue whereby 24-month-olds recognize that another's eye gaze movements are an indication of intent.

CONCLUSIONS AND FUTURE DIRECTIONS

In this chapter, we have presented three lines of research that demonstrate that infants view gaze direction as an intentional cue, rather than simply attentional cue, in word learning situations. First, evidence from children with autism suggests that they fail to rely on an adult's gaze direction to establish word-object mappings, despite having intact abilities to orient automatically to shifts in gaze direction. Second, studies have demonstrated that 24-month-old infants will rely on a gaze direction cue rather than on a cue that highlights the salience of an object when identifying the referent of a novel word. Finally, research from our lab has demonstrated that different processes may underlie 24-month-olds' reliance on a nonreferential cue versus an eye gaze cue in word learning situations. Moreover, our studies demonstrate that while attentional orientation can certainly play a role in word learning, infants' reliance on eye gaze direction cannot simply be reduced to a mechanistic reliance on attention.

The research reviewed in this chapter suggests that infants' appreciation of the intentionality of eye gaze direction in word learning is an emergent ability, becoming solidified between 18 and 24 months of age. This notion is in keeping with other research demonstrating advances in infants' understanding of gaze direction in other intentional arenas during this developmental period. For example, studies have demonstrated that infants' use of gaze direction as a marker of epistemic state (i.e., appreciating that seeing leads to knowing) is established during the second year of life (e.g., Poulin-Dubois, Demke, & Olineck, this volume).

The results of the research reviewed here suggest a number of important directions for future research into the development of infants' understanding of the intentional nature of eye gaze direction. First and foremost, the issue of what develops during this second year of life merits further investigation. That is, have infants developed a general understanding of others as intentional beings or have they acquired a very specific understanding about the intentional nature of gaze direction? In a related vein, how does this understanding of the intentionality of gaze direction relate to the ability to appreciate the intentionality of other cues such as facial expressions? Finally, given that this is also a developmental period during which rapid word acquisition occurs, the nature of the relation between this dawning understanding of the intentional nature of eye gaze direction and the putative vocabulary spurt merits further clarification. Although one might expect that understanding that gaze direction marks referential intentions would lead to more rapid acquisition of words, the specific causal nature of the relation remains to be determined. Gaining further insight into these and other related issues will lead to a more fulsome account of the critical role of gaze direction in early word learning.

ACKNOWLEDGMENTS

This research was supported by an operating grant awarded to the first author from the Social Sciences and Humanities Research Council of Canada and funding from the Canada Research Chairs program. The second and third authors were supported by graduate fellowships from NSERC of Canada and the Province of Alberta. We thank the parents, and children who participated in the studies. We also thank Chris Kelland Friesen, Cari Kilbreath, Jennie Neufeld, Amy Onysyk, and Hayli Stock for their invaluable assistance with these studies.

REFERENCES

Akhtar, N., Carpenter, M., & Tomasello, M. (1996). The role of discourse novelty in early word learning. *Child Development, 67,* 635–645.

Akhtar, N., Dunham, F., & Dunham, P. (1991). Directive interactions and early vocabulary development: The role of joint attentional focus. *Journal of Child Language, 18,* 41–49.

Akhtar, N., & Tomasello, M. (1996). Two-year-olds learn words for absent objects and actions. *British Journal of Developmental Psychology, 14,* 79–93.

Akhtar, N., & Tomasello, M. (2000). The social nature of words and word learning. In M. Marschark (Series Ed.), *Counterpoints: Cognition, memory, and language. Becoming a word learner: A debate on lexical acquisition* (pp. 115–135). New York: Oxford University Press.

Anglin, J. M. (1993). Vocabulary development: A morphological analysis. *Monographs of the Society for Research in Child Development, 58*(10, Serial No. 238).

Baldwin, D. A. (1991). Infants' contribution to the achievement of joint reference. *Child Development, 62,* 875–890.

Baldwin, D. A. (1993a). Infants' ability to consult the speaker for clues to word reference. *Child Language, 20,* 395–418.

Baldwin, D. A. (1993b). Early referential understanding: Infants' ability to understand referential acts for what they are. *Developmental Psychology, 29,* 832–843.

Baldwin, D. A., Markman, E. M., Bill, B., Desjardins, R. N., Irwin, R. N., & Tidball, G. (1996). Infants' reliance on a social criterion for establishing word-object relations. *Child Development, 67,* 3135–3153.

Baldwin, D. A., & Moses, L. J. (2001). Links between social understanding and early word learning: Challenges to current accounts. *Social Development, 10,* 309–329.

Baron-Cohen, S. (1989). Perceptual role taking and protodeclarative pointing in autism. *British Journal of Developmental Psychology, 7,* 113–127.

Baron-Cohen, S., Baldwin, D., & Crowson, M. (1997). Do children with autism use the speaker's direction of gaze strategy to crack the code of language? *Child Development, 68,* 48–57.

Baron-Cohen, S., Campbell, R., Karmiloff-Smith, A., Grant, J., & Walker, J. (1995). Are children with autism blind to the mentalistic significance of the eyes? *British Journal of Developmental Psychology, 13,* 379–398.

Bloom, P. (2000). *How children learn the meanings of words*. Cambridge, MA: MIT Press.

Brooks, R., & Meltzoff, A. M. (2002). The importance of eyes: How infants interpret adult looking behavior. *Developmental Psychology, 38*, 701–711.

Bruner, J. (1975). The ontogenesis of speech acts. *Journal of Child Language, 2*, 1–19.

Bruner, J. (1983). *Child's talk: Learning to use language*. San Diego, CA: Academic Press.

Butler, S. C., Caron, A. J., & Brooks, R. (2000). Infant understanding of the referential nature of looking. *Journal of Cognition and Development, 1*, 359–377.

Carpenter, M., Nagell, K., & Tomasello, M. (1998). Social cognition, Joint attention, and communicative competence from 9 to 15 months of age. *Monographs of the Society for Research in Child Development, 63*(4, Serial No. 255).

Carpenter, M., Pennington, B., & Rogers, S. (2002). Interrelations among social-cognitive skills in young children with autism. *Journal of Autism and Developmental Disorders, 32*, 91–106.

Chawarska, K., Klin, A., & Volkmar, F. (2003). Automatic attention cueing through eye movement in 2-year-old children with autism. *Child Development, 74*, 1108–1122.

Diesendruck, G., Markson, L., Akhtar, N., & Reudor, A. (2004). Two-year-olds' sensitivity to speakers' intent: An alternative account of Samuelson and Smith. *Developmental Science, 7*, 33–41.

Driver, J., Davis, G., Ricciardelli, P., Kidd, P., Maxwell, E., & Baron-Cohen, S. (1999). Gaze perception triggers reflexive visuospatial orienting. *Visual Cognition, 6*, 509–540.

Dunham, P. J., Dunham, F., & Curwin, A. (1993). Joint-attentional states and lexical acquisition at 18 months. *Developmental Psychology, 29*, 827–831.

Farroni, T., Johnson, M. H., Brockbank, M., & Simion, F. (2000). Infants' use of gaze direction to cue attention: The importance of perceived motion. *Visual Cognition, 7*, 705–718.

Farroni, T., Mansfield, E. M., Lai, C., & Johnson, M. H. (2003). Infants perceiving and acting on the eyes: Tests of an evolutionary hypothesis. *Journal of Experimental Child Psychology, 85*, 199–212.

Friesen, C. K., & Graham, S. A. (2002, June). *Lights, please: Attentional cues and early word learning*. Paper presented at the annual meeting of the Canadian Society for Brain, Behaviour, and Cognitive Science, Vancouver, B.C.

Friesen, C. K., & Kingstone, A. (1998). The eyes have it! Reflexive orienting is triggered by nonpredictive gaze. *Psychonomic Bulletin & Review, 5*, 490–495.

Graham, S. A., Neufeld, J., & Kilbreath, C. S. (2004). *The role of gaze cues and nonreferential cues in guiding 24-month-olds' word-object mappings*. Manuscript in preparation.

Hains, S. M. J., & Muir, D. W. (1996). Infant sensitivity to adult eye direction information. *Child Development, 67*, 1940–1951.

Hollich, G. J., Hirsh-Pasek, K., & Golinkoff, R. M. (2000). Breaking the language barrier: An emergentist coalition model for the origins of word learning. *Monographs of the Society for Research in Child Development, 65*(3, Serial No. 262).

Hood, B. M., Willen, D. J., & Driver, J. (1998). Adult's eyes trigger shifts of visual attention in human infants. *Psychological Science, 9*, 131–134.

Kingstone, A., Smilek, D., Ristic, J., Friesen, C. K., & Eastwood, J. D. (2003). Attention, researchers! It is time to take a look at the real world. *Current Directions in Psychological Science, 12*, 176–184.

Kylliäinen, A., & Hietanen, J. (2004). Attentional orienting by another's gaze direction in children with autism. *Journal of Child Psychology and Psychiatry, 45*, 435–444.

Langton, S. R. H., & Bruce, V. (1999). Reflexive visual orienting in response to the social attention of others. *Visual Cognition, 6*, 541–567.

Leekam, S., Baron-Cohen, S., Perret, D., Milders, M., & Brown, S. (1997). Eye-direction detection: A dissociation between geometric and joint attentional skills in autism. *British Journal of Developmental Psychology, 15*, 77–95.

Leekam, S., Hunnisett, E., & Moore, C. (1998). Target and cues: Gaze-following in children with autism. *Journal of Child Psychology and Psychiatry, 39*, 951–962.

Leekam, S., Lopez, B., & Moore, C. (2000). Attentional and joint attention in preschool children with autism. *Developmental Psychology, 36*, 261–273.

MacPherson, A. C., & Moore, C. (this volume). Attentional control by gaze cues in infancy. In R. Flom, K. Lee, & D. Muir (Eds.), *Gaze-following: Its development and significance.* Mahwah, NJ: Lawrence Erlbaum Associates.

Moore, C. (1999) Gaze-following and the control of attention. In P. Rochat (Ed.), *Early social cognition: Understanding others in the first months of life.* Mahwah, NJ: Lawrence Erlbaum Associates.

Moore, C., Angelopoulos, M., & Bennett, P. (1999). Word learning in the context of referential and salience cues. *Developmental Psychology, 35*, 60–68.

Moore, C., & Corkum, V. (1998). Infant gaze-following based on eye direction. *British Journal of Developmental Psychology, 16*, 495–503.

Poulin-Dubois, D., Demke, T. L., & Olinek, K. M. (this volume) The inquisitive eye: Infants' implicit understanding that looking leads to knowing. In R. Flom, K. Lee, & D. Muir (Eds.), *Gaze-following: Its development and significance.* Mahwah, NJ: Lawrence Erlbaum Associates.

Poulin-Dubois, D., & Forbes, J. (2002). Toddlers' attention to intentions-in-action in learning novel action words. *Developmental Psychology, 38*, 104–114.

Ristic, J., Friesen, C. K., & Kingstone, A. (2002). Are eyes special? It depends on how you look at it. *Psychonomic Bulletin & Review, 9*, 507–513.

Sabbagh, M. A., & Baldwin, D. A. (2004). Understanding the role of communicative intentions in word learning, In N. Eilan, C. Hoerl, T. McCormack, & J. Koessler (Eds.), *Joint attention: Communication and other minds.* Oxford: Oxford University Press.

Samuelson, L. K., & Smith, L. (1998). Memory and attention make smart word learning: An alternative account of Akhtar, Carpenter & Tomasello. *Infant Development, 69*, 94–104.

Scaife, M., & Bruner, J. (1975). The capacity for joint attention in the infant. *Nature, 253*, 265–266.

Smith, L., Jones, S., & Landau, B. (1996). Naming in young children: A dumb attentional mechanism? *Cognition, 60*, 140–171.

Symons, L. A., Hains, S. M. J., & Muir, D. W. (1998). Look at me: Five-month-old infants' sensitivity to very small deviations in eye-gaze during social interactions. *Infant Behavior & Development, 21*, 531–536.

Tipples, J. (2002). Eye gaze is not unique: Automatic orienting in response to uninformative arrows. *Psychonomic Bulletin & Review, 9*, 314–318.

Tomasello, M. (1992). The social bases of language acquisition. *Social Development, 1*, 67–87.

Tomasello, M., & Akhtar, N. (1995). Two-year-olds use pragmatic cues to differentiate reference to objects and actions. *Cognitive Development, 10,* 201–224.

Tomasello, M., & Barton, M. (1994). Learning words in non-ostensive contexts. *Developmental Psychology, 30,* 639–650.

Tomasello, M., & Farrar, J. (1986). Joint attention and early language. *Child Development, 57,* 1454–1463.

Tomasello, M., Strosberg, R., & Akhtar, N. (1996). Eighteen-month-old children learn words in non-ostensive contexts. *Journal of Child Language, 23,* 157–176.

Woodward, A. L., & Markman, E. M. (1998). Early word learning. In D. Kuhn & R. S. Siegler (Eds.), *Handbook of child psychology: Vol. 2. Cognition, perception, and language* (pp. 371–420). New York: John Wiley & Sons.

10

Eyes Wide Shut: The Importance of Eyes in Infant Gaze-Following and Understanding Other Minds

Andrew N. Meltzoff and Rechele Brooks
University of Washington

Why did they call him "Magic?" The skill that made Magic Johnson a unique basketball player is that he mastered the "no look" pass. He could pass the ball to a teammate without giving away his intentions through his pattern of gaze. Sometimes, in a particularly devious move, he "looked off" an opponent—he looked at a teammate just long enough to suggest that this player was going to receive the pass, but Magic really was attending to someone else, who was flipped the ball for an easy basket. In short, gaze direction and attention are separable. The former is usually a reliable indicator of the latter, but not always. For adults it is so natural to think that a person is attending where he is looking that one can deceive others by exploiting this default assumption. Psychologists have formal terms for capturing the difference: Gaze direction is a behavior; attention is a state of mind.

The Holy Grail for the developmental scientist is to discover the relation between infants' treatment of gaze as a bodily act versus an index of a state of mind. Key questions are: (a) whether infants grasp anything more than the behavioral level, and if so, (b) at what age they begin to make more sophisticated interpretations about "seeing" as a psychological connection between subject and object, and (c) how shall we characterize the attributions at different ages and what is the mechanism of change?

These questions, in turn, run into two familiar problems in developmental cognitive science. First, the words we use may be ill suited to describe infants' developing interpretations. We are trapped between using terms from behaviorism, such as "conditioning" and "cues" (which may be too lean) and philosophical descriptions based on a full-blown theory of mind, such as "making manifest a mutual awareness" and "representational intentional states" (which may be too rich). We lack a technical vocabulary that captures midway stations. Second, we lack critical data points, and without these it is difficult to propose a mechanism of change.

It is as if we are early biologists who had seen baby tadpoles and adult frogs, but had not yet documented the connecting steps. In such a primitive state of science, there will be some who claim that baby tadpoles are clearly different from adult frogs with no possibility of one being the progenitor of the other—who could be so silly as to suggest that legless, gilled swimmers are the baby versions of lunged four-legged creatures that can drown? It was only when biologists began to study the *metamorphs*—tadpoles who sprouted legs—that the underlying process became clear and the old black-white vocabulary was abandoned as insufficient.

Regarding the ontogeny of gaze-following, we think we have captured tadpoles with legs. We have located a 90-day window in which there are important transformations in infants' understanding of adult gaze. The critical time for the emergence of gaze-following is between about 260 days old to 350 days old, about 9 to 11 months of age. Based on these new findings, and converging work of others, we suggest that infants in the first 9 months of life do *not* understand gaze-following properly so called. They orient to where the adult's head is turning, but do not specifically take into account the adult's eyes, so they are not "gaze-following." By 10 to 11 months of age, infants begin to follow gaze, as shown in their dual tendency to (a) follow a person who turns to look at an object with open eyes, but (b) refrain from following if the person makes the same head turn with closed eyes. However, infants at this age understand certain types of gaze obstructions (eyes closed) but not others (blindfolds). We argue that infants may use their *own experiences* of eye closure as the basis for making psychological attributions about these behavioral acts in others—the "Like Me" hypothesis (Meltzoff, 2005; Meltzoff & Brooks, 2001). Once infants come to understand that eyes are the organs to monitor in assessing others' visual perceptions, they have made significant progress in acquiring a more adult-like understanding of the intentional states of others. (See Table 10.1.)

TABLE 10.1.
Developmental Changes in Understanding "Seeing"

9-month-olds	10- to 12-month-olds[a]	12- to 18-month-olds
Body following	Gaze-following	Target sharing Joint visual perception
Other as indicator, orienter	Other as looker with eyes differentiated as organ of seeing	Other has shared view which can be directed (e.g., by pointing)

[a]Infants at 12 months are at a transitional age, as discussed in the text.

ASSESSING INFANT GAZE-FOLLOWING: EYES OPEN/CLOSED TEST

Rationale

For adults, certain bodily movements are imbued with particular meanings. If a person looks up into the sky, bystanders follow his or her gaze. The adults are trying to see what the other person is looking at. Adults realize that people acquire information from afar and are in *perceptual contact with* external objects, despite the spatial gap between perceiver and object. When do infants ascribe such distal perception to others? Is there a stage when head turns are interpreted as purely physical motions with no notion that they are *directed toward* the external object—no notion of a perceiver, perception, or a psychological relationship between subject and object?

It is well established that young infants turn in the direction that an adult has turned, but there is a debate about the mechanism underlying this behavior (e.g., Butterworth, 2001; Carpenter, Nagell, & Tomasello, 1998; Deák, Flom, & Pick, 2000; Eilan, Hoerl, McCormack, & Roessler, 2005; Moore & Dunham, 1995; Tomasello, 1995). One conservative proposal is that the behavior is based on infants being attracted to the spatial hemi-field toward which the adult's head is moving (Butterworth & Jarrett, 1991; Moore, 1999; Moore & Corkum, 1994). The infant notices the adult's head motion and thereby swings his or her own head to the correct half of space without processing the adult's gaze to an object. On this view, infants do not understand anything about the adult as a perceiver of an external target, but simply process the salient movements in space caused by the head, regardless of what the organs of perception, the eyes, are doing.

We developed a test procedure that zeroed in on whether infants understand the "object directedness" or a primitive referential version of adult gaze (Brooks & Meltzoff, 2002, 2005). Two identical objects were used, and the adult turned to look at one of them with no verbal or emotional cues. The principal manipulation was that the adult turned to the target object with *eyes open* for one group and with *eyes closed* for the other group. If infants relied simply on gross head motions, they should turn in both cases. If they relied solely on an abstract rule to look in the same direction as a "contingent interactant" or "agent" has turned (e.g., Johnson, Slaughter, & Carey, 1998), they should also look whether the adult's eyes were open or closed, because it was the same person, with the same history of interactive behavior, who turned in both groups. If, however, infants understand that the eyes are relevant for connecting viewer and object, then they should differentiate the two conditions and turn to look at the target object in one situation and not the other.[1]

The reason such a manipulation is crucial for theory is that we do, in fact, see with our eyes and not with our head. Our eyes are the organs of (visual) perception. It is an important step toward gaining the adult psychological interpretation of "seeing" for infants to come to understand that the eyes are critical. It is, after all, the eyes that are the window to the soul—the head is not such a portal.

Empirical Findings and Interpretation

Brooks and Meltzoff (2002) used the Gaze-Following: Eyes Open/Closed test to assess 12-, 14-, and 18-month-old infants. Each infant at each age was randomly assigned to a condition in which the adult turned to the target with either open or closed eyes. The targets were silent 3-D toys placed equidis-

---

[1]This procedure has its own developmental roots. In the primate literature Povinelli (2000) measured food-begging responses to a person with open versus closed eyes, and reported no differentiation by chimpanzees. With older human children, Lempers, Flavell, and Flavell (1977) and O'Neill (1996) used verbal and manual measures to determine what older children know about open versus closed eyes. Of course, such techniques are not suitable for infants. The advance in Brooks and Meltzoff (2002) was to use a simple gaze-following measure within the capacity of young infants and to control for head movement by having the adult turn to an external object with open versus closed eyes. Contemporaneously, co-author Brooks also used eyes open/closed as one condition in another study (Caron, Butler, & Brooks, 2002), but this work may have dampened effects because it showed infants conflicting cues (e.g., eyes pointing ahead and head pointing to the side) in a within-subjects design. As argued in the text, indicating different directions to infants for the object location may confuse them across the test session.

tant from the infant, at approximately a 75° angle off midline. There were four trials (two to the left and two to the right in a counterbalanced order), and each trial was 6.5 s in duration. Thus, there were no linguistic or emotional cues as to where to turn, and no sound-localization cues because the targets were silent. The infant's behavior was videotaped and subsequently scored by an observer who remained blind to whether the adult turned with open or closed eyes and the direction of the adult turn. For each trial, an infant's first target look was categorized as a "correct look," when it aligned with the adult's target (+1), or an "incorrect look," when it aligned with the opposite target (−1). If infants looked at neither target, they received a score of 0 for "non-looking." As is standard in gaze-following procedures, the looking score was a total of the correct looks, incorrect looks, and non-looks (e.g., Butler, Caron, & Brooks, 2000; Flom, Deák, Phill, & Pick, 2004; Moore & Corkum, 1998). Thus, if an infant consistently looks at correct targets, she would have a positive score (with a maximum of 4), but if she frequently looks at incorrect targets, her score would be negative (with a minimum of −4).

The main findings are shown in Figure 10–1. Infants at all ages looked significantly more often at the target when the adult turned with open than with closed eyes. We also scored other behaviors beyond the traditional looking measure. We scored infants' average duration of correct looks. This revealed that infants *inspected the target longer* when the adult turned to it with open versus closed eyes. Also, more infants *vocalized* toward the correct target in the open-eyes than closed-eyes condition. Finally, significantly more

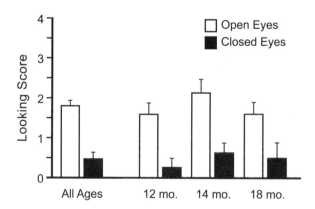

FIGURE 10–1. Infants look at the correct target more often in the open-eyes than the closed-eyes condition. (From Brooks & Meltzoff, 2002. Reprinted with permission of the American Psychological Association.)

infants *pointed to the targets* in the open-eyes condition than in the closed-eyes condition (Figure 10–2). This behavior is particularly striking because it is ostensive—the results show that infants are taking into account the perceptual status of the audience. They point when the social partner can see the objects, but refrain when the partner cannot (eyes closed), which Brooks and Meltzoff (2002) interpreted as evidence of "proto-declarative" pointing (see compatible interpretations about infant pointing by a set of converging studies using varying techniques: Bates, Benigni, Bretherton, Camaioni, & Volterra, 1979; Camaioni, Perucchini, Bellagamba, & Colonnesi, 2004; Franco & Butterworth, 1996; Liszkowski, Carpenter, Henning, Striano, & Tomasello, 2004).

We return now to the rationale for conducting this study. The lean interpretation of gaze-following is that a visible movement simply drags infants' attention to a hemi-field of space where they (happen to) see an interesting object. It is the adult's head movement that pulls infants' attention to the indicated side. The current findings indicate that such a mechanism does not provide a full explanation of the behavior of 1-year-olds, although it remains possible for younger infants. In the experiments reported here, head movement was controlled. The results show that infants are significantly more likely to look at the correct target when the adult has an unobstructed view of the target (open eyes) than an obstructed view (closed eyes).

The current work goes beyond the standard looking measure. We also analyzed how long infants look at the adult's target. Even if we select only correct looks at the target, these correctly oriented looks are longer when the adult

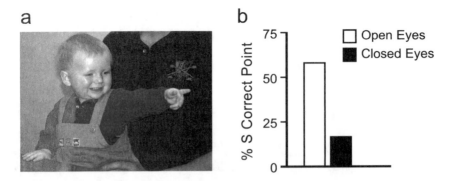

FIGURE 10–2.   (a) A 12-month-old boy pointing at the target. (b) Infants selectively point to the target when the social partner has her eyes open versus eyes closed. This suggests that points are used in a "proto-declarative" manner and not produced solipsistically.

turns toward the object with open eyes than with closed eyes. Put another way, even if the adult's head turning brings infants' attention to an object, the adult's open eyes prompt infants to inspect the object longer in one case than the other. This visual inspection is important because the object, in itself, is the same whether the adult turns with open or closed eyes. The object takes on special valence because it is looked at by another person. *It is as if having the adult shine her psychological spotlight on an inanimate object leaves a trace on it, an invisible mark—the mark of having been inspected by someone else.* This shows joint perception or joint visual exploration, not simply directionally appropriate looking.

What These Findings Add

We thus wish to argue that 12-month-old infants should be credited with gaze-following. At first blush, this may not seem new given other reports (Butterworth & Jarrett, 1991; Carpenter et al., 1998; Deák et al., 2000; D'Entremont, 2000; Flom & Pick, 2005; Morales et al., 2000; Mumme & Fernald, 2003; Scaife & Bruner, 1975). However, most of these studies are open to Moore's (1999; Moore & Corkum, 1994) critique that infants could simply be following the direction of head movement.

Corkum and Moore (1995) pitted the direction of head movement against eye movement to assess which one elicited a response from infants. They tested whether 6- to 19-month-old infants follow eye gaze in the following conditions in a within-subjects design: (a) turns of the eyes (with the head facing forward), (b) turns of both the head and eyes, (c) turns of the head (with eyes facing forward), and (d) head and eyes turning in opposite directions. There was no age at which infants followed the adult's gaze when only eyes were turned in the absence of head movement. Based on these results and others, a number of authors are hesitant to confirm that 1-year-olds gaze follow, and reserve such capacity for 18 months or older (Corkum & Moore, 1995; Moore & Corkum, 1998). It is important to realize, however, that when head and eyes point in different directions, this presents young infants with a conflict between cues. For example, showing the eyes turning left while the head moves to the right provides a display that indicates two contradictory places in space at the same time. This may dampen the effects. The Gaze-Following: Eyes Open/Closed test provides infants with a situation in which the head and eyes are not in conflict: It pits head direction + neutral eye information (eyes not looking anywhere because they are closed) against consonant head direction + eye direction information. Our finding that 1-year-old infants differentiate between the two conditions and respond appropriately in the eyes open condition shows that the status of the eyes is responsible for the effects.

Heads vs. Eyes: Can We Escape a Lean View?

We argued herein that 12-month-old infants can be credited with gaze-following given their success in our procedure, but a critic might question one aspect of the procedure. One might wonder whether infants are simply "disrupted" by the sight of a person with eyes closed. If so, they may turn less often in the closed-eyes condition because they were disrupted from turning, due to the novelty of the situation or the break in interaction. This is an interesting point, but there are four arguments weighing against this interpretation.

First, although confronting an infant with an *en face* adult who holds her eyes closed for a lengthy time may be disruptive, that was *not* the procedure. The adult's eyes were shut only slightly longer than the blink of an eye (half a second) before the turning toward the object for a 6.5 s response period. There is nothing in the literature suggesting this would be disruptive (the still-face paradigm does not come into play at these short time intervals, D'Entremont & Muir, 1997; Tronick, 1989; Tronick, Als, Adamson, Wise, & Brazelton, 1978). Second, we systematically reviewed the videotaped records and were not able to detect any difference in the emotional reactions as a function of condition. All infants displayed a calm or positive expression and rarely displayed any distress (see Brooks & Meltzoff, 2002, for a full analysis). Moreover, every infant looked at the adult's face as she began turning (after she closed her eyes).

Third, the duration measure is relevant, because it allows us to measure the length of looking *after* the infant has turned to the correct target. Disruption is not a parsimonious concept in this case, because the infant has chosen to follow the adult to the correct side. If we control for the fact that the infant is looking at the correct target (whether in the open- or closed-eyes condition), why would they inspect it *longer* in one case than another? A natural explanation is that the infant is visually inspecting the target just because the adult is looking at it—trying to see what the adult is looking at.

Fourth, infants marshal other target-directed acts, such as pointing at the target and vocalizing toward it when the adult can see the target. Increased pointing and vocalizing at the target indicates that infants are not simply turning to a hemi-field in space: Infants are generating actions that the adult did not produce. In short, the disruption idea is a logical possibility. However, the painstaking empirical work directed toward exploring this alternative provides both negative evidence (no signs of upset or disruption) and positive evidence (longer infant visual inspection and increased vocalizing and pointing to the target) that weigh against it.

A METAMORPHOSIS IN GAZE-FOLLOWING IN INFANCY

Rationale

The previous study showed that 12-month-olds gaze follow. The question remains as to when does this begin? The Gaze-Following: Eyes Open/Closed test provides a tool for looking at the ontogenesis of gaze-following before the child's first birthday.

Brooks and Meltzoff (2005) recently completed a study of infants during the tadpole era, from 9 months to 11 months of age. We used the same procedure as previously described, but tested infants within a remarkably controlled age window. The infants were recruited to fall at three discrete ages: 9, 10, and 11 months old, with each infant ±1 week of the target age. This was the equivalent of a cross-sectional microgenetic study—we assessed infants at three moments over a 90-day growth period to see if we could capture a metamorphosis in behavior.

Empirical Findings and Interpretation

As shown in Figure 10–3, 9-month-olds did not discriminate between the open- versus closed-eyes conditions. They turned equally often in both cases. However, there was a clear developmental shift 30 days later. For 10-month-olds, the looking scores in the open-eyes condition were significantly greater than in the closed-eyes condition; and a similar significant effect was also evident among 11-month-olds.

We also analyzed whether infants vocalized while looking at the correct target, categorized as a "correct gaze + simultaneous vocalization." (Infants

FIGURE 10–3.   At 9 months of age infants turn indiscriminately to the target, whether or not the adult can see it. But at 10 and 11 months old, they selectively follow the gaze of the adult in the open-eyes condition. Note the sharp decline in looking when the adult cannot see the target (eyes closed). (From Brooks & Meltzoff, 2005. Reprinted with permission of Blackwell Publishing.)

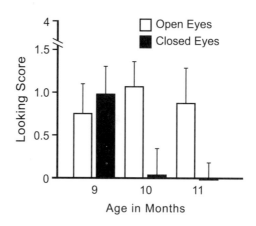

at these young ages rarely point, but they sometimes vocalize when looking at the target, which may serve a referential function.) The results were significant, with more infants in the open-eyes condition (16 of 48) producing correct gaze + simultaneous vocalizations than in the closed-eyes condition (8 of 48), $p < .05$.

An alternate interpretation is that closed eyes are odd/disruptive to 10- to 11-month-olds. Similar to the earlier study, we scrutinized the records and found that infants in the closed-eyes group gave no signs of being upset, either at the onset of the eye closure or during the brief (6.5 s) response period. As a statistical test, we examined how long infants stared at the experimenter, which could "disrupt" looking to the target. The results showed that infants spent the same amount of time looking at the experimenter in the open-eyes as the closed-eyes condition (average of 60% and 64%, respectively), and with a similar pattern at each of the three ages (see Brooks & Meltzoff, 2005, for full details). In sum, there was no evidence that these young infants were disrupted by the closed-eyes condition. Rather, we believe they did not interpret the adult turn with closed eyes as being "about" or referring to the external object.

What These Findings Add

An important detail about these results is the nature of the developmental change observed. The most significant change between 9 and 10 months of age is the sharp *decline* in turning to the closed-eyes condition (see Figure 10–3). It is not that the 9-month-olds fail to follow the adult's turn. Quite the contrary, in fact, *they follow too much*; they turn even when the adult turns with closed eyes.

This is key for theory because it makes sense of the literature claiming that infants gaze follow starting as early as 3 or 4 months old (e.g., Butterworth & Jarrett, 1991; D'Entremont, Hains, & Muir, 1997; Flom & Pick, 2005; Morales, Mundy, & Rojas, 1998; Scaife & Bruner, 1975; Striano & Stahl, 2005). At first, this might seem in contradiction to our claim about the development of gaze-following at 10 months of age. But there is no contradiction. We believe that infants turn to follow the direction of head movements at 9 months and younger, but that they do not selectively gaze follow properly so called (as shown by their turning to the closed-eyes condition). In fact, a supplementary analysis demonstrates that our findings are very compatible with the other findings in the literature. If we select 9-month-olds in the open-eyes condition, we, too, can show that they consistently turn in the correct direction. The looking scores of the 9-month-olds in the open-eyes condition (Figure 10–2) are significantly greater than 0 (where 0 equals chance, i.e., equal turning to the correct and incorrect side). Thus we replicate the common finding of correct turning. The problem is not a lack of turning, but that 9-month-olds turn even if the adult cannot possibly see the target.

In sum, our data support the idea that genuine gaze-following develops at about 10 to 11 months of life and emerges from simpler beginnings (more about this later). Although leaner views are possible, our interpretation is that *visual* contact between the looker and the object first becomes important at 10 to 11 months (Brooks & Meltzoff, 2005). Whereas 9-month-olds may understand others as "body orienters," older infants begin to understand others as "visually connected" to the external world and that the eyes are the critical organ. This is an important step in social cognition.

BIOLOGICAL VERSUS PHYSICAL OCCLUDERS

Rationale

There is a further important development that occurs at about 12 months of age. Eye closure is only one way to block the line of sight to an object. Another way is to use a physical object. From an adult perspective, blindfolds have the same function as closed eyes—both prevent visual access. Our results suggest that infants understand the consequences of eye closure (a biological motion) before they understand blindfolds (an inanimate object). This is fascinating because it opens the possibility that infants may use their *own experiences* of eye closure, and the result of not being able to see, as the basis for giving meaning to these similar behavioral acts in others—the "Like Me" hypothesis for gaze-following (Meltzoff, 2005; Meltzoff & Brooks, 2001). This hypothesis will be examined in the conclusion of this chapter. For now, it is relevant to summarize the relevant blindfold data.[2]

Empirical Findings and Interpretation

In our study of inanimate occluders, a person turned toward a target wearing either a headband or a blindfold (Brooks & Meltzoff, 2002; Experiment 2). In both instances, the same cloth covered part of the experimenter's face, but in one situation the opaque cloth was on the forehead and in the other it was over the eyes. We tested 12-, 14- and 18-month-old infants (all within 1 week

---

[2]Blindfolds are only one way of using an inanimate object to block a person's view. A wall or external barrier is another. We chose a blindfold in part because the occluder was on the face and completely obscured the organs of perception, the eyes, like eye closure does.

of stated age) using the same room set-up as in earlier studies. If infants were flummoxed by the novelty of the opaque cloth, they would stare at the adult and not look at the targets in either condition. If infants are simply following head turns, they would look at the external target but do so indiscriminately in both conditions. If infants recognize that a blindfold blocks visual access but headbands do not, they would look significantly more often at targets indicated by an adult wearing a headband compared to a blindfold.

The results showed that 14- and 18-month-old infants looked at the adult's target significantly more often in the headband than the blindfold condition. The 12-month-old infants did *not* distinguish between the two conditions. They looked at the indicated target just as often when the adult turned wearing the blindfold as the headband. Although they did not distinguish these two conditions, they were not behaving randomly or in a confused manner. The 12-month-olds looked at the correct target significantly more than the opposite target, resulting in their looking scores being greater than 0 (which would have been the chance level of responding). So once again we can say they were systematic in their response and turned to the correct side; their difficulty was that they failed to distinguish the two conditions of blindfold (when the experimenter could not possibly see) and headband (where the experimenter could) and indiscriminately turned in both.

These findings are interesting, especially when compared to the eyes open/closed test. The 14- and 18-month-olds responded just as they had in the earlier study. In both, they followed the adult's gaze when she had visual access to target, but refrained when she did not have visual access (i.e., blindfolded or closed eyes). However, the 12-month-olds, who had succeeded admirably on the eyes closed/open test, responded quite differently. They turned to follow the adult even when the adult wore a blindfold. This is not just a matter of blindfolds causing a general suppression of activity. Rather, infants make the mistake of following the "gaze" of the adult wearing the blindfold. In other words, they acted like the 9-month-olds did in the closed-eyes case. It is as if they had developed an understanding that eye closures block the adult's view, but do not yet understand that blindfolds block perception. Infants develop this latter understanding remarkably early in development, but not as early as they understand eye closure.

What These Findings Add

Not all occluders are equal in the eyes of infants. We have shown that there is a difference between understanding eye closure and blindfolds, with infants' understanding of simple eye closure being in advance. This research adds to other related work using different kinds of visual occluders, such as walls and detached screens. Taken together, this research suggests that infants come to understand nonbiological occluders to vision sometime around or soon after 1 year of age depending upon the nature of the occluder (Brooks & Meltzoff, 2002; Butler et al., 2000; Caron, Kiel, Dayton, & Butler, 2002; Dunphy-Lelii & Wellman, 2004; Moll & Tomasello, 2004). Future research could profitably be directed at examining the same age children, using the same paradigm, and systematically manipulating different types of barriers: eye closure, blindfolds, distal barriers such as walls/screens. Young infants may not come to understand all of these types of barriers to perception in the same way or at the same age.

AN INTERVENTION EXPERIMENT: THE "LIKE ME" HYPOTHESIS

Rationale

The foregoing research indicates that at least one kind of occluder to vision, eye closure, is understood quite early. One hypothesis is that this is because infants themselves have ample prior experience with the perceptual effects of eye closure. When they do so, the world goes black. The non-biological occluders should become more meaningful to an infant after repeated opportunities to learn that they block vision.

Empirical Findings and Interpretation

Meltzoff and Brooks (2004) gave 12-month-olds experience with blindfolds. Infants were randomly assigned to a baseline condition or two treatment groups, one of which involved blindfolds and the other involved the same black cloth but with an opening cut out of the middle of it. The infants experienced that the blindfold blocked their view. Their view was blocked when the blindfold was held in front of *their* eyes, and was restored again when the blindfold was removed. This experience had nothing to do with the experimenter's viewpoint; it was a first-person experience. In the critical test, the adult put the blindfold over her own eyes. This was the first time the infants were presented with the blindfolded adult. The results showed that infants now interpreted the blindfold correctly. They did not turn when the adult wore the blindfold. In the control groups (baseline and cloth with opening) the infants were allowed to familiarize themselves with the cloth, but without experiencing an obstructed view. This had no effect. As we expected, the control-group infants still mistakenly followed the blindfolded adult's "gaze."

What These Findings Add

This is the first study showing that infants use first-person experience about a mental state such as "seeing" to make interpretations about another person. We believe that first-person experience with blindfolds changes infants' understanding of the other's situation. Infants use first-person experience to make third-person attributions about perception. Other explanations may be possible, but we think these training effects are a case of "like me" projection (Meltzoff, 2005), with deep implications for infant development, as will be elaborated in the conclusions.

INDIVIDUAL DIFFERENCES IN EARLY GAZE-FOLLOWING PREDICTS LATER LANGUAGE ACQUISITION

Rationale

On theoretical grounds, there is good reason for thinking that gaze-following may be an important component of language acquisition (e.g., Baldwin, 1995; Baldwin & Moses, 2001; Bruner, 1983; Carpenter et al., 1998; Graham, Nilsen, & Nayer, this volume; Hollich, Hirsh-Pasek, & Golinkoff, 2000; Moore, Angelopoulos, & Bennett, 1999; Tomasello, 1995, 2003). Infants who understand adult gaze as an ostensive act are in a better position to use everyday interactions with adults to learn words as labels for external objects. Not all language refers to tangible entities that can be looked at (Gopnik, 1982, 1988; Gopnik & Meltzoff, 1986), and parents don't consistently label objects that are in the infants' current view (Sabbagh & Baldwin, 2005; Tomasello & Todd, 1983). Nonetheless, one basic format in the "initial word learning game" (Bruner, 1983) is for parents to point out salient objects through gaze and then to label them. Infants who are advanced on gaze-following, in particular (and perhaps in understanding referential intent in general), may have a leg up on learning language. In order to pursue this idea within our own data set, we conducted a longitudinal follow-up of the children who came into the lab at 10 to 11 months of age—the tadpoles we caught right at the onset of gaze-following.

Empirical Findings and Interpretation

Brooks and Meltzoff (2005) assessed whether gaze-following behavior at 10 to 11 months predicted later language development. Language development was assessed with the MacArthur-Bates Communicative Developmental Inventory (CDI; Fenson et al., 1994). The results showed that gaze-following behavior at 10 to 11 months predicted language development over 1 year later. Infants who produced the correct gaze + simultaneous vocalization act at 10 to 11 months had larger receptive vocabularies at 18 months than infants who did not ($p < .001$). The 10- to 11-month-old gaze-following behavior also predicted significantly more complex sentences ($p < .01$) and larger productive vocabulary at 24 months old. Those infants who showed gaze-following + simultaneous vocalization at 10 to 11 months had a 194 word advantage at 24 months over those infants who did not (521 vs. 327 words, $t(23) = 2.96$, $p < 01$).

We also examined the relationship between the average duration of looking to the correct target at 10 to 11 months and subsequent language. This infant gaze-following score at 10 to 11 months predicted by 24 months a significantly larger productive vocabulary size ($r = .63, p < .01$). For example, infants who earlier had low gaze-following scores (as measured by average duration at the correct target) produced utterances at 24 months that included structures such as "want more" or "cars voom." In contrast, infants who had high scores had sentences that included, "Sit right down here mommy, legs out, and play with spinning tops."

What These Findings Add

The current results complement recent empirical reports that infant gaze following predicts language development (Carpenter et al., 1998; Markus, Mundy, Morales, Delgado, & Yale, 2000; Morales et al., 1998, 2000; Mundy, Fox, & Card, 2003; Mundy & Gomes, 1998). The current findings agree with these pioneering reports, but also provide additional data. In the previous studies, the gaze-following procedures included adult vocalizations (and/or communicative points) in conjunction with the adult turning to look at the target. Consequently, it could have been that infants' responsiveness to these linguistic cues provided by the experimenter *during the gaze-following procedure* correlated with later language abilities. In the current study, the adult turned toward the targets silently and displayed no emotional or pointing cues. This control gives us confidence that the significant correlations rest on the predictive nature of infant gaze-following behavior (or more generally, social cognition). The findings strongly suggest that infants who are skilled at early gaze-following enter the language game with an advantage—a boost that persists through 24 months, over a year later.

ASPECTS OF A DEVELOPMENTAL THEORY

Why is gaze-following so fascinating? In adult commonsense psychology, gaze-following entails the ascription of a mental life to the viewer. We follow where another person looks because we want to see what they are seeing. When we see people direct their gaze somewhere, we wonder what object is catching their attention and want to seek out that interesting spectacle ourselves. Thus, a viewer's gaze is intentional in the philosophical sense—it is "about" a distal object. The "aboutness" is demonstrated by the fact that we turn to the same place in space to see, quite literally, *what the look was about.*

To a developmental psychologist, who may or may not care about the philosophy, this immediately raises classic issues: Do infants gaze follow on the same basis as adults? If not, how/when do they develop the adult framework? These empirical questions typically derive from two motivations. First, developmentalists are interested in the origins of adult behavior, and the ontogenesis of gaze-following, like the emergence of the pincer grip, can be charted. Second, we want to use gaze-following as a tool for illuminating the development of children's understanding of other minds or at least others' perceptions. Gaze-following is a window into social cognition.

Now comes the rub—the problem that bedevils all of developmental psychology. We cannot immediately "read off" infants' mental-state attributions based on the fact that they gaze follow. In order for infants to gaze follow, there must first be a stimulus change in the visual world, typically another person turns to look at an object. Although adults ascribe mental experience to the viewer, there may be a simpler basis for gaze-following. Indeed, there are at least two major levels: (a) a *physical* motion in space, and (b) a *psychological* connection between agent and object. Psychologists endlessly debate whether (a) or (b) applies to infants of a given age. Alas, there is no silver bullet for ending the debate. No single experiment will answer whether one or another level provides the best descriptor. As shown repeatedly in the history of psychology/philosophy, with schools of thought such as behaviorism, arguments can be mustered to show that even adults (no less infants) are simply smart readers of others' behavior and need not rely on making attributions of mind to other humans (Ryle, 1949). Nonetheless, empirical work provides grist for the debate.

THE IMPORTANCE OF EYES

In this chapter we discussed an integrated series of findings using the Gaze-Following: Eyes Open/Closed test. This technique provides a test of the leanest interpretation of gaze-following. According to the lean view, infants are attracted to the most salient movement in the stimulus, the head movement.

This movement drags them to the correct hemi-field in space where they happen to encounter an object, by chance. Presto! Infants succeed on the classical gaze-following test, but do not process *gaze* at all.

The Gaze-Following: Eyes Open/Closed test controls for head movements. Infants are randomly assigned to one of two groups. For one group, the adult turns with eyes open and for another group with eyes closed. Any difference between the groups cannot be due to the head movements, which are controlled. The studies allow us to address whether infants are taking into account the status of the eyes, by the logic of the design. The results show that 9-month-old infants turn regardless of whether eyes are open or closed, but that 10-, 11-, and 12-month-olds selectively turn to follow open rather than closed eyes. We conclude that 9-month-olds do not gaze follow, properly so called.

One response to these findings might be that it is "only a detail" that infants don't understand gaze. As long as infants follow the head, it matters little that they haven't isolated the eyes. Our response is that, from a developmental viewpoint, it matters a great deal. It matters for three reasons. First, infants who fail the eyes-closed test cannot be said to be gaze-following per se. Second, we humans do, in fact, see through our eyes. Until infants understand that eyes, not heads, are key, they will make many mistakes in real life in decoding the actions of adults. Third, it is a major advance in infants' understanding of persons and their perceptual-cognitive system for infants to grasp that eyes are the organ of visual information gathering. If one is interested in the development of the notion of perception, seeing, visual attention, and perspective taking, one needs to trace back to the earliest age at which infants begin to focus on eyes as the organ for seeing. Similarly, when infants begin to map their own eyes to the eyes of others, they have made a step forward in understanding self-other similarity.

THE IMPORTANCE OF DEVELOPMENT

The work discussed in this chapter suggests at least three developmental changes:

- Infants at 9 months and younger do not *gaze* follow. They turn even if the adult cannot possibly be looking at the target because she has her eyes shut.
- At 10 to 12 months infants gaze follow, turning to look at a target selectively according to whether the person has eyes open or not. But they do not yet have a general understanding that occluders block vision. They understand that some occluders (biological motion such as eye closure)

put the person out of perceptual contact, but do not fully understand that other occluders have this consequence.

- By 14 to 18 months of age, infants have a more generalized understanding that opaque occluders interposed between the eyes and the target block the adult's visual contact with this object. Also by this age, there is evidence that the majority of infants share their view with "perceiving others"—they selectively point to objects when the adult has eyes open versus eyes closed (Brooks & Meltzoff, 2002).

Having uncovered these developmental changes, it will be informative to use the eyes open/closed approach to investigate other topics. For studies tracing pointing development, the eye closure manipulation will be useful for clarifying when the infant does and does not deploy pointing as a proto-declarative act (Camaioni, et al., 2004; Franco & Butterworth, 1996; Liszkowski, et al., 2004). Also, it will be interesting for future work to more systematically compare infants' developing understanding of blindfolds to their understanding of free-standing barriers that block the line of sight but not all vision of the external world, such as walls and detached screens (cf., Butler et al., 2000; Dunphy-Lelii & Wellman, 2004; Moll & Tomasello, 2004).

Our current working hypothesis is that the earliest occluder of vision that infants understand is eye closure. Of course, eye closure is a biological motion over which infants have longstanding voluntary control. This raises the interesting possibility that infants have learned about the effects of eye closure by repeatedly opening and closing their eyes themselves.

A MECHANISM OF CHANGE: THE "LIKE ME" HYPOTHESIS

We have noted that there is developmental change in infant gaze-following. Whenever age-related changes are observed, multiple theories can be advanced to fit them. Two extreme options spring readily to mind—innateness and Skinnerian conditioning. Although no one may adhere strictly to either, it is worth considering what they entail. They often "lurk" in the background of discussions of gaze-following, and it is good for the debate to bring them into the open.

On the one hand, it might be suggested that gaze-following is innate. Infants might be born with the proclivity to follow gaze direction and do so on the same basis as older infants. They may not always demonstrate this core ability, but this could be due to "performance constraints" such as poor head control and so forth. An innate Eye Direction Detector (EDD) has been proposed that has this general flavor (Baron-Cohen, 1995). A strong nativist position is not especially compatible with the developmental timetable listed previously. Specifically, it would have been more convenient for this theory if young infants had differentiated eyes open versus closed. An EDD ought to lead 9-month-olds to follow in the presence of eyes and not their absence (eyes closed). This did not occur. This view is also stretched thin by the observed difference between eyes closed and blindfolds—1-year-olds follow one but not the other. There are no "eyes" to detect in either case. On the opposite extreme, it might be suggested that gaze-following is nothing more than a conditioned response. Infants learn that the adult head + eye stimulus is a reliable signal ("discriminative cue") for an interesting sight ("reinforcement") and infants are operantly conditioned to turn in the direction as the adults turn ("shaped by experience"). The question comes down to "what else" might be going on besides innate perceptual biases plus learning from the success of finding objects indicated by where adults point their heads and eyes?[3]

We think there is a large "what else." In order to understand the changing meaning that "turning to look at an object" has for infants, we find it useful to consider the "Like Me" hypothesis (Meltzoff, 1999, 2005; Meltzoff & Brooks, 2001; Meltzoff & Gopnik, 1993). The crux of this view is that infants use their own first-person experience to interpret the acts of others. In particular, we think that infants' interpretation of the adult's act of looking-to-target changes as they grow more experienced with their own behavior and map the similarities between self and other.

The intervention study with self-training on blindfolds at 12 months of age tests this idea. The prediction from the "Like Me" hypothesis is that if infants have experience with the consequences of blindfolds for their own perception, they can use this self-experience as background for understanding the situation of others. The conditioning view also emphasizes that infants learn from experience, but the crucial difference is that the experience is of a different kind. On the conditioning view, infants would need to learn that following blindfolded adults leads to finding nothing, whereas following sighted adults leads to a visual object (reinforcement). We did not give them *any* experience with the blindfolded adult at all. There was no opportunity for shaping their response to the cue of an adult-turning-with-blindfold; they were not trained on this. What differed is that infants obtained experience from the opaque cloth held to their *own* eyes. Then, the adult donned the blindfold for the first time. The results showed that infants who were given self-experience with

---

[3]We offer the extreme views in the spirit of mapping the conceptual space. There are few who argue that either extreme provides a full explanation of gaze-following in the first 12 to 18 months of life (see the subtleties of the eye-cuing studies by Farroni, Mansfield, Lai, & Johnson, 2003; Farroni, Massaccesi, Pividori, & Johnson, 2004; Hood, Willen, & Driver, 1998; and the learning studies by Corkum & Moore, 1998; and Moore & Corkum, 1998).

blindfolds did not follow where the blindfolded adult turned. This demonstrates the role of experience, but it is not the kind of experience that the behaviorists were talking about. Unlike either conditioning or nativist views, the "Like Me" hypothesis emphasizes the role of infants' own self-experience in interpreting the behavior of others.

Real-life Experience and the Development of Gaze-Following

A "Like Me" mechanism may play a role in everyday life, not just in the experimental setup where infants are specifically given experience. Given that the 9-month-old infants turn indiscriminately to eyes open and eyes closed, we must ask what this means. The current data do not allow firm conclusions, but we can offer three interpretations. First, 9-month-olds may be limited to tracking the adult head movements and run into the object by chance (building on Butterworth's ideas). Second, they may have learned that a head turn is a signal for seeing an object on the periphery, through conditioning or other training from parents (building on Moore's ideas). Third, *they may be body-orientation followers, rather than gaze followers* (building on Meltzoff's "Like Me" hypothesis).

The first two accounts have been described by others and will not be reviewed here. We wish to explore the third possibility. In this view, infants orient where another orients because they interpret bodily postures and familiar gross motor acts as being directed toward an external object. Importantly, however, this does not rely on training from adults. They could understand these behaviors in others based on their own previous experience with *their own acts*. Assuming that infants can at least relate their own gross body acts to those of others, as demonstrated in studies of imitation (Meltzoff, 1988, 1999, 2005), they have grounding for relating the bodily acts that they see to the ones they themselves have performed. Based on this connectedness between self and other, they may use their own experience with intentional body orientation as a template or framework for interpreting similar acts of others. The acts of others are imbued with meaning because they are like the intentional acts that are familiar to the infant in his or her own self-experience. This would allow infants who are 9 months old to turn where an adult is turning (as reported here and in the literature) without yet understanding the importance of eyes per se. Thus 9-month-olds may not understand object-directed gaze, but rather goal-directed bodily orientation.

If infants understand body orientation before gaze, the question naturally arises as to why this is the developmental ordering. One possibility may lie in the type of self-experience these acts entail. The proprioceptive feedback and intentionality involved in making orientation acts toward an object (positioning oneself, righting one's posture, orienting hands, head, trunk) would be especially salient for infants, who have to "work at this" to keep their balance. In everyday life, they may do less monitoring of their eyelids.[4]

GAZE-FOLLOWING AND THEORY OF MIND

We have discussed developmental changes in infants' understanding of the gaze of others. We suggested that one contributor to infants' interpretation of adult gaze is their own experience with their own bodies (their directed/intentional head and eye acts). Infants learn from their own bodily experience that eye closure blocks out the visual field, and they use this to interpret the behavior of others. In this way they come to imbue certain adult acts with felt meaning—not just as physical motions in space, but as acts having psychological correlates just like their own acts (see Meltzoff, 2005 for more details).

But as much development as occurs in the first year, there are later changes that build on these early achievements. The Magic Johnson story at the beginning of the chapter illustrates that adults make a differentiation between "seeing" and "attending." We do not think that 9-, 12- or (possibly even) 18-month-olds have a firm grasp on the adult notion of "attention." Attention is much farther "upstream" than seeing—farther from the action as it were. While seeing has an external marker that can be observed in others and felt in the self (for example, effortfully turning to look), attention has no such marker. My eyes can be pointed at a photograph, and my mind somewhere else. I can see things to which I do not attend; conversely, I can attend to that which I do not currently see. We do not think 1-year-olds can make this differentiation, though it is an essential aspect of our adult theory of mind.

We believe that infants' understanding of another's gaze is just one step, albeit a vitally important and early step, on the journey to understanding the richness of others' minds. The job of the developmental scientist is to document the critical transitions and discover the mechanism of change. At the same time, we must be aware that when we find the age when babies gaze follow, we have not moved down the age of the adult-like "theory of mind." What we have caught is a metamorph; there is little gained by arguing whether this is the same as a "real" frog or a frog with "performance constraints" (it can't jump).

---

[4]Here is a relevant thought experiment: Give infants special training on monitoring their own eye opening/closure through social games or eyelid-sensing technology to controlled external events. Concurrently, they could play imitation games that highlight the self-other mapping between their own and others' eye opening/closing. If the theory is correct, infants given such special training might succeed in our eyes open/closed gaze-following tests in an accelerated fashion.

Netting tadpoles is not trapping frogs. The value, of course, is that if you study the tadpoles, you will finally understand where in the world all those frogs come from. By studying the ontogenesis of gaze-following we are examining an essential foundation for developing the adult understanding of other minds.

ACKNOWLEDGMENTS

We thank Jacque Mullen, Ksenia Kosobutsky, Calle Fisher, and Craig Harris for help on many phases of this project, as well as Betty Repacholi for her valuable feedback. Work on this chapter was supported by the National Institute for Child Health & Human Development (HD-22514) and the Tamaki Foundation.

REFERENCES

Baldwin, D. A. (1995). Understanding the link between joint attention and language. In C. Moore & P. J. Dunham (Eds.), *Joint attention: Its origins and role in development* (pp. 131–158). Hillsdale, NJ: Lawrence Erlbaum Associates.

Baldwin, D. A., & Moses, L. J. (2001). Links between social understanding and early word learning: Challenges to current accounts. *Social Development, 10,* 309–329.

Baron-Cohen, S. (1995). *Mindblindness: An essay on autism and theory of mind.* Cambridge, MA: MIT Press.

Bates, E., Benigni, L., Bretherton, I., Camaioni, L., & Volterra, V. (1979). *The emergence of symbols: Cognition and communication in infancy.* New York: Academic Press.

Brooks, R., & Meltzoff, A. N. (2002). The importance of eyes: How infants interpret adult looking behavior. *Developmental Psychology, 38,* 958–966.

Brooks, R., & Meltzoff, A. N. (2005). The development of gaze-following and its relation to language. *Developmental Science, 8,* 535–543.

Bruner, J. (1983). *Child's talk: Learning to use language.* New York: Norton.

Butler, S. C., Caron, A. J., & Brooks, R. (2000). Infant understanding of the referential nature of looking. *Journal of Cognition and Development, 1,* 359–377.

Butterworth, G. (2001). Joint visual attention in infancy. In G. Bremner & A. Fogel (Eds.), *Blackwell handbook of infant development* (pp. 213–240). Oxford: Blackwell.

Butterworth, G., & Jarrett, N. (1991). What minds have in common is space: Spatial mechanisms serving joint visual attention in infancy. *British Journal of Developmental Psychology, 9,* 55–72.

Camaioni, L., Perucchini, P., Bellagamba, F., & Colonnesi, C. (2004). The role of declarative pointing in developing a theory of mind. *Infancy, 5,* 291–308.

Caron, A. J., Butler, S. C., & Brooks, R. (2002). Gaze-following at 12 and 14 months: Do the eyes matter? *British Journal of Developmental Psychology, 20,* 225–239.

Caron, A. J., Kiel, E. J., Dayton, M., & Butler, S. C. (2002). Comprehension of the referential intent of looking and pointing between 12 and 15 months. *Journal of Cognition and Development, 3,* 445–464.

Carpenter, M., Nagell, K., & Tomasello, M. (1998). Social cognition, joint attention, and communicative competence from 9 to 15 months of age. *Monographs of the Society for Research in Child Development, 63*(4, Serial No. 255).

Corkum, V., & Moore, C. (1995). Development of joint visual attention in infants. In C. Moore & P. J. Dunham (Eds.), *Joint attention: Its origins and role in development* (pp. 61–83). Hillsdale, NJ: Lawrence Erlbaum Associates.

Corkum, V., & Moore, C. (1998). The origins of joint visual attention in infants. *Developmental Psychology, 34*, 28–38.

D'Entremont, B. (2000). A perceptual-attentional explanation of gaze-following in 3- and 6-month-olds. *Developmental Science, 3*, 302–311.

D'Entremont, B., Hains, S. M. J., & Muir, D. W. (1997). A demonstration of gaze-following in 3- to 6-month-olds. *Infant Behavior & Development, 20*, 569–572.

D'Entremont, B., & Muir, D. W. (1997). Five-month-olds' attention and affective responses to still-faced emotional expressions. *Infant Behavior & Development, 20*, 563–568.

Deák, G. O., Flom, R. A., & Pick, A. D. (2000). Effects of gesture and target on 12- and 18-month-olds' joint visual attention to objects in front of or behind them. *Developmental Psychology, 36*, 511–523.

Dunphy-Lelii, S., & Wellman, H. M. (2004). Infants' understanding of occlusion of others' line-of-sight: Implications for an emerging theory of mind. *European Journal of Developmental Psychology, 1*, 49–66.

Eilan, N., Hoerl, C., McCormack, T., & Roessler, J. (Eds.). (2005). *Joint attention: Communication and other minds: Issues in philosophy and psychology.* New York: Oxford University Press.

Farroni, T., Mansfield, E. M., Lai, C., & Johnson, M. H. (2003). Infants perceiving and acting on the eyes: Tests of an evolutionary hypothesis. *Journal of Experimental Child Psychology, 85*, 199–212.

Farroni, T., Massaccesi, S., Pividori, D., & Johnson, M. H. (2004). Gaze-following in newborns. *Infancy, 5*, 39–60.

Fenson, L., Dale, P. S., Reznick, J. S., Bates, E., Thal, D. J., & Pethick, S. J. (1994). Variability in early communicative development. *Monographs of the Society for Research in Child Development, 59*(5, Serial No. 242).

Flom, R., Deák, G. O., Phill, C. G., & Pick, A. D. (2004). Nine-month-olds' shared visual attention as a function of gesture and object location. *Infant Behavior & Development, 27*, 181–194.

Flom, R., & Pick, A. D. (2005). Experimenter affective expression and gaze-following in 7-month-olds. *Infancy, 7*, 207–218.

Franco, F., & Butterworth, G. (1996). Pointing and social awareness: Declaring and requesting in the second year. *Journal of Child Language, 23*, 307–336.

Gopnik, A. (1982). Words and plans: Early language and the development of intelligent action. *Journal of Child Language, 9*, 303–318.

Gopnik, A. (1988). Three types of early words: The emergence of social words, names and cognitive-relational words in the one-word stage and their relation to cognitive development. *First Language, 8*, 49–69.

Gopnik, A., & Meltzoff, A. N. (1986). Relations between semantic and cognitive development in the one-word stage: The specificity hypothesis. *Child Development, 57*, 1040–1053.

Hollich, G. J., Hirsh-Pasek, K., & Golinkoff, R. M. (2000). Breaking the language barrier: An emergentist coalition model for the origins of word learning. *Monographs of the Society for Research in Child Development, 65*(3, Serial No. 262).

Hood, B. M., Willen, J. D., & Driver, J. (1998). Adult's eyes trigger shifts of visual attention in human infants. *Psychological Science, 9*, 131–134.

Johnson, S. C., Slaughter, V., & Carey, S. (1998). Whose gaze will infants follow? The elicitation of gaze-following in 12-month-olds. *Developmental Science, 1*, 233–238.

Lempers, J. D., Flavell, E. R., & Flavell, J. H. (1977). The development in very young children of tacit knowledge concerning visual perception. *Genetic Psychology Monographs, 95*, 3–53.

Liszkowski, U., Carpenter, M., Henning, A., Striano, T., & Tomasello, M. (2004). Twelve-month-olds point to share attention and interest. *Developmental Science, 7*, 297–307.

Markus, J., Mundy, P., Morales, M., Delgado, C. E. F., & Yale, M. (2000). Individual differences in infant skills as predictors of child-caregiver joint attention and language. *Social Development, 9*, 302–315.

Meltzoff, A. N. (1988). Infant imitation and memory: Nine-month-olds in immediate and deferred tests. *Child Development, 59*, 217–225.

Meltzoff, A. N. (1990). Origins of theory of mind, cognition and communication. *Journal of Communication Disorders, 32*, 251–269.

Meltzoff, A. N. (2005). Imitation and other minds: The "Like Me" hypothesis. In S. Hurley & N. Chater (Eds.), *Perspectives on imitation: From neuroscience to social science* (Vol. 2, pp. 55–77). Cambridge, MA: MIT Press.

Meltzoff, A. N., & Brooks, R. (2001). "Like me" as a building block for understanding other minds: Bodily acts, attention, and intention. In B. F. Malle, L. J. Moses, & D. A. Baldwin (Eds.), *Intentions and intentionality: Foundations of social cognition* (pp. 171–191). Cambridge, MA: MIT Press.

Meltzoff, A. N., & Brooks, R. (2004, May). *Developmental changes in social cognition with an eye towards gaze-following.* In M. Carpenter & M. Tomasello (Chairs), Action-based measures of infants' understanding of others' intentions and attention. Symposium conducted at the Biennial meeting of the International Conference on Infant Studies, Chicago, Illinois.

Meltzoff, A. N., & Gopnik, A. (1993). The role of imitation in understanding persons and developing a theory of mind. In S. Baron-Cohen, H. Tager-Flusberg, & D. J. Cohen (Eds.), *Understanding other minds: Perspectives from autism* (pp. 335–366). New York: Oxford University Press.

Moll, H., & Tomasello, M. (2004). 12- and 18-month-old infants follow gaze to spaces behind barriers. *Developmental Science, 7*, F1–F9.

Moore, C. (1999). Gaze-following and the control of attention. In P. Rochat (Ed.), *Early social cognition: Understanding others in the first months of life* (pp. 241–256). Mahwah, NJ: Lawrence Erlbaum Associates.

Moore, C., Angelopoulos, M., & Bennett, P. (1999). Word learning in the context of referential and salience cues. *Developmental Psychology, 35*, 60–68.

Moore, C., & Corkum, V. (1994). Social understanding at the end of the first year of life. *Developmental Review, 14*, 349–372.

Moore, C., & Corkum, V. (1998). Infant gaze-following based on eye direction. *British Journal of Developmental Psychology, 16*, 495–503.

Moore, C., & Dunham, P. J. (Eds.). (1995). *Joint attention: Its origin and role in development.* Hillsdale, NJ: Lawrence Erlbaum Associates.

Morales, M., Mundy, P., Delgado, C. E. F., Yale, M., Messinger, D. S., Neal, R., & Schwartz, H. (2000). Responding to joint attention across the 6- through 24-month age period and early language acquisition. *Journal of Applied Developmental Psychology, 21,* 283–298.

Morales, M., Mundy, P., & Rojas, J. (1998). Following the direction of gaze and language development in 6-month-olds. *Infant Behavior & Development, 21,* 373–377.

Mumme, D. L., & Fernald, A. (2003). The infant as onlooker: Learning from emotional reactions observed in a television scenario. *Child Development, 74,* 221–237.

Mundy, P., Fox, N., & Card, J. (2003). EEG coherence, joint attention and language development in the second year. *Developmental Science, 6,* 48–54.

Mundy, P., & Gomes, A. (1998). Individual differences in joint attention skill development in the second year. *Infant Behavior & Development, 21,* 469–482.

O'Neill, D. K. (1996). Two-year-old children's sensitivity to a parent's knowledge state when making requests. *Child Development, 67,* 659–677.

Povinelli, D. J. (2000). *Folk physics for apes: The chimpanzee's theory of how the world works.* New York: Oxford University Press.

Ryle, G. (1949). *The concept of mind.* London: Hutchinson.

Sabbagh, M. A., & Baldwin, D. A. (2005). Understanding the role of communicative intentions, in word learning. In N. Eilan, C. Hoerl, T. McCormack, & J. Roessler (Eds.), *Joint attention: Communication and other minds: Issues in philosophy and psychology* (pp. 165–184). New York: Oxford University Press.

Scaife, M., & Bruner, J. S. (1975). The capacity for joint visual attention in the infant. *Nature, 253,* 265–266.

Striano, T., & Stahl, D. (2005). Sensitivity to triadic attention in early infancy. *Developmental Science, 8,* 333–343.

Tomasello, M. (1995). Joint attention as social cognition. In C. Moore & P. J. Dunham (Eds.), *Joint attention: Its origins and role in development* (pp. 103–130). Hillsdale, NJ: Lawrence Erlbaum Associates.

Tomasello, M. (2003). *Constructing a language: A usage-based theory of language acquisition.* Cambridge, MA: Harvard University Press.

Tomasello, M., & Todd, J. (1983). Joint attention and lexical acquisition style. *First Language, 4,* 197–211.

Tronick, E. Z. (1989). Emotions and emotional communication in infants. *American Psychologist, 44,* 112–119.

Tronick, E., Als, H., Adamson, L., Wise, S., & Brazelton, T. B. (1978). The infant's response to entrapment between contradictory messages in face-to-face interaction. *Journal of the American Academy of Child Psychiatry, 17,* 1–13.

11

Preschoolers' Use of Eye Gaze for "Mind Reading"

Michelle Eskritt

Mount St. Vincent University

Kang Lee

University of Toronto

The ability to use eye gaze as source of information has a long evolutionary history. Animals, from reptiles to birds and mammals, show sensitivity to, and exhibit different behaviors based on another's direction of eye gaze (Burger, Gochfeld, & Murray, 1991; Burghardt, 1990; Gallup, Nash, & Ellison, 1971; Ristau, 1991). Adult humans are also sensitive to eye gaze, and their accuracy of determining direction of eye gaze is near the level of visual acuity (Cline, 1967; Gibson & Pick, 1963; Symons, Lee, Cedrone, & Nishimura, 2004). Furthermore, sensitivity to eyes is apparent at birth (Caron, Caron, Roberts, & Brooks, 1997; Farroni, Csibra, Simion, & Johnson, 2002; Haith, Bergman, & Moore, 1977), and by the second or third month, infants will react to shifts in adult gaze (Hood, Willen, & Driver, 1998; Muir & Hains, 1993; Vecera & Johnson, 1995).

Though a large range of animals use directional information from eye gaze, the type of information inferred from gaze direction can vary, and what an adult human interprets from eye gaze can be very different from what a snake or bird perceives. Povinelli and Eddy (1996a) distinguished between three levels of eye gaze comprehension. The most basic level is simple gaze-following where an organism notices the direction of eye gaze and may respond accordingly, but does not recognize what eye gaze may reflect about mental functioning. Povinelli and Eddy (1996b) argued that this first level of eye gaze comprehension can be useful to orient towards important events in the environment, but doing so does not require an understanding of others' minds. The second level of eye gaze comprehension starts to acknowledge the epistemic value of eye gaze. At this level there is awareness that eye gaze can indicate the attentional focus of another. The research done with animals usually reflects the first level of understanding rather than the second (e.g., Povinelli & Eddy 1996a, 1996b).

Within humans, one line of evidence for the second level of eye gaze comprehension is joint attention—that is, the realization that both the self and another are attending to the same object or event. Research with infants has found that 6-month-olds can use another person's eye gaze to orient to the same side as the person as long as head orientation is included (Butterworth & Grover, 1990), but it is not until 12 months of age that they can identify which object another is looking at (Butterworth, 1991; Brooks & Meltzoff, 2002). Eighteen-month-olds show a more sophisticated understanding with greater accuracy and can use eye gaze cues alone for this purpose (Butterworth, 1991; Butterworth & Jarrett, 1991; Moore & Corkum, 1998). By 24 months of age, children can use gaze along with other directional cues, to determine the referent of novel words (Baldwin, 1993, 1995; Poulin-Dubois & Forbes, 2002) and for social referencing purposes (Repacholi, 1998). However, this ability continues to develop through to at least 3 to 4 years of age (Anderson & Doherty, 1997; Doherty & Anderson, 1999).

The third level of eye gaze comprehension, and the focus of the present chapter, involves the realization that direction of eye gaze can indicate mental states (Povinelli & Eddy, 1996a). At this level of comprehension, direction of eye gaze is considered an ostensive behavior and can be used to determine the intention behind the behavior (Argyle, 1972; Rutter, 1984). This awareness includes an understanding of visual perception and its relationship to knowledge (e.g., Gopnik & Graf, 1988; Wimmer, Hoegrefe, & Perner, 1988), thinking (e.g., Flavell, Green, & Flavell, 1995), or desire (e.g., Lee, Eskritt, Symons, & Muir, 1998), and perhaps other mental states (e.g., emotion). Gopnik, Slaughter, and Meltzoff (1994) argued that the development of a theory of mind and the development of an understanding eye gaze are linked in that an understanding of visual perception may aid in developing a better understanding of mental states such as beliefs and false beliefs. Recognizing that people can perceive an event differently can help the development of the understanding that people can hold different beliefs about a situation. Gopnik et al. (1994) provide evidence that some aspects of visual perceptual understanding precede the development of false belief understanding. Baron-Cohen (1995a, 1995b) also suggested that children's ability to understand the ostensive function of eye gaze is an important building block for children's understanding of mind in general. He developed a model where the ability to follow eye gaze and detect intentionality feed into the ability to understand others' minds.

In the present chapter we would like to argue that the role between eye gaze and mental understanding is more complex than originally theorized. The relation between the two may be interactive rather than unidirectional; while eye gaze information provides a window for children to develop the understanding of the mind, the development of a theory of mind understanding may in turn facilitate children's use of eye gaze for mind reading purposes. An individual's eye gaze display may signal that the person is conveying a certain intentional state. However, children need to rely on many other sources of information (e.g., verbal and nonverbal behaviors of the individual) and their existing theory of mind knowledge to interpret exactly what intentional state is conveyed by the eye gaze display. For example, while a child may be able to detect that a person is looking at a cake, they must use the person's emotional behaviors (e.g., excited expressions) and verbal cues (e.g., "I am really hungry" or "Yum Yum") to infer that the person has a desire for the cake. Thus, the better a child's understanding of others' minds, the deeper an appreciation children will have for the intentional information provided by gaze.

In the chapter, we will examine existing evidence that is pertinent to this hypothesis. Specifically, we will first review existing studies on children's use of direction of eye gaze to infer another's desires, followed by their use of eye gaze information for inferring knowledge and thoughts. Based on the review of the existing literature, we will also discuss future studies that are needed to elucidate the relation between children's theory of mind understanding and their use of eye gaze for mind reading purposes.

INFERRING DESIRE

The first study examining children's ability to use direction of eye gaze to infer desire was conducted by Baron-Cohen, Campbell, Karmiloff-Smith, Grant, and Walker (1995). They showed 4-year-olds pictures of a cartoon face of a boy named Charlie looking at one of four chocolate bars. In the desire condition, children were asked to identify which chocolate bar the character wanted, and in the goal condition, children were asked to predict which chocolate bar Charlie was going to take. Four-year-olds had no difficulties using eye gaze to answer either of the questions. Their performance could not be attributed to the ability to detect eye direction alone because autistic children were unable to correctly determine what the character wanted even though they were able to indicate where Charlie looked. Furthermore, when eye gaze information was presented in conflict with an arrow cue, normal 4-year-olds continued to use gaze cues to answer the questions, whereas autistic children used the non-mentalistic arrow information. Thus, their results suggest that by 4 years of age typically developing children can use directional information from eye gaze to identify what another person desires, whereas autistic children appeared to have difficulty in establishing the linkage between a person's eye direction and the person's desired object.

Baron-Cohen et al. (1995) were interested in comparing autistic children to normally developing children and therefore their study did not investigate the developmental progression of children's ability to use eye gaze information to infer desire. Using a similar task to Baron-Cohen et al. (1995), we tested 3- to 6-year-olds' use of gaze information to determine what a cartoon character wanted (Lee et al., 1998). Our findings replicated those of Baron-Cohen et al., with older children relying on eye cues to answer the desire question. Three-year-olds, on the other hand, were at chance in guessing what the character wanted despite being able to use eye gaze to determine what the character was looking at. Therefore, their difficulty was not in being able to follow eye gaze, but to use it to impute a mental state. The problem was also not due to an inability to infer desire from behavioral cues in general, as 3-year-olds were able to do so using pointing or head orientation cues.

An important aspect of eye gaze information is the movement of the eyes. We wonder whether younger children's difficulty in using eye directional cues to infer desires was due to the fact that the eye gaze information was not displayed in a naturalistic and dynamic manner. We showed 2- and 3-year-olds a video that could capture this dynamic aspect of eye gaze (Lee et al., 1998). In the video, a clown was seated in front of three objects. The clown looked towards one of the objects and exclaimed, "I want that!" With the eye gaze information being presented via video, 3-year-olds were now able to determine the object of the clown's desire. In fact, 2-year-olds after a few trials also started using gaze cues to answer the desire questions.

When head orientation was placed in conflict with eye gaze, 3-year-olds continued to rely on gaze, but when pointing and eye gaze were contrasted, pointing information was used to respond to questions instead. In contrast, adults always relied on eye direction cues. These results suggest that there may exist a hierarchy of behavioral cues that children use to make inferences about another's desire. For adults, eye gaze cues are viewed to be more important than pointing, which is viewed more important than head orientation. Unlike adults, 2-year-olds viewed pointing and head orientation as more important than eye direction, whereas 3-year-olds viewed eye direction to be more important than head orientation, but less informative than pointing. In other words, while young children might be able to use behavioral information to infer desire, their understanding of the linkage between desire and eye gaze cues may be acquired after they have already understood the linkage between desire and other behavioral cues.

Although children as young as 2-year-olds can use eye gaze cues under some circumstances to infer desire, Montgomery, Bach, and Moran (1998) questioned the extent of their understanding. They showed 4- and 6-year-olds a video of a person in between two different objects. Like Lee et al. (1998), they were investigating if the children could use eye gaze to infer which of the two objects the person wanted. However, the person in the video looked at both objects, but only glanced at one and gazed at the other for a longer period of time. For adults, a prolonged look is more indicative of desire than a fleeting glance. Four-year-olds did not appear to differentiate between the looking times and were at chance for choosing the object of desire. On the other hand, 6-year-olds and adults picked the object looked at longer as the object of choice. In control trials where only one object was looked at, both groups of children chose the correct object. Therefore, like the findings of Lee et al. (1998), the 4-year-olds were able to use gaze information to infer desire, they were just unable to differentiate between different types of eye gaze cues. Einav and Hood (2006) also found that 5-year-olds begin to use duration as well as frequency of gaze to interpret desire.

Children's ability to interpret gaze information to infer desire appears to be intimately connected to their developing understanding of others' mental states. The few studies that have examined children's ability to use eye gaze to infer what another person might want have found that at quite a young age children can use eye gaze to infer desire. These findings correspond to other research on children's understanding of desire that suggests 2.5- to 3-year-olds can use desire to predict or explain another's behavior (Astington & Gopnik, 1991; Wellman & Woolley, 1990; Yuill, 1984). However, the ability to interpret desire from eye gaze is not simply a matter of detection, and there are more sophisticated levels of understanding as illustrated by Montgomery et al. (1998). For 4-year-olds, their understanding is still somewhat limited and their ability to infer desire appears to be related to their ability to reflect more deeply about another's mental state. For example, 4-year-olds are unable to differentiate between different types of eye gaze cues (Montgomery et al., 1998). Similar results have been found in research conducted on children's ability to infer knowledge and thinking based on eye gaze information.

INFERRING KNOWLEDGE

A large body of research covers the development of children's ability to use looking behavior to infer another's state of knowledge or what they might see or know. Piaget was one of the first to examine children's visual perspective-taking and whether children could determine another's visual experience in his famous three mountains task (Piaget & Inhelder, 1956). In this particular task, children are asked to either identify or reconstruct what a person might see from an orientation different from their own. He, as well as others, found that children were unsuccessful on the task until late childhood or early adolescence (Flavell, 1974; Flavell, Botkin, Fry, Wright, & Jarvis, 1968; Piaget & Inhelder, 1956).

However, by simplifying the tasks given to children, earlier evidence of competence at visual perspective-taking has been found. Thus, by 2.5 years of age children understand that for someone to see something, they must have their eyes open and the space between them and the object or event must be unobstructed (Lempers, Flavell, & Flavell, 1977; O'Neill, 1996). For example, young children would turn a card so that an observer could see the picture on it (Lempers et al., 1977). Three-year-olds recognize that an individual may not necessarily be able to see an object as they can (Flavell, 1978; Pillow, 1989) and that a person may be able to see an object that they cannot see, though this understanding continues to develop further in later preschool years (Lempers et al., 1977; Ruffman & Olson, 1989; Brooks & Meltzoff, 2002).

While 3-year-olds may be able to infer that another can see an object, they have difficulty recognizing that the other person may view it differently from themselves (Coie, Costanzo, & Farnill, 1973; Flavell, Everett, Croft, & Flavell, 1981; Flavell, Flavell, Green, & Wilcox, 1980; Liben, 1978; Masangkay et al., 1974), a distinction Flavell makes between Level I and Level II perspective-taking (Flavell, 1974, 1978; Flavell et al., 1981). Furthermore, for more complex visual experiences, such as predicting what would be seen if looking down a curved tube, even 5-year-olds have difficulty with this type of problem (Flavell, Green, Herrera, & Flavell, 1991).

Three-year-olds' understanding is limited in other regards. They do not necessarily understand that a person's knowledge of the shape or color of an object may vary depending on how they have experienced the object, such as having seen, touched, or heard an object (O'Neill, Astington, & Flavell, 1992; Pillow, 1993; Wimmer et al., 1988). This failure perhaps is not surprising because they also have difficulty attributing the source of their own knowledge (Gopnik & Graf, 1988; O'Neill & Gopnik, 1991; Povinelli & deBois, 1992; Wimmer et al., 1988). For example, Gopnik and Graf (1988) showed, told, or gave a strong hint to three-year-olds about an object in a drawer. While the children could identify the contents of a drawer, Gopnik and Graf found that children had problems identifying how they knew what the object was. Five-year-olds, on the other hand, had very little difficulty with the task. Younger children appeared to have difficulty understanding how perceptual experiences can lead to particular knowledge states, suggesting that children's developing understanding of how looking is related to knowing may be influenced by their developing understanding of knowing itself.

Previous research has typically focused on children's ability to use others' eye gaze cues in cooperative settings where the individuals intend to share their knowledge. A few studies have examined whether children were capable of hiding an object so that another could not find it or was unaware of its presence (Flavell, Shipstead, & Croft, 1978; Lempers et al., 1977; McGuigan & Doherty, 2002). For example, Flavell et al. (1978) found that by 2.5 years of age, children were able to hide an object behind a screen, suggesting that they understood the importance of not being able to see the object in hiding. However, this understanding is still fragile as even 3-year-olds were unable to move a screen in front of an object to hide it. Interestingly, McGuigan and Doherty (2002), using a similar procedure, found that children's performance at moving a screen to hide an object was related to children's ability to infer where another person was looking. Children who were better at identifying another's focus of attention seemed to better understand perceptual deprivation for hiding.

Eye gaze can also be informative in deceptive situations. Both lay people and theorists have suggested that nonverbal behavior, including eye gaze, can "leak" information about the truth when being deceptive (for review see De-Paulo et al., 2003; Kleink, 1986). Furthermore, research has found that adults will use an individual's eye gaze to detect deception (Hemsley & Doob, 1978; Kraut & Poe, 1980). In terms of children's understanding of eye gaze in this regard, another study conducted in our lab examined 3-, 4-, and 5-year-olds' ability to use eye gaze to infer the truth in a deceptive situation (Freire, Eskritt, & Lee, 2004). Children watched a video where they had to guess where a toy was hidden. In one experiment an actress claimed not to know the location of the toy but looked towards its hiding place. Four- and 5-year-olds were significantly above chance in determining the toy's location, whereas 3-year-olds were at chance. Three-year-olds were able to follow her eye gaze, as children from all three age groups were able to use direction of eye gaze to find the toy when the actress said she knew where the toy was located. The three-year-olds' performance also cannot be attributed to a failure to understand the actress's intent to deceive since they were specifically told she would try to trick them. Furthermore, they were able to use a hand concealing the location as a cue to the hiding spot. Finally, their failure cannot be attributed to eye gaze not being a salient enough cue, as 3-year-olds could not even use eye gaze with head orientation to determine where the toy was located. Freire et al. (2004) argued that 3-year-olds recognized that eye gaze can serve a referential function in a cooperative function, but they do not yet understand that eye directions can also serve as an intentional cue to indicate a "leak" of the true state of affairs in a deceptive situation.

In another experiment, Freire et al. (2004) examined whether 4- and 5-year-olds relied on eye gaze to determine the hiding place of the toy because it was the only cue available to use. That is, the gaze direction may have acted as an orienting cue, but that the children did not recognize its epistemic value. Freire et al. showed 3- to 5-year-olds a video where the actress looked at the hiding location of a toy, but said the toy was in another location. They were interested in whether children would rely on the verbal or eye direction information to solve the task. Three-year-olds guessed where the toy was hidden based on what the actress said, while 5-year-olds correctly used eye gaze information. Four-year-olds' responses were much more variable. Surprisingly, children's performance was not affected by feedback. Children continued to use the same cue, either verbal or eye gaze, regardless of whether they were told they were correct or not. Therefore, for 5-year-olds at least, their reliance on directional information in the previous experiment was not due to an orienting response. They appeared to recognize that eye gaze conveys more reliable information than verbal cues concerning what a deceiver knows about the true state of affairs.

As mentioned previously, it has been argued that visual perception can influence the understanding of mental states. For example, Gopnik et al. (1994) argued that children's ability to solve Flavell's Level II perceptual tasks, where they need to recognize that someone may see something differently from themselves, would help children understand false belief, or that someone could believe something they know to be incorrect. However, the research reviewed also suggests that the understanding of knowing may influence understanding of eye gaze. For example, the failure of 3-year-olds in using eye gaze cues in the deceptive situations suggests that they are relying on different information in these situations compared to older children and adults. For example, when verbal information was pitted against eye gaze information, 3-year-olds demonstrated a lexical bias where they relied on the verbal information to solve the task. However, it is not that these children cannot successfully use nonverbal information in general in a deceptive situation. When the actress said she did not know where the toy was hidden but used her hand to conceal the hiding place, they were able to correctly guess the location. Children appear to learn how to use different nonverbal behaviors to interpret deceptive situations at different ages. Thus, children's ability to correctly infer the significance of a person's eye gaze will be affected by their understanding of the intentionality behind the cue. In fact, the ability to use eye gaze to infer the true state of affairs may develop relatively early compared to some nonverbal behaviors since research has found that before the age of 7 or 8 years children often rely on verbal cues when verbal and nonverbal cues (e.g., facial expressions and vocal inflections) conflict with each other (Demorest, Meyer, Phelps, Gardner, & Winner, 1984; Eskritt & Lee, 2003; Friend, 2000, 2001; Friend & Bryant, 2000; Volkmar & Siegel, 1982).

INFERRING THOUGHT

A few studies have examined children's understanding of thinking in general. While they were not necessarily examining eye gaze per se, they were interested in children's ability to infer thinking and content of thought from various situational and behavioral cues, including looking behavior. For example, Baron-Cohen and Cross (1992) found that children as young as 3 years of age labeled a person who was looking upwards as "thinking." Flavell, Green, and Flavell (1993) asked children and adults whether a person would be thinking under various circumstances. Three-year-olds were not significantly different from chance in deciding whether a person looking at pictures was thinking, whereas 95% of 4-, and 6- to 7-year-olds, and adults thought the person would be. Surprisingly, children were better at deciding that a person looking at an object was thinking compared to a person solving a problem. Both 3- and 4-year-olds were at chance on the problem-solving question.

While Flavell et al. (1993) examined children's ability to identify whether a person was thinking by their behavior, they did not explore whether children could identify the contents of a person's thoughts. In another study, Flavell et al. (1995) asked children and adults to infer what a story character was thinking. Unlike Flavell et al. (1993), they found that 4- and 5-year-olds were at chance for using looking behavior to determine if a person was thinking. Furthermore, 88% of 4-year-olds answered that a person was thinking while solving a problem. Flavell et al. (1993) suggested that children's ability to infer mental activity from behavioral information is still quite fragile at this age and that they may not yet have acquired any general rules to process such information. Results from a study by Johnson and Wellman (1982) support this explanation as they found that children tend to understand that thinking is involved in intellectual activities like problem-solving more easily than for perceptual activities such as looking or hearing.

In terms of inferences about the content of thought, only 16% of 4-year-olds were able to determine that what a character was looking at was also what she was thinking. Perhaps this is not surprising since they were only at chance for deciding whether the character was even thinking at all. However, 5- and 7-year-olds were not particularly adept at drawing inferences either. Approximately half of them could use looking behavior to determine the object of thought. The problem cannot be that the children were unaware that thoughts have content, as Flavell et al. (1995) found that young children recognize that people think *about* something. It appears that while children may be able to use behavioral cues to ascertain whether someone is thinking, they are not necessarily able to use those cues to determine what is being thought about. One possible explanation for this discrepancy is that Flavell et al. (1995) also found evidence that children for the most part viewed thoughts as being infrequent and isolated from one another without any causes or effects. As a result, children could not be expected to recognize that viewing an object might mean you are thinking about it if they do not realize that seeing an object could cause you to think about it. Once again the understanding of a mental state, thinking, may influence children's realization that eye gaze can indicate thinking in general or even the content of thought. Regardless of whether Flavell et al. (1995) are correct in their supposition, the ability to draw inferences about content of thought from cues such as looking behavior takes time to develop and continues well past the age of 7 years.

SUMMARY AND CONCLUSIONS

The reviewed literature indicates that by preschool age, children can infer a great deal about mental states from eye gaze. They are able to use eye gaze to infer the object of desire (Baron-Cohen et al., 1995; Lee et al., 1998; Montgomery et al., 1998), what a person might see and therefore know (Flavell, 1978; Lempers et al., 1977; Pillow, 1989), and to some extent to determine if another is thinking (Flavell et al., 1993, 1995). Considering an early sensitivity to the eyes (e.g., Caron et al., 1997; Haith et al., 1977) and the importance of eye gaze in early interaction, such as joint attention (e.g., Butterworth, 1991), perhaps preschoolers' competence is not unexpected.

However, despite young children's proficiency at using eye gaze information, it is important to stress that the understanding of eye gaze continues to develop beyond preschool age. Gopnik et al. (1994) and Baron-Cohen (1995a, 1995b) have argued that an understanding of eye gaze aids in the development of understanding theory of mind. However, we believe the research on eye gaze reveals that the influence of development in these two areas is not one-sided in direction. Children's developing comprehension of mental states appears to feed back into their understanding of visual perception so that they can use this knowledge to interpret what another may be seeing and experiencing. Thus, children will be able to determine what another is thinking or wants from the focus of attention. Furthermore, understanding the intentions behind direction of eye gaze will be easier to identify. With a better understanding of the intentionality of gaze, children will be able to recognize that not only can gaze indicate what another wants, but why a person may want a particular object or that one would typically look more at what he/she wants as opposed to a quick glance (e.g., Montgomery et al., 1998).

While research has begun to outline when children are able to use gaze direction to infer some mental states, children's understanding of eye gaze information as an ostensive act that reveals the intentions of an individual is only starting to be understood in its more sophisticated forms. For example, while

4-year-olds can use direction of eye gaze to infer desire (Lee et al., 1998; Montgomery et al., 1998), Montgomery et al. (1998) found they cannot differentiate between different types of gaze information. They were equally likely to associate desire with a fleeting glance compared to a prolonged look. It was not until 6 years of age that children recognized that different types of perceptual activity could suggest something different about ongoing mental states. Flavell et al. (1995) found that even 7-year-olds had problems inferring what another was thinking by using eye gaze cues because they might not fully understand the causal relationships between mental states.

Thus, further research needs to examine how well children can link gaze information to various mental states to derive a deeper understanding of what eye gaze could imply. The findings of the studies reviewed suggest that children's ability to use eye gaze for "mind-reading" will depend on their understanding of the mind. To illustrate this link between understanding eye gaze and mental states, we tested 94 children between the ages of 3 to 6 years on a task very similar to that by Lee et al. (1998). We showed them pictures of a boy, Larry, looking at one of six objects surrounding him. One of the objects included in the pictures was edible and another was a type of drink. For some of the pictures we asked, "In this picture here, is Larry hungry or is he thirsty?" We compared the data from that question to another question, "In this picture here, what does Larry want?" that was reported in Lee et al. (1998). As can be seen in Figure 11–1, there was a significant difference in children's performance

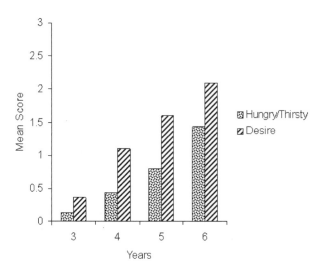

FIGURE 11–1.   Mean scores on the hungry/thirsty question and desire question for 3- to 6-year-olds (chance = 0.5).

across the two questions. Children were more likely to use eye direction to answer the desire question compared to the hungry/thirsty question. Also evident is a difference in performance across age groups. Children 4 years and older are above chance in correctly answering what Larry wanted (Baron-Cohen et al., 1995; Lee et al., 1998). However, in inferring whether Larry is hungry or thirsty, only 6-year-olds were above chance. Thus, while 4- and 5-year-olds were able to use eye gaze to determine what the boy might want, they were unable to take this knowledge a step further and reflect on why he might want that particular object to answer the hungry/thirsty question. The younger children could use gaze information to infer intention in another, but they could only understand it to a certain extent. Six-year-olds appeared to recognize the reason for why someone may want a certain object; they demonstrated a better grasp of the cause and effect of mental states.

Though both understanding of eye gaze and mental states may play a role in each other's development, the influence they have may shift with age. Gopnik et al. (1994) point out the significance that eye gaze understanding has in the recognition of shared attention (e.g., joint attention) as well as the development of Level II perspective-taking in the development of false belief. Thus, their argument suggests that eye gaze plays a significant role during the earlier years. On the other hand, mental state knowledge may have a more influential role on understanding visual perception at later ages. A more sophisticated theory of mind could better inform the interpretations one makes of eye gaze information.

FUTURE RESEARCH

Research on the relationship of eye gaze and mental states has been limited thus far. While the studies reviewed begin to address the development of eye gaze to infer mental states, more research is needed to fully understand the normative development of this skill, especially of the more subtle uses of eye gaze. Furthermore, research tends to present eye gaze information in simple, artificial situations. Thus, future research needs to address children's understanding of mental states under more complex and natural circumstances where the role of context becomes important. Sometimes the provision of context may aid performance in interpreting looking behavior. Thus, Lee et al. (1998) found that children performed better with video compared to static pictures because video included dynamic eye movement. Research in other areas of socio-cognitive development has also found benefits to performance when placed within context (e.g., Rice, Koinis, Sullivan, Tager-Flusberg, & Winner, 1997; Sullivan & Winner, 1993). However, context could potentially make the situation more difficult as well. For example, in terms of being able to use eye gaze in a deceptive situation, children need to be able to identify they are in a deceptive situation first, before they can look for nonverbal cues such as eye gaze to interpret the situation. Furthermore, the studies examining children's use of gaze cues are frequently under optimal conditions where the eye gaze is prolonged and highly visible. While this allows researchers to detect early competency in the ability to use eye gaze, this is not necessarily how gaze information is presented in the real world. In deceptive situations, for instance, eye gaze information is more likely to be more subtle glances.

Another issue is the importance of eye gaze in face-to-face interaction (Argyle & Cook, 1976). Eye gaze is typically used in association with a number of other cues such as body language, facial expression, and verbal information. How children use these different sources of information needs to be examined further. For example, three-year-olds in the study by Lee et al. (1998) were more likely to rely on pointing cues rather than eye gaze information to infer what another wanted. Freire et al. (2004) found that when verbal information contrasted with eye gaze, 3-year-olds demonstrated a lexical bias and relied on the verbal information to solve the task. These findings suggest that while children might be able to use eye direction information to interpret some situations, they may not necessarily rely on those cues over others. Furthermore, in situations where the cues from different sources do not necessarily conflict, children still need to learn to integrate these different types of cues. Depending on the context, different cues could indicate different types of information (e.g., liking, knowledge, deception). How children learn to coordinate these cues needs to be explored in greater detail.

The ability to use eye gaze with multiple cues in interaction is also important in examining atypical development of understanding eye gaze. Baron-Cohen et al. (1995) found that autistic children could not use gaze direction to infer desire, unlike normal 4-year-old controls. The difficulty could not be attributed to an understanding of the desire terminology since research has found that autistic children do use the word *want* spontaneously, unlike some other mental terms (Tager-Flusberg, 1993). Mental age of the autistic children was also matched with the mental age of children with William's syndrome, a disorder that does not impact on mentalizing skills. Children with William's syndrome performed significantly better than the autistic children in their use of eye gaze to infer desire, and their performance was similar to that of normal 4-year-olds. Furthermore, autistic children did use an arrow cue to determine what the character might want though normal controls, and children with William's syndrome chose eye gaze over the arrow in making their inference. These results suggest that autistic children have a problem interpreting the meaning behind eye gaze. However, autistic children could tell when someone was looking at them, suggesting they have at least some basic understanding of visual perspective taking (see also Tan & Harris, 1991). Thus it appears that the autistic child's problem is with inferring mental states from gaze information. Perhaps not surprising then, autistic children have also been found to have problems with theory of mind (Baron-Cohen, 1990; Baron-Cohen, Leslie, & Frith, 1985; Perner, Frith, Leslie, & Leekam, 1989). If autistic children have difficulty understanding different types of mental activity in others, then it should also be difficult to recognize the epistemic value of eye gaze. Of interest would be to see if this relationship holds in the typically developing child—whether children who do not perform as well on theory of mind tasks would also have difficulty with tasks that require them to have a deeper understanding of the mentalistic significance of the eyes such as the task by Montgomery et al. (1998).

As in other areas of research, the focus tends to be on children's comprehension rather than production. Research with autistic children has found that not only do they have trouble understanding eye gaze, but they can also have abnormal eye gaze patterns. Though they make about the same amount of eye contact (Philips, Baron-Cohen, & Rutter, 1992; Sigman, Mundy, Ungerer & Sherman, 1986; Volkmar & Mayes, 1990), autistic children do not seem to use eye contact in the same manner, such as in joint attention (Sigman et al., 1986), detecting goals (Philips et al., 1992), or regulating turn-taking (Miranda, Donnellan, & Yoder, 1983). Examining then production of eye gaze patterns of children in different populations in relation to social skills and understanding will give us a better awareness of how these abilities fit together. For example, in deceptive situations, do children use eye contact to help interpret the present state of affairs, and how is their use of eye contact related to their theory of mind understanding?

The present chapter reviewed the research conducted on children's understanding of how eye gaze can reflect mental states. Previous theorists have argued that appreciation of visual perception can aid in the development of a theory of mind. We have argued that the reverse is also true: that an understanding of others' minds is necessary to fully realize the information contained with direction of gaze. Unfortunately, research has only examined this issue indirectly and future studies are needed to fully elucidate the relationship between gaze processing and theory of mind understanding.

ACKNOWLEDGMENTS

The present chapter was supported in part by a Social Sciences and Humanities Research Council of Canada grant to the first author, and a NICHD grant (5 R01 HD46526-02) to the second author.

REFERENCES

Anderson, J. R., & Doherty, M. J. (1997). Preschoolers' perception of other people's looking: photographs and drawings. *Perception, 26,* 333–343.

Argyle, M. (1972). *The psychology of interpersonal behavior.* Harmondsworth: Penguin.

Argyle, M., & Cook, M. (1976). *Gaze and mutual gaze.* New York: Cambridge University Press.

Astington, J. W., & Gopnik, A. (1991). Developing understanding of desire and intention. In A. Whiten (Ed.), *Natural theories of mind: Evolution, development and simulation of everyday mindreading.* Oxford: Blackwell.

Baldwin, D. (1993). Infants' ability to consult the speaker for clues to word reference. *Journal of Child Language, 20,* 395–418.

Baldwin, D. (1995). Understanding the link between joint attention and language. In C. Moore & P. J. Dunham (Eds.), *Joint attention: Its origins and role in development.* Hillsdale, NJ: Lawrence Erlbaum Associates.

Baron-Cohen, S. (1990). Autism: A specific cognitive disorder of "mindblindness." *International Review of Psychiatry, 2,* 79–88.

Baron-Cohen, S. (1995a). *Mindblindness: An essay on autism and theory of mind.* Cambridge, MA: MIT Press.

Baron-Cohen, S. (1995b). The eye direction detector (EDD) and the shared attention mechanism (SAM): Two cases for evolutionary psychology. In C. Moore & P. J. Dunham (Eds.), *(Joint attention: Its origins and role in development).* Hillsdale, NJ: Lawrence Erlbaum Associates.

Baron-Cohen, S., Campbell, R., Karmiloff-Smith, A., Grant, J., & Walker, J. (1995). Are children with autism blind to the mentalistic significance of the eyes? *British Journal of Developmental Psychology, 13,* 379–398.

Baron-Cohen, S., & Cross, P. (1992). Reading the eyes: Evidence for the role of perception in the development of a theory of mind. *Mind and Language, 7,* 172–186.

Baron-Cohen, S., Leslie, A. M., & Frith, U. (1985). Does the autistic child have a 'theory of mind'?, *Cognition, 21,* 37–46.

Brooks, R., & Meltzoff, A. (2002). The importance of eyes: How infants interpret adult looking behavior. *Developmental Psychology, 38,* 958–966.

Burger, J., Gochfeld, M., & Murray, B. G., Jr. (1991). Role of a predator's eye size in risk perception by basking black iguana, *Ctenosaura similis. Animal Behavior, 42,* 471–476.

Burghardt, G. (1990). Cognitive ethology and critical anthropomorphism: A snake with two heads and hog-nosed snakes that play dead. In C. Ristau (Ed.), *Cognitive ethology: The minds of other animals.* Hillsdale, NJ: Lawrence Erlbaum Associates.

Butterworth, G. (1991). The ontogeny and phylogeny of joint attention. In A. Whiten (Ed.), *Natural theories of mind: Evolution, development & simulation of everyday mindreading.* Oxford, England: Blackwell.

Butterworth, G., & Grover, L. (1990). Joint visual attention, manual pointing and preverbal communication in human infancy. In M. Jeannerod (Ed.), *Attention and performance XIII.* Hillsdale, NJ: Lawrence Erlbaum Associates.

Butterworth, G., & Jarrett, N. (1991). What minds have in common is space: Spatial mechanisms serving joint attention in infancy. *British Journal of Developmental Psychology, 9,* 55–72.

Caron, A. J., Caron, R., Roberts, J., & Brooks, R. (1997). Infant sensitivity to deviations in dynamic facial-vocal displays: The role of eye regard. *Developmental Psychology, 33,* 802–813.

Cline, M. G. (1967). The perception of where a person is looking. *American Journal of Psychology, 80,* 511–523.

Coie, J. D., Costanzo, P. R., & Farnill, D. (1973). Specific transitions in the development of spatial perspective-taking ability. *Developmental Psychology, 9,* 167–177.

Demorest, A., Meyer, C., Phelps, E., Gardner, H., & Winner, E. (1984). Words speak louder than actions: Understanding deliberately false remarks. *Child Development, 55,* 1527–1534.

DePaulo, B. M., Lindsay, J. J., Malone, B. E., Muhlenbruck, L., Charlton, K., & Cooper, H. (2003). Cues to deception. *Psychological Bulletin, 129,* 74–112.

Doherty, M. J., & Anderson, J. R. (1999). A new look at gaze: Preschool children's understanding of eye-direction. *Cognitive Development, 14,* 549–571.

Einav, S., & Hood, B. (2006). Children's use of the temporal dimension of gaze for inferring preference. *Developmental Psychology, 42,* 142–152.

Eskritt, M., & Lee, K. (2003). Do actions speak louder than words? Preschool children's use of the verbal-nonverbal consistency principle during inconsistent communications. *Journal of Nonverbal Behavior, 27,* 25–42.

Farroni, T., Csibra, G., Simion, F., & Johnson, M. H. (2002). Eye contact detection in humans from birth. *Proceedings of the National Academy of Science, 99,* 9602–9605.

Flavell, J. H. (1974). The development of inferences about others. In T. Mischel (Ed.), *Understanding other persons.* Oxford, England: Blackwell & Mott.

Flavell, J. H. (1978). The development of knowledge about visual perception. In C. B. Keasey (Ed.), *Nebraska Symposium on Motivation* (pp. 43–76). Lincoln: University of Nebraska Press.

Flavell, J. H., Botkin, P. T., Fry, C. L., Wright, J. W., & Jarvis, P. E. (1968). *The development of role-taking and communication skills in children.* New York: Wiley.

Flavell, J. H., Everett, B. A., Croft, K., & Flavell, E. R. (1981). Young children's knowledge about visual perception: Further evidence for the level 1–level 2 distinction. *Developmental Psychology, 17,* 99–103.

Flavell, J. H., Flavell, E. R., Green, F. L., & Wilcox, S. A. (1980). Young children's knowledge about visual perception: Effect of observer distance from target on perceptual clarity of target. *Developmental Psychology, 16,* 10–12.

Flavell, J. H., Green, F. L., & Flavell, E. R. (1995). Children's understanding of the stream of consciousness. *Child Development, 64,* 387–398.

Flavell, J. H., Green, F. L., & Flavell, E. R. (1993). Young children's knowledge about thinking. *Monographs of the Society for Research in Child Development, 60* (Serial no. 243).

Flavell, J. H., Green, F. L., Herrera, C., & Flavell, E. R. (1991). Young children's knowledge about visual perception: Lines of sight must be straight. *British Journal of Developmental Psychology, 9,* 73–87.

Flavell, J. H., Shipstead, S. G., & Croft, K. (1978). Young children's knowledge about visual perception: Hiding objects from others. *Child Development, 49,* 1208–1211.

Freire, A., Eskritt, M., & Lee, K. (2004). Are eyes windows to a deceiver's soul?: Children's use of another's eye gaze cues in a deceptive situation. *Developmental Psychology, 40,* 1093–1104.

Friend, M. (2000). Developmental changes in sensitivity to vocal paralanguage. *Developmental Science, 3,* 148–162.

Friend, M. (2001). From affect to language. *First Language, 21,* 219–243.

Friend, M., & Bryant, J. B. (2000). A developmental lexical bias in the interpretation of discrepant messages. *Merrill-Palmer Quarterly, 46,* 140–167.

Gallup, G. G., Jr., Nash, R. F., & Ellison, A. L., Jr. (1971). Tonic immobility as a reaction to predation: Artificial eyes as a fear stimulus for chickens. *Psychonomic Science, 23,* 79–80.

Gibson, J., & Pick, A. (1963). Perception of another's looking behavior. *American Journal of American Psychology, 76,* 386–394.

Gopnik, A., & Graf, P. (1988). Knowing how you know: Young children's ability to identify and remember the sources of their beliefs. *Child Development, 59,* 1366–1371.

Gopnik, A., Slaughter, V., & Meltzoff, A. (1994). Changing your views: How understanding visual perception can lead to a new theory of mind. In C. Lewis & P. Mitchell (Eds.), *Children's early understanding of mind.* UK: Lawrence Erlbaum Associates.

Haith, M., Bergman, T., & Moore, M. (1977). Eye contact and face scanning in early infancy. *Science, 198,* 853–855.

Hemsley, G. D., & Doob, A. N. (1978). The effect of looking behavior on perceptions of a communicator's credibility. *Journal of Applied Social Psychology, 8,* 136–144.

Hood, B. M., Willen, J. D., & Driver, J. (1998). Adults' eyes trigger shifts of visual attention in human infants. *Psychological Science, 9,* 131–134.

Johnson, C. N., & Wellman, H. M. (1982). Children's developing conceptions of the mind and brain. *Child Development, 53,* 222–234.

Kleinke, C. L. (1986). Gaze and eye contact: A research review. *Psychological Bulletin, 100,* 78–100.

Kraut, R. E., & Poe, D. (1980). Behavioral roots of person perception: The deception judgments of customs inspectors and laymen. *Journal of Personality and Social Psychology, 39,* 784–798.

Lee, K., Eskritt, M., Symons, L. A., & Muir, D. (1998). Children's use of triadic eye gaze information for "mind-reading." *Developmental Psychology, 34,* 525–539.

Lempers, J. D., Flavell, E. R., & Flavell, J. H. (1977). The development in very young children of tacit knowledge concerning visual perception. *Genetic Psychology Monograph, 95,* 3–53.

Liben, L. A. (1978). Perspective-taking skills in young children: Seeing the world through rose-colored glasses. *Developmental Psychology, 14,* 87–92.

Masangkay, Z. S., McCluskey, K. A., McIntyre, C. W., Sims-Knight, J., Vaughn, B. E., & Flavell, J. H. (1974). The early development of inferences about the visual percepts of others. *Child Development, 45,* 357–366.

McGuigan, N., & Doherty, M. J. (2002). The relation between hiding skill and judgment of eye direction in preschool children. *Developmental Psychology, 38,* 418–427.

Miranda, P., Donnellan, A., & Yoder, D. (1983). Gaze behavior: A new look at an old problem. *Journal of Autism and Developmental Disorders, 13,* 397–409.

Montgomery, D. E., Bach, L. M., & Moran, C. (1998). Children's use of looking behavior as a cue to detect another's goal. *Child Development, 69,* 692–705.

Moore, C., & Corkum, V. (1998). Infant gaze-following based on eye direction. *British Journal of Developmental Psychology, 16,* 495–503.

Muir, D. W., & Hains, S. M. J. (1993). Infant sensitivity to perturbations in adult facial, vocal, tactile, and contingent stimulation during face-to-face interactions. In B. de Boysson-Bardies (Ed.), *Developmental neurocognition: Speech and face processing in the first year of life*. Netherlands: Kluwer Academic Publishers.

O'Neill, D. K. (1996). Two-year-old children's sensitivity to a parent's knowledge state when making requests. *Child Development, 67*, 659–677.

O'Neill, D. K., Astington, J. W., & Flavell, J. H. (1992). Young children's understanding of the role that sensory experience plays in knowledge acquisition. *Child Development, 63*, 474–490.

O'Neill, D., & Gopnik, A. (1991). Young children's ability to identify the sources of their beliefs. *Developmental Psychology, 27*, 390–397.

Perner, J., Frith, U., Leslie, A. M., & Leekham, S. (1989). Exploration of the autistic child's theory of mind: Knowledge, belief, and communication. *Child Development, 60*, 689–700.

Piaget, J., & Inhelder, B. (1956). *The child's conception of space*. London: Routledge & Kegan Paul.

Phillips, W., Baron-Cohen, S., & Rutter, M. (1992). The role of eye contact in goal detection: Evidence from normal infants and children with autism or mental handicap. *Development and Psychopathology, 4*, 375–383.

Pillow, B. H. (1989). Early understanding of perception as a source of knowledge. *Journal of Experimental Psychology, 47*, 116–129.

Pillow, B. H. (1993). Preschool children's understanding of the relationship between modality of perceptual access and knowledge of perceptual properties. *British Journal of Developmental Psychology, 11*, 371–389.

Poulin-Dubois, D., & Forbes, J. N. (2002). Toddlers' attention to intentions-in-action in learning novel actions words. *Developmental Psychology, 38*, 104–114.

Povinelli, D. J., & deBois, S. (1992). Young children's (*Homo sapiens*) understanding of knowledge formation in themselves and others. *Journal of Comparative Psychology, 106*, 228–238.

Povinelli, D. J., & Eddy, T. J. (1996a). What young chimpanzees know about seeing. *Monographs of the Society for Research in Child Development* (Serial No. 247).

Povinelli, D. J., & Eddy, T. J. (1996b). Chimpanzees: Joint visual attention. *Psychological Science, 7*, 129–135.

Repacholi, B. M. (1998). Infants' use of attentional cues to identify the referent of another person's emotional expression. *Developmental Psychology, 34*, 1017–1025.

Rice, C., Koinis, D., Sullivan, K., Tager-Flusberg, H., & Winner, E. (1997). When 3-year-olds pass the appearance-reality test. *Developmental Psychology, 33*, 54–61.

Ristau, C. (1991). Attention, purposes, and deception in birds. In A. Whiten (Ed.), *Natural theories of mind*. Oxford, England: Basil Blackwell.

Ruffman, T. K., & Olson, D. R. (1989). Children's ascriptions of knowledge to others. *Developmental Psychology, 25*, 601–606.

Rutter, D. (1984). *Looking and seeing: The role of visual communication in social interaction*. Chichester: Wiley.

Sigman, M., Mundy, P., Ungerer, J., & Sherman, T. (1986). Social interactions of autistic, mentally retarded, and normal children and their caregivers. *Journal of Child Psychology and Psychiatry, 27*, 647–656.

Sullivan, K., & Winner, E. (1993). Three-year-olds' understanding of mental states: The influence of trickery. *Journal of Experimental Child Psychology, 56,* 135–148.

Symons, L. A., Lee. K., Cedrone, C. C., & Nishimura, M. (2004). What are you looking at? Acuity for triadic eye gaze. *Journal of General Psychology, 131,* 451–469.

Tager-Flusberg, H. (1993). What language reveals about the understanding of minds in children with autism. In S. Baron-Cohen, H. Tager-Flusberg, & D. J. Cohen (Eds.), *Understanding other minds: Perspectives from autism.* Oxford: Oxford University Press.

Tan, J., & Harris, P. (1991). Autistic children understand seeing and wanting. *Development and Psychopathology, 3,* 163–174.

Vecera, S. P., & Johnson, M. H. (1995). Gaze detection and the cortical processing of faces: Evidence from infants and adults. *Visual Cognition, 2,* 59–87.

Volkmar, F. R., & Mayes, L. (1990). Gaze behaviour in autism. *Development and Psychopathology, 3,* 61–69.

Volkmar, F. R., & Siegel, A. E. (1982). Responses to consistent and discrepant social communications. In R. S. Feldman (Ed.), *Development of nonverbal behavior in children.* New York: Springer-Verlag.

Wellman, H. M., & Woolley, J. D. (1990). From simple desires to ordinary beliefs: The development of everyday psychology. *Cognition, 35,* 245–275.

Wimmer, H., Hogrefe, G. J., & Perner, J. (1988). Children's understanding of informational access as a source of knowledge. *Child Development, 59,* 386–396.

Yuill, N. (1984). Young children's coordination of motive and outcome in judgments of satisfaction and morality. *British Journal of Developmental Psychology, 2,* 73–81.

12

The Inquisitive Eye: Infants' Implicit Understanding that Looking Leads to Knowing

Diane Poulin-Dubois, Tamara L. Demke, and Kara M. Olineck
Concordia University, Montréal

Children's understanding of the significance of other people's eye gaze develops gradually. In particular, there are at least four critical levels of gaze sensitivity and understanding that can be traced (Povinelli & Eddy, 1996). At the first level, infants express a special sensitivity to eyes that is shared with many other species (see chapter 14 in this book). At the second level, which can be observed in the first few months of life, infants show a preference for eyes over other parts of the human face and engage with their caretakers in mutual gaze (Caron, Caron, Caldwell, & Weiss, 1973; Maurer & Barrera, 1981). By 3 to 6 months of age, infants progress to the third level of gaze sensitivity, and begin to engage in triadic interactions by shifting their gaze based on the other person's gaze direction. Gaze-following becomes more robust and more accurate between 6 and 18 months of age. By the end of the first year of life, infants advance to the fourth level of gaze sensitivity, which involves an understanding that there is some connection between the looker and the object of his or her gaze. This connection can take many forms, ranging from simple visual contact, to predicting mental states, emotional reactions, and other behaviors.

While the research supports this developmental progression, there is considerable controversy concerning the significance that researchers attribute to infants' gaze-following. Proponents of a lean interpretation argue that gaze-following is due to reinforcement, or that gaze-following simply represents an innate orienting response (Langton, Watt, & Bruce, 2000; Moore 1999). In contrast, proponents of a rich interpretation argue that gaze-following provides evidence for infants' understanding of visual attention or perception (Carpenter, Nagell, & Tomasello, 1998). Infants' ability to link visual perception with other people's knowledge plays a critical role in their development of "theory of mind" (Flavell, 1999). In particular, children's appreciation of knowledge formation in themselves and others, including the causal role that perceptual access plays in the acquisition of knowledge, has been the source of considerable controversy. Research suggests that children seem to have developed some understanding of the link between perception and knowledge by 3 to 4 years of age. They understand, for example, that someone who has looked inside a container will know its contents, whereas someone who has not will be ignorant (Pillow, 1989; Povinelli & deBlois, 1992; Pratt & Bryant, 1990; Wimmer, Hogrefe, & Perner, 1988; Woolley & Wellman, 1993). Thus, they understand that visual perception and knowing tend to go together, even if they do not appreciate that perception is a necessary condition for knowledge (Perner, 1991). For example, preschoolers do not understand that one cannot gain information about the color of an object by touch alone, or that knowledge cannot be acquired when perception is entirely absent (O'Neill, Astington, & Flavell, 1992; Pillow, 1989; Ruffman & Olson, 1989).

Surprisingly, even with the use of more simplified procedures (similar to those used with non-human primates), researchers have been unable to detect an explicit understanding of the seeing-knowing relation prior to age 3 (Povinelli & deBlois, 1992). However, it remains unclear whether younger children may have a more rudimentary, or implicit, understanding of the link between seeing and knowing. Based on recent research, it is plausible to expect that an implicit understanding of the seeing-knowing relation might emerge prior to a more well-developed understanding that is verbally accessible. For instance, toddlers' understanding of a story character's belief can be revealed by their anticipatory looking responses, even before they are able to explicitly demonstrate their understanding verbally (Clements & Perner, 1994). Similarly, a study by O'Neill (1996) provided some indirect evidence for an implicit understanding of the seeing-knowing relation in the second year. In this study, 27- and 31-month-old infants made more frequent and explicit attempts to communicate with their mother when she was ignorant to the location of an object compared to when she was not. Moreover, a recent study by Dunham, Dunham, and O'Keefe (2000), which included additional methodological controls, revealed a difference between 28- and 33-month-olds' ability to take their parent's knowledge into account. In this study, infants in both age groups pointed more often to convey information to a parent who had not witnessed a hiding event, compared to a parent who had witnessed it. However, 33-month-olds were better able to adjust their behavior depending on the parents' knowledge. Specifically, when a parent first covered his or her eyes but then reopened them during the placement of a sticker (i.e., peeking), the older infants considered the parent's new knowledge, and appropriately gestured less than when the parent did not peek. Together, these findings indicate that children possess an implicit understanding of the seeing-knowing relation by the end of the third year of life.

The series of studies presented in this chapter were designed to test the hypothesis that an implicit understanding of the link between visual experience and knowledge emerges *even earlier*, in the second year of life. This prediction is grounded in the observation that many of the building blocks necessary for an understanding of the association between vision and knowledge acquisition develop early, during the first year of life. As mentioned previously, attention to eyes or eye-like patterns appears very early in human development. Infants as young as 2 to 3 months show preferential attention to the eyes over other aspects of the human face, as well as an ability to follow the gaze of an adult when the target is within their immediate visual field (Caron, Caron, Roberts, & Brooks, 1997; d'Entremont, Hains, & Muir, 1997; Scaife & Bruner, 1975). Between 6 and 18 months, infants become both more likely to follow the gaze of another person and better able to turn correctly to objects outside their own visual field (Butterworth & Jarrett, 1991; Carpenter et al., 1998; Morissette, Ricard & Gouin-Décarie, 1995). Of course, such behaviors may simply demonstrate that infants have learned that following another's eye gaze results in positive experiences, such as the sight of an attractive object (Butterworth & Jarrett, 1991; Moore & Corkum, 1998).

However, recent research on social referencing and attentional focus suggests that infants might also possess the more sophisticated understanding that visual perception corresponds to a subjective connection to the external world. In particular, toddlers understand that looking involves an attentional focus. For instance, they realize that a person will see an object if, and only if, the person's eyes are directed toward the object and if her line of sight is not blocked by an obstacle (Flavell, 1992). Also, by 18 months of age, toddlers try to remove the hands covering their mother's eyes to show her a picture (Lempers, Flavell, & Flavell, 1977). Similarly, 18-month-olds are more likely to follow the gaze of an adult whose line of sight is unobstructed than when it is obstructed, while 14-month-olds behave similarly across these contexts (Butler, Caron, & Brooks, 2000). Nonetheless, by 14 months of age, infants are sensitive to the status of an adult's eyes, showing less joint attention behaviors when eyes are closed or when the adult wears a blindfold (Brooks & Meltzoff, 2002).

Other recent research suggests that the act of looking has a referential meaning for infants. For instance, studies on social referencing indicate that early in the second year of life infants use gaze to link emotional expressions to specific objects (Baldwin & Moses, 1994; Repacholi, 1998). Moreover, 16- to 18-month-old infants can use the eye gaze of a speaker to determine the correct referent of a new label, even when the object looked at and labeled by the speaker was different from the infant's attentional focus (Baldwin, 1991, 1995). Together, these studies provide evidence that between 12 and 18 months of age, infants begin to understand the attentional focus of another person as a psychological spotlight that can be intentionally directed at something in the environment.

Once infants are able to identify the referent of another person's attentional focus (i.e., they use eye gaze as a psychological spotlight), they progress to a more advanced understanding of looking, in which they are able to use this information to predict a person's subsequent behavior. In a recent study, Poulin-Dubois (1999) examined whether 18- to 30-month-old infants recognize the relationship between a person's attentional focus and his or her behavior. To do this, infants were presented with videotaped events in which a person was shown looking and pointing at one of two objects. Each event was followed by the presentation of two still frames, each showing the actor grasping towards one of the two objects. The results showed that infants looked significantly longer at the incongruent behavior (i.e., actor grasping the object not looked at) than at the congruent behavior (i.e., actor grasping the object looked at). This response suggested that infants expected the person to grasp the object that she had looked at previously and were surprised when the person reached for the previously ignored object. Recent studies, using the habituation paradigm, have demonstrated a similar understanding. For instance, Woodward (2003) demonstrated that even younger infants understand that gaze involves a relation between a person and the object of her gaze. In this experiment, 7-, 9-, and 12-month-old infants were habituated to an actor repeatedly looking at one of two toys. Infants were then presented with test events in which the actor either looked at a different toy in the same location or looked at the same toy in a different location. Overall, 7- and 9-month-old infants did not react when the object of the actor's attention changed (i.e., when the actor looked at a different toy in the same location); however, they were able to follow the actor's gaze to the toys. In contrast, 12-month-olds looked significantly longer at test events in which the object of the actor's attention changed (i.e., when the actor looked at a different toy in the same location) than at test events in which the location of the object changed (i.e., when the actor looked at the same toy in a different location). These results suggest that 12-month-olds, but not younger infants, expect a person who has looked at an object to subsequently act towards that object and are surprised if this link is violated. Moreover, this finding has been replicated when eye gaze is paired with positive affect (Phillips, Wellman, & Spelke, 2002; Sodian & Thoermer, 2002).

In sum, the current review suggests that beginning around the age of 1 year, infants seem to attend to the relation between a person and the object of his or her gaze. More specifically, infants have some grasp that gaze direction can be used to predict people's behavior. However, the extent of infants' knowledge about the nature of this relation remains to be determined. In particular, it remains unclear whether infants are able to use eye gaze to make inferences about other people's knowledge. Therefore, the following experiments represent a systematic attempt to shed light on this unresolved issue. In Experiment 1, we used an interactive search game, similar to the one used by Povinelli and deBlois (1992), to investigate whether infants understand that only the person who saw where an object was hidden would be able to help them find that object. In Experiments 2 and 3, a preferential looking procedure was designed to determine whether 18- to 24-month-old infants have some implicit understanding that seeing leads to knowing. Three-year-olds' anticipatory looking behavior suggests that they have a preliminary understanding of false belief even before they are able to make this understanding verbally explicit (Clements & Perner, 1994; Garnham & Ruffman, 2001). Therefore, we expected to observe a similar developmental pattern in infants' understanding of the seeing-knowing relation.

EXPERIMENT 1

In our laboratory, Bennett & Poulin-Dubois (1998) recently investigated whether 24- and 30-month-old infants possess an understanding that seeing allows another person to be "cognitively connected" to the world and that seeing leads to knowing. The experiment was comprised of two tasks, and the order in which infants completed these tasks was counterbalanced.

Task 1.   The goal of the first task was to examine 24- and 30-month-old infants' ability to recognize that responses to non-verbal communicative acts require that a person's eyes be unobstructed. As reviewed above, previous research has shown that by the end of the second year, infants understand that a person is able to see something only when the person's eyes are open. In order to ensure that infants understand the effect of a blindfold on visual access, a level-one perspective-taking task was administered (similar to the one used by Povinelli & Eddy, 1996). In the warm-up phase, infants were seated across from two actors who wore blindfolds around their necks and were trained to touch the hand of an adult actor in order to retrieve a toy. The experimenter placed a toy in the middle of the table and asked the actors to each place one of their hands on either side of the infant. The experimenter then said, "Let's play with the toy! Who can get the toy for you?" Infants were instructed to touch one of the actor's hands, and if they were reluctant, the experimenter demonstrated how to retrieve the toy by touching one of the actor's hands herself. In the experimental phase, there were four trials in which one actor was blindfolded and the other wore a blindfold around her neck. Each trial began with one of the actors placing a blindfold around her eyes. In order to emphasize to the infant that one actor could see and the other actor could not, the experimenter waved and greeted each of the actors, and only the actor who could see responded. The experimenter then placed a toy in the middle of the table and asked each of the actors to place one of their hands on either side of the infant. Infants were asked to touch an actor's hand in order to retrieve the toy. The investigators predicted that if infants have learned the importance of "seeing" by 2 years of age, they would preferentially enlist the help of the non-blindfolded actor in order to retrieve the toy.

The number of times the infant touched an actor's hand, as well as which actor's hand was touched, was coded for analyses. Only infants who touched an actor's hand in at least one trial were included in the final analyses ($N = 23$; ten 24-month-olds and thirteen 30-month-olds). If infants refused to touch the hand of an actor during one or more of the remaining trials, their response was coded as incorrect. In the first analyses, the dependent variable was the number of trials (out of 4) in which the infant touched the hand of the actor who could see (i.e., demonstrated an appropriate response). A planned comparison revealed no significant difference between the number of appropriate responses demonstrated by the 24-month-olds ($M = 2.00$, $SD = 1.05$) and the 30-month-olds ($M = 2.53$, $SD = 1.99$), $t(21) = -1.12$, ns. At first glance, these results seem to indicate that both 24- and 30-month-old infants have a relatively minimal understanding of the importance of the "seeing" relation to the world. However, it is likely that infants' performance on this task was negatively impacted by their unwillingness to touch the hands of the actors. Therefore, in subsequent analyses, the investigators examined the proportion of times the infants chose to touch the hand of the non-blindfolded actor out of the number of trials in which they actually touched an actor's hand. The analyses indicated that 24-month-old infants touched the hand of the "seeing" actor at a rate greater than expected by chance (62.50%), $t(9) = 1.90$, $p < 0.05$. Similarly, the 30-month-old infants also touched the hand of the "seeing" actor at a rate significantly different from chance (85.90%), $t(12) = 5.12$, $p < 0.05$. These results suggest that when infants' response rate was taken into account, both age groups preferentially touched the hand of the "seeing" actor when attempting to retrieve a toy. Overall, these data confirm that infants as young as 24 months of age understand that people's eyes have to be unobstructed in order for them to be connected to the world, which is a prerequisite for understanding the seeing-knowing relation.

Task 2. The purpose of the second task was to determine whether 24- and 30-month-old infants are capable of making inferences regarding another person's knowledge, based on whether or not she could see (i.e., had visual access) during the presentation of critical information. This task was a modified version of the procedure used by Povinelli and deBlois (1992). In the warm-up phase, infants were asked to watch two actors, who wore blindfolds around their necks, hide a toy underneath one of three cups. The actor who hid the toy placed her hand on top of the cup containing the toy, while the other actor placed her hand on one of the remaining cups. The experimenter then asked the infant, "Who has the toy? Where is the toy?" The actors pushed their respective cups forward, and the infant was told to find the toy by lifting up one of the cups. The purpose of the warm-up phase was to familiarize infants with the process of watching the actors select a cup and then deciding which actor may have correctly identified the cup containing the toy. In the experimental phase, there were four trials in which one actor's eyes were blindfolded during the hiding of the toy, while the other actor wore a blindfold around her neck. A screen was placed in front of the cups so that infants were unable to see where the toy was being hidden. Once the screen was in place, the experimenter showed a toy to the infant and pointed to the actors. It was emphasized to the infant that one actor could see and the other could not. The infant was then asked to watch the experimenter hide the toy. The actor who wore the blindfold around her neck saw where the toy was hidden, while the blindfolded actor did not. Once the toy was hidden, the experimenter removed the screen and the blindfolded actor removed her blindfold. Then the experimenter said, "Watch them. They are going to find the toy." The actor who had visual access during the hiding of the toy put her hand on the correct cup, while the blindfolded actor put her hand on an incorrect cup. After a short delay, the actors pushed their selected cups forward, and the infants were asked to find the toy by lifting one of the two cups chosen by the actors. It was predicted that if infants understand that seeing leads to knowing, they would choose the cup of the actor who had visual access (i.e., who could see) during the hiding of the toy. The accuracy of the infants' responses were coded.

The results indicated that there was no significant difference between the number of trials in which 24-month-olds ($M = 1.72$, $SD = 1.07$) and 30-month-olds ($M = 1.96$, $SD = .88$) correctly chose the cup containing the toy, $t(50) = .403$, ns. Neither the 24-month-olds nor the 30-month-olds chose the correct cup at a rate greater than one would expect given chance alone (55.90% and 53.41%, respectively). Taken together, these results indicate that 24- and 30-month-old infants do not yet possess an understanding that seeing leads to knowing. However, it is possible that these results may be partially due to methodological constraints, such as the complexity of the task and the memory requirements. For instance, infants may not have paid adequate attention to which actor had visual access and which actor did not have visual access during the hiding of the toy. Moreover, infants may have simply forgotten which actor was blindfolded during the hiding phase, as the blindfolded actor removed her blindfold before placing her hand on one of the cups. These methodological limitations led us to develop a preferential looking paradigm that would tap into infants' precocious ability to react to a violation of their expectancies.

EXPERIMENT 2

In a recent series of experiments conducted in collaboration with Beate Sodian and her colleagues, we tested the hypothesis that an implicit understanding of the link between visual experience and knowledge emerges in the second year of life (Poulin-Dubois, Tilden, Sodian, Metz, & Schöppner, 2003). Using the violation of expectancy paradigm, we examined infants' expectations about where a person will search for an object, based on that person's prior visual access to the hidden location of the object. We predicted that infants would expect a person who has seen a toy being hidden under a box to subsequently look for the toy in that location. This expectation would be violated if the person looked for the toy in a different location. In addition, we predicted that infants would have no expectation about where a person who did not see the toy being hidden would subsequently look for that toy.

To test these hypotheses, we presented videotaped scenarios to 18- ($N = 30$) and 24-month-old infants ($N = 30$) using the preferential looking paradigm. Infants sat facing two screens that displayed these scenarios, which differed in whether or not an actor was able to see the location of a hidden toy. Each scenario was divided into two phases. The first phase (information phase) was presented on one screen and showed a female actor seated at a table, with two identical overturned buckets on each side of the table. A second female actor stood behind the main actor, looked straight ahead, and called the infant's attention by saying, "Hi, we are going to play a game." In one condition, the second actor put a blindfold over the main actor's eyes (no visual access) and then lifted each of the buckets, one at a time, revealing a cup under one of the buckets. Meanwhile, the blindfolded actor remained silent and motionless throughout the uncovering of the buckets. In the second condition, the blindfold was placed over the main actor's mouth (visual access was maintained), and she leaned forward and looked at each bucket as it was lifted. In both conditions, after these actions were completed, the second actor walked off-screen while the main actor remained seated and removed her blindfold. Then, the voice of the second actor was heard from off-screen, asking the other actor to find a target object ("Hi Judy, Where is my cup?"). After a 1.5 second pause, during which both screens were blank, the test phase began. The test phase consisted of two still frames, which were presented simultaneously on the two screens for a duration of 10 seconds. One still image presented the main actor pointing at the bucket which contained the target object (correct action), and the other still frame presented her pointing at the other, empty bucket (incorrect action). Simultaneously, her voice was heard saying, "It's here."

Infants were administered two trials, one in the visual access condition and one in the no visual access condition. Across infants, the bucket under which the toy was located, presentation of the information phase (on left screen or right screen), and presentation of the correct action in the test phase (on left screen or right screen), was counterbalanced across trials. For each trial, the amount of time infants looked at the screen displaying the information phase and the amount of time they looked at each of the two screens during the test phase was measured.

To ensure infants encoded all of the relevant information in each film, only infants who looked at the screen for at least 80% of the total duration of the information phase, and at least 25% of the total duration of the test phase, were included in the final analyses. Overall, 18- and 24-month-olds demonstrated the same pattern of behavior, as depicted in Figure 12–1. Analysis of variance revealed a significant interaction, whereby infants' responses to the correct and incorrect actions were different in the visual access and no visual access conditions. Pairwise comparisons revealed that infants looked

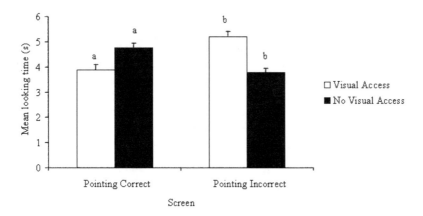

FIGURE 12–1.   Infants' mean looking time at the correct and incorrect actions as a function of visual access in Experiment 2.

significantly longer at the correct action when the actor's eyes were blindfolded ($M = 4.79$ s, $SD = 1.45$) compared to when she was able to see the event ($M = 1.53$ s, $SD = 1.53$). This indicates that infants were surprised to see the actor pointing to the correct location when she had not seen where the toy was hidden. In contrast, the opposite pattern was observed for the incorrect action. Infants looked longer at the incorrect action when the actor was able to see the event ($M = 5.19$ s, $SD = 1.63$) compared to when she was unable to see the event ($M = 3.77$ s, $SD = 1.27$). Thus, infants were surprised to see the actor pointing to the incorrect location when she had seen that the toy was hidden in a different location. To determine if infants looked differently at the actions within each condition (i.e., visual or no visual access), their looking times at the correct action was expressed as a ratio of their total looking times at both actions (expressed as a percentage) and compared to chance (50%). When the actor could not see the location of the hidden toy, infants of both ages looked longer at the correct action than expected by chance ($M = 55.49\%$, $t(29) = 2.20$, $p < .05$ for 18-month-olds and $M = 55.86\%$, $t(29) = 2.67$ for 24-month-olds, $p < .01$). When the actor was able to see the location of the hidden toy, 18-month-olds looked longer at the incorrect action than expected by chance ($M = 59.86\%$, $t(29) = 4.11$, $p < .001$), whereas 24-month-olds looked at the incorrect action at chance levels ($M = 54.30\%$, $t(29) = 1.39$, ns).

These findings suggest that at 18 months, infants expect that someone who saw the location of a hidden object will search for the object successfully, whereas someone who did not see the location of a hidden object will be unsuccessful. However, if the infants expected the blindfolded person to be ignorant, like adults, they should have expected the person to simply guess the location of the objects. Instead, infants seem to expect ignorance (i.e., no visual access) to lead to incorrect actions. Of course, an alternative interpretation is that infants simply computed an association between eye gaze and the object during the information phase, and therefore expected gaze and pointing to be associated with the object again in the test phase. Because it was not possible to compute such a correlation in the no visual access condition, infants could not predict where the actor would search and were surprised to see the actor point at the correct location. The following experiment was designed in order to clarify the interpretation of these findings.

EXPERIMENT 3

In Experiment 3, we attempted to clarify the nature of infants' implicit understanding of the seeing-knowing relation, while controlling for the possibility that infants were responding on the basis of a simple association between looking and the object. Infants were tested using a similar procedure, except that two objects were hidden during the information phase. As a result, the correct or incorrect action in the test phase was dependent on which specific toy the second actor requested, rather than a simple "perseveration" of behavior towards any object available, as could have been the case in Experiment 2. We predicted that if infants' knowledge is not simply based on behavioral regularities (i.e., that seeing leads to correct search, and not seeing leads to an incorrect search), infants would expect a person who has seen where the target toy is hidden to look in the correct location and would be surprised if that person looks in the wrong location. In contrast, we predicted that infants would have no clear expectation about where a person will look for a particular toy when they have not seen where it is hidden.

Eighteen-month-olds ($N = 27$) were presented with videotaped scenarios using the preferential looking paradigm. The scenarios were based on those used in the previous experiment, and the actors in the films followed the same procedure, with one primary exception. In the information phase, a different object was revealed under each of the two buckets (e.g., ball, cup). As in the previous experiment, the second actor requested the target object from off-screen, using the appropriate label for the object (e.g., "I'm looking for my ball. Where is my ball?"). Again, the test phase consisted of two still frames presented simultaneously for 10 seconds. One still image presented the actor pointing at the bucket that contained the target object (correct action), and the other still frame presented her pointing at the bucket that contained the other object (incorrect action).

In contrast to the previous experiment, infants were administered a total of four trials, using two different sets of objects (ball and cup; car and duck). Thus, each object was the target once. Each infant observed two trials where the actor had visual access to the location of the toy, and two where she did not have visual access. Across infants, the order of trials, target object, presentation of the information phase (on left screen or right screen), and presentation of the correct action in the test phase (on left screen or right screen), was counterbalanced across trials. As in the previous experiment, infants' visual fixation was measured for each trial. Because Experiment 2 consisted of two trials, infants' responses to the correct and incorrect actions were compared across the visual access and no visual access conditions in only the first two trials. Overall, there were no main effects or interactions, as shown in Figure 12–2. That is, there were no differences in infants' looking times at the correct and incorrect actions in the visual access condition ($M = 4.21$ s, $SD = 1.73$ and $M = 4.03$ s, $SD = 1.77$, respectively), or in the no visual access condition ($M = 4.32$ s, $SD = 1.51$ and $M = 4.67$ s, $SD = 1.70$, respectively).

Put simply, infants in Experiment 3 looked equally long at each action, across both the visual access and no visual access conditions. At first glance,

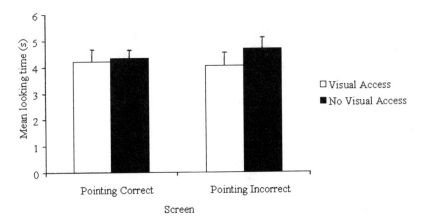

FIGURE 12–2.   18-month-olds' mean looking time at the correct and incorrect actions as a function of visual access in Experiment 3.

this pattern of results is consistent with the lean interpretation of the data from Experiment 2, whereby infants expect that if a person looks at an object, their subsequent behavior will merely be directed toward that object. Of course, it is possible that these results may also reflect the inherent difficulty of the task. Recall that the identity of each of the objects, their locations, and the visual experience of the actor (i.e., visual access or no visual access) all had to be remembered during the test phase. Although familiar objects were used, they were only labeled by the actor in the test phase. Thus, infants were required to quickly identify each of the objects in the short period of time when the objects were revealed from underneath the buckets. In addition, while infants have sophisticated object permanence skills at this age, the use of videotaped scenarios likely made it more difficult for infants to track the location of the objects. Therefore, infants' memory constraints may have also contributed to these results.

CONCLUSIONS

Like many other primate species, human infants follow the gaze direction of others. Moreover, infants expect a person to see an object only under certain conditions. For example, they expect that a person must have her eyes open and aimed in the direction of the object, and her eye gaze must be unobstructed (Hare, Call, Bryan, & Tomasello, 2000; Hare, Call, & Tomasello, 2001). Humans appear to have the unique ability to understand that eye gaze can be selective. In other words, humans recognize that people intentionally direct their eyes towards a particular object or person. Furthermore, only humans are able to understand that a person's visual experience influences their subsequent behaviors and beliefs about the world. By the end of the first year of life, infants recognize that people are more likely to look at and touch an object that they have looked at before, compared to an object that they have ignored (Woodward, 2003). Impressively, infants continue to do so, even if the two objects have switched location (Woodward, 2003). Around the same age, infants also maintain the link between a looker and an object over time. For example, they understand that people are more likely to show excitement towards an object that they have never seen before, compared to familiar objects (Tomasello & Haberl, 2003). Despite these achievements, data from recent experimental studies (particularly those conducted with habituation or familiarization procedures) may simply provide information about infants' ability to understand behavioral propensities.

Little is known about infants' or toddlers' ability to grasp less tangible outcomes of visual attention, such as the seeing-knowing relation. To date, research has indicated that 3-year-olds have a basic knowledge of the link between seeing and knowing (Flavell, 1999). However, slightly younger children also appear to demonstrate this understanding within communicative contexts (Lee & Homer, 1999). The present series of experiments represent the first systematic attempt to examine infants' ability to use visual perception to conceptualize other people's knowledge. By using an interactive search game and the violation of expectancy paradigm, we were able to assess infants' understanding of the seeing-knowing relation via procedures that are less dependent on language and are therefore more infant friendly.

Taken together, results from the present series of experiments suggest that infants have reached a new stage of visual perception understanding by the middle of the second year of life. In particular, the results of the second experiment suggest that infants predict that someone who has seen the location of a hidden object will later search successfully when asked to find that object. Recall that in Experiment 2, infants looked longer when the actor's behavior was incongruous with their visual access. That is, infants looked longer when the actor saw where the object was hidden, and yet later pointed at the incorrect location. Also, infants were confused when the actor did not see where the object was hidden (i.e., was blindfolded), yet later pointed at the correct location. These looking patterns are striking given that infants were privy to the correct location of the object and, therefore, may have been surprised to see the actor pointing at the incorrect location in both conditions. Instead, infants took the actor's visual experience into account and expected *different* behaviors as a function of that experience. We interpret these findings as evidence for the presence of an implicit understanding of the seeing-knowing relation by 18 months of age. However, we acknowledge that the data from Experiment 2 can be interpreted in a leaner fashion. That is, infants' looking time pattern may simply be attributed to rote expectations based on behavioral regularities (i.e., people point at objects they have just looked at). These two interpretations were directly examined in the third experiment, whereby infants were requested to find a specific object when *two objects* were hidden. We reasoned that if infants have an implicit grasp that seeing leads to knowing, the looking time pattern observed in Experiment 2 would be replicated. On the other hand, if infants were simply predicting that looking leads to subsequent looking and pointing behavior, infants would expect the actor who had visual access to two objects will point equally at both object locations, and they would be surprised to see the actor with no visual access pointing at any location.

Overall, the findings from Experiment 3 seem to support the leaner interpretation. Infants appear to understand that when a person looks at an object, they establish a long-term connection with that object and are able to maintain the connection even if the object is no longer visible. However, the results of Experiment 3 may not provide conclusive evidence regarding the two competing hypotheses described herein, because of the higher demands inherent in this task (e.g., greater memory load). In Experiment 3, infants had to keep track of the location of each object as well as the attentional state of the actor (i.e., seeing or not seeing) throughout the phase when the location of the hidden toys was revealed. Thus, it is possible that infants looked equally often at the two screens in the test phase because they could not recall the location of the target toy. This is in contrast with the task demands of Experiment 2, where only one object was hidden, making the location of that object very salient for the infant and presumably easier to recall. This potentially critical methodological limitation could be controlled for in future studies. One way to do this would be to label each toy as their location is revealed, while ensuring that no auditory cue is provided in the blindfolded condition (provide the labels with an off-camera voice). Another follow-up experiment that might clarify the nature of infants' ability to connect a looker with an object could be done using the present tasks, but eliminating all verbal information from the events. If the findings from Experiment 2 are replicated, this would confirm that the present patterns of results are based on behavioral regularities. The methodological limitations described above likely limit how conclusive our interpretations can be. However, we believe that we have been able to uncover a new step in infants' understanding of the link between looker and object. That new step involves an understanding that the connection between a looker and an object can be maintained even when the object is no longer visible, which corresponds to an implicit understanding that seeing leads to knowing.

The earliest age at which infants begin to understand the seeing-knowing relation remains to be determined. However, preliminary results from a recent follow-up study suggest that 14-month-olds do not seem to possess the same understanding as 18-month-olds (Metz, Sodian, & Poulin-Dubois, 2004). This follow-up experiment used the same procedure as in outlined in Experiment 2, and the results showed that 14-month-old infants looked equally at both still frames in the test phase. Based on these findings, it appears that there is a developmental shift between 14 and 18 months, whereby infants' understanding of the connection between a looker and an object emerges. At first glance, this developmental effect seems to be consistent with other research showing important changes in the way infants reason about the cause of other people's behavior in general, and of their understanding of visual perception in particular. For example, 18-month-olds, but not 14-month-olds, are more likely to follow an adult's gaze when her line of sight is unobstructed than when it is obstructed (Butler et al., 2000; Lempers et al., 1977). Also, between 12 and 18 months of age, infants develop an understanding of other people's intentions. Across these ages, infants perform better on the "failed intention" paradigm and prefer to imitate intentional, rather than accidental, actions (Bellagamba & Tomasello, 1999; Olineck & Poulin-Dubois, 2003). Thus, the present pattern of results is consistent with the development of a cluster of other abilities reflecting infants' understanding of other people's behavior (Meltzoff, Gopnik, & Repacholi, 1999; Poulin-Dubois, 1999). The experiments described in this chapter suggest that 18-month-olds understand that if people have visual contact with an object, this perceptual experience will subsequently influence their actions toward that object, even if the object is out of sight. We believe that this is a more advanced understanding of the looker-object link observed in 12-month-olds (Woodward, 2003). This understanding is more sophisticated because it requires granting others with a form of object permanence. Moreover, this understanding is impressive because it is based on a single exposure to the visual experience of another person.

Future research will be needed to address the precise nature of infants' connection between visual perception and others' epistemic and motivational states. One unresolved issue is whether infants appreciate that people's mental states are influenced by the quality of their perceptual connectedness to objects in the world. Adults and older children operate under the principle that a prolonged look at an object indicates that that particular object is more likely to be the actor's goal compared to an object that was either glanced at, or briefly touched by mistake (Montgomery, Bach, & Moran, 1998). In the present experiments, the actor looked desirously at one object (Experiment 2) and at two objects (Experiment 3). It remains to be determined whether a quick glance at one of the two objects would have had an impact on infants' performance. Recent research examining 14- and 18-month-olds' reenactment of intentional and accidental actions provides indirect evidence that by 18 months of age, infants are more likely to consider prolonged looking at and touching an object as markers of intentional action (Olineck & Poulin-Dubois, 2003). For this reason, 18-month-olds may be more likely than 14-month-olds to imitate intentional compared to accidental actions (Olineck & Poulin-Dubois, 2003).

In conclusion, the foundation for infants' explicit understanding that seeing leads to knowing is established during the second year of life. During this time, infants gradually come to appreciate that people's eye gaze can be used to predict their future behaviors toward objects. Infants also appreciate that they can refer to another person's perceptual experience when making inferences about that person's mental state. For example, infants can use eye gaze information to evaluate a person's knowledge about the location of an object and to infer whether the person has forged a long-lasting representation of that object. The transition from understanding eye gaze as a simple object-oriented behavior, to understanding eye gaze as a source of mental state knowledge, is still not well documented. Furthermore, there is debate about how existing evidence for this ability should be interpreted. It remains to be determined whether infants understand other people's eye gaze in purely behavioral terms, or whether their understanding of eye gaze provides a foundation for their knowledge about people's mental states. It is also possible that infants develop these two abilities in parallel, and consequently they might represent two separate systems for detecting and interpreting intentions (Povinelli, 2001). With regard to gaze, we believe that the available evidence suggests that infants' gaze understanding develops from a low-level, perceptually based system to a higher-level, inferentially based system. In order to recognize the incongruity between the actor's search behavior and their prior visual contact with the object, infants had to draw an inference about the actor's knowledge about the object location. This understanding represents a crucial developmental bridge between understanding gaze as a "behaviorist" to understanding gaze as a "cognitive" psychologist.

REFERENCES

Baldwin, D. A. (1991). Infants' contribution to the achievement of joint reference. *Child Development, 62*, 875–890.

Baldwin, D. A. (1995). Understanding the link between joint attention and language. In C. Moore & P. Dunham (Eds.), *Joint attention: Its origins and role in development* (pp. 131–158). Hillsdale, NJ: Lawrence Erlbaum Associates.

Baldwin, D. A., & Moses, L. J. (1994). Early understanding of referential intent and attentional focus: Evidence from language and emotion. In: C. Lewis & P. Mitchell (Eds.), *Children's early understanding of mind: Origins and development* (pp. 133–156). Hillsdale, NJ: Lawrence Erlbaum Associates.

Bellagamba, F., & Tomasello, M. (1999). Re-enacting intended acts: Comparing 12- and 18-month-olds. *Infant Behavior and Development, 22,* 277–282.

Bennett, P., & Poulin-Dubois, D. (1998, April). *Two-year-olds' understanding of attentional focus and seeing = knowing.* Poster session presented at the International Conference on Infant Studies, Atlanta.

Brooks, R., & Meltzoff, A. N. (2002).The importance of eyes: How infants interpret adult looking behaviour. *Developmental Psychology, 38*(6), 958–966.

Butler, S. C., Caron, A. J., & Brooks, R. (2000). Infant understanding of the referential nature of looking. *Journal of Cognition and Development, 1,* 359–377.

Butterworth, G., & Jarrett, N. (1991). What minds have in common is space: Spatial mechanisms serving joint visual attention in infancy. *British Journal of Developmental Psychology, 9,* 55–72.

Caron, A., Caron, R., Caldwell, R., & Weiss, S. (1973). Infant perception of the structural properties of the face. *Developmental Psychology, 9,* 385–399.

Caron, A. J., Caron, R., Roberts, J., & Brooks, R. (1997). Infant sensitivity to deviations in dynamic facial–vocal displays: The role of eye regard. *Developmental Psychology, 33,* 802–813.

Carpenter, M., Nagell, K., & Tomasello, M. (1998). Social cognition, joint attention, and communicative competence from 9 to 15 months of age. *Monographs of the Society for Research in Child Development, 63* (255).

Clements, W. A., & Perner, J. (1994). Implicit Understanding of Belief. *Cognitive Development, 9,* 377–395.

D'Entremont, B., Hains, S., & Muir, E. (1997). A demonstration of gaze-following in 3- to 6-month-olds. *Infant Behaviour and Development, 20,* 569–572.

Dunham, P., Dunham, F., & O'Keefe, C. (2000). Two-year-olds' sensitivity to a parent's knowledge state: Mind reading or contextual cues? *British Journal of Developmental Psychology, 18,* 519–532.

Flavell, J. H. (1992). Perspectives on perspective taking. In H. Beilin & P. Pufall (Eds.), *Piaget's Theory: Prospects and Possibilities.* (pp. 107–139). Hillsdale, NJ: Lawrence Erlbaum Associates.

Flavell, J. H. (1999). Cognitive Development: Children's Knowledge about the Mind. *Annual Review of Psychology, 50,* 21–45.

Garnham, W. A., & Ruffman, T. (2001). Origin and truth: Young children's understanding of imaginary mental representations. *Developmental Science, 4,* 94–100.

Hare, B., Call, J., Bryan, A., & Tomasello, M. (2000). Do chimpanzees know what conspecifics do and do not see? *Animal Behavior, 59,* 771–785.

Hare, B., Call, J., & Tomasello, M. (2001). Do chimpanzees know what conspecifics know? *Animal Behaviour, 61,* 139–151.

Langton, S. R. H., Watt, R. J., & Bruce, V. (2000). Do the eyes have it? Cues to the direction of social attention. *Trends in Cognitive Sciences, 4,* 50–59.

Lee, K., & Homer, B. (1999). Children as folk psychologists: The developing understanding of the mind. In A. Slater & D. Muir (Eds.), *The Blackwell reader in developmental psychology,* (pp. 228–252). Malden, MA: Blackwell Publishers.

Lempers, J. D., Flavell, J. H., & Flavell, E. R. (1977). The development in very young children of tacit knowledge concerning visual perception. *Genetic Psychology Monographs, 95*(1), 3–53.

Maurer, D., & Barrera, M. (1981). Infants' perception of natural and distorted arrangements of a schematic face. *Child Development, 52,* 296–202.

Meltzoff, A. N., Gopnik, A., & Repacholi, B. M. (1999). Toddlers' understanding of intentions, desires, and emotions: Explorations of the dark ages. In P. D. Zelazo, J. W. Astington, & D. R. Olson (Eds.), *Developing theories of intention* (pp. 17–41). Mahwah, N.J.: Lawrence Erlbaum Associates.

Metz, U., Sodian, B., & Poulin-Dubois, D. (2004, May). *Understanding of the seeing = knowing relation in the second year of life?* Poster submitted to the International Conference on Infant Studies, Chicago.

Montgomery, D. E., Bach, L. M., & Moran, C. (1998). Children's use of looking behavior as a cue to detect another's goal. *Child Development, 69*(3), 692–705.

Moore, C. (1999). Gaze-following and the control of attention. In P. Rochat (Ed.), *Early social cognition: Understanding others in the first months of life* (pp. 241–256). Mahwah, NJ: Lawrence Erlbaum Associates.

Moore, C., & Corkum, V. L. (1998). Infant gaze-following based on eye direction. *British Journal of Developmental Psychology, 16,* 495–503.

Morissette, P., Ricard, M., & Gouin-Décarie, T. (1995). Joint visual attention and pointing in infancy: A longitudinal study of comprehension. *British Journal of Developmental Psychology, 13*(2), 163–175.

Olineck, K., & Poulin-Dubois, D. (2005). Infants' ability to distinguish between intentional and accidental actions and its relation to internal state language. *Infancy, 8,* 91–100.

O'Neill, D. (1996). Two-year-old children's sensitivity to a parent's knowledge state when making requests. *Child Development, 67,* 659–677.

O'Neill, D. K., Astington, J. W., & Flavell, J. H. (1992). Young children's understanding of the role that sensory experience plays in knowledge acquisition. *Child Development, 63,* 474–490.

Perner, J. (1991). *Understanding the representational mind.* Cambridge, MA: The MIT Press.

Phillips, A. T., Wellman, H. M., & Spelke, E. S. (2002). Infants' ability to connect gaze and emotional expression to intentional action. *Cognition, 85*(1), 53–78.

Pillow, B. H. (1989). Early understanding of perception as a source of knowledge. *Journal of Experimental Child Psychology, 47,* 116–129.

Poulin-Dubois, D. (1999). Infants' distinction between animate and inanimate objects: The origins of naive psychology. In P. Rochat (Ed.), *Early social cognition: Understanding others in the first months of life* (pp. 257–280). Mahwah, NJ: Lawrence Erlbaum Associates.

Poulin-Dubois, D., Tilden, J., Sodian, B., Metz, U., & Schöppner, B. (2003). *Now you see it, now you don't: Implicit understanding of seeing = knowing in 14- to 24-month-olds.* Manuscript submitted for publication.

Povinelli, D. J. (2001). On the possibilities of detecting intentions prior to understanding them. In B. F. Malle & J. L. Moses (Eds.), *Intentions and intentionality: Foundations of social cognition* (pp. 225–248). Cambridge, MA: The MIT Press.

Povinelli, D. J., & deBlois, S. (1992). Young children's (Homo sapiens) understanding of knowledge formation in themselves and others. *Journal of Comparative Psychology, 106,* 228–238.

Povinelli, D. J., & Eddy, T. J. (1996). What young chimpanzees know about seeing. *Monographs of the Society for Research in Child Development, 61*(3, Serial No. 247).

Pratt, C., & Bryant, P. (1990). Young children understand that looking leads to knowing (so long as they are looking into a single barrel). *Child Development, 61,* 973–982.

Repacholi, B. M. (1998). Infants' use of attentional cues to identify the referent of another person's emotional expression. *Developmental Psychology, 34,* 1017–1025.

Ruffman, T., & Olson, D. R. (1989). Children's ascriptions of knowledge to others. *Developmental Psychology, 25,* 601–606.

Scaife, M., & Bruner, J. S. (1975). The capacity for joint visual attention in the infant. *Nature, 253,* 265–266.

Sodian, B., & Thoermer, C. (2002). *Infants' understanding of looking, pointing and reaching as cues to goal-directed action.* Manuscript submitted for publication.

Tomasello, M., & Haberl, K. (2003). Understanding attention: 12- and 18-month-olds know what is new for other persons. *Developmental Psychology, 39*(5), 906–912.

Wimmer, H., Hogrefe, G.-J., & Perner, J. (1988). Children's understanding of informational access as a source of knowledge. *Child Development, 59,* 386–396.

Woodward, A. L. (2003). Infants' developing understanding of the link between looker and object. *Developmental Science, 6,* 297–311.

Woolley, J. D., & Wellman, H. M. (1993). Origin and truth: Young children's understanding of imaginary mental representations, *Child Development, 64,* 1–17.

13

Look into My Eyes: The Effect of Direct Gaze on Face Processing in Children and Adults

Bruce M. Hood
University of Bristol, United Kingdom

C. Neil Macrae
University of Aberdeen, United Kingdom

"The difference in human features must be reckoned great, inasmuch as they enable us to distinguish a single known face among those of thousands of strangers, though they are mostly too minute for measurement. At the same time, they are exceedingly numerous. The general expression of a face is the sum of a multitude of small details, which are viewed in such rapid succession that we seem to perceive them all at a single glance." (Galton, 1883, pg. 3)

In this quote, Galton makes two important points in his observations of human face recognition. First, the capacity for recognizing thousands of faces is remarkable despite the fact that the differences between features of different faces seem remarkably small. Second, the processing is effortless with all features processed together rapidly. These observations have been borne out in recent years by careful measurements of face processing skills, as well as the underlying neural mechanisms that support this ability (for review see Bruce

& Young, 1998). The evidence from these studies suggests that humans are especially adept at detecting and processing faces in comparison to other categories of biological stimuli and that this specialization is supported by relatively dedicated brain regions of the posterior temporal cortex (for review, see Kanwisher & Moscovitch, 2000).

However, within the face, the eyes and, in particular, the direction of gaze, play a significant role in face processing. The direction of gaze has long been recognized by social psychologists as a rich, nonverbal channel of communication (Cook & Argyle, 1972). Many early empirical studies of gaze revealed considerable organization in the gaze interaction between individuals and demonstrated that patterns of mutual joint attention could reflect the social relationship between individuals communicating face-to-face. In these studies, the direction and duration of gaze were a barometer of the amount of attention that was being allocated (for review, see Kleinke, 1986).When two or more individuals coordinate visual attention through gaze to a shared point of reference, they are engaging in joint attention. We turn to see what others are looking at. This could be an object or event in or out of the field of view of the observers, as has been investigated in many studies of the development of joint attention using the original head turning paradigm (Scaife & Bruner, 1975). In this paradigm, it was found that infants towards the end of their first year will turn to look in the same direction as a adult who shifts gaze to the side. However, joint attention also includes periods of mutual gaze during which the attention mechanisms are still attracting information processing resources. When you look at me, your gaze triggers my attention to you. Thus, mutual gaze directs attention to each observer's face and may facilitate processing of faces to achieve the levels of expertise identified by Galton (1883).

Recently, cognitive neuroscientists have been investigating gaze as a mechanism for controlling attention. This arises from two distinct lines of research. The first comes from studies that have reported discrete brain activity related to the processing of gaze which is separable to mechanisms for processing of faces. Previously, theoretical models of face processing had not treated the eyes as a special category of stimulus that may be subserved by dedicated mechanisms (e.g., Bruce & Young, 1986). However, an influential hypothesis put forward by Baron-Cohen (1995) argued that there was evidence to support the existence of a specialized Eye Direction Detector (EDD). Various subsequent imaging studies did in fact find evidence for the EDD in humans using a variety of techniques including evoked response potentials (ERPs; Benton, Allison, Puce, Perez, & McCarthy, 1996; Puce, Allison, Benton, Gore, & McCarthy, 1998) functional magnetic resonance imaging (fMRI; Hoffman & Haxby, 2000) and positron emission topography (PET; Wicker, Michel, Henaff, & Decety, 1998). These studies all indicate that gaze processing may be supported by dedicated neural substrates. However, direction of gaze has also been shown to modulate brain activity related to processing of faces in general, by monkeys (single cell recording; Perrett & Mistlin, 1990), human adults (fMRI; Kampe, Frith, Dolan, & Frith, 2001) and human infants (ERPs; Farroni, Csibra, Simion, & Johnson, 2002). These latter findings are particularly important in that they demonstrate that brain activity generally thought to reflect attentional processing of faces is determined by whether the gaze on the face is directed towards the viewer. The mechanisms by which this attentional processing is modulated are not fully understood, but old psychophysiology studies indicate that general autonomic arousal as evidenced by the galvanic skin response (Nichols & Champness, 1971) and electroencephalogram (Gale, Kingsley, Brookes, & Smith, 1978) is elevated when viewing faces with direct gaze.

The second line of research to stimulate an interest in the direction of gaze comes from the finding that the control of one's own visual attention is determined by another's direction of gaze. This is based on the behavioral finding that gaze operates by triggering shifts of visual attention, very much like arrows and flashes of light can do so in traditional visual orienting paradigms. In his seminal work on orienting, Posner (1978) demonstrated that visual attention can be shifted by a visual cue such as an arrow, prior to the onset of the target, which produces enhanced or facilitated processing of the target location and identity. If cues are noninformative or indeed invalid by directing the observer to an incorrect location, this leads to a cost in terms of reaction time and accuracy as the observer has to re-orient attention to the correct location. These effects of costs and benefits under various cueing conditions led Posner to postulate an attentional system that can be driven by various internal and external cues much in the same way as a spotlight can move around a spatial layout, highlighting locations and objects for attention. While the spotlight metaphor of attention is controversial, the cost-benefit effects of invalid-valid cueing are a well-substantiated aspect of cueing visual attention.

Using similar logic of valid and invalid cueing, Jon Driver and colleagues (Driver et al., 1999) investigated whether the direction of gaze would cue another's visual attention. Participants were asked to identify targets presented on the left and right of a screen that were preceded by a face that had gaze directed towards the ensuing target location (valid), or away (invalid). Analysis of manual reaction times revealed significant costs of invalid cueing compared to valid cueing, indicating the direction of gaze had shifted the observer's own attention. Even when the study was setup so that there was either no relationship between gaze and targets, or the targets were reliably in the opposite direction to gaze, observers followed the gaze (Driver et al., 1999; Friesen & Kingstone, 1998). This led a number of researchers to conclude that gaze-following was an automated process that was almost obligatory in nature, though more recent work suggests that automated cueing effects are not restricted to gaze cues (Ristic, Friesen, & Kingstone, 2002; Tipples, 2002).

Nevertheless, the direction of gaze appears to be a compelling stimulus for capturing and directing another's attention. One recent study has suggested that gaze operates on the observer's own eye movement system through a process of behavioral mimicry. Observers were instructed to make an eye movement to a peripheral target. Before the target appeared, a face was presented with gaze in the same or opposite direction. When the gaze was opposite to the target position, this stimulus impaired the execution of the observer's saccades, which lead the researchers to conclude that a shift in someone else's gaze triggers a corresponding shift in our own eye movement system (Ricciardelli, Bricolo, Aglioti, & Chelazzi, 2002). Even when observers are told not to make an eye movement, a stimulus gaze shift quite often elicits an eye movement in the observer (Mansfield, Farroni, & Johnson, 2003). Thus, observing a gaze shift triggers both overt and covert movement of the observer's own gaze shifting mechanisms, producing the various orienting effects even when the participant was told to ignore gaze, maintain fixation, and press a button. That eye movements can affect manual responses is consistent with models of the orienting system, which suggests that many attentional cueing effects reflect a central multimodal premotor system that has a very strong input from the midbrain eye movement mechanisms (Buchtel & Butter, 1988).

Taken together, these findings from imaging and behavioral studies strongly support the idea that direction of gaze, as signaled predominantly by the eyes, is processed by separable neural mechanisms that serve to shift the observer's attention in the same direction as that of the viewed person. This mechanism is very strong and difficult to ignore and may be the basis for Baron-Cohen's (1995) EDD. It follows then that when gaze is directed to the observer, the observer's attention is focused on the gaze and the face surrounding the eyes. Thus, attention to faces is likely to be enhanced when the direction of gaze is mutual. Such an effect would be especially beneficial in face processing. As a category of stimulus, faces are more alike than dissimilar, and yet in comparison to other categories of stimuli, humans are remarkably good at distinguishing, recognizing, and remembering faces. Direct gaze may facilitate face processing by directing the necessary attentional resources to address the commonality problem of faces highlighted by Galton (1883). In this chapter, we present some recent empirical data to support this contention that gaze modulates face processing. We begin by reviewing research that indicates that sensitivity to gaze is an early emerging capacity.

EARLY EMERGENCE OF SENSITIVITY
TO DIRECT GAZE

The visual resolution of the newborn infant is fairly poor in terms of acuity and contrast sensitivity (Atkinson, 2002). The child's vision meets the criterion for being effectively blind, and yet this limited visual ability is sufficient for processing gaze in static faces. Newborns presented with photographs of an adult woman with either her eyes shut or open with direct gaze preferentially spend longer time looking at the picture with open eyes (Batki, Baron-Cohen, Wheelwright, Connellan, & Ahluwalia, 2000). One could argue that this simply reflects a preference for the presence of eyes, but Farroni and colleagues (2002) also demonstrated that newborns prefer to fixate photographs of a female face with direct gaze compared to the same face with eyes averted to the side. The effect was pronounced, with newborns spending an average of 106 seconds fixating the staring eyes compared to 64 seconds directed to the face with averted eyes. The ability to discriminate direct from deviated gaze is also evidenced in older infants presented with cartoon faces. Vecera and Johnson (1995) reported that 3- to 4-month-olds could tell the difference between the direction of gaze, though they did not report a preference for staring eyes. This attention to the eyes is borne out by the earlier studies of Maurer and Salapatek (1976) who tracked the infant's eye movements when viewing faces and found a significant shift in the pattern of scanning at around 2 months of age, when infants begin to concentrate their fixations on the eye region of the face. While behavioral preferences and discrimination abilities are informative, important questions remain as to the effects and functional significance of maintaining mutual gaze. To begin to answer this sort of question, we must look for effects of staring eyes on the nature of the interaction.

Darwin Muir and his colleagues (Hains & Muir, 1996) began to answer these sorts of questions by examining mutual gaze in paradigms where adults interacted with babies. They discovered that looking directly at babies triggered social smiling in infants. Social smiling as opposed to spontaneous smiling occurs in response to the interaction by another and has particular universal significance in marking a transition in the infant's social development (Stern, 1977). Hains and Muir (1996) found that by training adults to alternate between periods of looking directly at the infant with periods of looking away, the direction of gaze was important in determining whether 3-month-olds smiled. Like other studies, they found a fixation preference for faces with staring eyes, but more importantly a corresponding increase in the amount of smiling by the baby when the adult's gaze was directed towards the child. Furthermore, this sensitivity to the direction of gaze was remarkably good as 5-month-olds in this mutual gaze paradigm modulated their smiling based on a shift of the focus of eye gaze from the infant's eyes to either the infant's ears or chin (Symons, Hains, & Muir, 1998). At the viewing distances concerned, this corresponded to a discrimination of about 5° of visual angle. So babies are tuned to respond socially when we stare at them during interaction. As the adults were trained to interact with the infants and their own behavior was contingent on that of the infant, it is not clear whether adult behavior is also spontaneously triggered by infants staring back at them. Anecdotally, parents find the absence of mutual gaze quite distressing. In the course of studying healthy infants at the Visual Development Unit in Cambridge, the first author often had to reassure parents that 1-month-olds who tend not to engage in mutual gaze were not blind, but reflexively attracted to high-contrast regions in a room such as the windows and lights. Hood (1995) coined the term "sticky fixation" to refer to this attentional capture phenomenon that is present around the first month, but disappears with increasing higher visual function.

This reciprocal social interaction of smiling and mutual gaze is important. Parents of blind children can experience rejection in the absence of social smiling (Frailberg, 1974). These children show normal spontaneous smiling in the early weeks, but this eventually drops out. However, training techniques substituting tactile interaction by the parent can reinstate social smiling even in the absence of visual feedback. Mutual gaze also facilitates face recognition in young infants (Blass & Camp, 2001). In this study, an experimenter administered sucrose to 3- to 4-month-old infants and either maintained eye contact with the infant or looked above the infant's head for 3.5 minutes. After this session, the infant was presented with the experimenter and a stranger in a paired comparison. Both 9- and 12-week-olds formed a reliable visual preference for the experimenter compared to a stranger if the experimenter had maintained gaze during the sucrose administration.

The visual preference for direct gaze in the newborns (Farroni et al., 2002) is followed by automatic gaze-following at 10 to 12 weeks of age. Using the same Posner orienting paradigm described earlier, Hood and colleagues (Hood, Willen, & Driver, 1998) found that infants were faster to orient to a peripheral target preceded by a face with gaze in the same direction compared to trials where the gaze was in the opposite direction. In this study, a female face was presented with eyes directed towards the infant. See Figure 13–1.

When the infant stared at the face, the picture was replaced with the same face, but with the eyes directed to the left or right. This produced an impression that the eyes had deviated from central to peripheral focus. A target was then presented at the corresponding or opposite peripheral location. As there was no predictive relationship between gaze and target location, this supports an early mechanism that may be triggered by behavioral mimicry described earlier. This finding has been replicated, though there was a question about whether the attentional effects could be attributed to perceived apparent motion when the eyes move from aligned to deviated gaze rather than a gaze detecting mechanism per se (Farroni, Johnson, Brockbank, & Simion, 2000). However, it seems likely that while perceived motion could play a role, it is not the full explanation as attentional cueing is significantly attenuated by inverting the face, which should have no effect on low-level perceptual effects of apparent motion (Farroni, Mansfeld, Lai, & Johnson, 2003). Furthermore, the cueing effects in adults are found when apparent motion is not an issue.

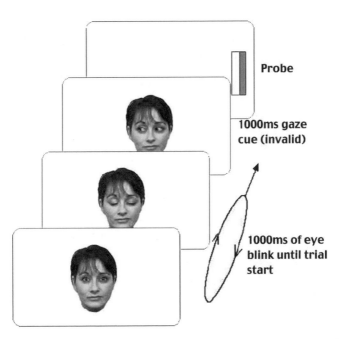

FIGURE 13–1.   Schematic representation of the temporal sequence of cue and probe in the infant gaze cueing experiment.

Attentional cueing by perceived gaze shifts in young infants raises an interesting question. If the attention to eye gaze is present early and the automated gaze-following can be demonstrated at 3 months, why does normal joint attention to eye gaze using the Scaife and Bruner (1975) paradigm not occur until at least one year later? The answer may be related to sticky fixation, as Hood and colleagues (Hood et al., 1998) found that no reliable orienting to gaze occurred at 3 months if the face modeling the gaze was still in the infant's field of view. The orienting effect was only found in those trials where the face was extinguished as the peripheral target appeared. Otherwise, infants continued to stare at the face. It would seem then that for babies, faces are more captivating than peripheral targets—even when the faces are not looking at you. This finding is consistent with a wealth of data that indicates that selective attention is very impoverished in young infants but shows substantial improvements and flexibility over the first year (Butcher, Kalverboer, & Geuze, 2000; Hood, 1995; Hood & Atkinson, 1993; Matsuzawa & Shimojo, 1997). By 6 months of age, infants possess sufficient attentional flexibility, which enables them to readily shift their own visual attention to objects or areas of interest despite competition from other potential targets such as faces.

Hence, the ability to engage in normal joint attention starts to appear more reliably from then on, though there are still some restrictions on where infants will shift their gaze (Butterworth & Jarrett, 1991).

In summary, the work with infants suggests a built-in mechanism for attending to the direction of gaze as proposed by Baron-Cohen's EDD (1995). Initially, this mechanism works well for focusing the infant's processing of faces, especially when they are returning mutual gaze. This supports a number of important functions that can be seen to stimulate early social interaction in a dyadic relationship. Gaze as a means for shifting joint attention to other potential targets of interest in a triadic relationship does not become functional and well established until towards the end of the first year.

GAZE AND PERSON PERCEPTION

Beyond infancy, gaze behavior continues to play an important role in social interaction though there is comparatively little research on gaze behavior during the period between infancy and adulthood. Furthermore, most research follows the tradition of interpreting gaze behavior as an additional channel of nonverbal communication (Argyle & Cook, 1976), though there are notable exceptions such as the study of gaze as a mechanism for recruiting attention in schoolchildren (Doherty-Sneddon, Bruce, Bonner, Longbotham, & Doyle, 2002) or as means for supporting deception (Lee, K. this volume). However, in recent years, with the increased interest from cognitive neuroscientists, gaze has been generating considerable research efforts from those workers focused on the social-cognitive role of the direction of eyes. As noted earlier, direction of gaze is an effective mechanism for manipulating another's attention. It follows then that direct gaze is likely to influence the processing of the face in which the eyes are situated. Classification by sex is one of the primary functions of face processing, as it occurs before the face is processed for identity (Bruce & Young, 1986). In a study of sex classification, Campbell and colleagues (Campbell, Wallace, & Benson, 1996) demonstrated that subjects were faster to make the correct classification of faces if the gaze was directed towards the viewer rather than deviated downwards. The authors concluded that the vertical upper-lid-to-brow distance was smaller in men than women when the eyes were deviated downwards, which could serve as the basis for a difference in discrimination speed. Note that this explanation is based on a perceptual difference rather than one that appeals to the effects of attentional capture. In contrast, Macrae et al. (Macrae, Hood, Milne, Rowe, & Mason, 2002) speculated that gaze was primarily an attentional mechanism that would modulate categorical thinking both in terms of sex classification and associated information from semantic memory (Macrae & Bodenhausen, 2000). Identifying the sex of the individual is just the first step in the chain of person-construal processes. Once the sex of an individual is identified, the observer can formulate an appropriate pattern of interactions based on semantic information. To test this, Macrae et al. (2002) first demonstrated that direct compared to deviated gaze facilitated sex classification of faces. In a second experiment, they presented a face as a prime to classify stereotypical words (e.g., cigar, lingerie), counter stereotypic words, and nonwords. As predicted, the priming effects of faces was determined by both the sex of the face and whether or not gaze was direct. However, an alternative account for the finding was that faces with direct gaze are more typical than faces with deviated gaze and hence act as a stronger priming cue (see gaze and face recognition following). Importantly, Macrae et al. (2002) checked to see if the facilitation of direct gaze could also be demonstrated with 3/4 profile faces with the eyes directed back towards the observer as in Figure 13–2.

The effects were upheld, indicating that it was gaze which determined the attentional cueing rather than the representativeness of faces with direct gaze. However, the findings from this study diverge in one important respect with Campbell et al.'s (1996) study which did not find a difference between direct gaze and laterally deviated gaze in the sex classification. Their result was only found between direct gaze and downwards gaze. However, their deviated gaze stimuli used faces that were 3/4 profiles, as well as deviated eyes, making a comparison between direct gaze (face straight) and deviated gaze (3/4 profile) problematic. Any effect of deviated gaze could have been offset by the ease of categorizing sex on the basis of profile.

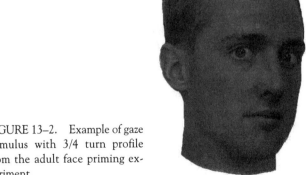

FIGURE 13–2. Example of gaze stimulus with 3/4 turn profile from the adult face priming experiment.

GAZE AND FACE RECOGNITION

Another significant component of person construal is the ability to recognize faces. As noted earlier, individuals who share a significant social interaction engage in mutual gaze. It seems plausible then that we are more likely to recognize faces in which the gaze is directed towards the viewer. This was tested in a study of face recognition in both children and adults who were presented with faces to recognize that had the gaze either direct or deviated (Hood, Macrae, Cole-Davies, & Dias, 2003). This was a forced-choice paradigm in which the direction of gaze was manipulated over the course of the initial presentation and subsequent test phase. In one condition, the faces to be remembered were initially presented with the eyes open with either direct or deviated gaze. Participants then had to make a forced-choice decision to recognize the old from novel face when both sets of eyes were closed. In a second condition, the opposite presentation sequence was used where the faces to be remembered were initially presented with closed eyes, and participants were tested with a forced-choice decision between pairs of faces where the eyes were open with either direct or deviated gaze.

Both 6-year-olds and adults correctly recognized more faces with direct gaze in the first condition. This supports the supposition that direct gaze facilitates the encoding of facial features, which leads to a better substantiated representation in memory compared to faces with deviated gaze. What was remarkable was that the effect of gaze was also found in the second condition. Faces that were initially presented with closed eyes were better recognized if they were presented at test with eyes open and directed towards the participants rather than deviated. This raises the possibility that direct gaze facilitates both the encoding and retrieval stages of face memory. In these studies, no instructions were given to the children or adults during the initial presentation phase. They were simply told to look at the faces. In the recognition test, they were to choose which of the two faces they had seen before.

However, presenting a sequence of faces is likely to have alerted the adult participants at least that they were to be tested on some form of memory for the stimuli. This does not explain the reported effects between deviated and direct gaze, but if strong claims for the automaticity of gaze processing are to be upheld, then studies should demonstrate that gaze influences processing even when participants are unaware that they are taking part in a face memory task. This was tested in a replication of the direction of gaze and recognition memory for faces in adults (Mason, Hood, & Macrae, 2004). Participants were told to imagine that they were bouncers at the door of a club and that they had to make judgments about whether individuals where beyond the legal drinking age of 21 years based on their photographs. Photographs were presented with either direct or deviated gaze. Participants initially thought they were making a judgment about age, but they were then given a recognition memory test. Again, there was a significant advantage for recognizing faces that had been presented with direct gaze.

One potential problem for these recognition studies is the conclusion that better memory for faces with direct gaze reflects the attentional benefits of direct gaze. As noted earlier, an alternative explanation for the advantage of direct gaze is that faces are encoded and retrieved from a prototypical representation or "face space" in which the eyes and face are directed towards the viewer (e.g., Valentine, 1991). Thus, it is easier to encode and store face information when the gaze conforms to the prototypical template. However, as noted above, Macrae et al. (2002) demonstrated that the gaze effects occurred when the faces were 3/4 profiles in their studies of sex categorization and priming effects. It remains a possibility that the recognition memory effects are attributable to the template account, though the template account does not readily explain the effect of gaze when the faces were initially presented with eyes closed. (Hood et al., 2003). Nevertheless, we are currently conducting recognition studies where the orientation of the faces changes between presentation and test. Also, template models of face encoding are heavily experiential and have been used to explain the own-race bias where individuals are better at processing and recognizing faces from their own race compared to other races (Valentine, 1991). Template models advocate that more numerous opportunities better substantiate the representation of features for faces from one's own race compared to other races where there is less contact (Chiroro & Valentine, 1995). It is therefore pertinent to find that infants also recognize faces with direct gaze better than faces with deviated gaze at 4 months of age (Teressa Farroni and Mark Johnson, personal communication). This would suggest that it is the attentional aspects of an early EDD mechanism, rather than a template account, that explain our findings.

In conclusion, developmental, experimental sociocognitive, and cognitive neuroscience research has converged on the study of gaze as a significant component of social interaction. The evidence supports an account of an early emerging mechanism, but one that is dependent on appropriate environmental feedback. It eventually comes to serve as a rapid processing cue for establishing who others are, though there are significant gaps in our understanding of how gaze is used to categorize others prior to adulthood. It also seems likely that the cue is not passive, but rather is a reciprocal mechanism that is used to interpret interactions. So it is probably not too surprising to find that we rate others as more attractive if they stare back at us and that the brain area associated with reward prediction (ventral striatum) becomes active during this type of encounter (Kampe et al., 2001). What could they be thinking?

ACKNOWLEDGMENTS

This work was supported by a grant (S16736) from the Biotechnology and Biological Sciences Research Council of Great Britain to the first author. We thank
Karen Hector for helping to prepare this work and Shiri Einav for comments.

REFERENCES

Argyle, M. (1972). Non-verbal communication in human social interaction. In R. Hinde
(Ed.) *Non-verbal communication.* Oxford: Cambridge University Press. xiii: 443.

Argyle, M., & Cook, M. (1976). *Gaze and mutual gaze.* Oxford: Cambridge University Press.

Argyle, M., & Cook, M. (1972). *Gaze and mutual gaze.* New York: Cambridge University
Press.

Atkinson, J. (2002) *The developing visual brain.* Oxford: Oxford University Press.

Baron-Cohen, S. (1995). *Mindblindness: An essay on autism and theory of mind.* Cambridge,
MA: MIT Press.

Batki, A., Baron-Cohen, S., Wheelwright, S., Connellan, J., & Ahluwalia, J. (2000). Is there
an innate gaze module? Evidence from human neonates. *Infant Behavior and Development, 23, 223–229.*

Benton, S., Allison, T., Puce, A., Perez, P., & McCarthy, G. (1996). Electrophysiological
studies of face processing. *Journal of Cognitive Neuroscience, 8, 551–565.*

Blass, E. M., & Camp. C. A. (2001). The ontogeny of face recognition: Eye contact and
sweet taste induce face preference in 9- and 12-week-old human infants. *Developmental Science, 37, 762–774.*

Bruce, V., & Young, A. (1986) Understanding face recognition. *The British Journal of Psychology, 77, 305–327.*

Bruce, V., & Young, A. (1998) *In the eye of the beholder: The science of face perception.* New
York: Oxford University Press.

Buchtel, H. A., & Butter, C. M. (1988). Spatial attentional shifts: Implications for the role
of polysensory mechanisms. *Neuropsychologica, 26, 499–509.*

Butcher, P. R., Kalverboer, A. F., & Geuze, R. H. (2000). Infants' shifts of gaze from central
to a peripheral stimulus: A longitudinal study of development between 6 and 26 weeks
of age. *Infant Behavior and Development, 23, 3–21.*

Butterworth, G. E., & Jarrett, N. L. M. (1991). What minds have in common is space:
Spatial mechanisms serving joint attention in infancy. *British Journal of Developmental
Psychology, 9, 55–72.*

Campbell, R., Wallace, S., & Benson, P. J. (1996). Real men don't look down: Direction of
gaze affects sex decisions on faces. *Visual Cognition, 3, 393–412.*

Chiroro, P., & Valentine, T. (1995). An investigation of the contact hypothesis of the
own-race bias in face recognition. *Quarterly Journal of Experimental Psychology, 48A,
879–894.*

Doherty-Sneddon, G., Bruce, V., Bonner, L., Longbotham, S., & Doyle, C. (2002). Development of gaze aversion as disengagement from visual information. *Developmental
Psychology, 38, 438–445.*

Driver, J., Davis, G., Kidd, P., Maxwell, E., Ricciardelli, P., & Baron-Cohen, S. (1999). Shared attention and the social brain: gaze perception triggers automatic visuo-spatial orienting in adults. *Visual Cognition, 6,* 509–540.

Farroni, T., Johnson, M. H., Brockbank, M., & Simion, F. (2000). Infants' use of gaze direction to cue attention: The importance of perceived motion. *Visual Cognition, 7,* 705–718.

Farroni, T., Csibra, G., Simion, F., & Johnson, M. H. (2002). Eye contact detection in humans from birth. *Proceedings of the National Academy of Sciences, 99,* 9602–9605.

Farroni, T., Mansfield, E. M., Lai, C., & Johnson, M. H. (2003). Infants perceiving and acting on the eyes: Tests of an evolutionary hypothesis. *Journal of Experimental Child Psychology, 85,* 199–212.

Frailberg, S. H. (1974). Blind infants and their mothers: An examination of the sign system. In M. Lewis & L. Rosenblum (Eds.) *The effect of the infant on the caregiver.* New York: Wiley.

Freire, A., Eskritt, M., & Lee, K. (2004). Are eyes windows to a deceiver's soul: Children's use of another's eye gaze cues in a deceptive situation. *Developmental Psychology, 40,* 1093–1104.

Friesen, C. H., & Kingstone, A. (1998). The eyes havit it! Reflexive orienting is triggered by nonpredictive gaze. *Psychonomic Bulletin & Review, 5,* 490–495.

Gale, A., Kingsley, E., Brookes, S., & Smith, D. (1978). Cortical arousal and social intimacy in the human female under different conditions of eye contact. *Behavioural Processes, 3,* 271–275.

Galton, F. (1883). *Inquiries into human faculty and its development.* London: Macmillan.

Hains, S. M. J., & Muir, D. W. (1996). Infant sensitivity to adult eye direction. *Child Development, 67,* 1940–1951.

Hoffman, E. A., & Haxby, J. V. (2000). Distinct representations of eye gaze and identity in the distributed human neural system for face perception. *Nature Neuroscience, 3,* 80–84.

Hood, B. (1995). Gravity rules for 2- to 4-year olds? *Cognitive Development, 10,* 577–598.

Hood, B., & Atkinson, J. (1993). Disengaging visual attention in the infant and adult. *Infant Behavior & Development, 16,* 405–422.

Hood, B.M., Macrae, C. N., Cole-Davies, V., & Dias, M. (2003). Eye remember you! The effects of gaze direction on face recognition in children and adults. *Developmental Science, 6,* 69–73.

Hood, B. M., Willen, J. D., & Driver, J. (1998). An eye direction detector triggers shifts of visual attention in human infants. *Psychological Science, 9,* 53–56.

Kampe, K. K. W., Frith, C. D., Dolan, R. J., & Frith, U. (2001). Reward value of attractiveness and gaze. *Nature, 413,* 589.

Kanwisher, N., & Moscovitch, M. (2000). *The Cognitive Neuroscience of Face Processing.* Dorchester: Psychology Press.

Klienke, C. L. (1986). Gaze and eye contact: A research review. *Psychological Bulletin, 100,* 78–100.

Macrae, C. N., & Bodenhausen, G. V. (2000). Social cognition: Thinking categorically about others. *Annual Review of Psychology, 51,* 93–120.

Macrae, C. N., Hood, B. M., Milne, A. B., Rowe, A. C., & Mason, M. F. (2002). Are you looking at me? Eye gaze and person perception. *Psychological Science, 13,* 460–464.

Mansfield, E. M., Farroni, T., & Johnson, M. H. (2003). Does gaze perception facilitate overt orienting? *Visual Cognition, 10*, 7–14.

Mason, M. F., Hood, B. M., & Macrae, C. N. (2004). Look into my eyes: Gaze direction and person memory. *Memory, 12*, 637–643.

Matsuzawa, M., & Shimojo, S. (1997). Infants' fast saccades in the gap paradigm and development of visual attention. *Infant Behavior and Development, 20*, 449–455.

Maurer, D., & Salapatek, P. (1976). Developmental changes in the scanning of faces by young infants. *Child Development, 47*, 523–527.

Nichols, K. A., & Champness, B. G. (1971). Eye gaze and the G.S.R. *Journal of Experimental Social Psychology, 7*, 623–626.

Perrett, D., & Mistlin, A. (1990). Perception of facial characteristics by monkeys. In W. C. Stebbins and M. A. Berkley (Eds.) *Comparative perception, Vol. 2: Complex signals. Wiley series in neuroscience, Vol. 2.* Oxford: John Wiley & Sons.

Posner, M. I. (1978). *Chronometric Explorations of the Mind.* Hillsdale, N.J.: Lawrence Erlbaum Associates.

Puce, A., Allison, T., Benton, S., Gore, J. C., & McCarthy, G. (1998). Temporal cortex activation in humans viewing eye and mouth movements. *Journal of Neuroscience, 18*, 2188–2199.

Ricciardelli, P., Bricolo, E., Aglioti, S. M., & Chelazzi, L. (2002). My eyes want to look where your eyes are looking: Exploring the tendency to imitate another individual's gaze. *NeuroReport, 13*, 2259–2264.

Ristic, J., Friesen, C. K., & Kingstone, A. (2002) Are eyes special? It depends on how you look at it. *Psychonomic Bulletin & Review, 9*, 507–513.

Scaife, M., & Bruner, J. S. (1975). The capacity for joint visual attention in the infant. *Nature 253*, 265–266.

Stern, D. (1977). *The first relationship.* Cambridge, MA: Harvard University Press.

Symons, L. A., Hains, S. M. J., & Muir, D. W. (1998). Look at me: Five-month-old infants' sensitivity to very small deviations in eye-gaze during social interactions. *Infant Behavior and Development, 21*, 531–536.

Tipples, J. (2002). Eye gaze is not unique: Automatic orienting in response to uninformative arrows. *Psychonomic Bulletin & Review, 9*, 314–318.

Valentine, T. (1991). A unified account of the effects of distinctiveness, inversion and race in face recognition. *The Quarterly Journal of Experimental Psychology, 43A*, 161–204.

Vecera, S., & Johnson, M. (1995). Gaze detection and the cortical processing of faces: Evidence from infants and adults. *Visual Cognition, 2*, 59–87.

Wicker, B., Michel, F., Henaff, M. A., & Decety, J. (1998). Brain regions involved in the perception of gaze: A PET study. *NeuroImage, 8*, 221–227.

14

Gaze Processing in Nonhuman Primates

Shoji Itakura

Kyoto University, Japan

Lopamudra Das and Arash Farshid

University of California, San Diego

The evolution of human beings has brought about the sophistication of many cognitive abilities including one of our chief social skills—the ability to follow gaze. Gaze-following has been defined as, "looking where someone else is looking" (Butterworth & Jarrett, 1991; Corkum & Moore, 1995) see Figure 14–1. Emerging very early in life, it is considered to be an essential component of attention (Caron, Kiel, Dayton, & Butler, 2002) and is regarded as the bedrock to the theory of mind. This chapter starts with research providing evidence of gaze-following in nonhuman primates, followed by the age of emergence of nonhuman gaze-following through a developmental perspective. Subsequently, it explores existing milestones in parallel research in domesticated animals while emphasizing the significance of theory of mind as it relates to gaze-following. The chapter concludes with a brief compendium on recent neurophysiological research and the prospects of future research.

GAZE-FOLLOWING IN NONHUMAN PRIMATES

Immense research has been devoted to examining the gaze-following abilities in nonhuman primates. One experiment tested 11 primates consisting of nine species of monkeys and two species of great apes (Itakura, 1996). Facing each

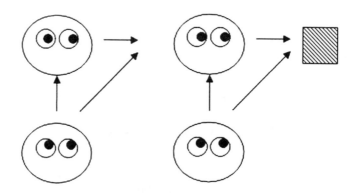

FIGURE 14–1.   Schema of Gaze-Following and Joint Visual Attention.

subject, the experimenter would obtain the subject's attention. The experimenter then looked straight past the subject to a spot either to the left or right of the subject. While the monkeys failed to perform above a chance level, the great apes were found to reliably follow the experimenter's head + eye and pointing cues (Itakura, 1996). Moreover, gaze-following efficiency improved when subjects were exposed to the experimental situation for greater periods of time. See Figure 14–2.

FIGURE 14–2.   Gaze monitor.

Subsequent researchers modified the simple gaze-following paradigm (Itakura, 1996; Povinelli & Eddy, 1996) to include opaque barriers like gutter, board, walls, and even a different room (Tomasello, Hare, & Agnetta, 1999). These barriers were positioned to prevent the chimpanzee from seeing the end of the experimenter's line of gaze. The experimenter used head and eye movements to look at an object out of the chimpanzee's range of vision. The chimpanzees tried to look around or over the barrier, and they did so more when the experimenter looked around and over the barrier compared to other directions (Tomasello et al., 1999). Chimpanzees also followed human gaze to target locations, instead of getting disoriented by distracter objects. The chimpanzee's reactions to the aforementioned studies conveys cognizance of the presence of another unseen object behind the barrier from the experimenter's eye movements. Though debatable, the ability to comprehend beyond the apparent could suggest the underlying presence of a theory of mind in chimpanzees.

While there is excellent evidence of gaze-following in chimpanzees (Tomasello, Call, & Hare, 1998), the evidence so far in monkeys is rather controversial. Using an experimenter-given object choice task, researchers reported that capuchin (*Cebus apella*; Anderson, Sallaberry, & Barbier, 1995) and rhesus monkeys (Anderson, Montant, & Schmitt, 1996) could find the location of hidden food using pointing and gaze + pointing cues. In a slightly modified object choice paradigm, capuchin monkeys were trained to cues like tapping, pointing, glancing, and two types of gazing (Itakura & Anderson, 1996). In the tapping phase, the experimenter looked at an object and tapped it with an index finger. During the pointing stage, the experimenter gazed and pointed to an object using the index finger. In the glancing stage, the experimenter glanced at the target object, avoiding any kind of head movement. In the first kind of the two gaze tasks, the experimenter faced the target object from 15 cm, while in the second task, the experimenter gazed at the target object from a distance of 60 cm. The capuchin monkeys successfully followed all the above cues except glancing. See Figure 14–3.

However, conflicting evidence exists regarding monkeys' ability to follow gaze (Anderson et al., 1995, 1996; Itakura & Anderson, 1996). Nine species of monkeys [viz., brown lemur (*Eulemur fulvus*), black lemur (*Lemur macaco*), squirrel monkey (*Saimiri sciureus*), brown capuchin (*Cebus apella*), white-faced capuchin (*Cebus capucinus*), stumptailed macaque (*Macaca arctoides*), rhesus monkey (*Macaca mulatta*), pigtailed macaque (*Macaca nemestrina*), and tonkean macaque (*Macaca tonkeana*)] failed to follow human gaze beyond chance level (Itakura, 1996). By comparison, the monkeys performed consistently better when the gaze cues were presented by conspecifics instead of human experimenters. For example, four species of monkeys [viz., rhesus (*Macaca mulatta*), stump-tailed (*Macaca arctoides*), pigtailed (*Macaca nemestrina*) and sooty mangabeys (*Cercocebus atys*)] could reliably follow the gaze of conspecifics (Tomasello, Call, & Hare, 1998). Furthermore, rhesus monkeys could

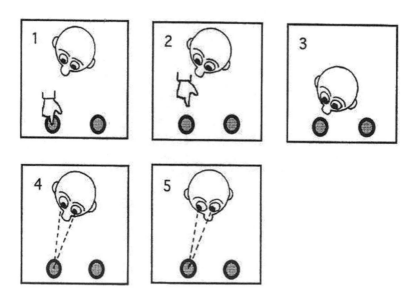

FIGURE 14–3.   Five cues of experimenter-given cues tasks.

also follow gaze cues of videotaped conspecifics on to a specific location on the video screen (Emery, Lorincz, Perrett, Oram, & Baker, 1997). Researchers have put forth insufficient motivation as a probable cause for monkeys failing to follow human gaze. Nevertheless, the underlying reason for the apparent discrepancy in the gaze-following patterns of monkeys remains unexplained.

In a study using a paradigm described by Itakura and Anderson (1996), chimpanzees, orangutans, and human infants successfully located hidden food and toys by using cues such as gazing, glancing, and pointing (Itakura & Tanaka, 1998). The researchers attributed the performance of the orangutan and the chimpanzee to their enculturation. Their history of extensive exposure to human beings was considered critical to their acute perception of human gestural cues. Chimpanzees also used social cues to locate hidden food (Itakura, Agnetta, Hare, & Tomasello, 1999). In the first experiment, the subject chimpanzee was given a local enhancement cue and a gaze + point cue. Both cues were provided in turn by humans and conspecifics. In the second experiment, the chimpanzees were given a gaze cue combined with a vocal cue. The vocal cue was either a legitimate word or a sound referred to as the "food bark" due to its association with food. All subjects were competent with the local enhancement cues regardless of whether the cue was provided by humans or conspecifics. Some of the enculturated subjects were skillful with the gaze + point cue, regardless of experimenter type. Most subjects responded correctly to the gaze + vocal cues with marginally better results with the "food bark."

Interestingly, in spite of their inferior status to the great apes in the phylogenetic hierarchy, white handed gibbons (*Hylobates lar*) seem to be able to use human glance as a deictic cue (Inoue, Inoue, & Itakura, 2004). This experiment had four conditions. In the near pointing condition, the experimenter pointed at the baited cup with one finger from a distance of 5 cm with their bodies oriented towards the cup. In a similar far pointing condition, the experimenter pointed at the baited cup from a distance of 20 cm. In the full body orienting condition, the experimenter's eyes and body were oriented towards the baited cup, with the eyes 50 cm away from the cup. In the eye direction condition, the experimenter's body remained straight and motionless, while providing cues using only eye movements. See Figure 14–4.

FIGURE 14–4. Experimental scene of gibbon.

FIGURE 14–4.   (*Continued*)

In studies so far, the great apes (viz., chimpanzee and gorilla) used gaze and pointing cues successfully, but failed to use human glance as a deictic cue (Peignot & Anderson, 1999; Povinelli, Bierschwale, Reaux, & Cech, 1999). Enculturation has been postulated as a possible explanation for the surprising adeptness of gibbons, a "lower ape" with supposedly lower cognitive abilities in using human glance as a deictic cue. Researchers believe that the effect of human eye movements or human gaze may be dependent on the degree of enculturation of the subjects, because some of the most positive data have been collected from highly enculturated subjects. Enculturation could be a powerful factor in the development of gaze-following because even species with previously unreliable gaze-following data (e.g., macaques) have followed gaze and alternated between gazing at the food and the experimenter after intensive gaze-following training (Kumashiro, Ishibashi, Itakura, & Iriki, 2002).

GAZE-FOLLOWING FROM A
DEVELOPMENT PERSPECTIVE

Previous studies reported in this chapter do not shed any light on the longitudinal development of gaze-following abilities in primates because most of these studies were conducted on adult primates. In this section we study the emergence of gaze-following abilities across the years. Eleven pigtailed monkeys (*Macaca nemestrina*), ranging between 6 and 12 years in age, were tested in a cross sectional study devised to explore the developmental stages of gaze-following. There were three experimental conditions. In the head + eyes condition, the experimenter's head was oriented 70° up, down, left, or right. The eyes were aligned with the head. In the eye condition, the experimenter moved the eyes up, down, left, or right to extreme corners of the orbit. In the trunk condition, the experimenter's trunk was turned 60° to the left or right. The data showed that gaze-following skills improve dramatically with age. Compared to adults, juveniles displayed a marked lack of understanding of human or conspecific gaze by employing eye cues alone (Ferrari, Kohler, Fogassi, & Gallese, 2000). This prompted Ferrari et al. (2000) to propose that the orientation of the head and eyes together provided more salient cues about the direction of gaze than those provided by eyes alone.

In a longitudinal study based on the paradigm described above, a subject chimpanzee was tested regularly from 6 to 13 months of age. Four types of gestural cues were provided—tap, point, head turn, and glance. The chimpanzee responded to the tap condition at around 8 months, the point condition at 9 months, head turn condition by 10 months, and the glance condition by 13 months (Okamoto et al., 2002). However, to eliminate the effect of local enhancement or nonsocial peripheral cues, the researchers conducted another experiment with two conditions, incongruent point and incongruent head turn. In the incongruent point condition, the experimenter gazed and pointed to the target object with an index finger, from the side of a distracter object. In the other condition, the experimenter oriented head and eyes toward the target object from the side of the distracter object. It was hypothesized that if the subject relied on local enhancement cues, then it would choose the distracter object. On the other hand, if the subject used social cues, then the target object would be chosen. The results indicated that the subject chose the socially cued object more often under both conditions, suggesting that the subject chimpanzees probably utilized similar social cues presented by the experimenter in the first part of this study (Okamoto et al., 2002).

In yet another developmental study, researchers focused on the evolution of gaze-following in rhesus macaques (*Macaca mulatta*) and chimpanzees (*Pan troglodytes*). The researchers utilized an integrated cross sectional, longitudinal experiment design to ensure a more precise and fine-tuned estimation of the actual onset of gaze-following in their subjects. There were experimental and control conditions. In the experimental condition, the experimenter looked straight up in the air moving both head and eyes while the experimenter's body remained facing the subject. In control conditions, the experimenter looked directly at the subjects. The findings suggest that rhesus infants began to follow human gaze direction at the age of about 5.5 months. On the other hand, chimpanzees were unable to follow human gaze reliably until 3 to 4 years of age (Tomasello, Hare, & Fogleman, 2001).

Following these experiments, researchers extended the previous experiment for additional testing of the rhesus and the chimpanzee infants. They exposed both rhesus monkeys and chimpanzees of various ages to an experimenter gazing into thin air at no particular target for many trials in succession (Tomasello et al., 2001). They wanted to ascertain whether gaze-following was a relatively fixed response in chimpanzees and rhesus macaques, or if at some point of development it could be modified by learning. The data suggested that rhesus and chimpanzee infants and juveniles never really habituated to the procedure. They kept following the experimenter's gaze onto nowhere. Yet, adult rhesus macaques and chimpanzees learned to ignore the experimenter's gaze consistently. This lead the researchers to conclude that somewhere in between infancy and adulthood, individuals of these two species learn to integrate their gaze-following skills with behavioral and sociocognitive information about other animate beings (Tomasello et al., 2001).

The inconsistency in the age of emergence of gaze-following in chimpanzees between Okamoto et al. (2002) and Tomasello et al. (2001) could be attributed to the difference in methodology employed in the two experiments. Okamoto et al. (2002) trained a chimpanzee infant to use human gaze cues, whereas Tomasello et al. (2001) relied on a simple gaze-following paradigm without any training. However, the discrepancy remains to be fully explained.

GAZE-FOLLOWING IN DOMESTICATED ANIMALS

Given that humans and nonhuman primates share a common ancestor, it is not surprising that many of the cognitive abilities inherent in humans are also present in other primates (McKinley & Sambrook, 2000). With this in mind, humans and nonhuman primates have been the focus for comparative research. For example, such research has shown that enculturation may be more prominent in species with a greater degree of behavioral sophistication, such as in great apes. Enculturation may also be seen in animals that have had a long history of domestication (e.g., dogs and horses), as the evolution of these animals have been largely shaped by humans. In this vein, domesticated animals should have sociocognitive abilities similar to those of enculturated great apes.

The following studies report on the ability of domesticated dogs (*Canis familiaris*) and horses (*Equus caballus*) to follow human gaze.

Based on the original paradigm described by Anderson et al. (1995, 1996) and modified to suit the species under investigation (Itakura & Anderson, 1996; Itakura & Tanaka, 1998), it has been demonstrated that domesticated dogs have the ability to follow human gaze by using experimenter-given cues (Miklósi, Polgárdi, Topál, & Csányi, 1998). Each dog was presented with a series of containers, one of which represented the correct target. The experimenter provided the dog with a behavioral cue(s) to point out the target container. The behavioral cues included pointing, bowing, head-turning, nodding, and glancing. 1) *Pointing*. The experimenter faced the dog and briefly pointed toward the target, after which the experimenter's arm returned to the resting position near the thigh. 2) *Bowing*. The experimenter bowed by bending the upper torso approximately 30° from the vertical in the direction of the target container, while making eye contact with the target. 3) *Head-turning*. The experimenter turned his/her head in the direction of the target. 4) *Nodding*. The experimenter turned his/her head in the direction of the baited target and nodded once. 5) *Glancing*. The experimenter knelt, facing the dog; while keeping the head turned toward the dog, the experimenter glanced at the target. Not only were domesticated dogs capable of using various behavioral cues from humans to find the target container, but also the dogs were able to generalize the same cues from one person to another, given that the experimenter was familiar.

Research conducted by Hare and Tomasello (1999) demonstrated that dogs could use behavioral cues in a more versatile manner than previously thought. A total of 10 dogs were used as subjects. Behavioral cues were presented by either a human experimenter or a conspecific. The results were as follows: 8 of 10 responded correctly to human local enhancement cues; 5 of 10 responded correctly when given human gaze and pointing cues; 6 of 10 responded correctly to conspecific local enhancement cues; and 4 of 10 responded correctly when given conspecific gaze cues. The results suggested that the ability of dogs to utilize conspecific cues may have arisen from their long history as pack hunters (Emery, 2000).

Another study was conducted to compare the abilities of two of the most common domesticated animals—dogs and horses—to use behavioral cues in an experimenter-given cue paradigm (McKinley & Sambrook, 2000). A total of 16 dogs and 4 horses were tested for their ability to use behavioral cues presented by a human experimenter in an object choice task. The behavioral cues presented to each dog were as follows: 1) *Point*. While facing forward, the experimenter pointed toward the correct location twice. 2) *Head*. The experimenter knelt, facing the correct location; shortly thereafter, the experimenter looked at the dog and then looked back at the correct location. 3) *Gaze*. The experimenter stared straight ahead and turned his/her eyes to gaze at the correct location.

The behavioral cues presented to each horse were as follows: 1) *Touch.* The experimenter knelt behind two food containers, touching the target container by moving one hand up and down (movement is an important element of the equine visual system). 2) *Point.* The experimenter pointed toward the correct container twice, while moving the same hand up and down until the horse chose one of the containers.

When dogs were tested in the aforementioned paradigm, it showed that these domesticated animals were skillful in using pointing as a cue to locate hidden food; dogs were also able to effectively use head and gaze (eye movements alone) cues in conjunction with one another. While these results were consistent with previous findings, one key result was not. Novel to any previous finding (McKinley & Sambrook, 2000), dogs were able to solely use eye gaze as a cue, as two dogs were significantly more likely to choose the object being looked at by the experimenter. This finding could not be replicated, however, by Hare, Call, and Tomasello (1998) who conducted a similar experiment with domesticated dogs. While it was found that dogs could use the head and gaze cues together (as well as the pointing cue alone) to locate hidden food, dogs were unable to use eye gaze alone as a cue. McKinley and Sambrook (2000) explained this discrepancy by pointing out a critical difference between their study and the Hare et al. (1998) study in terms of how salient the eye gaze cue was presented. In the Hare et al. (1998) study, the experimenter presented the gaze cue from a standing position, whereas the experimenter in the McKinley and Sambrook (2000) study sat on the ground when presenting the gaze cue, a position much closer to the dog's eye level. Presenting the gaze cue closer to the dog's eye level may have made the cue more salient. Notwithstanding this point of divergence, dogs clearly exhibit some kind of sensitivity to human eye movement.

However, horses displayed no such sensitivity to human gaze when tested in an object choice task, and the results reported individual differences (McKinley & Sambrook, 2000). Two of the four horses tested were able to find the target container when the experimenter used the touching cue, while only one horse was able to identify the target using the pointing cue.

More recent research (Hare, Brown, Williamson, & Tomasello, 2002) has been conducted to examine whether wolves, a closer relative to dogs than horses, share a similar ability to use behavioral cues presented by human experimenters. Dogs and wolves that were domesticated from birth were tested in an object choice task. Unlike dogs, wolves did not show a comparable ability to read human communicative signals to locate hidden food. Puppies, even as young as a few weeks old that have had little human contact, were able to exhibit these skills. Hare et al. (2002) suggested that dogs were probably selected for domestication based upon their unique set of sociocognitive abilities that has aided them to communicate with humans.

SEEING IS KNOWING

One of the most important and central questions to the study of social cognition in nonhuman animals is to what degree individuals know about the psychological processes of others (Hare, Call, Agnetta, & Tomasello, 2000). There is a growing amount of evidence supporting the notion that many nonhuman animals, including nonhuman primates, can reliably follow the gaze direction of a conspecific or human experimenter. This forms the basis for postulating that these animals have the ability to understand that the direction of another's gaze could lead this other individual to have a different vantage point of the world. In other words, these animals may have the capability for theory of mind and hence the understanding that a relationship exists between "seeing" and "knowing." Unfortunately, only a handful of studies have been conducted to examine this issue in a controlled environment (Hare et al., 2000).

Using an ingenious paradigm, Hare et al. (2000) demonstrated that chimpanzees could recognize what a conspecific could and could not see. In a series of experiments, a subordinate and dominant chimpanzee were placed in competition over two pieces of food, strategically placed in different locations relative to the two chimpanzees. Whichever chimpanzee that had better visual access to the pieces of food often succeed in obtaining them (i.e., one chimpanzee could see the pieces of food, while the other could not). By recognizing what a conspecific was able to see, chimpanzees were able to effectively devise sociocognitive strategies in naturally occurring food competition situations (Hare et al., 2000).

Unlike chimpanzees, however, capuchin monkeys were not found to be as sensitive to what a conspecific could see (Hare, Addessi, Call, Tomasello, & Visalberghi, 2003). Capuchin monkeys were tested in much the same way chimpanzees were in the Hare et al. (2000) experiment. While subordinate capuchin monkeys were sensitive to the *behavior* of the dominant capuchin monkeys, there was little evidence that they assessed what the conspecific did and did not see with respect to food sources.

Hirata and Matsuzawa (2001) suggested that not only can chimpanzees recognize what a conspecific can see, but that they can also grasp what a conspecific *knows* in instances of competition. The experiment involved two chimpanzees in an intricate setup. A human experimenter hid a piece of food in one of five containers placed in an outdoor enclosure. While one chimpanzee could see where the food was hidden ("witness") the other could not ("witness-of-witness"). The witness-of-witness chimpanzee, however, could observe the witness watching the baiting procedure. In other words, the witness-of-witness chimpanzee could infer where the food was hidden simply by watching the gaze of the other chimpanzee. Once the two chimpanzees were released into the enclosure, each used a strategy to mislead the other. For example, the witness-of-witness chimpanzee developed certain tactics to forestall the witness, thereby providing more time to find which container housed the piece of food. The ability of the witness-of-witness chimpanzee to be flexible in its tactics to obtain the food suggests an understanding of what the witness knew about the baited food's location.

Based on the paradigm previously used by Povinelli, Nelson, and Boysen (1990), researchers have found that capuchin monkeys share a similar ability to that of chimpanzees in understanding the association between "seeing" and "knowing" (Kuroshima, Fujita, Fuyuki, & Masuda, 2002). Capuchin monkeys were trained to observe a human experimenter who either viewed or did not view a baiting procedure. If the experimenter saw the baiting procedure, he/she would tap the correct container; if the experimenter did not see the baiting procedure, he/she would tap a container at random. The capuchin monkey had to approach the container that was tapped only when it saw the experimenter view the baiting procedure. Capuchin monkeys were able to perform this task after a short period of learning. The results suggested that capuchin monkeys were capable of understanding the relationship between observing another individual's gaze and the knowledge that individual gained from that experience. This was the first such reported instance that a non-ape primate demonstrated this ability.

Interestingly, a similar ability was reported in a nonprimate species—scrub jays (*Aphelocoma coerulescens*), a corvid bird species. Like other corvids, scrub jays remember where conspecifics cache their food, pilfering them when given the chance, but also altering their own caching strategies to avoid pilfering by others. To examine this further, Emery and Clayton (2001) allowed scrub jays to cache either in private or with a conspecific present, and then to privately recover their caches. It was found that the scrub jays that had prior experience pilfering another bird's cache subsequently re-cached the food to a new location during recovery trials, only after those scrub jays had been observed caching by a conspecific. Although there is no evidence to support that scrub jays are able to follow eye gaze or exhibit joint attention, results of the study suggest that these birds may understand on some level the association between seeing and knowing when observing a conspecific.

CONCLUSION

The ability to follow eye gaze not only allows nonhuman primates to obtain important information about the location of objects, but also allows them to engage in complex forms of social cognition, such as deception, empathy, visual-perspective taking, and theory of mind (Emery, 2000).

The problem is, however, that it is not known how to best evaluate the phenomenon of shared attention in nonhuman primates. In the case of human infants, and showing behavior is one of the best available procedures in testing for shared attention. With the exception of gorillas (Gomez, 1991), there have been no reported instances of nonhuman primates exhibiting such behavior. Hence, it is not clear whether nonhuman primates, such as the apes, are capable of exhibiting shared attention. While great apes do not possess a human-like theory of mind, they have at the very least some understanding of the seeing-knowing relationship. If it is the case that the understanding of this relationship is a critical component to shared attention, then it could be inferred that great apes would have the capacity for shared attention despite the lingering absence of an adequate paradigm to support this assumption. With evidence to support that great apes can understand on some level the psychological states of others (Tomasello, Call, & Hare, 2003), researchers have sought to model this behavior through cognitive means.

From a cognitive perspective, the question is how nonhuman primates understand the visual gaze of other individuals. Tomasello et al. (1999) suggested two possible models, referred to as the "low-level" and "high-level" models. The low-level model states that nonhuman primates have a tendency to look in the direction that others are looking. Because this often results in seeing interesting and important events, nonhuman primates learn that the gaze direction of others serves as a reliable cue for such experiences. In the high-level model, nonhuman primates come to understand that other individuals are seeing something when they look in a particular direction, resulting in a mental perspective different from one's own. Attempts to provide a cognitive model for this capacity have led some (Perrett, Hietanen, Oram, & Benson, 1992; Perrett & Mistlin, 1990; Perrett et al., 1985) to approach the issue from a neurophysiological perspective.

The fact that monkeys have not always shown the ability to follow gaze from a behavioral standpoint (Emery, Lorincz, Perrett, Oram, & Baker, 1997; Itakura 1996; Anderson et al., 1995, 1996) does not necessarily imply that these animals lack the cognitive capacity for this ability. Single-cell recordings of neurons in the cortex have provided some insight as to how monkeys, such as macaques, are able to follow the gaze of other individuals. For example, cells selectively responsive to faces have been found in several sub-areas of the temporal cortex in macaques, including the amygdala (Perrett et al., 1985, 1992; Perrett & Mistlin, 1990). These cells have been reported to be sensitive to particular gaze and head orientations (Perrett et al., 1985). The sensitivity to head view suggests that these cells enable an analysis of social attention, that is, they signal where other individuals are directing their attention. Some of these cells code the direction of attention rather than the geometric features belonging to each and every face orientation. Cells sensitive to head and gaze direction generalize across different orientations so long as the available cues suggest that attention is maintained in a given direction (Perrett et al., 1985, 1992; Perrett & Mistlin, 1990). The results suggest that monkeys have the neural mechanism necessary for detecting gaze direction.

While the neurophysiological evidence introduced here is encouraging, it only scratches the surface of the potential of this research. In addition to conducting more single-cell recording studies in other primate species, several steps must be taken to garner a better understanding of the underlying neural mechanisms inherent in gaze processing. First, existing behavioral research should be supplemented with neural-imaging studies (e.g., functional Magnetic Resonance Imaging and Event Related Potential) to provide a more conclusive linkage between primate behavior and the biological processes involved in gaze-following. By approaching this research from multiple perspectives, it allows us to achieve a more global understanding of gaze-following that has been presently lacking.

Second, more behavioral research should be conducted to examine primates in their natural habitats. Data obtained under controlled conditions render the ecological validity of the data questionable because of its often deficient simulation of real-life conditions. Anyway, past research results can assert greater ecological validity if future research can evince that primates exhibit theory of mind in naturally occurring situations (e.g., instances of food competition, deception, and perspective taking).

Third, more ingenious behavioral studies need to be created to facilitate the long-held belief that an association exists between gaze-following and theory of mind. Recent behavioral findings showing macaques' ability to follow visual gaze (Tomasello et al., 1998; Emery et al., 1997) shed some light on the possibilities available from developing new paradigms. It is imperative to clarify social gaze parameters through research in various species to advance our knowledge of how we process gaze, attention, and mental states of other beings. By expanding the scope of gaze-following research, we could be opening the floodgates to a realm of endless exciting possibilities.

REFERENCES

Anderson, J. R., Montant, M., & Schmitt, D. (1996). Rhesus monkeys fail to use gaze direction as an experimenter-given cue in an object-choice task. *Behavioral Processes, 37,* 47–55.

Anderson, J. R., Sallaberry, P., & Barbier, H. (1995). Use of experimenter-given cues during object-choice tasks by capuchin monkeys. *Animal Behaviour, 49,* 201–208.

Butterworth, G., & Jarrett, N. (1991). What minds have in common is space: Spatial mechanisms serving joint visual attention in infancy. *British Journal of Developmental Psychology, 9,* 55–72.

Caron, A. J., Kiel, E. J., Dayton, M., & Butler, S. C. (2002). Comprehension of the referential intent of looking and pointing between 12 and 15 months. *Journal of Cognition & Development, 3,* 445–464.

Corkum, V., & Moore, C. (1995). Development of joint visual attention in infants. In C. Moore & P. J. Dunham (Eds.), *Joint attention: Its origins and role in development* (pp. 61–83). Hillsdale, NJ: Lawrence Erlbaum Associates.

Emery, N. J. (2000). The eyes have it: The neuroethology, function and evolution of social gaze. *Neuroscience & Biobehavioral Reviews, 24,* 581–604.

Emery, N. J., & Clayton, N. S. (2001). Effects of experience and social context on prospective caching strategies by scrub jays. *Nature, 414,* 443–446.

Emery, N. J., Lorincz, E. N., Perrett, D. I., Oram, M. W., & Baker, C. I. (1997). Gaze-following and joint attention in rhesus monkeys (Macaca mulatta). *Journal of Comparative Psychology, 111,* 286–293.

Ferrari, P. F., Kohler, E., Fogassi, L., & Gallese, V. (2000). The ability to follow eye gaze and its emergence during development in macaque monkeys. *Proceedings of the National Academy of Sciences, 97,* 13997–14002.

Gomez, J. C. (1991). Visual behavior as a window for reading the mind of others in primates. In A. Whiten (Ed.), *Natural theories of mind: Evolution, development, and simulation of everyday mind reading* (pp. 195–207). Oxford: Blackwell.

Hare, B., Addessi, E., Call, J., Tomasello, M., & Visalberghi, E. (2003). Do capuchin monkeys, Cebus apella, know what conspecifics do and do not see? *Animal Behaviour, 65,* 131–142.

Hare, B., Brown, M., Williamson, C., & Tomasello, M. (2002). The domestication of social cognition in dogs. *Science, 298,* 1634–1636.

Hare, B., Call, J., Agnetta, B., & Tomasello, M. (2000). Chimpanzees know what conspecifics do and do not see. *Animal Behaviour, 59,* 771–785.

Hare, B., Call, J., & Tomasello, M. (1998). Communication of food location between human and dog (Canis familiaris). *Evolution of Communication, 2,* 137–159.

Hare, B., & Tomasello, M. (1999). Domestic dogs (Canis familiaris) use human and conspecific social cues to locate hidden food. *Journal of Comparative Psychology, 113,* 173–177.

Hirata, S., & Matsuzawa, T. (2001). Tactics to obtain a hidden food item in chimpanzee pairs (Pan troglodytes). *Animal Cognition, 4,* 285–295.

Inoue, Y., Inoue, E., & Itakura, S. (2004). Use of experimenter-given directional cues by a young white-handed gibbon (Hylobates lar). *Japanese Psychological Research, 46,* 262–267.

Itakura, S. (1996). An exploratory study of gaze-monitoring in nonhuman primates. *Japanese Psychological Research, 38,* 174–180.

Itakura, S. (2004). Gaze-following and joint visual attention in nonhuman animals. *Japanese Psychological Research, 46,* 216–226. (there is no citation for this ref.)

Itakura, S., Agnetta, B., Hare, B., & Tomasello, M. (1999). Chimpanzee use of human and conspecific social cues to locate hidden food. *Developmental Science, 2,* 448–456.

Itakura, S., & Anderson, J. R. (1996). Learning to use experimenter-given cues during an object-choice task by a capuchin monkey. *Current Psychology of Cognition, 15,* 103–112.

Itakura, S., & Tanaka, M. (1998). Use of experimenter-given cues during object-choice tasks by chimpanzees (Pan troglodytes) and orangutan (Pongo pygmaeus), and human infants (Homo sapiens). *Journal of Comparative Psychology, 112,* 119–126.

Kumashiro, M., Ishibashi, H., Itakura, S., & Iriki, A. (2002). Bidirectional communication between a Japanese monkey and a human through eye gaze and pointing. *Current Psychology of Cognition, 21,* 3–32.

Kuroshima, H., Fujita, K., Fuyuki, A., & Masuda, T. (2002). Understanding of the relationship between seeing and knowing by tufted capuchin monkeys (Cebus apella). *Animal Cognition, 5,* 41–48.

McKinley, J., & Sambrook, T. D. (2000). Use of human-given cues by domestic dogs (Canis familiaris) and horses (Equus caballus). *Animal Cognition, 3,* 13–22.

Miklósi, A., Polgárdi, R., Topál, J., & Csányi, V. (1998). Use of experimenter-given cues in dogs. *Animal Cognition, 1,* 113–121.

Okamoto, S., Tomonaga, M., Ishii, K., Kawai, N., Tanaka, M., & Matsuzawa, T. (2002). An infant chimpanzee (Pan troglodytes) follows human gaze. *Animal Cognition, 5,* 107–114.

Peignot, P., & Anderson, J. R. (1999). Use of experimenter-given manual and facial cues by gorillas (Gorilla gorilla) in an object-choice task. *Journal of Comparative Psychology, 113,* 253–260.

Perrett, D. I., Hietanen, J. K., Oram, M. W., & Benson, P. J. (1992). Organization and functions of cells responsive to faces in the temporal cortex. *Philosophical Transactions: Biological Sciences, 335,* 23–30.

Perrett, D. I., & Mistlin, A. J. (1990). Perception of facial characteristics by monkeys. In W. C. Stebbins & M. A. Berkley (Eds.), *Comparative perception* (Vol. 2, pp. 187–215). Oxford, England: John Wiley & Sons.

Perrett, D. I., Smith, P. A., Potter, D. D., Mistlin, A. J., Head, A. S., Milner, A. D. (1985). Visual cells in the temporal cortex sensitive to face view and gaze direction. *Proceedings of the Royal Society of London Series B, Biological Sciences, 223,* 293–317.

Povinelli, D. J. (1993). Reconstructing the evolution of mind. *American Psychologist, 48,* 493–509.

Povinelli, D. J., Bierschwale, D. T., Reaux, J. E., & Cech, C. G. (1999). Do juvenile chimpanzees understand attention as a mental state? *Journal of Comparative Psychology, 17,* 37–60.

Povinelli, D. J., & Eddy, T. J. (1996). Chimpanzees: Joint visual attention. *Psychological Science, 7,* 129–135.

Povinelli, D. J., Nelson, K. E., & Boysen, S. T. (1990). Inference about guessing and knowing by chimpanzees (Pan troglodytes). *Journal of Comparative Psychology, 104,* 203–210.

Tomasello, M., Call, J., & Hare, B. (1998). Five primate species follow the visual gaze of conspecifics. *Animal Behaviour, 55,* 1063–1069.

Tomasello, M., Call, J., & Hare, B. (2003). Chimpanzees understand psychological states— the question is which ones and to what extent. *Trends in Cognitive Sciences, 7,* 153–156.

Tomasello, M., Hare, B., & Agnetta, B. (1999). Chimpanzees, Pan troglodytes, follow gaze direction geometrically. *Animal Behaviour, 58,* 769–777.

Tomasello, M., Hare, B., & Fogleman, T. (2001). The ontogeny of gaze-following in chimpanzees, Pan troglodytes, and rhesus macaques, Macaca mulatta. *Animal Behaviour, 61,* 335–343.

Author Index

Dawson, G., 23, 25, 27, 28, 29, 31, 45, 46, 134, 138
Dayton, M., 229, 238, 297, 310
Dayton, M., 78, 80, 81, 82, 87, 90,
de Haan, M, 7, 13, 15
de Schonen, S., 34, 49, 117, 132, 134, 137, 139, 140
Deák, G. O., 87, 91, 98, 102, 104, 105, 109, 219, 221, 223, 239
deBois, S., 248, 260, 264, 267, 269, 281
DeCasper, A.J., 95, 109, 116, 138
Decety, J., 4, 16, 19, 20, 25, 38, 48, 51, 178, 179, 188, 189, 191, 284, 296
Deckner, D. F., 107, 108
Dehaene, S., 172, 189
Dehaene-Lambertz, G., 172, 189
Delaney, S., 115, 141, 148, 170
Delgado, C., 20, 21, 22, 36, 39, 44, 48, 49, 51, 77, 84, 85, 87, 92, 223, 231, 240, 241
Demke, T. L., 98, 110, 212, 215
Demorest, A., 258
D'Entremont, B., 19, 33, 45, 53, 54, 60, 74, 79, 80, 81, 82, 83, 88, 89, 91, 93, 97, 109, 132, 139, 148, 168, 223, 224, 226, 239, 265, 279
DePaulo, B. M., 249, 258
Deruelle, C., 117, 140
Desjardins, R. N., 175, 182, 184, 188, 194, 195, 213
Detwiler, A. C., 124, 141
DiAdamo, C., 89, 92
Dias, M., 292, 293, 295
DiCorcia, J. A., 101, 110, 113, 140, 149, 153, 154, 156, 157, 159, 168, 169
Diesendruck, G., 197, 214
Dilavore, P. C., 180, 189
Doehring, P., 25, 48
Doherty, M. J., 244, 249, 257, 258, 259
Doherty-Sneddon, G., 290, 294
Dolan, R.J., 7, 15, 16, 25, 27, 46, 47, 285, 293, 295
Donnellan, A., 256, 259
Doob, A. N., 249, 259
Dowd, J. M., 120, 140
Doyle, C., 290, 294
Drew, A., 22, 31, 45, 50
Driver, J., 1, 7, 8, 9, 15, 19, 25, 33, 36, 46, 47, 55, 56, 57, 58, 59, 60, 61, 62, 66, 67, 69, 72, 74, 83, 91, 96, 110, 148, 169, 177, 183, 184, 189, 198, 199, 207, 214, 235, 240, 243, 259, 285, 288, 289, 295
Dubner, R., 132, 140

Dunham, F., 85, 91, 194, 195, 213, 214, 264, 279
Dunham, P. J., 85, 91, 194, 195, 213, 214, 219, 240, 264, 279
Dunphy-Lelii, S., 82, 91, 229, 234, 239
Dziurawiec, S., 5, 15, 34, 4,

Eacott, M., 26, 45
Eastwood, J. D., 198, 214
Eddy, T. J., 243, 244, 260, 263, 267, 281, 299, 312
Eilan, N., 219, 239
Einav, S., 247, 258
Eisele, J., 181, 188
Ellenberg, J. H., 123, 140
Ellis, H., 34, 47
Ellison, A. L., 243, 259
Emde, R. N., 99, 110, 145, 170
Emery, N. J., 25, 26, 37, 45, 178, 190, 300, 305, 308, 309, 310, 311
Eskritt, M., 244, 246, 247, 249, 250, 252, 253, 255, 254, 258, 259, 290
Estes, A., 25, 27, 28, 29, 31, 45
Everett, B. A., 248, 258

Fabre-Grenet, M., 117, 140
Fagen, J. W., 34, 37, 46, 154, 169
Fantz, R., 34, 37, 46, 95, 109
Farah, M., 34, 46
Farnill, D., 248, 258
Farrar, M. J., 93, 183, 190, 194, 195, 216
Farroni, T., 5, 6, 11, 12, 13, 14, 15, 58, 59, 60, 61, 66, 67, 71, 72, 74, 96, 109, 110, 114, 135, 139, 198, 214, 235, 239, 243, 258, 285, 286, 287, 288, 295
Faw, B., 35, 46
Feldman, J., 41, 50
Fenson, J., 181, 188
Fenson, L., 231, 239
Fernald, A., 99, 101, 102, 110, 145, 146, 147, 148, 153, 154, 155, 165, 169, 223, 241
Ferrari, P. F., 303, 311
Field, T.M., 95, 109, 116, 117, 120, 122, 134, 139, 140
Fifer, W., 95, 109
Filipek, P., 23, 46
Fillion, T. J., 115, 131, 132, 138, 141
Fitzgerald, E., 115, 138
Fitzsimmons, C. M., 183, 191
Flaisch, T., 35, 36, 48
Flavell, E. R., 220, 240, 244, 248, 249, 251, 252, 253, 258, 259, 265, 277, 280

Subject Index